Christian Friedrich Schlenker

A Collection of Temne Traditions, Fables and Proverbs

With an English Translation

Christian Friedrich Schlenker

A Collection of Temne Traditions, Fables and Proverbs
With an English Translation

ISBN/EAN: 9783337080204

Printed in Europe, USA, Canada, Australia, Japan

Cover: Foto ©Thomas Meinert / pixelio.de

More available books at **www.hansebooks.com**

A Collection

of

Temne Traditions,

Fables and Proverbs,

with an English Translation:

as also some

Specimens of the Author's own Temne Compositions and Translations;

to which is appended

A Temne - English Vocabulary.

By

The Rev. *C. F. Schlenker*,
Missionary of the Church Missionary Society.

Printed for the Church Missionary Society, Salisbury Square.
London. 1861.

Printer: J. F. Steinkopf in Stuttgart.

Preface.

§ 1.

The Collection of Temne Traditions, Fables etc., as contained in the I. Part of the following pages, was received by the author from one of the oldest Temne men living at Port-Loko about twelve years ago, who has since died. These Traditions etc. were of course delivered orally not in writing.

As regards the Traditions about the creation of the world, and about the first people; we may discover some traces of how sin and death came into this world; though of course much deviating from the truth, as represented to us by the Mosaic accounts.

It seems, however, that some Mohammedan traditions have been mixed up with the original Temne ones.

The translation of these Traditions, etc. in Part I. was made somewhat free; which the author thought himself justified to do; as there is a full Vocabulary appended for this Collection of Temne literature, by which the literal translation may be made out by the reader himself, if required.

§ 2.

The signification of the term: Témne seems to be „an old man himself." They derive it, as the author was told, from: ǫ-tem, „an old man, an old gentleman," to which is affixed the reflexive suffix -ne, „self"; because they believe that the Temne nation will ever exist.

The word ought, therefore, to be written „Témne", and not „Timne", as is often done, or even „Timmanee".

§ 3.

The Temne country, as to its extension, reaches about from 11° 15′ to 13° 10′ of western longitude, and from 8° 15′ to 9° 6′ northern latitude.

As regards the number of its inhabitants, it is difficult to state a sum which comes near the truth. The author is, however, of opinion that they will amount to from 90,000—100,000. But the Temne is understood in the Bolom country, and in those districts, which border immediately on the Temne country.

The Temnes have by no means those strong characteristic negro features, which the tribes farther down to the south have. Their features come nearer to those of the Susus and Mandingoes, who live to the north of the Temne country.

§ 4.

a) The principal Temne tribes are the following:
1. Aṅ-Témnę a-tǫ́roṅ, „the eastern Temnes."
2. Aṅ-Témnę a-pil, „the western Temnes."
3. Am-Mabánta, „the Mabanta Temnes."
4. Aṅ-Kwéa, „the Quea Temnes."

The two latter tribes are on the right bank of the Rokel river; the Mabantas are higher up the river, and the Queas lower down close to the Colony of Sierra-Leone.*)

b) The Port-Loko territory belongs to the western part of the Temne country, bordering on the Bolom country on the west.

c) The town Port-Loko is in Temne called Báke Lǫ́kǫ, which signifies literally „Wharf of the Lokos." This town is situated at the top, or end of the Port-Loko creek, about 60 miles north-east from Freetown. The Lokos are a people of their own, having their own language or dialect. They were formerly inhabiting Port-Loko, from whence they were driven by the Temnes more to the interior north-east, where they are

---

*) A tract of the Quea-Country has been lately ceded to the English Government at Sierra Leone.

now living, between the Temne and the Limba country. From this nation the town Port-Loko derives its name.

d) Also the Baka people were living at Port-Loko in former times; from whence they were driven by Bey Farma the Conqueror. They then went down to Sierra Leone, and from thence up to the Isles de Loss, where they settled again, and where their descendants are still living. (Cf. Traditions pag. 3.)

§ 5.

Bey Foki, they say, preceded the first Álikáli Kindo, also called Álikáli Mórba. The Gbara family gave the country into the hands of Mórba, and named him Álikáli; because they had the government of the Port-Loko territory. They did so, because the country was in a bad state that time. Kindo, or Mórba lived before Álikáli Fatima's time. Fátima Bréma was the predecessor of Namina Módu, who was Álikáli of the Port-Loko territory at the time, when the author was residing at Port-Loko.

As to the derivation and signification of the term „Álikáli" see the word in the Vocabulary. — It ought properly to be written Álikáli, not Ali Káli.

§ 6.

The Temnes affirm that this present world is the second which God made, and the people inhabiting it the second race of men, and that when the present world comes to an end, and all its inhabitants are in Hades; God will make another world, and other people in the same way as he had done for the first and second world. (Cf. Traditions pag. 15.)

As they affirm that the present world is the second, which God made; may we not here have a trace of the flood in Noah's time, by which the first world was destroyed?

They also affirm that the first people, which God made, were neither white nor black; but of a Mulatto complexion, or of a brown or tawny colour.

§ 7.

The traditions about the conduct of the first people, whom God made, are very descriptive of the character of the Temnes; thus they are at this day. Eating and drinking, and the lusts of the flesh, are still the objects for which they care most. Their God is their belly. These Traditions also serve to show what notions they have of God, or of the Supreme Being, and how contrary these notions are to the attributes of God, as revealed to us in the Bible.

While the author resided at Port-Loko, he was frequently asked by the natives for what they called „child medicine," i. e. a medicine to procure children with for persons who were barren. They would have given any thing for it, if he could have procured it for them. Of course he told them that he was not in the possession of such a medicine, and that it was God alone who could give us children, as they where his gift. (Cf. Traditions pag. 17. 19.)

§ 8.

If one commits adultery with the woman of another man, they consider it a very serious offence, and the offender is severely punished for it. If a man marries a woman, and finds her defloured, or not a virgin, he may send her back to her family; but if he finds her a virgin, he will, a few days after the marriage, send a present to her parents in token of her virginity, which present is called: a-bóla, and generally consists of a gun, or of an iron pot, or of tobacco, which is sent along with a white cloth, which latter article is always necessary for this purpose. (Cf. Deut. 22, 13. etc.

§ 9.

The Temnes use to kill deformed children after their birth. The persons, who perform this cruel act, are not the parents themselves; but particular persons called r'a ra-sam, pl. y'etr e-sam, lit. „a holy" or „sacred thing," or „a thing set apart from common use for some particular object;" and then as applied to persons: „people set apart from common use for a particular object." Thus the name of the work, which these people do, is applied also to the persons who do it, and we have here an Abstractum pro Concreto, as is sometimes the case in Temne. (For r'ā ra-saṃ is generally not used of animate objects; though they may say r'ā rā-ñésam, „a living creature;" but here it is the adjective, which makes the word to signify an animate being.) These persons are said to perform this cruel act at night, when no other person is allowed to be present, while engaged in it. They either burn these unhappy creatures, or strangle them by stopping their breath.

This accounts for the circumstance, that we see no deformed, or crippled children or persons among the Temnes, or but very very seldom.

The reason why they act in this manner is no doubt because they attach some superstitious fear to such a deformed offspring, thinking that such a child would not only become an unlucky being itself; but also bring evil or misfortune upon the family.

§ 10.

a) Of a proper resurrection of the dead on the last day, the Temnes have no idea; though they believe in some kind of judgment or retribution after death, or that their state after death will depend on their conduct here in this world. They believe that all men, who live in this world will go to the Hades (i. e. ro-kriti,*) „place" or „abode of departed spirits"), when they die, and will remain there for ever without a body; some in a happy, some in an unhappy state, according to their behaviour here. They also believe, that they will get their slaves again in Hades; provided they tie a rope round their neck when they die, and let the rope reach out of the grave, fastening it to a stick pinned on the grave for this purpose. (Cf. Traditions pag. 39.)

b) But the Temnes believe that a person may by a sort of

---

*) See the term: kriti, ro-, in the Vocab. behind.

transmigration escape from the grave, which they express by the word „fálaṅ". They affirm that some persons having been put to death innocently, have come to life again, and that they were then living in a far country in great wealth. E. g. Alikáli ọ dif ọ-wọntr ka Dálu Mọ́du; kẹ́rẹ ọ fálaṅ, ọ yi ri ro ka an-tọf ña aṅ-Súlima; ọ bā a-trar a-laī, dẹ a-kála a-ġbáti, ọ yi ọ-yóla ọ-bána. „Alikáli put to death a brother of Dalu Modu; but he transmigrated, he is there in the country of the Sulimas; he has many slaves, and much property, and is a great gentleman."

It deserves to be remarked, that the country, in which these persons are said to live again, is always a very distant one.

c) They also assert that a child, which has died and been buried, may be born again in a natural way, which they express by the verb kal kōm, „bring forth again, bear again." They prove this assertion from certain marks on the body of the new-born child agreeing exactly with those which the child had that died.

d) The place of torment or hell is in Temne called: an'ántr, „the fire," or also: an'ántr na-tabána, „the everlasting fire." They also call it: Yahánnama; but this is of Arabic origin, and introduced by the Mohammedans.

e) The place of happiness they call: ọd'ẹ́r ọ-ma-bọ́ne, „the place of joy," in opposition to which they call the place of torment also: ọd'ẹ́r ọ-lạs, „the bad place." Otherwise they call the place of happiness also: riánna, „heaven", and: fírdaus, „paradise", which two terms are, however, also of foreign origin, and derived from the Arabic, and have also been introduced by the Mohammedans. (Cf. Temne Gramm. § 6.)

f) The state or condition of the happy they express by: ma-trạ́ma ma-fíno, „a prosperous" or „happy condition," and that of the unhappy by: ma-trạ́ma ma-lạs, „a bad" or „unhappy condition," or also by: m'ọ́ne ma-bána, „great misery." (Cf. Traditions pag. 37. 39.)

g) But the Temnes seem to believe that both places, i. e. the place of happiness and the place of torment, are contained in the Hades itself, and not existing somewhere else, or separately. (Cf. the word krifi, ro-, in the Vocabulary behind.)

§ 11.

a) As regards the object of their worship, it may be said that they believe in the existence of a Supreme Being, which they call: K'úrumasäba, which is the most solemn name of the Deity; otherwise they call this Being also: K'úru,* which, however, signifies also „sky, heaven; deity." What the sense of the „masaba" is, which is joined to K'úru, we have not been able to find out. Perhaps it is for: ma sa ba, = sa ma ba, which signifies „we have," when the full sense of the word would be „the God we have;" but this is only a conjecture.

They do, however, not believe that this Being exercises any providence over men. They think that, after having created the world, he does not farther care about it, nor about the concerns of men; and, therefore, they also do not worship him.

b) The objects of their worship are rather what they call: a-krifi,**) „krifis, tutelary spirits." For these they care much more than for the Supreme Being, and pay them much greater attention; because they believe that these Krifis exercise a much greater influence upon their condition than God, and that their happy or unhappy condition in this world depends on the goodwill, or upon the ill-will of these Krifis. Hence the many sacrifices which they make to them, by which they endeavour to keep them well disposed towards them, in order that they might do them no harm. For any evil, which befalls a person, is attributed to the ill-will of the Krifi, who, as they say, has been offended by the person, on whom he sent the evil, either by not having made sacrifices to him, or by not having cared for him properly, and the Krifi must then be reconciled by sacrifices; while on the other hand every good, with which one may meet,

---

*) Cf. the word k'úru in the Vocabulary.
**) See the word: krifi, both the noun and the adjective in the Vocabulary behind.

is attributed to the good-will of the Krifi, for which they then bring him a sacrifice of thanksgiving.

c) There are good and evil Krifis, as also male and female ones. They believe that they not only take care of men, but also of towns, houses, and farms etc., as long as they are well disposed. Hence we frequently meet with a small hut before a town, or at its entrance, which is dedicated to the Krifi, or tutelary spirit of the town; before whom they set food from time to time, or at certain periods.

But the concrete noun o-krífi is also used for the abstract, and they use o-krífi for „luck", as: o bā o-krífi o-fíno, „he has good luck," lit. „he has a good krifi;" — o bā o-krífi o-las, „he has bad luck," lit. „he has a bad krifi."

A male Krifi they call: o-krifi o-rúmi, and a female one: o-krifi o-béra.

The sacrifices which they bring to these Krifis, and which are called: s'ádka*) (which is a word of Arabic origin, and introduced by the Mohammedans; cf. Temne Gram. § 6), generally consist of food, as of cooked rice, or of cakes, etc.

§ 12.

a) The Krifis themselves, they say, cannot be seen by any body, except by those who have four eyes, as they call it, that is by the: añ-sóki, „the wizards, the augurers," or by „those possessed of second sight." But they have representatives of these Krifis in their houses, which consist of stones taken from the graves of relatives, never from those of strangers. These stones they call: am-báki, lit. „the dead ones, the manes," or „the shades of the departed." To these stones they bring their sacrifices; and we may often hear them saying: 'a ko trond am-báki, „they go to cook for the dead," or „for the manes;" or: o trond o-krifi, „he cooks for the Krifi."

b The immortal part of man they call: añ'úmpal, pl. am'úmpal, sometimes also: ey'úmpal. It properly signifies „the shadow

---

*) See this word in the Vocab. behind.

of a person," or „of a tree, as caused by standing in the sun."
As applied to a person it is said to walk sometimes, hence
„departed spirit, soul," = the Gr. τὸ πνεῦμα. It is also used
of the shade of an animal slaughtered for sacrifice, which is said
to appear in the Hades in behalf of him, for whom the sacrifice
was made. They even apply it to the Deity.

In the whole they rather dread than revere these Krifis, and
try by sacrifices to keep them favourably disposed towards them,
so as not to be harmed by them.

Note. They do not apply the term Krifi to the spirit of man.
But from the circumstance that the stones taken from the
graves of relatives are the representatives of the Krifis; one
might be induced to believe that these Krifis are their de-
ceased ancestors, deified, as it were, after their death, as
is the case with the Bassutos in South-Africa.

§ 13.

a) The Krifis are said to reside in the wood or bush, and
sometimes to make a noise before sun-rise, as if one were striking
a tin-pan. Some, they say, look like White men, some like the
Mori-men (Mohammedans), i. e. of a Mulatto complexion. They
assert that God made the Krifis, and that they are invisible; only
certain persons (as stated in the preceding section) can see them.

Sometimes, they say, a shine may be seen like the glimmer
of a lamp early in the morning, which, they say, is the Krifi
when passing round the town.

b) „The diamond snake," or „the devil snake," or „the
magic snake" called: añ-yáro in Temne, they believe to be a
Krifi. They affirm that it is able to part the water in two, so
that a canoe cannot pass on. If a black man sees it, and is
able to give something to the snake, the man can get rich, for
this Krifi will give him plenty of rice, etc. This yáro is said to
come to people in the form of another person, to talk to them,
and to tell them: „How do you do?" If he comes to a house
at night to sleep with a person, no other person can come to
that house; the house, they say, is then very hot. There is a

little island on the other side of Port Loko, close to that part of the town Port-Loko, which they call: Old Port Loko, where the Krifis are said to beat drums, and to dance in the day-time; but no man can see them.

Many more such superstitious things might be stated of these Krifis by the author; but those given above will suffice.

Note. As regards the sacrifices of those Temnes, who have become Mori-men, or Mohammedans, and their belief that the shadows of the victims go to the Hades, see „Church Missionary Record for June 1851, pag. 129."

§ 14.

The Temnes firmly believe that by witchcraft a person may turn himself into a leopard, or into an alligator in order to hurt others in a secret manner. Yea, they affirm that such persons may come at night to the house of another, rub against the door, and imitate the voice of some person, and pretend to have something to say to the person in the house. But when the person opens, it is a leopard, who then kills him. In the year 1854 they burned a man at Port-Loko, because he was charged with having done such a thing. They tied his hands and feet together, thrust a stick through them, and then suspended him over a fire, and burned him to death.

In April 1850 one was burned at night quite secretly, about which see „Church Miss. Record for June 1851, pag. 131."

§ 15.

Charms or Amulets are also extensively used among the Temnes, which, they say, are to protect them from evil. Some are to protect the owner against rain; others against the ball of a gun; again others against the stroke of a cutlass, etc. The wearing of such charms seems to prevail much among the African tribes.

§ 16.

As the Temnes ascribe events, as they happen, generally to chance or fortune; we cannot be surprised at meeting with many words in their language referring to this, such words as convey the sense of „luck, fortune; good luck, bad luck; a good krifi, or a bad krifi." Still we may now and then hear one say at the death of a person: „God has called him away."

Another thing in the Temne language worthy of remark is that many words occur referring to the cultivation of rice, which shows that this is one of their principal articles of food among them, and so it is.

§ 17.

The Bondo-Institution among the Temnes called: am-bóndo, is a secret institution, where they practise female circumcision; the oldest woman of the king is generally the headwoman of it, whom they call „bom rigba." Every female before getting married is to be initiated into it. The Temnes have received this custom from the Kossos. A member of this institution is called o-ko-bóndo, pl. a-ko-bóndo. *)

§ 18.

a) The Porro Association is a secret society called: am-póro, and a member of it is called: o-ko-póro, pl. a-ko-póro.* It is for men only, and exists chiefly on the Rokel. All the members of it are tattooed on their nape. It is chiefly of a political nature, and they assume a great deal of power, and are very violent, especially when offended by one not initiated into their society, upon whom they look as unclean, calling him: o-gbórka, which signifies „any one not initiated into the great institutions of the country," or „one ceremoniously unclean." Thus a woman not initiated into the Bondo institution is called by that name. The Pórros will demand satisfaction for all what they may call an offence done to them.

b) They frequently excommunicate persons by fixing a Gree-gree called: a-póro at their yard, or at their farms, consisting of a stick, at the top of which they tie some leaves or grass,

---

*) For an analysis of these forms see the Temne Grammar § 23.

and by which they prevent the respective person from leaving his yard, or from touching any thing in his farm, and thus cut him off from all communication with others. Thus they may say: 'a raf ri a-pǫ́rǫ, „they fixed there a pǫ́rrǫ," or „they fixed a pǫ́rrǫ greegree," or „the sign of excommunication there;" — 'a ráfar-ko am-pǫ́rǫ, „they excommunicated him," lit. „they fixed the pǫ́rro greegree for him."

Note. The author was once an eyewitness of the violent character of these people. Already their look indicates their character. When the author went once down the Rokel to Sierra Leone, he was obliged to stay at some little town on shore to wait for the tide. One of his boat-crew happened to spit on the foot of such a pǫ́rro man, not intentionally but accidentally. The pǫ́rro man immediately asked for a satisfaction on account of this offence; and as the Liberated African had nothing to give him, he took away the iron pot in which they cooked their food on shore. To regain the pot the author gave his man some heads of tobacco to redeem the pot with it. It would have been of no use for the author to speak to this saucy person, and the simplest way of settling the matter was to give the desired satisfaction; especially under the circumstances in which he and his crew were then placed.

§ 19.

a) With regard to the Traditions there are sometimes various readings, which have been given at the bottom of the page. This is also the case with some of the Fables.

b) As regards the Fables some of them seem to be intended to convey a moral precept; others to state the occasion, on which an animal assumed its present form, and again others the reason why some animal lives at such and such a place. (Cf. also what has been stated under a, with regard to various readings.)

§ 20.

Though Proverbs collected from the Natives are in some respects of great use for the acquisition of the language; yet they will not always enable the student to form general rules for the construction of the language; because with Proverbs the construction is often very peculiar, and the expressions so concise; as would not be tolerated in common language or conversation; and as regards the collection of materials for a Grammar, Fables and Stories are far more preferable for this purpose.

This observation applies at least to most of the Temne Proverbs, and may probably apply also to those of other African languages.

§ 21.

With regard to the Temne Addresses in P. II. Chapt. II. they are expressed in plain Temne, the same truth being sometimes imparted in different ways; as may be expected, and as was necessary with such an audience as that one was to which they were delivered.

§ 22.

a) The Vocabulary has been adapted to the Contents of this book only, and those words only (with a few exceptions) have been inserted, which occur in this publication. The original sense of each word has been given; but not all the other senses derived from it. It may be observed here, that what we have called relative verbs, whose suffix is -na, or -a, generally govern two, and sometimes even three Accusatives; one of which sometimes expresses the object in whose behalf, or in whose favour or disfavour the energy of the verb is exercised; and sometimes the instrument by which the action, indicated by the verb, is performed; and sometimes the material of which a thing is made. Another class of rel. verbs have the suff. -ar, or -r, which expresses various prepositions. As regards verbal nouns with the prefix ka-, see the observation under this prefix in the Vocabulary.

b) In order to make the Vocabulary more intelligible to the reader, it may be well to notice here in short, what has been stated in the Grammar more fully, that the Prefix, which is prefixed to nouns, might also be called the Article; that it assumes various forms, and that it has an indef. as well as a def. form in both numbers. Most of them are made def. by the vowel prefix a-, and a few by e-, and some by o-, which vowels see in the Vocab in their respective places. But the emph. vowel prefix is sometimes dropped, especially at the beginning of a proposition, or when the connection sufficiently shows that the def. state is intended. It must also be borne in mind, that the prefix, at least as regards the one used with inanimate or neuter nouns, always influences the form of the poss. preposition, and that of all the various pronouns, as of the rel., — dem., — poss., — etc. With animate nouns this is less the case.

> Note 1. The various Forms or Conjugations of the Temne verb are but sparingly represented in the Traditions, Fables and Proverbs; though there is a great variety of them.
>
> Note 2. As the Author's Temne Grammar has not yet been published, he has thought himself justified in giving a more copious explanation of certain words in the Vocabulary than he would have done otherwise, in order to make it more useful and intelligible to the reader.
>
> Note 3. The author does not think that any word, occurring in the Traditions, Fables etc., has been omitted in the Vocabulary; nor is he aware that any word, occurring in the examples of the Vocabulary itself has been left out; though it is possible that a few may have escaped his notice.*)

May the following pages serve, in some measure at least, to promote the spread of Christ's Kingdom in benighted Africa; so that the dark places of this great Continent also may soon become enlightened with the glorious Gospel of Truth!

C. F. Schlenker.

Kirchheim u. Teck, Württemberg, October 15. 1861.

---

*) A few words omitted in the Vocabulary will be found under the »Addenda« behind.

Pronounciation of Letters.

As not every reader of the following pages may have at hand the Standard Alphabet of Professor Lepsius of Berlin, according to which the Traditions, etc., contained in the following pages, as also the Grammar, are written; we subjoin here, for the convenience of the reader, a table representing the sounds used in the Temne language —

1. Vowels.

a) Primary and intermediate vowels.

ā sounds like a in — father.
ă   „ „ the ger. a in — Mann.
ē   „ „ the ger. e in — legen.
ĕ   „ „ the ger. e in — wenn.
ê   „ „ the ger. ä in — Bär.
ĕ̂   „ „ a in — happy, fat.
ī   „ „ ee in — see.
ĭ   „ „ i in — sin.
ō   „ „ o in — no, home.
ŏ   „ „ the ger. o in — von, wollen.
ǭ   „ „ a in — all, water.
ǫ̆   „ „ o in — hot, not.
ū   „ „ u in — rule.
ŭ   „ „ oo in — foot.

b) Imperfect vowel sounds.

a̯   This is the only one used in Temne, and is a short deep pectoral sound. As to its power it comes nearest to the u in — but, or in — tub. See Tem. Gram. § 16, 1. b.

c) Diphthongs.

ai sounds like the ger. ai in — Kaiser, or like the engl. i in — mine.
au ,, ,, ou in — house, or like the ger. au in — Haus.
ei ,, ,, the ger. ei in — leiden, or like the engl. ey in — eye.
oi ,, ,, the gr. οι in — κοινός, as pronounced on the Continent.
ọi ,, ,, oi in — oil, join.
ui ,, ,, the lat. ui in — fui, as pronounced on the Continent; or somewhat like the engl. ui in congruity, if it would be pronounced like a diphthong.
a̯i Both vowels have their proper sound; but are so contracted in pronouncing them as to form a short diphthong.

2. Consonants.

a) Simple.

The letters b, d, f, k, l, m, n, p, r, s, t, have the usual english sounds.

g like g in — gold.
h ,, h in — horse.
ṅ ,, ng in — king, or like the ger. ng in — Gesang.
š ,, sh in — shṓw,
w ,, w in — we, waft.
y ,, y in — year.

b) Compound.

Of these there are only two, viz —
gb and tš. The latter sounds like ch in — church.

Note 1. Whenever the forms mm, ṅṅ, and rr are met with at the end of a word, which is the case with some adverbs, the voice dwells upon them, not on the vowel preceding them, on which account these consonants have been doubled. E. g. tam͡m, „very".

Note 2. Long vowels are marked as usually by (¯), as: ā, ē, etc. Though the short vowels have been marked in the preceding table by the usual sign (¯) to show their corresponding sound in other languages; yet for brevity's sake this mark will be left away in the following pages. It is, therefore, to be borne in mind, that every vowel not having the mark of a long one, is short.

Note 3. Long diphthongs have the usual sign of length placed on the second vowel, thus: aī. When they receive the accent, it is always placed on the last of the two vowels, e. g. atreí.

Note 4. Extreme length of vowels has been marked by doubling them with the usual mark of length, and when receiving an accent, it is placed on the first of them; e. g. tralíi. Diphthongs pronounced very long have been marked in the same way, that is by doubling them, as: laūaū.

Note 5. If two vowels standing together are to be sounded distinctly or separately, the usual mark of diaeresis has been employed, as: a-réï, „a day."

Note 6. If r follows t, and is to be pronounced together with t, as is often the case both at the beginning and at the end of a word; the r is pronounced rather faint, much like tr in „true" or in „truth".

Note 7. The accented syllable is indicated by the accute accent; e. g. fálir. If a word has two accents the stronger one is marked by a double accent; e. g. K'úrumasäba.

Contents.

Part I.

Collection of Temne Traditions, Fables and Proverbs.

		Page.
Chapter I.	Traditions about the ancient Heroes of the Temnes	1—13
Chapter II.	Traditions respecting the Creation of the World and of the first Men . . .	13—35
Chapter III.	Traditions concerning the State of Man after Death 1. and 2 . . .	35—41
Chapter IV.	Fables.	
	Fable I. The Iguana and the Dog . . .	41—45
	» II. The Spider, and the Ant-Eater and Mr. Tamba	45—57
	» III. The Child and the Bird	57—61
	» IV. The Elephant and the Goat . . .	61—67
	» V. The Spider, and the Bushgoat, and the Deer, and the Antelope, and the Bushcow, and the Fillentamba . . .	67—73
	» VI. The Spider, and the Bushgoat, and the Ant-Eater, and the Leopard . .	73—87
	» VII. The King, and his Daughter, and Mr. Tamba	87—97
Chapter V.	Proverbs .	98—101

Part II.

Specimens of the Author's own Temne Compositions and Translations.

Chapter I.	Colloquial Phrases.	
	1. Salutations	105—110
	2. Of Worship	110—112

		Page.
3. Of the School		112—113
4. Of the House		113—114
5. Of Eating and Drinking		114—115
Chapter II. Addresses delivered to the Temnes.		
1. On John 14, 6.		115—119
2. On 2 Cor. 5, 19. 20.		119—123
3. On Jude v. 14. 15.		123—127
4. On Luke 10. 10—16.		127—131
Chapter III. The ten Commandments		132—133
Chapter IV. Translation of some Psalms.		
Psalm I.		133
» XXIII.		134
» CXXVI.		134—135
Chapter V. Hymns		136—138
Chapter VI. The Lord's Prayer		138

Part III.

Temne English Vocabulary 139—298

Corrigenda et Addenda.

1. Corrigenda.

Page.	Line		For	Read
15,	9	from top,	ake	take.
24,	11	,, ,,	me e-súma	mo e-súma.
37,	4	from bottom,	returnes	returns.
105,	10	,, ,,	Nothing but trouble!	Nothing at all!
107,	1	,, ,,	yéfa-i?	yéfa-e?
107,	5 and 8	,, ,,	sen	sen'.
108,	5	from top,	sen-e	séne.
110,	4. 5 and 8	from bottom,	sen nan	sen' nan.
146,	11	,, ,,	a rope and rope	a rope.
247,	13	,, ,,	so, v. n.	so, v. a.

2. Addenda

Page.

105. Line 2 from bottom, after: „Thou, how art thou?" add: or „Thou, what news?"

107. Line 1 from bottom read:
re ma yéfa-e? or }
ro ma yéfa-e? }

168. Fil, v. a. „turn round" as a sling; „move" or „turn to and fro; swing to and fro" (as a hammock); e. g. tsê fil ow'ahét, „do not turn the child to and fro."

179. I, pr. subj. „I"; e. g. I poṅ ama-pant, „I have done with the work."

,, I-, pref. indef. „a, an;" its pl. form is always ma-, never e-. E. g. i-yári, „a cat."

228. P'in, adj. num. „one kind, one sort;" e. g. pg-lā p'in, „one sort of rice."

Part I.

A Collection

of

Temne Traditions Fables and Proverbs.

Ara-bomp I.

Ma-Káne ma-kur trạka añ-Kélfa a-báki ña an-Témne.

Bē Fárma o yéfa ro-tóroñ, o woṇ ri, o yi o-kélfa o-bána. Pạ tási trạ-kómra tr'éme trạ-sas mo o yi tạ́pañ.

Añ-lo ña-tši an-Témne[1]) ña bā he a-píñkar, ña bā he a-gbato; ña bā gbo tr'aṇtr, de e-sor, de e-bạ́ntra, de ma-séno, de e-bóka, de e-tis trạka tšim. O dim an-tof be. O yóka ra-kélfa ro-tóroñ, o tšim an-tof a-tóroñ, o poñ-ñi. Kóno mot sóto a-kála, de e-piñkar, de p'ólpala, de e-gbáto, de y'etr e-tšíma be. O won ro-tóroñ, o tor he lemp ro-Báke Lóko.[2]) O dif a-Límba, de o tíla-ña; o woṇ ri; o dif a-Lóko, ko o dim ri tamm.[3]) O der ka an-tof ña an-Témne, o yíra ro-Bélia.[4])

Ko o tšim Bē Yáre, owó gbúke, ko o woñ ro-m'antr de añ-wut-ñ'oñ be, de añ-kála-ñ'oñ be, de apa-lā-p'oñ be, de e-šemy'oñ e-trol be; ko Bē Fárma o tšia o yíra ri; ko o wur, o tšim an-tof ña an-Témne be, o poñ-ñi. Ko o bal am-Báka, añá yi ro-Báke Lóko tạ́pañ, ña tor ro-bil, ña kóne ro-pil; de am-Marúñ, de añ-fam be ña gbúke; ko o bal am-Bólam de añ-Kwéa, ña yéfa ro-Báke Lóko; o poñ bal ro-Kel be, ka ña be ña gbúke.

---

1) See the Preface § 2.
2) See about the name of this town Preface § 4. c.
3) Lit. „he destroyed there entirely", i. e. he dispeopled the country so much that it became almost a desert.
4) A river in the Loko country. A town lying near it was called „Yare".

Chapter I.

Traditions about the ancient Heroes of the Temnes.

Bey Farma came from the East, where he was for a long time; he was a great warrior. More than three hundred generations have passed away since he lived.

At that time the Temnes had no gun, and no cutlass; they had only sticks, and spears, and bows, and arrows, and billhooks, and knives to fight with. He destroyed the whole country. He took upon him the office of a captain of the army in the East, and waged war against the East-country, and went all over it. He was the first who got money, and guns, and gunpowder, and cutlasses, and all sorts of arms. He stayed a long time in the East, and did not straightways come down to Port-Loko. He killed Limbas, and sold (some of) them; he was long there;[1] he killed Lokos, and he destroyed it (country) entirely. He came into the Temne country, and lived at Belia.

Then he fought against Bey Yare, who ran,[2] and went into the water with all his children, and with all his property, with all his rice, and with all his cattle; and Bey Farma remained and lived there; then he went forth, and waged war against all the Temne country, and went all over it. He expelled the Bakas, who where formerly at Port-Loko, and who went down the river in canoes toward the West;[3] and the Maruns,[4] and all the people fled; he also expelled the Boloms and the Queas, and they came away from Port-Loko; he entirely expelled (the people) on the whole of the Rokel, and they all fled.

---

1) That is in the Limba country.
2) Or „fled".
3) See what is stated about this people in the Preface § 4. d.
4) By this name the Settlers were called, who first settled at Sierra Leone.

— 4 —

Ko o yíra ka an-tof ña Kwéa, o tšim he so; o fi, ko pa tšía toñ, ña tšim fe so. Kon' o tróri a-fam ka-tšim; ka-tšim ka yi he tápañ. Bĕ Fárma o tóra am-bántra.[1]) Fárma Támi o šek o-póto,[2]) o ko faī; o šek o-baī,[2]) o ko faī, mo o tási-ko. Tr'eī tra yi he so, ko pa won 'a tšim fe so (or: ko pa won ka 'a móta tšim). Ko pa won ka ka-tšim ka ma der, ha Pā Korómbo o yókane o-kélfa; o dim an-tof a-témne be, o tšim hā o bĕk no-Báke Lóko. O tšim he no-Báke Lóko, o tíla gbo ka am-póto. Mo o pai ka-der no-Báke Lóko, ka-petr[2]) aká o díra, o yif a-fet a-rúni; o yóka-ña, o kára-ña, o re tíla. Mo o bap o-kómra, o kóri o-kómra, o wúra tr'óta de ma-ber, o soñ o-kómra, o pā ho: „Be ow'án-ka-mu o bĕka am'ólo, I tši tílako." O wúra a-píñkar, o soñ-ñi ka o-rúni. Ña gbáli he dif-ko; 'a trap-ko, añ-gbáto ña woñ fe; 'a sútara-ko a-píñkar, ama-pílor ma wop he ko; o gbáli fálir. Be o der ra-petr, o tóñkla añ-fam, o tit-ña, o tíla-ña. Añ-gbáto-ñ'oñ ña yi k'óno.

Korómbo o ñatr, o dim tra-petr tramát ro kin, ko o pā ho: „I tšim fe so." O-kélfa ka Korómbo, Ya Fúra, o tráma kadí, o ko trap aka-tšim; ko o gbip a-fam, o dif a-fam táñkañ. An-tof a-tóroñ ña tóñkla r'áfa ra-bána, 'a re gbañ-ko ka as'oñ be, ka ar'áfa ra trap ka-tšim ro-tóroñ.

Korómbo Fúnti kóno yi o-kélfa o-báki, ka 'a tšim an-

---

1 Lit. „B. F. brought down the bow", which phrase is equivalent to: „B. F. b. d. the war." They assert that there was no rainbow before his time, and that none was seen till he came; for which reason they call the rain-bow to this very day: am-bántra ña Farma, „Farma's bow;" or also: am-b. ña k'úru, „the bow of heaven."

2) The Singular for the Plural.

Then he settled in the Quea country, and did not wage war again; he died, and it remained so then, they did not fight again. He taught people the art of war; there was no war before. Bey Farma was the first who waged war. Farma the Conquerer tied white men (Europeans), and went and cut their throat; he tied kings, and went and cut their throat; because he was superior to them. There was no matter again, and for a long time they did not fight again, (or: and it was long before they warred again). It was long before war was coming, till Mr. Korombo rose up as a warrior; he destroyed the whole Témne country, he fought till he reached here to Port-Loko.¹) Here at Port Loko he did not fight, he only traded with the Europeans. When he was ready to come here to Port Loko, at the towns, where he slept, he asked for boys; he took them and brought them, and went and sold them. When he met with a woman in childbed, he saluted (or: went to see) the woman in childbed; he took out cloths and palmwine (or: liquor), and gave (them) to the woman, and said: „When thy child is worth the amount, I shall sell it." He took out a gun, and gave it to the husband. They were not able to kill him; they chopped him, (but) the cutlas did not enter (his body); they shot at him with a gun, (but) the balls did not hit him; and he was able to fly. When he came to a town, he assembled the people, selected (a number of) them, and sold them. His sword was a turkish sabre.

Korombo went up the country, and destroyed six towns; then he said: „I do not fight again." An officer of Korombo, Ya Fura, he placed himself at the head, he went and began the war; he caught people, and killed many of them. The East-country collected a large army, they went and prevented²) him in all the roads, and the army began war in the East.

Korombo Funti was an old captain, and they invaded the

---

1) It is to be borne in mind that the speaker lived at Port Loko, and that it was written there.
2) Or: „way-laid him etc."

tọf a-témnẹ bẹ; ka 'a kọ tšim an-tọf a-lọ́kọ bẹ, ka 'a poṅ ṅi dim, hā w'úṅi k'in ọ tšía hẹ ri. Ka 'a kọ́nẹ ka an-tọf a-límba, 'a tšim ri sọ, ka 'a poṅ-'i; ka 'a poṅ dim trạ-tọf tramát ro ṅ'áṅlẹ. An-tọf aṅá bēka trofátr-ẹ, Ya Fúra ọ pā họ: „I kọ́nẹ, ar'ạ̈fa-ra-mi ra lásạr." Koróṁbo ọ pā rọṅọ́ṅ: „Tšē kọ;" kẹ́rẹ ọ kọ́nẹ, ọ tšía Koróṁbo ọ-k'ẹ́lfa ọ-báki; kọ ọ kọ tšim an-tọf aṅá bēka trọfátr, ọ dim-ṅi. Aṅá bēka trọfátr ṅ'in-e ọ kọ tšim ri, ọ bēk ratrọ́ṅ. Ka aṅ-fạm, aṅá ọ poṅ bal ka trạ-tọf tramát ro kin, ṅa kal, ṅa der ṅa máṅknẹ Ya Fúra; kẹ́rẹ kọ́nọ tr'a hẹ tši. R'ạ̈fa ra-bána ra der tšim-kọ, ṅa bal-kọ; ọ der yíra ratrọ́ṅ; ṅa der tšim-kọ ri, kẹ́rẹ ṅa gbạ̈li hẹ. Kọ ọ sōm ọ-kẹ́lfa ọ-lọm ka Koróṁbo trạ̈ka kánẹ-kọ họ: „'A tšim-mi, der mar-mi." Kẹ́rẹ ọ-kẹ́lfa, owọ́ ọ sōm, ọ bạp ro-r'oṅ aṅ-fạm, aṅá máṅknẹ Ya Fúra, ka 'a tšim-kọ ma-réï tramát ro kin. Kọ ọ-kẹ́lfa ọ-báki ọ kálanẹ ka Ya Fúra; kẹ́rẹ aṅ-fạm-ṅ'ọṅ ṅa kọ́nẹ ka Koróṁbo, ṅa kánẹ-kọ họ: „'A poṅ-su ro-r'oṅ." Dẹ ọ-kẹ́lfa ọ-báki ọ kọ kánẹ sọ Ya Fúra họ: „Ṅa poṅ-su ro-r'oṅ." Ma Ya Fúra ọ trạl atšé, ọ yókanẹ dẹ ar'ạ̈fa-r'ọṅ bẹ, ṅa der tšim ro-r'oṅ y'of yẹ-rạṅ, kọ ọ fọï-hẹ-tas. Kọ Koróṁbo ọ yéfa ro-pil, ọ der gbaṅ's Ya Fúra ro-r'oṅ trạ̈ka mar-kọ tra tšim. Ya Fúra ar'ạ̈fa-r'ọṅ ra yi k'ẹ́mẹ k'in; ṅa bēk sọ kạ-petr kạ-lọm, ka aṅ-fạm ṅa ka-petr ṅa dim-ṅa. Ka ar'ạ̈fa, ará yi roráraṅ-e, ra laï, ṅa re tas bẹ, ka ṅa šek aṅ-fạm bẹ, ṅa tọï ẹ-set-'ẹ-ṅaṅ; kẹ́rẹ aṅá 'a gbip, ṅa dif hẹ ṅa. Ka ṅa der bạp sọ kạ-petr kạ-lọm; aṅá ma trạ̈ma rodí, ṅa poṅ ṅa dif whole Temne country; then they went and invaded the whole Loko country, and destroyed it entirely, so that not one person was left there. Then they went into the Limba country, and invaded it also, and destroyed it; and they destroyed nine countries entirely. Respecting the tenth country, Ya Fura said: „I go, my army is complete." Korombo said to him: „Do not go;" but he went, and left to Korombo an old captain; then he went and invaded the tenth country, and destroyed it. With regard to the eleventh he went and invaded it, and reached the middle (of it). And the people, whom he had expelled from six countries, returned, they came and way-laid Ya Fura; but he did not know it. A large army came to fight against him, they drove him away; he came and sat down between (them); they came to fight with him there, but did not succeed. And he sent some officer to Korombo to tell him: „They fight against me, come and help me." But the officer, whom he sent, met in the road with the people, who way-laid Ya Fura, and for six days they fought with him. Then the old officer returned to Ya Fura; but his people went to Korombo, and said to him: „They have destroyed[1] us in the road." And the old officer went and told also Ya Fura: „They have destroyed us in the road." When Ya Fura heard this, he rose up and all his army, they came and fought in the road two months, and it was not easy to pass. And Korombo departed from the West, and came to meet Ya Fura in the road, and to help him to fight. As to Ya Fura's army it amounted to one hundred (men); they arrived again at another town, and the people of the town destroyed them. And the army, which formed the rear,[2] was numerous, they came and passed all along, and they tied all the people, and burned their houses; but they whom they took prisoners, they did not kill them. And they came and met again another town; as to those who were in advance,[3] they entirely killed them

---

1) Or: „routed."
2) Lit. „which was behind".
3) The avant-guard.

bẹ; kẹ́rẹ a-laī n̂a bēk sọ, n̂a tšim, ka n̂a dif an̂-fạm, n̂a tas. N̂a der sọ bạp kạ-petr kạ-lọm, ka an̂á trạ́ma rodí, n̂a yi tr'ẹ́mẹ trạ-rạn̂, n̂a dim-n̂a sọ bẹ; kẹ́rẹ ar'ạ́fa ra-laī rorárạn̂ ra bēk, n̂a tšim an̂-fạm, n̂a dif-n̂a, ka n̂a tas. Ma n̂a kọ bạp sọ kạ-petr kạ-lọm, Ya Fúra ọ pā họ: „Man̂ gbán̂'sanẹ ka-petr." Ka n̂a gbán̂'sanẹ ka-petr ka-tši, 'a tšim ri ma-réï tramát ro kin; ka 'a pon̂ dif ar'ạ́fa ra Ya Fúra, n̂a tšía gbo a-tan. Ma n̂a der kánẹ ar'ạ́fa, an̂á mán̂knẹ Ya Fúra họ: „Korómbo ọ bēk!" n̂a gbúkẹ; ka Ya Fúra ọ tọī ri bẹ, ọ tas, ọ kọ bạp Korómbo. Korómbo ọ kánẹ-kọ họ: „Man̂ kálanẹ; I kánẹ-mu tápan̂: tšē kọ. Mạ nạn̂k ma n̂a pon̂ dif an̂-wut n̂a an̂-fạm-i?" Ka n̂a kálanẹ sọ. An̂á pon̂ kọ kán̂ka Ya Fúra, n̂a trạ pon̂ ko na wop, mọ Korómbo ọ bēk, ọ der bal an̂-fạm. Ya Fúra, mọ ọ kal-e, ọ der gbo yíra ha ọ fi; w'úni ọ dif hẹ kọ. Kẹ́rẹ atra-petr-tr'ọn̂ bẹ w'an dúni ọ yi hẹ ri sọ, a-fẹt gbo dẹ a-bom; a-lán̂ba n̂a yi hẹ ri, n̂a pon̂ n̂a dif ro-tọ́rọn̂. Kọ Korómbo ọ kal botr a-lán̂ba ri bẹ ka tra-petr tra-tši bẹ, kọ ọ tšía sọ ọ-kẹ́lfa ọ-bána sōn; ọ tam an̂-fạm ka 'ra-rū bẹ, am-póto ó am-bi ó bẹ. Ka ka-lạ́psọ n̂a dif kọ.

Korómbo, mọ ọ tam a-fạm bẹ, tšían̂ n̂a bótra-kọ yán̂fa trạ́ka mẹ́mar kọ dif. Ka n̂a son̂-kọ a-bẹ́ra a-gbáti; 'a kánẹ am-bẹ́ra n̂a-tši, ma n̂a ma rū-kọ an̂-fon-e, káma n̂a kára an̂-fon-n̂'ọn̂. Am-bútu, ro ọ mọ botr ara-bomp-r'ọn̂, mọ ọ fạ́nta, an̂-lọ n̂a ma kọ yak-e, am'ántr amá 'a wẹk, n̂a botr am'ántr ma-tši ka all; but many arrived again, and they fought, and killed the people, and passed on. They came and met again another town, and those who were in advance,¹) amounted to two hundred (men), and they destroyed the whole of them also; but the gross of the army (which was) behind²) arrived, they fought against the people, and killed them, and then passed on. When they went and met again another town, Ya Fúra said: „Let us surround the town." And they surrounded that town, and fought there six days, and they entirely killed the army of Ya Fúra, only few were left. When they came and told the army, which way-laid Ya Fúra: „Korombo has arrived!" they fled; then Ya Fúra burned the whole place, and passed on, and went to meet Korombo. Korombo said to him: „Let us return; I told thee before: do not go. Doest thou see how they have killed the children of the people?" And they returned again. As to those, who had gone and enclosed Ya Fúra on all sides, they would have apprehended him, if Korombo had not arrived, who came and drove away the people. As to Ya Fúra, when he returned, he just came and settled in a place till he died; nobody killed him. But as regards all his towns there was no youth again, (but) only children and women; young men were not there, they had killed them all in the East. And Korombo located again young men every where in all those towns, and he was left the only great warrior again; he vanquished the people in the whole world, both all the white and the black men. At last they killed him.

As to Korombo, because he conquered all people, therefore they acted deceitfully against him in order to try to kill him. They gave him many women, and told those women (that) when they were plaiting his hair, they might bring his hair. As for the pillow, whereon he was putting his head, when he lay down (they told them), that when they were going to wash (it), the water which they wring out, they should put that water into

---

1) The avant-guard.
2) That is, the rear!

a-bítra, ña kére-ña ka am-Móri. Mọ ọ gbạk ẹ-sántrạk, ọ pā ka am-bẹ́ra: „Kọ fíta-mi-yi." Ka ña yóka ña kére-yi ka añ-fạm, añá tẹn-kọ ara-bomp-e. Ma ña káne-ko họ: „Mañ kọ́nẹ gbán-nẹ;" ña kọ gbo ka añ-gbánnẹ ña-tši. Kọ Korómbo ọ bā r'ạ́fa ra-bána: kére ar'ạ́fa-r'ọñ o bā, ña poñ kọ wọñ yáñfa. Ña tóntọ Korómbo, káma o der tráka dif-kọ; kére kọ́nọ tr'a he tši Ka am-baī ña tẹn r'ạ́fa ra-bána; ña poñ kóne tratrák ro ka Korómbo. Mọ ọ der gbánnẹ-ña, ar'ạ́fa ra gbạ́tro ro-kant bẹ; a-baī tramát ro kin ña der yíra ka k'ạntr k'in. O-baı, owọ́ yi ọw'úmi-k'ọñ gbeñ. ọ yíra ka ak'ạ́ntr. Mọ Korómbo ọ bēk, ña kúlọ, ña liñ-kọ, ọ yíra ka ka-troñ ka a-baī ña-rạñ, ña trạ kúlọ; Korómbo ọ tra kúlo. Ña yif-ko họ: „W'an-ka-su, ko tr'eī tra mạ poñ-su-e?" Ko owọ́ liñ-ko, o botr-ko ka ẹ-lañk-y'ọñ, o tra kúlo. O-baī o-lọm ọ noī-ko, o botr-ko ka ẹ-lañk-y'oñ. Korómbo o láktẹ, o fántạ ka ẹ-lañk ya o-baī, ọwọ́ bā a-bálma. Kọ ọ-baī ka-tši ọ wúra am-bálma, o rok-kọ ka ka-lim, ọ faī-kọ; am-baī a-lom bẹ ña gbúkẹ, ña woñ ro-kant. Korómbo ọ yókanẹ, ọ pā họ: „Man tšim nạñ!" Kọ ọ dif a-kẹ́lfa trọfátr. Mọ ọ kal botr añ-gbátọ-ñ'ọñ ka am-bom-ña-tši, ọ fúmpọ, kọ ọ fi.

Ar'étr ra gbépar gbeñ, kọ ọ fúmpo; ka ma ar'étr ra mọ́tra, ña nañk fẹ ri sọ, hā pạ bēka ma-ré͞ı tramát ro kin. Añá béka ma-ré͞ı tramát dẹ rạñ, ma ar'étr ra gbépar 'ra-bomp ratrọ́ñ, ka ña mọt ri nañk. Kére Korómbo, ña poñ kọ dif; kére o trạ gbálap; hā ña mañk-kọ ọ trạ gbálap. Ka añ-gbátọ-ñ'ọñ, w'úmi ó w'úmi ọ gbáli hẹ ñi wúra ka am-bom; ta ọw'án-k'ọñ, kọ́nọ der a bottle,[1]) and carry it to the Mori-men. When he cut the nails, he said to the women: "Go and throw them[2]) away for me." And they took (them), and carried them to the people, who sought his life.[3]) When they said to him: "Let us go and meet together;" they just went to that meeting. And Korombo had a large army; but his army which he had, had entered into a conspiracy against him. They coaxed Korombo, that he might come in order to kill him; but he did not know it. And the kings raised a large army; they had gone to Korombo's place at night. When he came to meet them, the army was all around the wood (where they met); six kings came and sat upon one log of timber. A king, who was of his own family, sat upon the log. When Korombo came, they cried, they drew him close, and he sat between two kings, they were crying; Korombo was crying. They asked him: "Friend,[4]) why hast thou destroyed us?" And he who had drawn him close, put him upon his lap, and was crying. Another king took him, and put him upon his lap. Korombo looked up, he lay in the lap of a king, who had a dagger. Then that king took out the dagger, cut him into the neck, and cut his throat; all the other kings fled, and went into the wood. Korombo got up and said: "Let us fight together!" And he killed ten captains. When he had put the cutlass again into its sheath, he fell down and died.

The sun had just reached the Meridian, when he fell down; and when the sun set, they did not see it again, for the space of six days. On the seventh day, when the sun reached the Meridian, then only they saw it. But as regards Korombo, they had killed him; but he was (still) twinkling with the eyes; till they buried him he was twinkling with the eyes. As to his sword, nobody was able to unsheath it; except his son, he came

---

1) That is: 'they should put the water, which they wring out, into a bottle etc.'
2) That is 'the cuttings of them'.
3) Lit.: "who sought his head."
4) Lit. "Our friend etc."

wúra-ṅi. Mo o poṅ fi, w'úni ó w'úni o yóka ra-kẹ́lfa, ka ṅa tšim.

Ka̱-tšim ka̱ poṅ tabána, pa̱ tọ́f'la ka an-tọf a-témnẹ bẹ;[1] 'a tšéla am-póto, 'a der gbánnẹ. Ka am-baī ó, am-póto ó, ṅa fọf d'im r'in, ṅa pā ho: „Tr' 'a tšē yō so r'a̱fa ra-bána, támbe r'a̱fa tra̱-gbā tra̱-raṅ, dẹ tra̱-gbā tra̱-sas gbo; pa̱ poṅ. Be w'úni o yō r'a̱fa tra̱-gba tr'áṅlẹ, o fúmpo k'áši, tr' o ram; pa̱kášifẹ o yéma la̱sa̱r an-tọf. Yo Koróṁbo o yō ta̱paṅ, o la̱sa̱r an-tọf.

Ara-bomp II.

Ma-Ká̱nẹ ma an-Témnẹ ma-kur trá̱ka ka-Trá̱pi ara-Rū dẹ aṅ-Fa̱m a-trọ́trọko.

Aṅ-kas-'a-su ṅa ká̱nẹ bẹ su o-lai trá̱ka ka-bémpa 'ra-rū, ṅa ká̱nẹ-su gbo fo[2] mo K'úru o bémpa ara-rū-e, o reṅ'-ri ka 'ra-bomp ra w'úni bána,[3] owọ́ yi roráta. Ow'úni owé kọ́no sára ara-rū. Ṅa kà̱nẹ-su fo ey'íntr bẹ, dẹ ak'éreṅ bẹ, dẹ ey'étr bẹ, eyé lọ́ko ka 'ra-rū, e yi aṅ-fon ṅa 'ra-bomp ra ow'úni owé; dẹ ey'étr e-ṅésa̱m bẹ e yi atr'ár tra 'ra-bomp-r'oṅ.[4] Owọ́ 'a reṅ ta̱paṅ ara-rū ka 'ra-bomp-e, o poṅ fi, w'úni lom kọ́no

---

1) Or: „the whole Temne country became quiet (pacified)."

2) Or: fo ara-rū aré ra rénsa ka 'ra-bomp ra w'úni bána, etc., „that this world was on the top of the head of a giant, etc."

3) According to some: -ra a-sẹm a-bána, „of a large animal, etc."

4) Or: R'áka ó r'áka ka 'ra-rū bẹ, ak'éreṅ, dẹ ey'íntr bẹ, e yi aṅ-fon-ṅ'oṅ. E-lop ó r'a ra-ṅésa̱m bẹ, añá yi ro-tọf dẹ ro-m'antr ṅa yi atr'ár-tr'oṅ. „Every thing in this world, the grass and all the trees are his hair. The fish and every living creature, which is on the earth or in the water, are his lice."

and unsheathed it. When he was dead, every one took upon him the office of a captain of the army, and they fought together.

War was now at an end for ever,¹) and there was peace in all the Temne country; they called the white people; they came and met together. And the kings and the white people made an agreement, they said:²) Let none raise a large army again, except an army of forty, or of sixty (men) only; it is sufficient. If any one raises an army of eighty (men), he becomes liable to a fine, he must pay (for it); because he wants to spoil the country. Thus Korombo did before, and spoiled the country.

Chapter II.

Traditions of the Temnes respecting the Creation of the World and of the first Men.³

Our fathers did not tell us much about the creation of the world, they only told us that when God made the world, he put it on the head of a giant, who was below (it).⁴) This person carries the world on the head. They told us that all the trees, and all the grass, and all things, which grow on this earth,⁵) are the hair of the head of this giant; and all living creatures are the lice of his head. He, on whose head the world was put before, has died, and another man

---

1) Little quarrels excepted as mentioned before.

2) Sense: „And the Chiefs and the Europeans made an agreement to this effect that none should raise an army exceeding, etc."

3) We may head this Chapter also as follows:
An Account of the Creation of the World and of man as received by the Temnes according to the Traditions delivered to them by their Ancestors.

4) The Temnes believe the earth to be a round flat body. In the same way the sacred books of the Hindus represent the earth as resting on the back of a turtle of an immense size, and that earthquakes arise in consequence of a movement of this turtle.

5) Lit. „in this world, etc."

kal sára ara-rū aré. Ma 'a reṅ-kọ 'ra-rū, ọ yíra, ọ sā̰kẹ ro-tọ́rọṅ. Na káṅe-su fọ ọw'úni ọwé ọ sā̰kẹ; kérẹ ọ sā̰kẹ sọī, hā a-fa̰m ṅa gbā̰li hẹ tši trára; támbe aṅ-lọ ṅa mọ sā̰kẹ ro-pil, a-fa̰m ṅa trára-tši; pa̰kášifẹ aṅ-lọ ṅa-tši an-tọf ṅa bọ́nẹ,[1]) hā ẹ-set dẹ y'intr ẹ fúmpọ. Aṅ-lọ ṅaṅ ọw'úni ọwé ọ mọ fúmpọ, ọ fi-e, ara-rū bẹ ra poṅ, dẹ r'áka ó r'áka ka 'ra-rū aré ra tra̰ dínnẹ. Pa̰ won gbo-e K'úru ọ yóka ara-rū aré, káma ọ kal botr ra-rū ra-fu. K'úru ọ bẹ́mpa hẹ ra-rū ra-bak tabána; pa̰ won ọ kal botr ra-rū ra-fu. Atrá aṅ-fa̰m a-bi, dẹ am-póto ṅa tra̰ pā trā̰ka ara-rū, fọ ara-rū aré ra tra̰ poṅ lọ́kọ lọm, tra̰ yi tra̰-tšeṅ.

Ka ka-tra̰p, mọ K'úru ọ bẹ́mpa ara-rū, ọ bẹ́mpa a-fa̰m ṅa-ra̰ṅ ka an-tọf,[2]) ọ-rúni rẹ ọ-béra. Aṅ-lọ ṅaṅ K'úru ọ bẹ́mpa 'ra-rū, w'úni ó w'úni ọ yi hẹ ri hā ka aṅ-réï mọ K'úru ọ bẹ́mpa ọ-rúni dẹ ọ-béra. Mọ K'úru ọ poṅ bẹ́mpa-ṅa, ṅa yíra gbo, ọ sọṅ fẹ ṅa r'ā ra-di. Ṅa trā̰lnẹ d'or, ka ṅa pā ka K'úru: „Ma̰ poṅ bẹ́mpa-su; kérẹ ko r'áka sa̰ ma di-e?" Ka aṅ-lọ ṅa-tši ṅa tr'a hẹ r'áka ó r'áka. Tšíaṅ K'úru ọ káṅe-ṅa fọ ọ tra̰ sọṅ-ṅa r'ā ra-di. K'úru ọ sọṅ-ṅa pa̰-lā pa̰-féra, káma ṅa yọ̄-pi a-gbéra; ṅía ma rúṅka̰tr rẹ m'antr, ṅa yọ̄-ṅi ka̰-bō, ṅa di.[3]) Ṅa ta na̰m fẹ sọ

1) Or: mo ọ sā̰kẹ gbo ro-pil-e, ara-rū bẹ ra bọ́nẹ, etc., „as soon as he turns towards the West, there arises an earthquake, etc."

2) Or: Mọ K'úru ọ trā̰pi ara-rū bẹ, ọ wúra a-fa̰m ṅa-ra̰ṅ, etc. „When God created the whole world, he took out two persons, etc."

3) Or: Ṅa trā̰lnẹ d'or, 'a pā ka am-boi (ọwó mọ yọ̄ mapant ka-trọ́ṅ-ka-ṅaṅ dẹ ka-trọ́ṅ ka K'úru): „Mọ K'úru ọ wúrasu anọ́, ko sa̰ ma re di-e?" Am-boi ọ kọ́nẹ, ọ kọ káṅe K'úru. K'úru ọ wúra pa̰-lā pa̰-féra, o sọṅ ka am-boi, ọ kérẹ-pi. O wúra tra̰-romp dẹ tra̰-dir, o sọṅ ka am-boi, ọ kára-tši. Apa-la pía ma kọ gba̰m, 'a rúṅka̰tr-ṅi rẹ m'antr; ṅía ṅa ma di. „They felt hungry, and they said to the servant (who was transacting matters between them and between God): „As God has taken us out here, what shall we go eat?" The servant departed, and

carries this world again on the head. When they put the world on him, he was in a sitting posture, and turned towards the East. They told us that this person turns himself, but that he turns softly, so that people cannot know it;[1]) except that time when he turns towards the West, then men know it;[2]) because at that time there arises an earthquake,[3]) so that houses and trees fall down. At that time when this person falls down, and dies, the whole world is at an end, and every thing in this world will perish. After a long time God will ake this world away, that he may put again a new world. God did not make a world lasting for ever; after a long time he will put a new world again. What the black and the white people say respecting the world, that this world will be at an end some day, is truth.

In the beginning, when God made the world, he made two persons on the earth, a male and a female. At that time when God made the world, there was no man in it till the day when God made the male and the female. When God had made them, they just sat down, he did not give them any thing to eat. They felt hungry, and they said to God: „Thou hast made us; but what thing shall we eat;" At that time they did not know any thing. Therefore God told them that he will give them something to eat. God gave them clean rice, that they might make flour of it; this they were to mix with water, and to make a cake of it, and to eat it. They had not yet seen

went and told (it) to God. God took out clean rice (i. e. deprived of the husks), and gave (it to the servant, and he carried it. He took out pestles and mortars, and gave (them) to the servant, who brought them. As for the rice, they were to go and beat it to powder, and to mix it (i. e. the flour of it) with water; and this they were to eat."

1) Or: „are not aware of it."
2) Or: „are aware of it."
3) Lit. „the earth moves, etc.

r'ā ra-di ra-lọm. K'úru ọ sọṅ fẹ ṅa n'antr aṅ-lọ ṅa-tši.
Ar'á ra-di aré ṅa di kạ-reṅ k'in. Ka-ráraṅ-ka-tši ṅa yif K'úru
sọ: „Aré ría sa ma di gbo lọ́kọ ó lọ́kọ-i?" ¹) Tšíaṅ K'úru ọ
káne-ṅa: „Trạ bā hẹ tr'eī, l tši sọṅ-nu sọ r'a ra-di ra-lọm trạ́ka
di. Ka ka-reṅ aká béka trạ-rạṅ-e K'úru ọ sọṅ-ṅa y'ẹtr ẹ-di
bẹ. ²) dẹ ẹ-šẹm aṅá yi ọ-lómpi trạ́ka di; ọ sómra ka am-bọī.
káma ọ kérẹ-yi, yía ṅa ma kọ di. Ka aṅ-lọ ṅa-tši ọ trọ́ri-ṅa
sọ ẹ-šẹm, aṅá ma tšē di-ẹ. E-lọm 'a ma tšē di-ẹ. Ọ kára-yi
bẹ rọkín, ọ gbáski-yi; ọ botr ẹyé 'a ma di-ẹ tọ́kọ; ẹyé 'a ma
tšē di-ẹ, ọ botr-yi tọ́kọ; ọ trọ́ri-ṅa ẹyé 'a ma di, dẹ ẹyé 'a ma
tšē di. Aṅ-lọ ṅa-tši ṅa tr'a hẹ tr'eī ó tr'eī, támbe trạ́ka kạ-di
gbo. Ka-rárạṅ-ka-tši K'úru ọ trọ́ri-ṅa ẹ-trọl bẹ, dẹ ẹy'étr bẹ
trạ́ka yọ̄ ma-pant ka an-tof, kạ-trála, dẹ a-sápạr, dẹ kạ-bap, dẹ
a-bóka; ọ sọṅ-ṅa sọ n'antr. Na trạ́ma a-tšiṅ, ṅa bā hẹ y'ẹtr
ẹ-lópra.

Ma 'a nạṅk ṅa bā y'ẹtr ẹ-di ẹ-laī, ṅa sōm am-bọī, káma
ọ kọ káne K'úru họ: „Téte sạ bā y'ẹtr ẹ-di ẹ-laī; kérẹ sạ yi
gbo ṅa-rạṅ: tro sạ ma yọ̄-ẹ sạ yi a-laī-e?" K'úru ọ pā: „Trạ
bā hẹ tr'eī; kar-mi." K'úru ọ kọ baṅ a-trọl, trạ-bot tramát rẹ
sas, ọ sọṅ ka am-bọī, káma ọ kérẹ-tši, dẹ káma ṅa di-tši. ³)

1. Or: Na ta nạm fẹ sọ r'ā ra-di ra-lọm. Tšíaṅ ṅa kúnẹ
sọ am-bọī, káma ọ kọ kánẹ K'úru fọ yē: „Eyé yía sạ ma di gbo
lọ́kọ ó lọ́kọ-i?" „They had not seen as yet any other food.
Therefore they told the servant again, that he might go and tell
God thus: „These things them we shall eat only always?"

2) Or: K'úru o kal wúra y'ẹtr ẹ-di bẹ, „God took out again
all sorts of victuals."

3) Or: Ma ṅa yif K'úru yaṅ-e, K'úru ọ kálane; kọ téte ọ
sōm am-bọi-ṅ'ọṅ. Am-bọi ọ kára-ṅa ẹ-trọl ẹ-lọm, káma ṅa di-yi,
káma ṅa yi a-lai. „When they asked God thus, God returned;
and presently he sent his servant. The servant brought them
some medicines, that they might eat them, (and) that they might
increase." Or also: Ma ṅa yif K'úru yaṅ-e, K'úru ọ pā: „Trạ
bā hẹ tr'eī, kar-mi." Kọ K'úru ọ kọ baṅ a-trọl, trạ-bot tramát
rẹ sas; atra-rạṅ trạ-fḗra ọ sọṅ ka am-bọī, káma ọ kérẹ-tši.
Am-bọi ọ kérẹ an-trọl, ọ kọ sọṅ-ṅa. Q-béra ọ pā fọ, etc. „When
they asked God thus, God said: „It is of no consequence, wait

any other food. God did not give them fire at that time. This food they ate for one year. Afterwards they asked God again: "This only we shall eat always?" Therefore God told them: "It does not matter, I shall give you also some other thing to eat." In the second year God gave them all sorts of victuals, and animals which were proper to be eaten; he sent (them) by the servant, that he might carry them, and these they were to go to eat. At that time he showed them also the animals, which they were not to eat. Some they were not to eat. He brought them all together, and separated them; he put those which they were to eat by themselves; those which they were not to eat, he put by themselves; he showed them those which they were to eat, and those which they were not to eat. At that time they did not know any thing but to eat only. Afterwards God showed them all kind of medicines, and all sorts of tools to do work with in the ground,[1]) as a hoe, and a digger, and an axe, and a bill-hook; he also gave them fire. They were naked, and had no clothes.

When they saw that they had plenty of victuals, they sent the servant, that he might go and tell God: "Now me have plenty of food; but we are only two: what (how) must we do to increase?" God said: "It is of no consequence; wait me." God went and fetched medicine, eight pills, and gave (them) to the servant, that he might carry them, and that they might eat them.

---

me." Then God went to fetch medicine, eight pills; the two white ones he gave to the servant, that he might carry them. The servant carried the medicine, and gave (it) to them. The woman said that, etc."

1) I. e. ,agricultural implements.'

Fǫ K'úru ǫ bémpa-ña ña-rǫ̇ñ ña trára-tši; kérę ña tr'a he, ma 'a ma yō ña yi a-lai. Ma am-bǫī ǫ kára ę-trǫl-e, ǫ-béra ǫ pā fǫ kǫ́nǫ mǫ mǫt di an-trǫl; kérę am-bǫī ǫ šélǫ hę trąka tši, ǫ pā: „Kar-mi, káma I kǫ trǫ́ri-tši ka Pā." Tšiañ ǫ kálanę trąka kánę K'úru, atrá ǫ-béra ǫ poñ pā-e. K'úru ǫ pā ka am-bǫī: „Kǫ sǫñ-kǫ atra-bána trą-rąñ, káma ǫ mǫt tši di." Ka am-bǫī ǫ kǫ́nę, ǫ sǫñ-kǫ-tši; kǫ ǫ-béra ǫ di atra-rąñ. Tšiañ ǫ-béra ǫ tas trąka a-féla; tšiañ a-béra bę ña ma trū k'or, ma añ'óf ña las, talǫ́m ma añ'óf ña fi.¹) Am-bǫī ǫ wúra an-tramát ro kin, atrá tšía, ǫ sǫñ ǫ-rúni trą-sas rę ǫ-béra trą-sas. Ǫ-rúni ǫ di an-trǫl-ñ'ǫñ, ǫ mun sǫ m'antr.²) Ma ña poñ di ę-trǫl-e, ña bā fǫ́sa trąka sǫ́tǫ a-wut; kérę atr'eí atšé trą gbąli hę yi, támbe 'a lękanę. K'úru ǫ yif am-bǫī fǫ: „Ña di an-trǫl-i?" Am-bǫī ǫ wósa. Kǫ K'úru ǫ sǫñ-kǫ a-trǫl a-lǫm, ǫ pā: „Kǫ botr ma-lap ka ǫw'úni bom, kǫ botr kạ-bak ra-fǫr ka ǫw'áñ dúni. Tšiañ a-fąm a-rúni bę ña yi a-báki ra-fǫr; tšiañ sǫ a-fąm a-bom ña bā ma-lap. Añ-féla ña bak-ña ña-rąñ tra lękanę; kérę ǫ-béra ǫ gbąli hę trąp,

1) Or: Am-bǫī o kǫ́nę, o ko bēk ka K'úru, o pā: „O-béra ǫ pā hǫ kǫ́nǫ mǫ mǫt di an-trǫl." K'úru ǫ kánę-ko fǫ káma ǫ yǫ́ mǫ ǫ-béra ǫ yéma, káma o mǫt di an-trǫl. E-trǫl e yi trą-bot tramát rę sas: ǫ-béra ǫ yóka atrá ta yi trą-báma, ǫ di-tši. Tšiañ a-béra bę ña yeñk hę sǫ ma-der ka añ'óf a-fi, dę ka añ'óf a-las." The servant departed, and went and came to God, and said: „The woman said that she must first eat the medicine." God told him that he might do as the woman wanted, and that she might first eat the medicine. The medicines consisted of eight pills: the woman took the two larges ones, and ate them. This is the reason that all women are not well again at new moon, and at full moon."

2) Or: Ma ña ña-rąñ 'a poñ di ę-trǫl-'e-ñañ, ña yéranę e-trǫl tramát ro kin, eyé tšía; ǫ-béra o sǫ́to ę-sas, ǫ-rúni ǫ sǫ́tǫ ę-sas. Ma ña poñ di, etc. „When they both had eaten their medicine, they divided the six medicines, which were left among each other; the woman got three, and the man got three. When they had eaten, etc."

That God made them two they knew it; but they did not know, how (what) they must do to increase. When the servant brought the medicine, the woman said that she must first eat the medicine; but the servant was not willing for it, he said: „Wait me, that I may go and inform the Master of it." Therefore he returned in order to tell God, what the woman had said. God said to the servant: „Go and give her the two large ones, that she may eat them first." And the servant went, and gave them to her; and the woman ate the two. This is the reason that the woman has a stronger (sexual) desire; this is the reason that all women have the menses when the moon is full, or when the moon is new.[1] The servant took out the six (pills), which were left, and gave three to the man and three to the woman. The man ate his medicine, and drank also water. When they had eaten the medicine, they had power[2] to get children; but this thing could not happen, unless they had a sexual commerce with each other. God asked the servant: „Did they eat the medicine?" The servant answered in the affirmative. And God gave him another medicine, and said: „Go and put modesty on the woman, and boldness on the man." This is the reason that all men are bold; this is also the reason that women are modest. The desire to have a sexual commerce with each other was strong with both of them; however the woman could not begin,

---

1) Lit. „is dead", — „is done".
2) Or „ability".

ọ lap trặka yọ̄-tši; kére ọ-rúni kọ́nọ ta báki ra-fọr, kọ́nọ
kọ trạp tra yọ̄-tši.¹) Ma 'a fạnta, ọ-béra ọ yóka k'or. Ma
am-bọī ọ der, o-béra ọ trọ́ri-kọ ak'ór; am-bọī ọ kọ trọ́ri
K'úru, fọ ọ-béra ak'ór-k'ọṅ ka bána. K'úru ọ sọṅ-kọ y'etr
ẹ-lópra tra kọ sọṅ-ṅa, ka ọ-béra rẹ ọ-rúni. Ọ kára-yi, ọ re
sọṅ-ṅa. Ma ak'ór-k'ọṅ ka poṅ bak, ọ kōm w'ahẹ́t rúni o-bi.
Ọ kal yóka k'or, kọ ọ kōm w'ahẹ́t béra ọ-féra. Ọ-béra ọ kal
sọ yóka k'or, ọ kōm trạ-bári, w'ahẹ́t rúni rẹ w'ahẹ́t béra; ọ-rúni
ọ yi ọ-féra, kọ ọ-béra ọ yi o-bi. Ma am-bọī ọ der, 'a káne-
kọ, káma ọ kọ káne K'úru fọ: „Sạ sọ́tọ a-fạm ṅ'áṅle." Am-bọī
ọ kọ́ne, ọ kọ káne K'úru, fọ aṅ-fạm, aṅá ọ bémpa, ṅa poṅ sọ́tọ
a-wut; aṅa-rúni ṅa rạṅ, de aṅa-béra ṅa rạn.²) Mọ ọ kọ káne
K'úru, K'úru ọ yif fọ: „Tro ṅa yi-e?" Kọ ọ pā họ: „O-rúni
ọ bi, ọ-béra ọ féra, kọ ọ-rúni ọ-lọm ọ féra, de ọ-béra ọ-lọm ọ
bi; tšíaṅ 'a pā, káma l re yif-mu fọ tro 'a ma yọ̄-ṅa-e." K'úru
ọ pā: „Kọ́ne, kọ gbáski-ṅa; kére aṅa-féra ro-m'antr rayẹ́r; aṅa-
bi botr-ṅa ro-gbaṅ." Am-bọī ọ der, ọ gbáski-ṅa, ọ yọ̄ mọ K'úru
ọ sōm-kọ; ọ kọ trọ́ri K'úru fọ: „I poṅ yọ̄ ma mạ poṅ pā."
K'úru ọ wúra y'etr be, ọ sọṅ sọ ka am-bọī, ọ pā „Kọ́ne". Aṅá
ro-gbaṅ ọ sọṅ, káma ọ kére-ṅa y'etr ẹ-yọ́na ma-pant be ro-tọf;

1) Or — — kọ́nọ yọ̄-tši. Ka-rárạṅ-ka-tši ọ béra ọ yóka
k'or, kọ ọ kōm w'ahẹ́t rúni ọ-bi. Ọ-béra ọ yóka sọ k'or, kọ
ọ re kōm w'ahẹ́t béra ọ-féra. Aká béka ma-sas-e ọ kōm trạ-
bári, o-rúni ọ féra, ọ-béra ọ bi. Am-boī o der, 'a káne, etc.
„— — he did it. After this the woman conceived, and she brought
forth a black boy. The woman conceived again, and she brought
forth a white girl. At the third time [lit. (at the parturition) which
amounted to three (times)] she brought forth twins, the boy was
white, and the girl was black. The servant came, they told, etc".

2) Or: Ma am-bọī ọ der, ọ nạṅk-ṅa, ọ kọ́ne, ọ kọ káne
K'úru, fọ aṅ-fạm — — — ṅa rạṅ. Tšíaṅ K'úru ọ sōm-kọ
sọ, káma ọ gbáski aṅ-wut. Kọ ọ der, ọ gbáski aṅ-wut a-féra
ka aṅ-wut a-bi." When the servant came, and saw them, he
left, and went and told God, that the people — — — were two.
Therefore God sent him again, that he might separate the children. And he came, and separated the white children from the
black children."

she was ashamed to do it; but the man he was more bold, he began to do it. When they lay down, the woman conceived. When the servant came, the woman showed him (her) pregnancy;¹) (and) the servant went and informed God, that as for the woman she was pregnant.²) God gave him clothes to go and give them to them, to the woman³) and to the man. He brought them, (and) came and gave them to them. When her pregnancy had come to the full time, she brought forth a black boy. She conceived again, and brought forth a white girl. The woman conceived once more, and brought forth twins, a boy and a girl; the boy was white, and the girl was black. When the servant came, they told him, that he might go and tell God: „We have got four persons." The servant left, and went and told God, that the people, whom he had made, had got children; the boys were two, and the girls were two. When he went to tell God, God asked him: „Of what kind are they?" And he said: „A boy is black, and a girl is white, and another boy is white, and another girl is black; therefore they said, that I might come and ask thee what (how) they must do with them." God said: „Go and separate them;⁴) carry the white ones to the water side; as to the black ones locate them in the country." The servant came, and separated them, he did as God sent⁵) him (to do); and went and told God: „I have done as thou hast said." God took out all sorts of implements, and gave them to the servant, and said: „Go." For those in the country he gave (to the servant), that he might carry to them all sorts of agricultural implements;⁶)

---

1) Lit. „the woman showed him the belly."
2) Lit. „that the woman her belly was great" or „big".
3 To this day, when a girl gets betrothed to her future husband, the latter gives her clothes, as she wears none before that time.
4) Lit. „Depart, go and separate etc."
5) Or: „caused him etc."
6) Lit. „things to do all sort of work with in the ground."

aṅá ro-m'antr, ọ kọ yer-ṅa y'etr e-yọ́ua ma-pant be rom'antr. Ka aṅ-féra ọ soṅ a-fạm a-trol, de aṅá sọt-aṅ, de aṅá gbal. Aṅá ro-gbaṅ, ọ soṅ-ṅa a-kábi. Aṅ-fạm a-trol ṅa bémpa e-set tráka aṅ-fạm a-féra, de trạ-bil trạ-póto tráka kọt ro-baṅ; káma ṅa sótọ a-kála, kọ káma ṅa yi a-yóla; kọ ọ botr-ṅa rom'antr rayér. Aṅ-wut a-bi ọ botr ro-gbaṅ, de ka trạ-tšeṅ, de ka trạ-gbọ́ṅkọ; ọ tạ́k'sa-ṅa tráka bémpa e-set e-népạl, de e-set e-sọr, de tráka baf k'ọr, kọ ọ yọ̄-ṅa tra yọ̄ ma-pant ma-báki be; kére a-fạm a-féra ṅa bā he kạ-yọ̄ 'ma-pant amé, ṅa bā he kạ-yọ̄ e-trọl, ṅa túpạs he; ama-treī amé be 'a botr-ṅa ka aṅ-fạm a-bi gbo. Tšíaṅ aṅ-fạm a-féra, K'úru ọ reṅ-ṅa rokọ́m ka aṅ-fạm a-bi trạ́k' a-fọ́sa ó, trạ́k' a-kála ó, tráka kạ-tšemp ó; tšíaṅ w'úni féra, háli ọ yi gbo w'ahét rúni, a-fạm a-bi ṅa yi-kọ roráta, ṅa mínta he kọ. Atrá-bóna be ka ra-rū aré ṅa yéfa ka aṅ-wut aṅé a-féra, de ka aṅ-wut aṅé a-bi.

Am-boī ọ kọ káne K'úru fọ: „I poṅ yer-ṅa." Mọ ọ poṅ gbáski-ṅa, aṅa-féra ṅa kọ kōm a-wut tramát ro kin, aṅa-bi ṅa kōm tramát ro kin; aṅa-féra a-béra a-sas de a-rúni a-sas; aṅa-bi a-rúni a-sas de a-béra a-sas. Ma aṅ-wut ṅa-tši ṅa poṅ bak, ṅa kal sọ kōm, aṅé tramát ro kin, aṅé tramát ro kin. Aṅa-bi ya ṅa kōm sọ, aṅa-féra ya ṅa kōm sọ. Am-boī ọ kọ káne K'úru fọ: „Aṅ-fạm ṅa ma la-aṅ." K'úru ọ pā ka am-boī:

as to those close the water side, he went and gave them all sorts of shipping implements.¹) To the white people he gave artisans, and taylors, and clerks. As to those in the country he gave them blacksmiths. The artisans made houses for the white people, and ships²) for to walk on the sea; that they might get money, and that they might be gentlemen; and he put them close the water side. The black children he put in the country, and on hills, and in forests; he taught them to make grass-houses and mud-houses, and to make farms, and he made them to do all laborious work; but white people have not to do this work, they have not to make country-medicines,³) they do not practise divination;⁴) as regards all these things, he put them only on the black people. Therefore, as regards the white people, God made them superior to the black people in power, and in property, and in intelligence; therefore, as regards a white person, although he be but a boy, black people are inferior to him, they dare not vie with him. All nations in this world descend from these white children, and from these black children.

The servant went and said to God: „I have shared out to them."⁵) When he had separated them, the white (people) went and brought forth six children, the black (people) went and brought forth six children; the white ones three females and three males; the black ones three males and three females. When those children had grown up, they also brought forth children again, these six, (and) these six. The black ones brought forth black children again,⁶) the white ones brought forth white children again.⁶) The servant went and told God: „The people are increasing." God said to the servant:

---

1) Lit. „things to do all sort of work with at sea."
2) Lit. „white man's canoes," or „european canoes."
3) Or „charms, amulets."
4) Or „fortune telling."
5) That is ‚the various objects, as artisans, blacksmiths etc.'
6 Lit. „the black (or white) ones in the same way they brought forth again.

„Ko yer-ña tra-bóna." O kóne, o ko yer tra-bóna seňk. Aňaféra ña ba tra-bóna-tra-ñań, o-béra re o-rúni o-k'in, o-béra re orúni o-k'in. Aña-bi, o ko yer-ña tra-bóna, mo o poń yer aňaféra be; kére aňa-féra ña yi ra ka-petr k'in, de aňa-bi ña yi ra ka-petr k'in. Ma ña ma béka a-laī-e, am boī o ko káne K'úru fo: „Ań-fam-'a-mu 'a gbáti toů-e." K'úru o pā: „Tr' 'a ko soń-ña an-tof ña tra-bóna-tra-ñań." Mo o der-e, o yer ampó!o tra-tof tra-gbánte be; o kal yer ań-fam a-bi tra-tof tragbánte, ma tra-bóna tra yi tra-laī.

Ka ka-trap, mo K'úru o bémpa w'úni, a-fam ña yi fe tráka fi, me e-súma yē ka ra-trū, de ka ka-báńsa ma-der. Ań-lo ñatši ra-trū ra yi he, ra-fi ra yi he. Aů-lo ña-tši ań-fam, aňá K'úru o mot kára ká ra-rū-e, ña tra káli ka-bak ka-bána; a-lom ña káli ña béka tra reń tr'éme tramát ro kin,[1]) a-lom tr'éme tramát re sas, a-lom ña tása yi;[2]) ña fi he. K'úru o sōm gbo, 'a re bań-ña. K'úrumasába o botr tápań m'etr ma-bóli ka w'úni ó w'úni, o re bań he ko lemp. Be K'úru o yéma yóka w'úni, o mot sōm am-boī-ń'oń ronóń, owó mo re káne-ko, fo K'úru o sōm-ko tra re kóri-ko, de tráka káne-ko, fo ań-lóko-ń'oń ña poń, káma o bénene. Ow'úni, ma am-boī o poń káne-ko yań-e, o bénene tráka aka-tret ań-ñań; o sōm ka ań-fam-ń'oń be, de ań-máne-ń'oń, o lémne-ña. Mo o poń yō yań-e, ma ań-lóko ña-tši ña běk-e; am-boī ña K'úru o der so, ow'úni o yókane, o kóne gbo re am-boī, o naůk fe ra-fi. Ye pa yi tráka w'úni ó w'úni ań-lo ña-tši.

1) Or: a-lom ña bak tra-reń tr'éme tramát ro kin, „some got six hundred years old," etc.
2) Or: a-lom ña tási; „some exceeded (this age)."

„Go and divide them into nations." He left, and went and divided all the nations. The white (people) had their nations, always a woman and one man at a time.¹) As to the black (people), he went and divided them into nations, as he had divided all the white ones; but the white ones were in one town, and the black ones were in another town. When they were amounting to many, the servant went and said to God: „Thy people are numerous now." God said: „Let them go and give them the country of their nations." When he came, he gave to the white people all (their) various countries; (then) he returned and gave to the black people (their) various countries, because the nations were numerous.

In the beginning, when God made man, men had not to die, as at this time by sickness and by bodily pain. At that time there was no sickness, there was no death. At that time the people, whom God brought first into the world, were living to a great age; some were living (till) they reached six hundred years, some eight hundred, some more than that; they did not die, God only sent, (and) they came to fetch them. God fixed formerly a long time for every person, he did not come to fetch them quickly.²) When God wanted to take away a person, (then) he first sent his servant to him, who was coming to tell him, that God had sent him to come and see him, and to tell him, that his time was up, that he might make himself ready. The man, when (after) the servant had told him thus, made himself ready for the departure from his family: he sent to all his people, and to his friends, and had farewell to them. When he had done thus, (and) when that time (spoken of) arrived; the servant of God came again, the man got up, and just went with the servant, he did not see death. Thus it was with every person at that time.

---

1) Lit. „a woman and one man, a woman and one man," or: „a woman with one man, etc.:" i. e. each couple formed one nation, as one the French, another the English, etc.

2) Or „abruptly".

Kérɛ ka a-lóko lọm 'a re kōm o-láṅba, ọwṍ yi w'úni lạs, dẹ w'úni kásra; kóno yi sọ w'úni bána, o ba a-kála a-gbáli, dẹ a-trar a-laī, dẹ y'ẹtr ẹ-trol ẹ-laī, dẹ ẹ-boī ẹ-laī; ọwó tšē trára w'úni ó w'úni r'áka, ọ yọ gbo mọ o yéma; o botr m'ọ́nẹ ka aṅ-ṅaṅ bẹ: kónọ rẹ trạ́pi kạ-fi ka 'ra-rū. Mọ K'úru o soṅ-kọ a-fósa a-bána, o yi o-kḗlfa, o yi o-yóla. Am-boī o kọ kánẹ K'úru fo. „Ọw'án-ka-mu o yi w'úni lạs." K'úru o pā ka am-boī: „Kónẹ, baṅ-kọ; kánẹ-ko, fọ aṅ-lọ-ṅ'ọṅ ṅa poṅ." Ma am-boī o der trạ́ka ọw'úni ọwé tra re baṅ-kọ, o kánẹ-ko mọ K'úru o sōm-ko; kḗrẹ o pā: „I šélọ hẹ. I kọ hẹ; min' láṅba rạs."[1]) Ka trạ-reṅ trạ-laī am-boī o der tra baṅ-ko lókọ ó lókọ; kḗrẹ o šélọ hẹ; kọ o pā ka ka-lápso fọ o gbáli hẹ ri ko kókō. Am-boī o kálanẹ, o kọ kánẹ K'úru fo: „Ọw'án-ka-mu o šélọ hẹ trạ́ka der." Mọ K'úru o tral atšé, o pā ho: „Yáo, pạ bónẹ-mi ma mạ kánẹ-mi atšé; kḗrẹ I tši sōm a-fạm a-lọm." K'úru o wúra a-fạm a-laī, o pā roṅáṅ: „Kọ na baṅ-kọ." Ṅa der, ṅa laī, ṅa pa: „Pā, sạ re baṅ-mu." O pā: „I kọ hẹ ri." Ṅa pā sọ: „Sạ trɛi fẹ mu, maṅ kónẹ." Tšiaṅ o yókanẹ, o sap-ṅa. Ṅa kálanẹ, 'a kọ kánẹ K'úru ho: „Pā, ọw'án-ka-mu o sap-su, o foī hẹ kára." K'úru o pā: „Yíra nạṅ, I tši sōm ọwó mo kọ baṅ-kọ o-tófạl-ẹ; I tši sōm ẹ-boī ṅa-rạṅ, aṅá ma kára-ko soī." Trạ-reṅ trạ-rạṅ trạ las, o sōm fẹ w'úni; ka-reṅ kạ-lọm, aká béka trạ-sas-ẹ, K'úru o mọt sōm Pā Ra-trū, o pā: „Kọ wop-ko, trạ́ma kạdí, o-ṅa-mu o trạ bạp-mu."[2])

---

1) Or: Tšíaṅ, ma am-boī o der trạ́ka ọw'úni ọwé tra re baṅ-kọ, o šélo hẹ tra ko rẹ am-boī, ma aṅ-lókọ-ṅ'ọṅ ṅa poṅ. Ka trạ-reṅ trạ-laī, etc. „Therefore, when the servant came for this man to fetch him, he was not willing to go with the servant, when his (appointed) time was up. For many years, etc."

2) Or: Yaṅ K'úru o mọt sōm Pā Ra-trū, kọn' o yi w'úni báki; o kónẹ ka aṅ-sɛt ṅa ọw'úni, o wop-ko, o pā: „I rẹ baṅ-mu;" kḗrẹ ṅa naṅk fẹ ko kókō. Ọw'úni o fạ́nta, o gbáli hẹ sọ yókanẹ, o gbáli hẹ sáke. Ka ka-bat Pā Ra-fi, ọwó yi, etc. „Thus God first sent Mr. Sickness, he was an old person; he went into the house of the person, took hold of him, and said: „I come to fetch thee;" but they did not see him at all. The

But at a certain time a man was born, who was a wicked person, and a violent person; he was also a great man, he had plenty of money, and many slaves, and plenty of cattle, and many servants; who did not care for any one,[1]) and did just as he pleased, and troubled all his people: he became the author of death in the world.[2]) As God gave him great power, he was a warrior, (and) he was a gentleman. The servant went and said to God: „Thy child is a bad person." God said to the servant: „Go and fetch him; tell him, that his time is up." When the servant came for this man to fetch him, he told him as God caused him (to say); but he said: „I will not, I do not go; I am still a young man." For many years the servant came to fetch him from time to time; but he was not willing; and at last he said that he would not go there at all. The servant returned, and went and told God: „Thy child is not willing to come." When God heard this, he said: „Well, I am glad that thou didst tell me this; but I shall send other people." God picked out many persons, and said to them: „Go ye and fetch him." They came, they were many, and they said: „Sir, we come to fetch thee." He said: „I do not go there." They said again: „We do not leave thee, let us go." Therefore he got up, and beat them. They returned, and went and told God: „Sir, thy child beat us, he is not easy to bring away." God said: „Sit ye down, I shall send one who will go and fetch him quietly; I shall send two servants, who will bring him away softly." Two years passed away, he did not send a person; the next year, which was the third, God first sent Mr. Sickness, and said: „Go, take hold of him, go thou before, thy companion will meet thee."

---

man lay down, he could not get up again, nor could he turn himself. In the morning Mr. Death, who was etc."

1) Lit. „who did not know any thing for any person."
2) Lit. „he came to begin dying in the world."

Pa Ra-trū o yi w'úni báki; o kóne ka aṅ-sel ṅa ow'úni, o baṇ-ko o fặnta ka an-tẹnta-ṅ'oṅ; o pa roṅọ́ṅ: „I wop-mu tẹnoṅ. Ma 'a re baṅ-mu, ma káši, mína Ra-trū I re baṅ-mu, I wop-mu tẹnoṅ." Ow'úni o yókane, o kạli-kạli, o naṅk fe w'úni. O tšéla am-boi-ṅ'oṅ, o pā: „Tšéla aṅ-fạm-'a-mi be." Am-boī o tšéla-ṅa; aṅ-fạm ṅa der, ṅa re yíra ka aṅ-set be, ṅa yif-ko: „Ko ne-e?" O pā: „Pā Ra-trū o wop-mi; kére I naṃ fe ko." Pā Ra-trū o pā ho: „Mína wop-ko; mo o lā káši fo o ko he, tšíaṅ o trū, I wop-ko tẹnoṅ." Aṅ-fạm be, aṅá yi ri, ṅa traļ ar'ím ra Pā Ra-trū; kére ṅa naṅk fe ko kókō. Ow'úni o fặnta, o sóko gbes, o díra he, o gbạ́li he so yókane, o gbạ́li he sáke. Aka-baṭ Pā Ra-trū o pā ho: „Ra-trū ra bak-mu-e." Ka ar'étr ra-baṭ Pā Ra-fi, owó yi o-láṅba, o bēk. Ma Pā Ra-fi o der, o káne o-máne-k'oṅ Pā Ra-trū, fo ow'úni o-kásra owé o gbạ́li he yíra so anó o-bóli, fo kon' o gbạ́li he bā-ko i-nei, fo o gbạ́li he piára anó tẹnoṅ, fo o traļ kére-ko. Ṅa be ro-set ṅa traļ ar'ím-ra-ṅaṅ; kére ṅa gbạ́li he naṅk-ṅa.¹) Ma Pā Ra-fi o poṅ pā yaṅ-e, o yóka aṅ-ṅésam

---

1) Or: Ka ar'étr ra-baṭ Pā Ra-fi o bēk. Mo o der-e, o pā ho: „Pā Ra-fi o bēk, ma Pā Ra-trū o wop-mu; kére mína I bēk, ma piára he anó tẹnoṅ, I tši kére-mu." Ṅa be ṅa traļ atra-fof-tra-ṅaṅ; kére ṅa naṅk fe ṅa. Pā Ra-fi o wúra téte aṅ-ṅésam ṅa ow'úni, ṅa kóne, ṅa ko trọ́ri K'úrumasäba ho: „Sạ poṅ ama-pant, amá ma soṅ-su." Am-boī o yif K'úrumasäba ho: „Tro ma yō-e, mo ow'úni o fi-e?" K'úru o wúra y'etr e-bésa ro-tof, o soṅ-ko; o wúra y'etr e-lópra, de e-gbáta, o pā: „Be aṅa-féra etc." At the early sun Mr. Death arrived. When he came, he said: „Mr. Death has come, because Mr. Sickness took hold of thee; even I have come, thou wilt not be here to day all day, I shall carry thee away." They all heard their words; but they did not see them. Presently Mr. Death took out the breath (life) of the man, they left, (and) went,*) and said to God: „We have done with the work, which thou gavest us (to do)." The servant asked God: „How must they do, as the man is dead?" God took out tools to dig in the ground with (i. e. digging tools), and gave (them) to him; he took out clothing, and mats, and said: „If the white (people) etc."

*) That is Mr. Sickness and Mr. Death went, etc.

Mr. Sickness was an old person; he went into the house of the person, and met him lying down in his hammock; he said to him: „I take hold of thee to day. As they came to fetch thee, (and) thou didst refuse, I Sickness come to fetch thee, I take hold of thee to day." The man got up, and looked all about; (but) he did not see any person. He called his servant, and said: „Call all my people." The servant called them; the people came, they sat down all over the room, they asked him: „What is the matter?" He said: „Mr. Sickness took hold of me; but I do not see him." Mr. Sickness said: „I took hold of him; as he always refused and did not go, therefore he is sick, I took hold of him to day." All the people, who were there, heard the voice of Mr. Sickness; but they did not see him at all. The man lay down, he was awake all night, and did not sleep, he could not get up again, and could not turn (himself). In the morning Mr. Sickness said: „The sickness is getting heavy upon thee." At the early sun[1]) Mr. Death, who was a young man, arrived. When Mr. Death came, he told his friend Mr. Sickness, that this violent man would not live here again long, that he would have no pity on him, that he would not be here all day to day, (and) that he would carry him away. They all in the house heard their voice; but they could not see them. When Mr. Death had said this, he took away the breath

---

1) i. e. ‚when the sun was not up long get‘, or ‚early‘.

ña ọw'úni, ko ọw'úni ọ fi. Ña kọ́nẹ, ña kánẹ K'úrumasäba fọ ña poñ yọ̄ ama-pant-ma-ñañ. fọ ọw'úni o poñ fi.

Ka añ-fạm-ñọñ bẹ, dẹ añ-wut-ñ'ọñ, dẹ an-trar-ñ'oñ, ña trạp tra kúlọ, ña pä họ: "O-kas-ka-su o fi! O-kas-ka-su ọ fi!" Fọ añ-lọ ña-tši ña ta tr'a bẹ bōk trạ́ka w'úni fi.

Añ-lo ña-tši am-boï ọ kánẹ K'úru: "Ọw'úni ọ fi, tro 'a ma yọ̄-kọ-e?" K'úru ọ wúra y'etr ẹ-bẹ́sa ẹ-lọm, a-sápar, dẹ kạtrála, ọ sọñ-yi ka am-bọï; ọ wúra sọ tr'óta, dẹ a-gbáta; ọ trọ́rikọ sọ, tro ma yọ̄-e trạ́ka bẹ́nẹ ọwọ́ fi-e, ọ pä: "Be aña-féra 'a fi-e, tr' 'a bẹ́mpa k'úma, 'a botr-kọ ri, 'a mañk-kọ ro-tọf; bẹ w'úni bi ọ fi-e, tr' 'a bes, 'a botr-kọ ka tr'óta, dẹ a-gbáta, 'a mañk-kọ; bẹ w'úni mọ́ri ọ fi-e, tr' 'a wọñ's-kọ y'áñkra y'in, dẹ r'úma r'in, dẹ a-lápra ñ'in, 'a mañk-kọ." Tšïañ am-bọï ọ kára ẹy'ẹ́tr ka añ-fạm, ọ trọ́ri-ña, atrá ma yọ̄ trạ́ka 'ra-fi. Añ-lọ ñatši ña trára trạ́ka mañk a-fạm, ẹ-bóna bẹ ka 'ma-yọs-ma-ñañ; añfạm a-féra ka tr'úma; an-Témnẹ ka a-gbáta, dẹ tr'óta, dẹ tr'ạntr. Trạ́ka ọwọ́ fi-e, K'úru ọ pä: "Kọ nạ bẹ́nẹ-kọ, nạ wọñ's-kọ ẹy'ẹ́tr ẹ-lópra." Ña kọ́nẹ, ña kọ bẹ́nẹ-ko. Ma 'a poñ kọ bẹ́nẹ, 'a ko kánẹ K'úru fọ. "Sạ poñ kọ bẹ́nẹ." K'úru ọ kọ wúra a-bítiñ, dẹ k'éñkẹ, dẹ ma-ber, ọ sọñ-ña, ọ pä: "Tra ña kọ bōk-họ, káma ña of the man, and the man died. (Then) they went,¹) and told God that they had done their work, (and) that the man was dead.

Then all his people,²) and all his children, and his slaves, began to cry, they said: „Our father is dead! Our father is dead!" For at that time they did not yet know to weep (mourn) for a dead person.

Then the servant said to God: „The man is dead, how must they with do him?" God took out some digging tools, a digger, and a hoe, and gave them to the servant; he also took out clothing, and a mat; he also informed him, how they must do in order to bury the one who died, he said: „If the white people die, let them make a coffin, and put him into it, and bury³) him in the ground; if a black man dies, let them dig, and put him into clothes, and into a mat, and bury him; if a Mori man dies, let them put him on a pair of trowsers, and a shirt, and a cap, and bury him."⁴) Therefore the servant brought the things to the people, and showed them, what they must do with the one who died.⁵) At that time they knew to bury people, every nation according to their customs; the white people in coffins; the Temnes in a mat, and with clothes, and sticks. With regard to the one who died, God said: „Go ye and bury him, and put him on the clothing." They left, and went and buried him. When they had buried him, they went and told God: „We have buried him." God went and took out a drum, and a cymbal,⁶) and liquor, and gave it⁷) (to the servant), and said: „Let them go and bewail him, that they

---

1) That is Mr. Sickness and Mr. Death went etc.
2) i. e. ‚the people of the man who died.'
3) Or lit. „hide him etc."
4) In this way they bury the respective persons to this very day, the sticks, which are used for the burial of Temne people, are laid across the grave over the corpse, leaving some space between the corpse and the sticks, and the earth is then put upon the sticks; so that the earth does not fall on the corpse.
5) Lit. „with the death." (Abstractum pro concreto.)
6) See the word k'ĕṅkĕ in the Vocabulary.
7) i. e. ‚the liquor.'

mun ma-ber, káma 'a tšis, káma 'a tómo, káma 'a tšē so nésa."
Ma ra-fi ra yi ra-nínis-e, a-fạm ña woṅ ra-nēs: tšíaṅ o sōm amboī-ṅ'oṅ, o pā roṅóṅ: „Kére ey'étr eyé, káma o-nínis o poṅ."
Tšíaṅ d'er ó d'er w'úni o fi, 'a putr ara-fi, 'a trạ fer, 'a trạ tómo, 'a trạ mun ma-ber. Trạ woṅ ka a-fạm a-bi be, be w'úni o fi, 'a trạ wol, 'a trạ tómo.

Ka ka-rárạṅ-ka-tši K'úru, mo o kạ́li a-fạm o-nósi neī, o sómra so r'áka ka 'ra-rū, An'émi, aná bálane ma a-ténta; tša o náne, fo w'úni lom o gbạ́li he so yókane mo owó yi tápaṅ. An'émi ané na yi tra yéṅkạs so w'úni ma-der, be o trū. Be w'úni lom o trū-e, 'a, botr-ko ka an'émi, 'a lạ́ṅka-ko, o trạ kal yeṅk ma-der. Am-boī o soṅ an'émi trạ́ka a-fạm be; kére w'úni kásra o yi so, owó soṅ fe an'émi ka w'úni ó w'úni, ma 'a ma trū; kére o maṅk an'émi ka ak'úma-k'oṅ. Mo K'úru o nạṅk-tši, o lạ́sạr an'émi ka ak'úma, ro o maṅk-ni-e, ow'úni o tr'a be tši. Tšíaṅ mo kóno-kónone o trū, o sōm káma ña wúra an'émi ka ak'úma trạ́ka yéṅkạs-ko ma-der; kére ma ña kára-ni, 'a botr-ko ri, 'a lạ́ṅka-ko win-e; ara-béña ra an'émi ra píma, koṅ' o fúmpo ro-tof, o fi.

Ka ka-rárạṅ aké K'úru o soṅ a-fósa ka Ra-trū de ka Ra-fi, káma ña kot d'er ó d'er ka 'ra-rū be; táni lóko lom w'úni lom o yókane, o yō so mo owé o yō tápaṅ-e. Am-boī ña K'úru, mo K'úru o sōm-ko, o ko káne Ra-trū de Ra-fi tra wop w'úni lom.[1]) Aṅ-lo ña-tši a-fạm ña trạ trạl, fo ow'úni owé o trū; téte so 'a trạ trạl,

---

1) Or: Ka ka-rárạṅ aké Ra-trū de Ra-fi ña bā fósa ka ra-rū; de am-boī ña K'úru, mo K'úru etc. „After this Sickness and Death had power in the world; and the servant of God, as God etc."

may drink liquor, that they may be drunk, that they may dance, (and) that they may be no more afraid." As death is terrible, people became alarmed (at it): therefore he sent his servant, and said to him: „Carry these things, that the terror may have an end." This is the reason, that everywhere, where a person dies, they make the death known.¹) they are making music, they are dancing, (and) they are drinking liquor. It became fashion among all black people, if a person dies, they are playing and dancing.

After this, God, as he looked with pity upon people, sent again something into the world, (viz.) the Némi, which resembled a hammock; for he thought, that another person would not arise again as the one who was before. This hammock was to make a person well again, if he was sick. If some one was sick, they put him into the hammock, they swung him, (and) he was getting well again. The servant gave the hammock for all people; but there was again a violent man, who did not give the hammock to any one, when they were sick, but (who) hid the hammock in his box. When God saw it, he spoiled the hammock in the box, where he hid it, the man did not know it. So when he himself got sick, he sent that they might take out the hammock from the box to make him well again; but when they brought it, and put him into it, and swung him once; the rope of the hammock broke, (and) he fell down on the ground, and died.

After this God gave power to Sickness and Death, that they might walk all about²) in the whole world; lest some time another person arise, and act again as this one did before. The servant of God, as God sent him, went and told Sickness and Death to take hold of some³) person. That time people were hearing, that this person was sick; presently also they were hearing,

---

1) Thus the Temnes do to this very day. As soon as one dies, they discharge muskets, making known the death thereby.
2) Or: „every where in etc."
3) Or: „of such and such etc."

fo o fi. Kẹrẹ o lomp fe fo w'úni ó w'úni o yọ o lạs; pạkášifẹ a-fạm tramát rẹ sas ṅa rạp-kọ; ṅa-rạṅ ṅa yi ka ka-trā-k'ọṅ kạ-díọ; ṅa-rạṅ ṅa yi ka ka-trā-k'ọṅ kạ-mẹ́rọ; ṅa-rạṅ ṅa yi rodí; ṅa-rạṅ ṅa yi rorárạn-k'ọṅ, mọ w'úni o mọ kọt. Aṅé ṅa ma kánẹ K'úru tr'eī ó tr'eī atrá w'úni mọ yọ: ṅa ma mar aṅ-fạm a-féra ka kạ-tšim, dẹ ka tr'eī trạ-lạs bẹ. Tšíaṅ a-fạm a-féra ṅa túpạs hẹ, ṅa fak hẹ ọ-krífi, ṅa šek hẹ a-trọl, ṅa bā hẹ a-séṅa trạ́ka tšim; kẹ́rẹ ṅa trạ tam ka kạ-tšim.

Ara-bomp III.

Ma-Kánẹ ma an-Témnẹ ma-kur trạ́ka 'ma-Trạ́ma¹) ma W'úni ka-rárạṅ ka ra-Fi.

1.

Bẹ w'úni o fi bạt, o piára ro-krífi páli, o kal ra-foı, o trạ́sạm-trạ́sạm. Aṅ-lọ ṅa-tši a-fạm ṅa yif-kọ: „Tro pẹ-ẹ?" O wósa, o pā hẹ: „Tr'eī ó tr'eī, o báki gbo!" 'A pā sọ: „Ma mạ piára ro-krífi páli, mạ kal sọ, ko r'áka ra yọ-mu-ẹ?"²) O wósa sọ:³) „Aṅ-fạm a-báki bẹ ṅa der baṅ-mi, ko ọ-kas-ka-mi o bal-mi, o pā hẹ: „Kálanẹ, kọ kánẹ-ṅa:

---

1) Or: ma-yi, „state".

2) Or: Ko r'áka ra báṅ'sa-mu-ẹ? „What thing did hurt thee?"

3) Or: Bẹ w'úni o fi bạt, o piára páli ro-krífi. Aṅ-lọ ar'étr ra tọ́tlọ gbo, o trạ́sạm. Aṅ-lọ ṅa-tši aṅ-fạm a-báki ṅa trạ kọ rọṅ'ọṅ: ṅa yif-kọ: „Ko tr'eī ma naṅk ka ro-krífi-ẹ? Kánẹ-su. Ma ma piára ro-krífi hā ma kal so der, ko tr'eī tra mạ kal-ẹ?" Téte o wósa-ṅa: „I kal hẹ tr'eī ó tr'eī, 'a sōm-mi gbo." Aṅ-lọ́kọ ṅa-tši o kánẹ-ṅa atrá o naṅk, ro o piár'-ẹ; bẹ o naṅk d'er o-ma-bónẹ, o pa-tši; etc. etc. „If a person dies in the morning, he spends all day in Hades. When the sun gets cool, he sneezes. At that time the old people are going to him, and ask him: „What thing didst thou see in Hades? Tell us. As thou hast been in Hades till thou didst come back again, why didst thou return?" Presently he answers them: „I did not return for any matter, they just sent me." At that time he tells them what

that he was dead.¹) But it is not proper for any one to act wrong; because eight persons surround him; two are at his right hand; two are at his left hand; two are before (him); (and) two are behind him, when he is walking. These are telling God every thing which man does; they are helping the white people in the war, and in every danger. Therefore white people do not use country fashion, they do not set up a Krifi.²) they do not tie on amulets,³) (and) they have no Greegree for war; but they are victorious in battle.

Chapter III.

Traditions of the Temnes concerning the State of Man after Death.

1.

If a person dies in the morning, he spends the whole day in Hades, he returns in the evening, and sneezes repeatedly. Then people ask him: „How is it?"⁴) He answers, and says: „Nothing but trouble!"⁵) They say again: „As thou wast all day in Hades, and didst return again, what thing happened to thee?" He answers again: „All the old people came to fetch me, and my father drove me, he said: „Return, and tell them:

---

he saw, where he was all day: if he saw a place of joy (gladness), he states it; etc. etc."

1) This may also be given as follows: „The servant of God, when God sends him, goes and tells Sickness and Death to take hold of such and such a person. Then people will hear, that this person is sick; and soon afterwards again they will hear, that he is dead."

2) That is for worshipping it.

3 Or „charms", lit. „medicine".

4) Or: „What news?"

5) Lit. „Every trouble, it is but hard!"

w'úni ó w'úni tra o nésa K'úrumasäba, tra o nésa 'ra-rū, tra o tšē yọ tr'eī tra-lạs, tra o nésa sọ w'úni bom;¹) tra o nésa w'úni mọ́ne¹) dẹ w'úni báki." ¹)

„Be w'úni bom o bála, tra o nésa o-wos-k'oṅ; be o nésa he o-wos-k'oṅ-e, ọ yō he ko o-tọt-e; m'óne ma-bána ma tra kar-ko ro-krífi, be o poṅ fi. Be o-béra o bótrar he am-méra ka o-wos-k'oṅ; be o fi, o tra sóto m'óne ma-bána ka ro-krífi. Rúni so. be o nántra o-béra, owó yō-ko tr'eī tra-ffno, be o-wos-k'oṅ o sap-ko ka-tšiṅ; kére o-ráni-k'oṅ o nal he ko, o yóka he a- púre, ko be o-wos-k'oṅ o bótrar he am-méra ka o-ráni-k'oṅ; be ow'úni ka-tši o fi, o tra kọ́ne ka an'ántr, ka m'óne ma-bána."

„Trạ́ka pa-lā sọ ña sōm-mi tra káne-nu, káma na bótrar am- méra tráka pa-lā, káma na tšē lásar pa-lā. Be w'úni o lásar pa-lā, o tra kọ́ne ka an'ántr, be o fi. Ma a-fam ña ma lásar apa-lā;²) tšía sōm K'úru o tóra e-láma dẹ tš'er tra lásar apa-lā."

Aṅ-lo ña-tši o káne-ña so atrá o naṅk, ro o piár'-e. Be o naṅk d'er o-ma-bóne, o pā-tši; be o naṅk d'er o-las, o pā- tši. O pa: „I naṅk d'er o-ma-bóne, ma-pant ó ma-pant ma yi he ri, ma-bóne gbo; 'a piára gbo ña bóntras aṅ'és ña K'úru- masäba páli gbes."

„Atšé, atrá ña pā, I der tra trọ́ri-nu." Mo o poṅ pā atšé, ow'úni o fi so, o kálane ro-krífi; o gbáli he fof ka aṅ-réï a- mọ́ta, ka aṅ-réï a-trándo, ka aṅ-réï aṅá béka ma-sas, hāṅ ña béka ma-réï m'áṅle o mọ́ta fof ro-krífi.

1) The Singular for the Plural.
2 Or: „Because people are wasting rice; therefore etc."

Every man let him fear¹) God: let him fear the world; let him not commit sin, let him also honour women; let him honour the poor people and the old people."

"If a woman marries, let her honour her husband; if she does not honour her husband, and does not do him good; great trouble will await her in Hades, when she is dead. If the woman does not care for her husband; when she dies, she will get great trouble in Hades. A man also, if he marries a woman, who treats him well, if her husband beats her without cause; but his wife does not abuse him, and does not take a lover, and if her husband does not care for his wife; if that man dies, he will go into the fire (hell), into great misery."

"Concerning rice also they sent me to tell you, that ye should take care of rice, that ye should not spoil²) rice. If one spoils rice, he will go into the fire (hell), when he dies. As people were wasting the rice; therefore God sent down locusts and rats to spoil the rice."³)

At that time he tells them also what he saw, where he was all day; if he saw a place of gladness (joy), he states it; if he saw a bad place, he states it. He says: "I saw a place of joy, no work whatever is there, nothing but joy; they are only engaged in praising the name of God all day (and) all night."⁴)

"These (words), which they said, I came to tell you." When he has said these (things), the man dies again, and returnes to the Hades; he is not able to speak on the first day, nor on the second day, nor on the third day, till on the fourth day then only he can speak again in Hades.

---

1) Or also: "honour, respect etc." Sense: "let every one fear God etc."

2) Or: "waste."

3) Lit. "this caused God to bring down locusts etc."

4) Lit. "they spend all day only they praise the name of God all day all night."

2.

W'úni o yi ri ka an-lo ṅa Fátima Bréma. aṅ'és-ṅ'oṅ Lénsene, owó fi ro-Ráka,¹) ka 'a kára-ko ro-Kábata, 'a béne-ko ri; ko pa won mo o-trar-k'oṅ o fi ro-Gbóṅko. O fi gbo, o bap Pā Lénsene ro-kríft. Pā Lénsene o pā roṅóṅ: „Kálane, I tši sōmmu. Be ma ko-e, káne Móri Lámina tráka tra-bap, atrá ṅa ma tens-e, tra yi roráraṅ. Tra ṅa láfti aṅ-sar, tra ṅa bes ri; dí-aṅ tra-bap tra-pólo tra yi, dí-aṅ an-tásale ṅa yi; tra ṅa káli aṅ-sar, aṅá fatr ro-kuṅk-e, káma ṅa fáli-ṅi, káma ṅa bes ri; dí-aṅ tra-bap tra-témne tra yi. Tra ṅa ko káli ro-bat, ṅa ṅatr akabat, ṅa ko káli ka atr'ántr tra-bána, káma ṅa káli ak'ólo, ro atr'ántr tra gbép'trane; rí-aṅ ak'úma ka yi; tr' 'a ko wúra-ki. Be 'a wúra-ki, Móri Lámina tra o béne-ki tráka Lahai ow'áṅ-k'oṅ. Be o tra béne ak'úma, tra o ten a-tróko a-féra, de a-gbéra, káma o bémpa ak'úma seṅk, káma o soṅ-ki ka ow'án k'oṅ, be o sólo a-méra.²) Káne so Móri Lámina: „„Be ma bā tráka ram w'úni a-kála, ram-ko o-fíno. Míne, me I tšē bā rabeī ra w'úni,³) I bap o-fíno ro-kríft.“" Káne-tši a-yóla seṅk, be w'úni o bā a-kála ṅa w'úni,⁴) be o ram fe; ka-trak ka-báki ka yi ro-kríft tráka tr'oṅ. Tra ṅa nésa yáṅfa; w'úni ó w'úni owó tšē nésa yáṅfa, be o fi-e, o tra tráma ka m'óne ma-bána ro-kríft."

---

1) The camp of Fatima Brema while engaged in a war.
2) Lit. „when he gets sense."
3) Lit. „because I had no debt of a person."
4) Lit. „if one has money of a person," = „if one owes money to a person."

2.

There was a man in the time of Fatima Brema,¹) whose name was Lensene, who died in the Camp, and they brought him to Kabata, and buried him there; and it is long since his slave died at Gbonko. As soon as he was dead, he met Mr. Lensene in Hades. Mr. Lensene said to him: „Return, I will send thee. When thou goest, tell the Mori-man Lamina about the axes, which they were seeking, they are behind. Let them turn up the stone, let them dig there; there are the European axes, (and) there is the pray-kettle;²) let them look at the stone, which is near to the fence, that they may move it away, and that they may dig there; there the country axes are. Let them look at the brook, and go up at the brook, and go and look at the large timber trees, that they may look at the hollow, where the timber trees join together; there the box is; let them take it out. When they take it out, Lamina the Mori-man shall keep (preserve) it for Lahai, his son. When he is keeping the box, let him look for a white fowl, and for rice flour, that he may perform all the ceremonies requisite for the keeping of the box,³) that he may give it to his son, when he arrives at the years of discretion. Tell also Lamina the Mori-man: „„If thou hast to pay money to one, pay him well. I, because I did not owe a debt to a person, fared well in Hades.““ Tell it to all gentlemen, if one has to pay money to a person, and does not pay, there is a heavy palaver for him in the future world. Let them be afraid of deceitful dealing; every one who is not afraid of deceitful dealing, will be in great misery in the future world."

---

1) Fatima Brema was the predecessor of Namina Modu, the late Alikali, or Chief at Port-Loko, who was Alikali there, when the author resided at that town.

2) It is a brass-pan used by the Mohammedans for their ablutions.

3) That is by making a sacrifice of the fowl and flour in behalf of the person, who buried the box, and who sent the slave, and by putting the sacrifice a little while in the box for the Krifi.

O-trar o der ka Móri Lámina, o káne-ko ama-trei amé be;
ko mo o poṅ káne seṅk, o pä ho: „Me I fi-e, I tši wur he so
ro-krifi, I kóne toṅ tabána." Mo o poṅ pa atšé, o fi so, o kal
he so der.

Ara-bomp IV.

M'ump.

Aṅ'ump I.

Pa Kámu de Pä Tran-aṅ.

¹) Pa Kámu de Pä Tran ṅa yi ri tápaṅ. Pa Kámu o yi
ro-kant ro-petr rayér; Pä Tran o yi ro-petr. Pä Kámu o tra
tral ar'im ra Pä Tran lóko ó lóko ro-petr, o tral 'a tra bontr-
ko aṅ'és lóko ó lóko. Mo o naṅk Pä Tran-a, o pä ho: „W'an,
mun' mári-tr'eī ro-petr!" Pä Tran o pä: „Yáo, maṅ kóne."
Ṅa kóne ro-petr. Pä Tran o pä so: „I tši rána-mu, ma ma

---

1) Or: Pa Kámu o yi ri tápaṅ. O tral 'a tra tséla Pä
Tran lóko ó lóko. Pä Kámu o tséla Pä Tran, o pä ho: „Pä
Tran, mun' mári-tr'eī!" Pa Tran o pä ho: „Min' mári-tr'eī-i?"
O wósa-ko a-lo ṅ'in, ka Pä Tran o pä ho: „Maṅ kóne, rénsa-
mi ro-mut." O rénsa Pä Tran; o kére-ko ra-gbóṅkto. Ṅa yóka
ka-lápatr, 'a nap-ko-ki ro-mut. Pä Kámu o fai, o pä ho: „O
báki, Pa Tran!" Pä Tran o pä ho: „Ma naṅk-i? O báki-mi,
be I kot-e; múino ma naṅk gbo yaṅ-e, ma pä ho min' mári-
tr'eī: tšía sōm ma naṅk yaṅ."*) Pä Kámu o paī ro-tof, o won'
do-kant.

*) Lit. »it sent thou didst see thus (so).«

The slave came to Lamina the Mori-man, and told him all these things; and when he had told all, he said: „When I die again, I shall not come out again from Hades, I shall now go for ever." When he had said these (words), he died again, and did not come back again.

Chapter IV.

Fables.

Fable I.

The Iguana and the Dog.[2])

There was once an Iguana and a Dog. The Iguana was in the bush close to the town; the Dog was in the town. The Iguana was always hearing the voice of the Dog in the town, he heard that they were always calling him by his name. When he saw the Dog, he said: „Friend, thou art fortunate in town!" The Dog said: „Yes,[3]) let us go." They went into the town. The Dog said again: „I will carry thee on my back, as thou

---

1) Or: There was once an Iguana. He heard that they were always calling the Dog. The Iguana called the Dog, and said: „Mr. Dog, thou art lucky!" The Dog said: „I lucky?" He answered to him once in the affirmative,*) and the Dog said: „Let us go, get on my back." He got on the back of the Dog, he carried him into a kitchen. They took a burning stick, and knocked him with it on the back. The Iguana got a burn, and said: „It is hard, Mr. Dog!" The Dog said: „Doest thou see? It is hard for me, when I go about; as for thee, it only appeared so to thee**) (when thou saidst that I was lucky: this is the reason that thou hast made such experience." The Iguana jumped down to the ground, and went into the bush.

*) Or: »he was willing for him for once,« i. e. either granting that he was lucky; or to take the Iguana once with him to town.
**) Lit »thou, thou only seest thus, thou saidst that I etc.«

2) Lit. „Mr. Iguana and Mr. Dog."
3) Or: „Well, let etc."

tšē trára ro-petr-e." O rána-ko, o kére-ko ra-gbǫ́ŋktǫ; ña baṗ¹)
'a botr o-šem ka k'áro. Pä Tran o yóka o-šem ro-k'áro. Qw'a-
bét o pä ho: „O gbo, yä! Pä Tran o yóka o-šem!" O-bórko
o yóka ka-lápatr, o sap Pä Kámu ro-mut ka Pä Tran. Pä Tran
o gbúke (o bä Pä Kámu), ña ko yíra rokáñ. 'A botr a-nak a-
tan, 'a re soñ Pä Tran-añ; kére añ-nak, ma ña yi a-tan, ña bē'
he tra ña ña-rañ. Ma 'a poñ som o-šem 'a wúra tra-bant, 'a
re fáka Pä Tran-añ. Pä Tran-añ o pa ka Pä Kámu: „W'an,
man di o-šem." Pä Kámu o pä: „O-šem-'o-mi táho; I bä he
e-šek tra som tra-bant. Ma Pa Tran o poñ som tra-bant, o
pä: „Mañ kóne toléñken." Na ko bēk roléñken, ña baṗ¹) 'a
tra di. Pä Tran o ko mun am'ántr; 'a yóka k'etr, 'a gbánta Pä
Kámu; mo o rénsa Pä Tran, ak'étr ka be'²) he Pä Tran. Pä
Tran o wur, ña ko yíra rokáñ. Pä Kámu o pä ho: „I yéma
kóne." Kére Pä Tran o pä: „Tšē ko, w'an; min' mári-tr'eī.
ma tra sóto téñoñ a-bóya." 'A bä tra-bant, 'a re fáka-ña-tši.
Pä Tran o pä: „W'an, der, sa re som o-šem." Pä Kámu o
pä: „Di gbo; mína, I bä he e-šek." Pä Tran, mo o poñ som
atra-bant, o pä: „Mañ kóne roléñken." Na ko baṗ³) roléñken
'a tra ros. Pä Tran o ko loñ am'ántr, 'a yóka k'etr, 'a sap-
ko; kére Pä Kámu kóno mo sóto ka-sap gbo. 'A bal-bal Pä
Tran-añ, o gbúke. Pä Kámu o pä so: „I yéma kóne." Pä
Tran o pä: „Tšē ko, añ-lámbe-'a-su ña yi rodí, mañ kóne." 'A
kóne roléñken, 'a baṗ¹) 'a tra di. Pä Kámu o yi ro-mut ka
Pä Tran-añ. Pä Tran o ko loñ am'ántr, 'a wop Pä Tran-añ,

---

1) For: bap-ña 'a etc., „met them they etc."
2) Or: bap, „meet."
3) For: bap-ña r. etc., „met them etc."

doest not know how to shift for thyself in town." He carried him on his back, and carried him into a kitchen; they met them putting meat into a bowl. The Dog took the meat in the bowl. The child said: „O dear, mother! The Dog took the meat!" The damsel took a burning stick, and knocked the Iguana on the back of the Dog. The Dog ran (he had the Iguana), and they went and sat without. They put a little cooked rice (into a bowl), and came and gave (it) to the Dog; but the rice, as it was a little, was not sufficient for both of them. When they had eaten the meat, they took out the bones, and went and threw (them) for the Dog. The Dog said to the Iguana: „Friend, let us eat the meat." The Iguana said: „This is no meat for me,[1] I have no teeth to eat bones." When the Dog had eaten the bones, he said: „Let us go yonder." They went and came to the other yard, they met them eating. The Dog went and lapped the soup; they took a whip, they beat the Iguana: as he was on the back of the Dog, the whip did not reach the Dog. The Dog went out, they went and sat without. The Iguana said: „I want to go away." But the Dog said: „Do not go, friend; I am lucky, thou wilt get a present to day." They had bones, they came and threw them for them. The Dog said: „Friend, come, we will eat the meat." The Iguana said: „Do but eat; as for me, I have no teeth." The Dog, when he had eaten the bones, said: „Let us go yonder to the other yard." They went and met them taking out boiled rice from the pot[2] in the other yard. The dog went and upset the soup; they took a whip, and flogged him; but the Iguana only was getting the whipping. They drove the Dog away, he ran. The Iguana said again: „I want to go away." The Dog said: „Do not go, our present is before, let us go." They went into the other yard, they met them eating. The Iguana was on the back of the Dog. The Dog went and upset the soup; they took hold of the Dog,

---

1) Lit. „My meat not at all etc.," or „Meat of me not at all."

2) Or „serving up boiled rice etc."

'a sap,¹) 'a wúra kọ rokáṅ ka sap-aṅ. Pä Trạn ọ gbúkẹ, ọ kọ́nẹ ro-kanl, ro 'a yéfa, ṅa Pä Kámu-e. Pä Tran ọ pä: „Maṅ kọ́nẹ." Pa Kámu ọ pä: „I kọ hẹ so, ọ báki ro-petr." Pä Kámu ọ gbúkẹ, ọ kọ máṅknẹ. Pä Trạn o pä: „I kọ́nẹ." Pä Kámu ọ pä: „Kọ́nẹ, ọ báki ro-petr, I der hẹ sọ." Pä Trạn ọ pä: „Der, sạ kọ́nẹ, ma mạ pä min' mári-tr'eī ro-petr-e." Pä Kámu ọ pä: „I kọ hẹ sọ."

Tšíaṅ Pä Kámu ọ mínta hẹ sọ w'úni, ọ der hẹ ro-petr; ọ yi gbo ro-kanl. Pä Trạn ọ nạṅk gbo sọ Pä Kámu, ọ gbip-kọ, ọ kára¹) ro-petr, 'a re poṅ-kọ sọm. 'A yif Pä Trạn-a fọ: „Ko ṅẹ mạ ma kíra Pä Kámu-e?" Kọn' ọ pä: „I trọ́ri-kọ kạ-mártr'eī; mọ ọ pä min' mári-tr'eī." Tšíaṅ Pa Kámu ọ mínta hẹ sọ w'úni; ọ mínta hẹ sọ Pä Trạn-aṅ; ọ mínta hẹ sọ ro-petr.

Aṅ'úmp II.

Pä Nēs-aṅ, ṅa Pä Traṅk-aṅ, ṅa Pä Tába.

²) Yẹ táhọ Pä Nēs ọ yi ri tạ́paṅ-i? Ọ-baī ọ trọl tra-nä-tr'ọṅ, ka Pä Nēs ọ kọ kạ́li atra-nä;

---

1) Object: kọ, „him" dropped, as is someting the case.

2) Or: Ọ-baī ọ trọl tra-nä-tr'ọṅ, ka Pä Nēs ọ kọ kạ́li-ṅa, kọ ọ re kánẹ Pä Tába fọ: „Ọ-nä ka ọ-baī ọ-bána, maṅ kọ difkọ." Pa Tába ọ pä họ: „Tru sa ma yō-e?" Kérẹ Pä Nēs ọ pä fọ: „Mína trára sọt; bẹ pa poṅ bía, maṅ kọ́nẹ." Ma a-fam ṅa poṅ díra, ọ kọ támi Pä Tába, ọ pa họ: „Maṅ kọ́nẹ." Kọ ọ yókanẹ, ṅa kọ́nẹ. Ma ṅa kọ bēk ka ọ-nä-e, Pa Nēs ọ sut ọ-nä, ọ pä:

they flogged (him) and pulled him out while flogging. The Dog ran, and went into the bush,¹) from whence they came, he and the Iguana. The Dog said: „Let us go." The Iguana said: „I do not go again, it is hard in town." The Iguana ran, and went and hid himself. The Dog said: „I go." The Iguana said: „Go, it is hard in town, I do not come again." The Dog said: „Come, let us go, because thou saidst I was lucky in town." The Iguana said: „I do not go again."

Therefore the Iguana does not dare again to come near a person, he does not come to town; he is only in the bush. As to the Dog, as soon as he but sees again the Iguana, he catches him, and brings (him) to town, (and) they come and devour him entirely. They asked the Dog: „Why art thou troubling the Iguana?" He said: „I show him (what) luckiness (is); because he said I was lucky." Therefore the Iguana does not venture again to come near a person; he does not venture again to come near a Dog; he does not venture to town again.

Fable II.

The²) Spider, and the Ant-Eater, and Mr. Taba.³)

Is it not so that there was once a Spider? A (certain) king took care of his cows, and the Spider went to look at the cows;

---

1) Or: „wood."
2. Lit. „Mr. Spider, and Mr. Anteater etc."
3) The name of a fabulous person.
4 Or: A certain king took care of his cows, and the Spider went to look at them, and he came and told Mr. Taba: „As to the large cow of the king, let us go and kill it." Mr. Taba said: „How shall we manage (it)?" But the Spider said: „I know an artifice; when it has got dark, let us go." After people had gone asleep, he went and awoke Mr. Taba, and said: „Let us go." And he rose up, (and) they went away. When they came to the cow,*) the Spider stroked**) the cow, and said:

*) Lit. »When they went and arrived at the cow etc.,« or »when they go arrive at the cow etc.«
**) Or rather: »rubbed.«

ko mo o naṅk o-nā o-bána; o der káne Pā Tába fo: „O-nā ka o-baī, owọ́ yi o-bána, maṅ kọ́ne dif-ko tra som." Pā Tába o pā: „I mínta he, tro sạ ma yō-e?" Pā Nēs o pā: „Mína, I trára sot." Pā Tába o pā: „Ko a-sot ṅaṅ aṅó-e?" Pā Nēs o pā: „Maṅ kọ́ne ro-lal, ro atra-nā ṅa ma wont-e." Na kọ́ne ro-lal, ṅa ko bap Pā Traṅk-a, o trạ bēs ro-tof. Pā Nēs o pā roṅọ́ṅ: „Ma mam bes anọ́-a? Be atra-nā tra o-baī ṅa woṅ ka am-bi-e, ma trạ sọ́to a-pā de kạ-trạk." Ma Pā Traṅk-a o trạl atśé, o nésa, o kọ́ne roléṅken, o kára e-tof tra botr ka am-bi, aṅá o bémpa. Pā Traṅk o pā so: „I yéma ko fótane." Pā Nēs o pā: „Maṅ kọ́ne ro romú, ro maṅ díra-e." Kére o bótra Pā Traṅk-a yáṅfa, káma o trára, ro o mo díra. Na ko so. Ma ṅa ko bē' ri-e, Pā Nēs o pā ho: „I tśi kálane." Pā Traṅk-a o pā ho: „Kọ́ne, ma-rē ma bā-mi." Pā Nēs o kọ́ne, o ko baṅ o-nā o-bána ka o-baī, o kára-ko, o re wọ́ṅa-ko ro-bi; od'ér, ro Pā Traṅk-a o fạ́nta, o fatr ri, o kálane ro-petr. O-baī o pā ka aṅ-fet-ṅ'oṅ: „Kọ́ne naṅ, kạ́li atra-nā ro-lal, pạ yéma bía." Na ko baṅ-ṅa. Na ko bap o-nā o yi ro-bi, o wúra gbo 'rabomp. Aṅ-fet ṅa gbúke, ṅa ko káne o-baī fo: „O-nā o woṅ ro-bi, o yéma fi." Mo o-baī o trạl atśé, o tśéla aṅ-fạm be, o

„Na śite! Na śite!" Ko o-nā o śite, ṅa woṅ' etc.

and when he saw a large cow, he came and told Mr. Taba: "As to the cow of the king, which is large, come let us kill it to eat (it)." Mr. Taba said: "I do not dare, how shall we manage (it)?" The Spider said: "As for me, I know an artifice." Mr. Taba said: "What artifice is that?"[1]) The Spider said: "Let us go to the grass-field, where the cows are grazing." They went to the grass-field, they went and met the Ant-Eater, he was making a hole in the ground. The Spider said to him: "Why art thou digging here?[2]) If the cows of the king get into the hole, thou wilt get a matter and a palaver." When the Ant-Eater heard this, he was afraid, and went to some distance, and brought earth to put (it) into the hole, which he had made. The Ant-Eater said again: "I want to go and rest myself." The Spider said: "Let us go yonder to thy place, where thou doest sleep." But he acted deceitfully against the Ant-Eater, that he might know, where he was sleeping. They went again. When they reached there,[3]) the Spider said: "I shall return." The Ant-Eater said: "Go, I am sleepy." The Spider left, and went and fetched the large cow of the king, he brought it, and came and put it into the hole; the place, where the Ant-Eater lay down, was near to it, (and) he returned to town. The king said to his children:[4]) "Go ye, and look after the cows on the grass-field, it wants to get dark." They went to fetch them. They went and met a cow in the hole, she only put forth the head. The children ran, and went and told the king: "A cow got into a hole, and is about to die." When the king heard this, he called all the people, and

"Cow, break the wind! Cow break the wind!" And the cow broke the wind, (and) they went into etc."

1) Lit. "What artifice that this?"

2) Seems rather to be an elliptical expression, for: "What art — — here for? (Take care what thou art about.) If the cows etc."

3) Lit. "When they go reach there," or "when they went and reached there etc."

4) Or "boys".

pā roñáñ: „Mañ kọ́nẹ wúra nañ ọ-nā ro-bi." Ṅa bẹ ña ko ri, ña bạp ọ-nā ọ fi tọñ. Añ-fạm ña bẹs, ña wúra ọ-nā ka am-bi. Ọ-baī ọ pā họ: „Atr'ei atšé tra kẹ́ta-mi, ọ-nā o-bána ọ der fi anọ́; ko tr'ei-e?" Pā Nēs ọ pā họ: „Tr' 'a tšéla Pā Trañk-a, kónọ yi ro-lal." Ṅa pā họ: „Ma sạ tšē trára ro ọ yi-e." Pā Nēs ọ pā sọ: „Tr' 'a tšéla-kọ, ọ fatr anọ́." Ọ-baī ọ tšélakọ; Pā Trañk-a ọ wósa. Ọ-baī ọ pā sọ: „Der ba lẹmp-a!" Pā Trañk ọ bēk. Ọ-baī ọ pā so: „W'an-ka-mi, der ba, kạ́li tr'cī-a!" Mọ ọ bēk ri, ọ-baī ọ pā roñọ́ñ: „Káne yọ̄ ama-pant amé, káma ọ-nā-ka-mi ọ der fi rẹ-e?" Pā Trañk ọ pā họ: „Mína yọ̄ ama-pant amé; kẹ́rẹ min' táhọ kára ọ-nā anọ́; min' táhọ dif-kọ." Pā Nēs ọ kọ fatr Pā Tába, ọ káne-kọ sọi: „Pā Trañk-a, sạ tra som-kọ ténọñ." Ọ-baī dẹ Pā Trañk 'a tra tọ́ñka. Ọ-baī ọ pā: „Pa Nēs, Pā Trañk-a kon' táhọ yi ro-lal-i?" Pā Trañk ọ pā: „Mína yi ro-lal; kẹ́rẹ min' táhọ dif ọ-šẹm." Pā Nēs ọ pā họ: „Ma tra tọ́ñka-i? Me I la káne-mu-e: tšē bẹs ro-lal, ri-añ ẹ-šẹm ña ma wọnt; be ọ-nā ọ der gbo, ọ wọñ ro-bi-e, o fi gbo-e, múnọ dif-kọ." Ọ-baī ọ yif Pā Trañk-a: „Múnọ bẹs ẹ-bi y'áñlẹ ẹyé-i?" Ọ wósa. Ọ-baī ọ pā sọ: „W'an, ma dífa-mi ọ-nā!" Pā Nēs ọ kọ́nẹ sọi ka ọ-sántki, ọ kọ kánẹkọ: „Wop-kọ ngñ, kọnọ dif ọ-nā." Pa Trañk-a ọ tra tọ́ñka dẹ ọ-baī-añ. Ọ-sántki ọ wop Pā Trañk-a, ọ pā: „Ma tọ́ñkas ọ-baī ka-tšiñ;" ọ pā: „Mọ ọ dif ọ-nā ka ọ-baī-añ, tr'a dif-kọ ngñ."

said to them: „Let us go, and pull out the cow from the hole."
They all went there, they found that the cow was dead already.
The people digged, and pulled out the cow from the hole. The
king said: „This thing puzzles me, the large cow came and died
here; how is this?" The Spider said: „Let them call the Ant-Eater,
he is on the grass-field." They said: „When we do not know where
he is."[1]) The Spider said again: „Let them call him, he is close
by." The king called him; the Ant-Eater answered. The king said
again: „Come here quickly!" The Ant-Eater arrived. The king
said again: „My friend, come here, look at something!" When
he came there, the king said to him: „Who did this work, that
my cow came to die here?" The Ant-Eater said: „I did this
work; but it was not I who brought the cow here; it was not
I who killed it." The Spider went and came near to Mr. Taba,
and told him softly: „As for the Ant-Eater, we shall eat him
to day." The king and the Ant-Eater were debating the matter.
The king said: „Mr. Spider, was it not the Ant-Eater who was
on the grass-field?" The Ant-Eater said: „I was on the grass-
field; but it was not I who killed the beast." The Spider said:
„Art thou expostulating? When I used to tell thee: do not
dig at the grass-field, there beasts are grazing; if but a cow
comes, and goes into the hole, and dies, thou doest kill it."
The king asked the Ant-Eater: „Didst thou dig these four holes?"
He answered in the affirmative. The king said again: „Friend,
thou hast killed me the cow!" The Spider went softly to the
minister of the king, he went and told him:[2]) „Take ye hold
of him, he killed the cow." The Ant-Eater was expostulating
with the king. The minister of the king took hold of the Ant-
Eater, and said: „Thou doest expostulate in vain with the king;"
and said: „As he killed the cow of the king, let them kill him"[3])

---

1) That is: „When we — — — is (how can we call him?)"
It is rather an elliptical expression.

2) Lit. „he go tell him: (as the Lib. Africans say) = „he
went to tell etc."

3) Lit. „let them kill him ye."

Pā Nēs ǫ pā: „Áwa, tr' 'a dif-kǫ;" mǫ ǫ yéma di¹) Pā Trañk-a. Na dif Pā Trañk. Ǫ-baī ǫ pā: „Mañ kérę-kǫ, káma są kǫ bę́nę-kǫ ro-petr." Kę́rę Pā Nēs ǫ pā: „Tr' 'a tšē kǫ bę́nę ro-petr, bę́nę-kǫ ka ro-lal ka ka-petr-k'ǫñ." Ma Pā Nēs ǫ pā yañ-e, ña bę́nę Pā Trañk ka am-bi, ro ǫ-nā ǫ fi. Ma ña poñ bę́nę-kǫ, ǫ-baī ǫ pā: „Mañ kǫ́nę ngñ ro-petr, káma I kǫ yer o-nā." Na kǫ bēk ro-petr, ǫ-baī ǫ yer ǫ-nā señk. Ǫ-baī ǫ pa sǫ: „Pā Nēs kǫ́nǫ sōm I trára ǫwǫ́ dífa-mi ǫ-nā-e, tr' 'a soñ-kǫ a-lañk." Na soñ-kǫ. Añ-fąm ña sákanę, 'a kǫ́nę fą́nta. Ma añ-fąm ña poñ díra-e, Pā Nēs ǫ wur, ǫ tšéla Pā Tába; ña kǫ bañ Pā Trañk ro-lal, ña kérę-kǫ ka añ-set-ñ'ǫñ roráraņ; ña kǫ poñ kǫ tšen señk, ǫ yer Pā Tába. Ka Pā Tába ǫ pā hǫ: Pā Nēs, mą foī hę tr'cī!" Pā Nēs ǫ pā: „Mę I pā mą tr'a hę sǫt-i?" Ka ña sǫm-ko hā añ'óf ña fi. Pā Tába ǫ pā hǫ: „Yáwe, añ-lǫ ñañ ką-sǫm ǫ-šem!" Pā Nēs ǫ pā: „Mañ kar tánì tratrák, są trą sǫm anína ǫ-šem." Ma pą bía, ka a-fąm ña poñ díra, ǫ kǫ tšéla Pā Tába; ña kǫ́nę, ña kǫ bap tra-nā tra ǫ-baī, ña kótąr-ña. Pā Nēs ǫ wúra an-trǫl-ñ'ǫñ, ǫ kǫ sut ǫ-nā ǫ-bána, ǫ pā: „Nā, šítę! Nā, šítę!" Ǫ-nā ǫ šítę, ña wǫn' do-k'or-k'ǫñ, ña Pa Tába. Pā Nēs ǫ trǫ́ri Pā Tába ka ka-but, ǫ pa hǫ: „Tšē gbąk aņǫ́." Ǫ wúra a-tis, ǫ soñ Pā Tába; kérę

---

1) Or: sǫm, „devour".

The Spider said: „Well, let them kill him;" because he wanted to eat the Ant-Eater. They killed the Ant-Eater. The king said: „Let us carry him away, that we may go and bury him in the town." But the Spider said: „Let them not bury him in town, bury him on the grass-field in his town." When the Spider said this, they buried the Ant-Eater in the hole, where the cow died. When they had buried him, the king said: „Let us go to town, that I may go and share the cow." They went and arrived at the town, (and) the king shared out the whole of the cow. The king said again: „As to the Spider, he caused me to know who killed me the cow, let them give him a leg." They gave (it) to him. The people dispersed, they went and lay down. When the people had gone asleep, the Spider went out, and called Mr. Taba; they went and fetched the Ant-Eater at the grass-field, they carried him behind his house; they went and cut him up entirely, he shared (the meat) with Mr. Taba. And Mr. Taba said: „Spider, thou doest not joke!"[1]) The Spider said: „When I said that thou didst not know cunning?" And they ate of it (meat) till the month was done. Mr. Taba said: „Oh dear, that time (of) eating meat (is over)!"[2]) The Spider said: „Let us wait till to night, we shall eat meat to morrow." When it got dark, and people had gone asleep, he went and called Mr. Taba; they left, and went and met the cows of the king, they had tied them on.[3]) The Spider took out his medicine, and went and stroked[4]) a large cow, and said: „Cow, break the wind! Cow, break the wind!" The cow broke the wind, and they went into her belly, he and Mr. Taba. The Spider showed Mr. Taba the heart, and said: „Do not cut here." He took out a knife, and gave (it) to Mr. Taba; but

---

1) Lit. „Mr. Spider, thou makest no joke of a thing," or „thou doest etc.!"

2) This is an elliptical expression.

3) That is the kings people had tied them on.

4) Or „rubbed".

Pā Tába o pā: „I tr'a hẹ tši;¹) gbạk, káma I kạ́li." O pā: „Yáo, kára ka-mọ́tẹ." Pā Nēs ọ tra gbạk, ọ sọṅ Pā Tába; kọ́nọ botr ka ka-mọ́tẹ. Ṅa lásạr ka-mọ́tẹ. O wúra sọ an-trọl, ọ sul o-nā, o pa: „Nā šítẹ! Nā, šítẹ!" O-nā ọ šítẹ, ṅa wur, ṅa kọ di ọ-šẹm ka-tši ma-ré̈ï m'áṅlẹ. A-lọ́kọ lọm tratrák Pā Nēs ọ kọ tšéla Pā Tába, ọ pā: „Maṅ kọ́nẹ." Ṅa kọ bạp atra-nā tra ọ-baī. Pā Nēs ọ der, o wúra an-trọl, ọ sul ọ-nā, ọ pā: „Nā, šítẹ! Nā, šítẹ!" O-nā o šítẹ, ṅa wọṅ-ko ro-k'or. Pā Nēs ọ wúra a-tis, ọ sọṅ Pā Tába, ọ káṅẹ-kọ tọ họ: „Kọ ka tšen-aṅ ro-kạ́patr." Kọn' o kọ́nẹ ka tšen ka aṅ-fi-aṅ. Pā Tába ọ kọ bap m'áro ma-laī ka ka-but, ọ kọ gbạk ara-béṅa ra ka-but; ọ-nā o fúmpọ, ọ fi. Pa Tába o tr'a hẹ tši; kẹ́rẹ Pā Nēs o tráratši. Pā Nēs ọ pā ho: „Pā Tába, o-nā ọ fi!" Pā Tába o pā: „Tro sạ ma yō-e, mo ọ-nā ọ fi-e?" Pā Nēs o pā: „Ma máṅknẹ: mína, I tši máṅknẹ ka am'ím." Pā Tába o pā: „Mína, me I tšē trára sọt-e, I tši yíra anọ́." Pā Nēs ọ máṅknẹ ka am'íni; Pā Tába o wọṅ ka am-pútu. Ma pạ poṅ sọk bạt, aṅ-fẹt ṅa o-baī ṅa pā: „O gbo, Pā, ọ-nā ọ fi!" Ṅa kọ tšen ọ-nā. Ma ṅa ma tšen ọ-nā, 'a trápa kạ-bap ka tra-sạk. Pā Nēs o pā ro-k'or ka o-nā: „Tr' 'o mạ trap-mi-e! Tr' 'o mạ trap-mi-e!" Mọ ọ pā yaṅ-e, ṅa nésa; 'a kọ káṅẹ o-baī, fọ r'áka ra fọf ka ọ-šẹm rokór. O-baī o bēk, o pā: „Trap nạ ba sọ-a!" Kẹ́rẹ Pā Nēs

---

1 Or: I tr'a hẹ yi: „I do not know thus," = „I cannot do this."

Mr. Taba said: „I do not know it; cut, that I may look at."
He said: „Yes,¹) bring the basket." The Spider was cutting,
and gave (the meat) to Mr. Taba; he put (it) in the basket.
They filled the basket. He pulled out again the medicine, and
stroked²) the cow, and said: „Cow, break the wind! Cow, break
the wind!" The cow broke the wind, they came out, and went
and ate of that meat for four days. Another time at night the
Spider went and called Mr. Taba, and said: „Let us go "
They went and met the cows of the king. The Spider came,
he took out the medicine, he stroke²) the cow, and said: „Cow,
break the wind! Cow, break the wind!" The cow broke the
wind, they went into her belly. The Spider took out a knife,
and gave (it) to Mr. Taba, and told him now: „Go and cut at
the breast." He he went and cut at one of the loins.³) Mr. Taba
went and met with much fat at the heart; he went and cut
the heart-strings; the cow fell down, and died. Mr. Taba did
not know it; but the Spider knew it. The Spider said: „Mr. Taba,
the cow is dead!" Mr. Taba said: „How must we do, as the
cow is dead?" The Spider said: „Let us hide ourselves: as
for me, I shall hide myself at the liver." Mr. Taba said: „As
for me, because I do not know cunning, I shall sit down here."
The Spider hid himself at the liver; Mr. Taba went into the
rectum. When it had fully dawned, the children of the king,
said: „Oh dear, Sir, the cow is dead!" They went and cut
up the cow. When they were cutting up the cow, they chopped
with an axe at the ribs. The Spider said within the cow:
„Mind, that thou doest not chop me! Mind, that thou doest not
chop me!"⁴) When he spoke thus, they were afraid; they went
and told the king, that something talked within the beast. The
king came, and said: „Chop ye now here again!" But the Spider

---

1) Or: „Well, bring etc."

2) Or „rubbed".

3) Lit. „Go in (by) cutting at the breast." He he went in
(by) cutting at the loin. = „Go be cutting at the breast." He
he was cutting etc.

4) Lit. „Not that thou chop me! Not that — — me!"

o kal mánkne roléṅken ka ro-k'or. Ma ṅa poṅ trap e, 'a ko naṅ'-ko de ka-móte-k'oṅ; 'a wúra-ko de ka-móte, ṅa ko šek-ko. Ma 'a poṅ tšen o-šem seṅk, ṅa ko sap Pa Nēs-aṅ. O baī o pā: „Pa Nēs-aṅ, kónoṅ mo póṅa-mi o-šem, tr' 'a sap-ko." Ma 'a gbánta-ko win-e, o kúlo, o pā: „Šya Tába, šya yi! Šya Tába, šya yi!" O-baī o pā: „Tr' 'a trei ba ka-sap-ko-a, tr' 'a yif-ko ba." Ṅa yif Pā Nēs: „Nya káne der tra dif o-šem-e?" O pā: „Šya Tába, šya dif o-šem." Ṅa pā: „Kóna Tába?" O pā: „I tr'a he ro o ko-e." Ko o baī o pā: „Ma yémsa Tába; mun' sōn, múno dif-ko." Kére Pa Tába o yi ka am-pútu, o máṅkne. Ṅa* wúra am-pútu, 'a soṅ aṅ-fet tra ko yak ro-bat. Ṅa kóne ro-bat, ṅa ko gbaī am-pútu, ṅa won am-pútu ro-m'antr. Ma ṅa won-ṅi ro-m'antr yaṅ-e, Pā Tába o wur, o ko trálpe romóri, o pā ho: „Ko na yō-mi yaṅ-e?" Aṅ-fet ṅa pā: „O gbo, Pā-ka-mi, sa tr'a he tši!" W'ahét o-lom o ko tróri-tši ka o-baī; o-baī o der, o káli Pā Tába, o pā roṅóṅ: „Ko ṅe-e?" Pā Tába o pā: „Aṅ-fet ṅa yō-mi gbo ka-tšiṅ, ṅa sákar-mi gbo e-nin ya o-nā!" O-baī o ko baṅ r'úma, de y'áṅkra, o kára, o soṅ Pā Tába, o pā: „Búko, w'an-ka mi!" Mo o poṅ búko, ṅa wur ro-petr. Pā Nēs o pā so: „Pā Tába šya yi." Kére kon' o péṅša. Ṅa pā ho: „Tšéla o-ráni ka Pa Tába, káma sa hid himself again in another place of the belly. When they had done with chopping, they went and saw him and his basket; they pulled him out and the basket, and went and tied him. When they had cut up the whole of the beast, they went and flogged the Spider. The king said: „The Spider, he was destroying me the beast, let them flog him." When they struck him once, he cried, and said: „I and Taba, we were together! I and Taba, we were together!"¹) The king said: „Let them leave off now from flogging him, let them ask him now." They asked the Spider: „Thou and who²) came to kill the beast?" He said: „I and Taba, we killed the beast." They said: „Where is Taba?" He said: „I d'ont know where he went to." And the king said: „Thou doest tell a lie about Taba; thou alone, thou didst kill it." But Mr. Spider was in the rectum, he hid himself. They took out the rectum, and gave (it) to the children to go and wash (it) at the brook. They went to the brook, and went and burst the rectum, and shook out the bag into the water. While they thus shook it out into the water, Mr. Taba came out, and went and jumped to the other side, and said: „Why treat ye me in this way?" The children said: „Oh dear, Sir,³) we did not know it!" Some child went and informed the king of it. The king came, he looked at Mr. Taba, and said to him: „What is the matter?" Mr. Taba said: „The children treated me but in a vile manner, they just bespattered me with cow-dung!" The king went and fetched a shirt, and a pair of trowsers, and brought (them), and gave (them) to Mr. Taba, and said: „Wash thyself, my friend!" When he had washed himself, they went into the town.⁴) The Spider said again: „It was Mr. Taba and I." But he denied (it). They said: „Call the wife of Mr. Taba, that we

1) Lit. „We Taba, we were! We T. we were!" But the Plur. form is in such cases used also for the Singular; and the copula implied in the pronoun.

2) Lit. „Ye who came etc.?"

3) Lit. „my Sir."

4) That is: „they went out (from the water) into the town."

yif-ko." Ma ña tšéla-ko, ña yif-ko. O pā ho: "Pā Tába o díra he anó, ar'étr ra laī dis mo o wur ro-set, o kóne." O-baī o pā ho: "Pā Nēs kónoñ; mo o pā fo kon' de Pā Tába ña dif o-nā-e, o yémsa-ko gbo." Pā Tába o pā: "Káli-mi anó; o yémsa-mi; be šya yi nañ-e, na bap-mi ka ro-k'or ka o-nā."

Ňa pā to: "Tr' 'a sap Pā Nēs-añ, kóno dif o-nā." Ňa kére-ko ka a-batr, 'a gbak ka-róñko ka am-batr, 'a sápa-ko karóñko. Tšíañ o wur tr'átrak tra-laī. O-bai o pā: "Tr' 'a tšer-ko." Ma ña tšer-ko, o kóne, o ko trū; o yókane, o bā tr'átrak tra-gbáti; o gbúke, o kóne ro-kant.

Añ'úmp III.
Ow'ahét de am-Bamp-añ.

W'ahét o yı ri tápañ, o gbatr ma-téli ka a-tan' dáta, ko o sápas a-bamp. Ambá, mo o poñ ko som, o kal so lómpar ama-téli, ko o kal sápas a-bamp; ko o gbúke o kótši am-bamp, ko o kére-ko ro-báñka; kére o-kára-k'oñ o bal-ko ro-gbántrani tra ko bal e-bamp. Ko ow'ahét o pā ho: "Ya, toísa-mi') am-bamp." O-kára-k'oñ o pā ho: "Iyóō." Ambá, mo ow'ahét o kóne, o-kárak'oñ o dif am-bamp, ko o túši-ko, o ko tois-ko, o som-ko tárap. Mo ow'ahét o der-e, ko o yif o-kára-k'oñ tra am-bamp, o-kára-k'oñ o pa ho: "I poñ ko som." Ko ow'ahét o bōk, o pā ho: "Bom, soñ-mi am-bamp-'a-mi! Bom, soñ mi am-bamp-'a-mi, owó I dif ro-tan' dáta, tánta, tan' dáta!"[2]) Ambá, o-bom o soñ-ko tra-mañk, ko

---

1) Or: "broil."

2) The preposition ro- before the first tan' dáta belongs here also to the following tánta and tan' dáta.

may inquire of her." When they had called her, they inquired of her. She said: „Mr. Taba did not sleep here; the sun was still high yesterday when he went out of the house, and went away." The king said: „It is the Spider; when he said that he and Mr. Taba killed the cow, he only told a lie against him." Mr. Taba said: „Look me here; he told a lie against me; if it had been I,[1]) ye would have met me in the belly of the cow."

They then said: „Let them flog the Spider, he killed the cow." They led him to a young palm-tree, and cut a branch from the young palm-tree, they flogged him with the palm-leaf.[2]) This is the reason that he got many legs. The king said: „Let him go."[3]) When they left him, he departed, and went and was sick; he recovered,[4]) he had many legs; he ran, and went away into the bush.

Fable III.

The Child and the Bird.

There was once a child who set a trap under a root, and he caught a bird. Well, when he had eaten it, he returned and set the trap again, and he again caught a bird; and he ran and loosed the bird; and carried it into the hut; but his mother drove him to the outskirts of the farm to go and drive birds away. And the child said: „Mother, roast me the bird." And his mother said: „Yes." Well, when the child was gone, his mother killed the bird, and plucked it, and went and roasted it, and ate it entirely. When the child came, and asked his mother for the bird, his mother said: „I have eaten it." And the child cried, and said: „Mother, give me my bird! Mother, give me my bird, which I killed under the root, at the waterfall, under the root!" Well, the mother gave him maize, and

---

1) Lit. „if it were we," but the Plural is here used for the Singular.
2) Or: „palm-branch."
3) Lit. „Let them leave him."
4) Or: „he got up."

o reṅ-tši ro-lákat rokóm; ke me e-mórka ña poṅ tši som, ọw'ahét
o pä ka e-mórka: „Mórka, sọṅ-mi tra-maṅk-tra-mi! Mórka, sọṅ-
mi tra-maṅk-tra-mi, atrá ọ-bom ọ sọṅ-mi! Ọ-bom ọ sọm am-
bamp-'a-mi, ọwọ́ l dif ro-tan' dáta, tánta, tan' dáta." Ambá, e-mórka
ña sála-ko e-bọl; ko ọ kére-yi ro-bat ka ka-tánta tráka kut. Ka ma
ka-tánta ka ma wọtr e-bọl eyáṅ, ọ pä họ: „Tánta, sọṅ-mi e-bol-
'e-mi! Tánta, sọṅ-mi e-bọl-'e-mi, eyé e-mórka ña sọṅ-mi!
E-mórka ña sọm tra-maṅk-tra-mi, atrá ọ-bom ọ sọṅ-mi; ọ-bom
ọ sọm am-bamp-'a-mi, ọwọ́ l dif ro-tan' dáta, tánta, tan' dáta."
Ka-tánta ka sọṅ-ko a-fak; ka ma a-bar o mọ yóka-ko, ọ pä họ:
„Bar, sọṅ-mi aṅ-fak-'a-mi! Bar, sọṅ-mi aṅ-fak-'a-mi, ọwọ́ Tánta
ọ¹) sọṅ-mi! Tánta ọ¹) wọtr e-bọl-'e-mi, eyé e-mórka ña sála-
mi; e-mórka ña sọm tra-maṅk-tra-mi, atrá ọ-bom ọ sọṅ-mi; ọ-
bom ọ sọm am-bamp-'a-mi, ọwọ́ l dif ro-tan' dáta, tánta, tan'
dáta." Ambá am-bar o fáka-ko k'úpọ k'in. Ambá, ma aṅ-fef
ña ma kére-ki, ọ pä họ: „Fef, sọṅ-mi ak'úpọ-ka-mi! Fef, sọṅ-
mi ak'úpọ-ka-mi, aká aṁ-bar ọ sọṅ-mi! Am-bar ọ sọm aṅ-fak-
'a-mi, ọwọ́ tánta ọ sọṅ-mi; tánta ọ wọtr e-bọl-'e-mi, eyé e-
mórka ña sála-mi; e-mórka ña sọm tra-maṅk-tra-mi, atrá ọ-bom
ọ sọṅ-mi; ọ-bom ọ sọm am-bamp-'a-mi, ọwọ́ l dif ro-tan' dáta,
tánta, tan' dáta." Ambá, aṅ-fef ña kóña-ko ma-lel ma-laï.
Ambá, ma tra-wóto ña poṅ di ama-lel-e, ọ pä họ: „Wóto, sọṅ-
mi ama-lel-ma-mi, amá aṅ-fef ña kóña-mi! Aṅ-fef ña kére
ak'úpọ-ka-mi, aká am-bar ọ sọṅ-mi; am-bar ọ sọm aṅ-fak-'a-mi,
ọwọ́ tánta o sọṅ-mi; tánta o wọtr e-bọl-'e-mi, eyé e-mórka ña sála-
mi; e-mórka ña sọm tra-maṅk-tra-mi, atrá ọ-bom ọ sọṅ-mi; ọ-bom
ọ sọm am-bamp-'a-mi, ọwọ́ l dif ro-tan' dáta, tánta, tan' dáta."

---

1) The Cataract is here personified, hence the pronoun ọ, „he".

he put it on the top of the stump of a tree; and when the termites had eaten it, the child said to the termites: „Termites, give me my maize! Termites, give me my maize, which the mother gave me! The mother ate my bird, which I killed under the root, at the water-fall, under the root." Well, the termites made[1]) him earthen pots; he carried them to the brook at the water-fall to scoop water with. And when the cataract was breaking those earthen pots, he said: „Cataract, give me my earthen pots! Cataract, give me my earthen pots, which the termites gave me! The termites ate my maize, which the mother gave me; the mother ate my bird, which I killed under the root, at the water-fall, under the root." The cataract gave him a skate (fish); and when a hawk was taking it away, he said: „Hawk, give me my skate! Hawk, give me my skate, which the cataract gave me! The cataract broke my earthen pots, which the termites made[1]) for me; the termites ate my maize, which the mother gave me; the mother ate my bird, which I killed under the root, at the water-fall, under the root." Well, the hawk dropped a feather for him. Well, when the wind was carring it away, he said: „Wind, give me my feather! Wind, give me my feather, which the hawk gave me! The hawk ate my skate, which the cataract gave me; the cataract broke my earthen pots, which the termites made for me; the termites ate my maize, which the mother gave me; the mother ate my bird, which I killed under the root, at the water-fall, under the root." Well, the wind made many country-beans to fall down for him. Well, when baboons had eaten the beans, he said: „Baboon, give me my country-beans, which the wind made to fall down for me! The wind carried away my feather, which the hawk gave me; the hawk ate my skate, which the cataract gave me; the cataract broke my earthen pots, which the termites made for me; the termites ate my maize, which the mother gave me; the mother ate my bird, which I killed under the root, at the water-fall, under the root."

---

1) Lit. „formed".

Ambá, ra-wóto ọ pa họ: „I bā he r'áka trạka sọń." Kọ ọ šek ara-wóto; kọ mọ ọ poń kọ Sek, o kére-ko ro-petr.

Ań'úmp IV.

Pā Rańk re Pā W'ir-ań.

Pā Rańk de Pā W'ir ńa yi ri tápań; ka ńa gbákane kạ-wọnt ro-lal. Pā Rańk, kọnọ pā họ: „Mína tas-mu trạka kạ-wọnt." Pa W'ir-ań o pā họ: „De, mạ yéma; mína tas-mu." Pā Rańk o pā họ: „Tro mạ tas-mi-e?" Pa W'ir-ań ọ pā họ: „Ma sọkọ wọnt, sạ piára wọnt." Pā Rańk ọ pā họ: „Mań kọ ka Pa Sóńala, káma sạ tọńka." Ambá, ńa kọne ka Pā Sóńala. Pā Sóůala ọ pā họ: „Pā Rańk, ko ńe-e, na der-e?" Pa Rańk ọ pā họ: „Pā W'ir ọ fárki-mi; Pā W'ir o lọl, mína bána; ọ pā fọ o tas-mi ka-wọnt." Pā Sóńala ọ pā họ: „I ta rọk he am-pā; mań kọne nạn ro-lal." Pā W'ir ọ pā họ: „Be sạ trạ kọ ro-lal-e, mań trap nạn ano-kant kạ-wont." Pā Rańk o pā họ: „I Sélọ." Pa Sóńala ọ pā họ: „Áwa!" Pā Rańk ọ yi ka ka-trā kạ-dío ro-r'oń; Pā W'ir ọ yi ka ka-trā kạ-mérọ; Pā Sóńala o tráma ro-r'oń. Pā Rańk o kére ka-trā rokóm, ọ šim ey'íntr, o tra som e-bópar-ya-tši, ko ọ pā họ: „Pā W'ir o kólone ka-tšiń, I tas-kọ." Pa W'ir ọ pa họ: „Mań ko gbo, be pạ yi họ mạ tas-mi." Pa Sóńala ọ pā họ: „Mań ko nạn gbo, nyań I me kạli-ań." Ka ar'étr ra ka-tro Pa Sóńala o pā họ: „Ma wur nạń ro-lal." Ma ńa bēk ro-lal-e, Pā W'ir-ań ọ pa ho: „Ma wọnt nạn, mań gbákane nạń."

Well the baboon said: „I have nothing to give." And he tied the baboon, and when he had tied him, he carried him into the town.

Fable IV.

The Elephant and the Goat.

There was once an Elephant and a Goat; and they contended with each other in grazing on the grass-field. As to the Elephant, he said: „I surpass thee in grazing." The Goat said: „No, thou doest tell a lie; I surpass thee." The Elephant said: „How doest thou surpass me?" The Goat said: „Let us graze all night and all day."¹) The Elephant said: „Let us go to the Lion, that we may debate the case together." Well, they went to the Lion. The Lion said: „Mr. Elephant, what is the matter that ye come?" The Elephant said: „The Goat despises me; the Goat is little, I am big; he said that he surpasses me in grazing." The Lion said. „I do not yet decide the matter; let us go to the grass-field." The Goat said: „If we are going to the grass-field, let us begin grazing here in the bush." The Elephant said: „I am willing." The Lion said: „Very well!" The Elephant was to the right hand of the road; the Goat was to the left hand; the Lion stood in the road. The Elephant put up the trunk,²) he broke the trees, and was eating the leaves of them, and said: „The Goat boasts in vain, I surpass him." The Goat said: „Let us but go, whether it be so that thou surpass me." The Lion said: „Let us just go, it is you I am looking at." About 4 o' clock³) the Lion said: „Let us go out to the grass-field." When they arrived at the grass-field, the Goat said: „Let us graze, let us vie with each other."⁴)

---

1 Lit. „Let us graze all night, we graze all day", or rather: „let us spend all night in grazing, we spend all day in grazing."

2) Lit. „the hand," but here „the proboscis of the Elephant."

3) Lit. „At the sun of beating rice (for supper)," that is about two hours before sun-set, when they begin to beat rice for supper.

4) That is: „let us contend with each other in grazing."

Ar'étr ra woṅ, ka Pā W'ir o pā ho: „Mína, I ta nám'ra he."
Pā Raṅk o pā ho: „Sa ma fa̧nta he o-tan-i?" Pā W'ir o pā:
„Ma wont na̧n hā ka-ren' datrǫ́ṅ ka bēk." Ka-ren' datrǫ́ṅ ka
bēk-e, ka Pā Sóṅala o pā ho: „Maṅ kǫ́ne toṅ ro-gbálaṅ."
Aṅ-gbálaṅ 'a bána, e-búma e yi he ri tra̧ka wont. Ṅa wur
ka aṅ-gbálaṅ ratrǫ́n gbeṅ. Aṅ-Sóṅala o pā ho: „Ma fótane
na̧ṅ, man díra naṅ o-tan." Ṅa fa̧nta ro-gbálaṅ. Pà Raṅk o ko
fa̧nta ka aṅ-gbálaṅ, ro ṅa yi a-fíno; Pā W'ir o ko fa̧nta, ro aṅ-
gbálaṅ ṅa gbópe, dí-aṅ¹) o botr ara-bomp-r'oṅ. Pā Raṅk o
díra; Pā Sóṅala o díra; Pā W'ir o díra; kére o tra̧ trom. Pà
Sóṅala o ta̧me, o tra̧l Pā W'ir o tra̧ trom ma̧ra̧t-ma̧ra̧t. Pā
Sóṅala o pā ho, „Pā W'ir, ko maṅ som-e?" Pā W'ir o pā
ho: „I ta nám'ra he." Pā Sóṅala o pā ho: „Pā Raṅk, ma̧ tra̧l
ma Pā W'ir o mo som-i?" Pā Raṅk o pā: „Ko o mo som-e?"
Pā Sóṅala o pā ho: „I tr'a he ar'á raṅ o mo som-e, yit-ko."
Pā Raṅk-a o pā ho: „Ma sa̧ fa̧nta ka aṅ-gbálaṅ ratrǫ́n, e-búma
e yi fe ri. Pà W'ir, ko ma̧ ma som-e?" Pā W'ir o pā ho:
„I tši som aṅ-gbálaṅ, I na̧m̃ fe e-búma." Pā Raṅk o pā ho:
„Be ma̧ poṅ aṅ-gbálaṅ-e, ko ma̧ ma som-e?" O pā ho: „I tši
som r'a ra-bǫ́ti-som." Pā Raṅk o yókane, o ko rodí, o ko
fa̧nta. Pā Sóṅala o pā ho: „Ma fátrane na̧ṅ, mína yi tra rok
an-tǫ́ṅka, I ta rok he ṅi." Ṅa kǫ́ne ka Pā Raṅk, ṅa ko fatr-
ko; hálisa Pā W'ir o tra̧ trom gbo ma̧ra̧t-ma̧ra̧t. Pā Raṅk o
pā ho: „Maṅ kǫ́ne na̧ṅ ka wont-aṅ!" Pā Sóṅala o pā ho:
„Áwa, ma ra̧p na̧ṅ aṅ-gbálaṅ ka wont-aṅ." Ma ṅa poṅ wont be,

---

1) Or: dí-a.

The sun set, and the Goat said: „As for me, I have not yet enough." The Elephant said: „Shall me not lie down a little?" The Goat said: „Let us graze till midnight comes." Midnight came, and the Lion said: „Let us now go on the rock."

The rock was large, there was no green for grazing. They went out to the very middle of the rock. The Lion said: „Let us now rest, (and) let us sleep a little." They lay down on the rock. The Elephant went and lay down on the rock where it was good;[1]) the Goat went and lay down, where the rock was rugged, there he put down his head. The Elephant slept; the Lion slept; the Goat slept; but he was chewing the cud. The Lion awoke, he heard that the Goat was chewing the cud making marat-marat.[2]) The Lion said: „Mr. Goat, what art thou eating?" The Goat said: „I am not yet satisfied." The Lion said: „Mr. Elephant, doest thou hear how the Goat is eating?" The Elephant said: „What is he eating?" The Lion said: „I d'ont know that thing which he is eating, ask him." The Elephant said: „When we lay down on the middle of the rock, there was no green there. Mr. Goat, what art thou eating?" The Goat said: „I am eating the rock, I do not see green." The Elephant said: „When thou hast done with the rock, what wilt thou eat?" He said: „I shall eat something sweet to eat."[3]) The Elephant rose up, and went forwards, and lay down. The Lion said: „Let us come close together, I have to settle the matter, I did not yet settle it." They went to the Elephant, they went near him; the Goat was but still chewing the cud making marat-marat. The Elephant said: „Let us go grazing!" The Lion said: „Well, let us go round the rock while[4]) grazing." When they had grazed all about,

---

1) That is „even" or „smooth, not rugged".
2) This is an onomatopoetic adverb. See it in the Vocabulary.
3) Or: „something delicious to eat."
4) Or: „in grazing."

ńa wur ro-gbálań, ńa tráma. Pā W'ir ǫ sánnę, ǫ pą́ntńę, ǫ trą trǫm. Pā Rańk ǫ pā hǫ: „A, w'an ǫwé mǫ nám'ra hę!" Tśía ba Pa Sóńala ǫ pā hǫ: „Ań-lǫ́kǫ ńa ka-rǫk an-tǫ́ńka ńía bēk-ań. Pā W'ir-ań, tśē wúra-kǫ ro-pętr ka a-fąm; mǫ o tśē nám'ra, káma a-fąm ńa mar-kǫ tra soń-ko y'ętr ę-di." Pā Sóńala ǫ botr Pā Rańk ro-kant. Pā Rańk o nésa Pā W'ir-ań, ǫ gbúkę-kǫ. Pa Sóńala ǫ pā hǫ: „Ko ńę-ę?" Pa Rańk ǫ pā ho: „I mínta hę Pā W'ir-ań ka-wǫnt-k'oń; ǫ tr'a hę ar'á rań ǫ mǫ sǫm-ę; ǫ trą díra, o trą wǫnt." Pā Sóńala ǫ pa ka Pā Rańk: „Mą gbą́li hę yi rǫkín rę a-fąm, mą trą lą́sar ę-sęt ya a-fąm, de ę-kuńk; a-fąm ńa mínta hę mu; yi ro-kant; mą tą́na hę Pā W'ir ką-wǫnt. Ma Pa W'ir ǫ poń sǫm ań-gbálań, ǫ trą sǫm-mu." Tśíań Pā Rańk ǫ gbúkę, ǫ kǫ́nę ro-kant, ǫ wur hę sǫ ro-pętr.

O kǫ nat Pā Síp-ań, ǫ pā róńǫ́ń: „Są gbákanę ką-wǫnt, mína de Pā W'ir-ań, kǫ o bun mi sǫm; o sǫm ę-búma; są kǫ fą́nta rą-gbálań, kǫ ǫ sǫm ań-gbálań. Ko ań-gbálań ńa gbópę-gbópę, dí-ań Pa W'ir ǫ fą́nta, ǫ pā hǫ: „Bę I poń sǫm ań-gbálań, I tśi sǫm r'ā ra-bǫ́ti sǫm." Tśíań Pā Rańk ǫ gbúkę, ǫ kǫ nat Pā Sip-ań, ǫ pā rǫń'ǫ́ń: „Gbípa-mi Pā W'ir-ań; táńkań, ro mą ngń'-kǫ bę, gbip-kǫ. I tr'a hę ro są ma gbáńanę, I mínta hę kǫ sǫ; lánsa ro są ma gbáńanę, ǫ trą poń mi sǫm. I bóya-mu Pa W'ir-ań, gbípa-mi-kǫ." Tśíań ǫ-Sip ǫ mǫ gbip tǫń Qw'ír; Pā Rańk kǫ́nǫ bóya-kǫ tápań ka Pa Síp-a. Pa Rańk they went out on the rock, and stood. The Goat bent himself down, and raised himself again, and was ruminating. The Elephant said: „Ah, this boy is not satisfied!" Therefore the Lion said: „The time of settling the matter arrives. As regards the Goat, do not take him out from town with the people; because he does not get satisfied, that people may assist him to give him food." The Lion located the Elephant in the wood (bush). The Elephant was afraid of the Goat, and ran away from him. The Lion said: „What is the matter?" The Elephant said: „I do not dare to vie with the Goat (as regards) his grazing; he does not know that which he is eating; he is sleeping, and is grazing."[1]) The Lion said to the Elephant: „Thou canst not be together with people, thou art spoiling people's houses, and fences; people do not dare to cope with thee; be thou in the wood; thou art not able to keep up with the Goat in grazing. As the Goat has eaten (of) the rock, he will devour thee." Therefore the Elephant fled, and went into the wood, and did not come out into town again.

He went and challenged the Leopard, and said to him: „We were contending with each other in grazing, I and the Goat, and he almost devoured me; he ate green; we went and lay down on a rock, and he ate (of) the rock. Where the rock was very rough, there the Goat lay down, and said: „If I have eaten the rock, I shall eat something delicious to eat." Therefore the Elephant fled, and went and challenged the Leopard, and said to him: „Catch me the Goat; at all times, wherever thou doest see him, catch him. I do not know where we may meet each other, I do not dare to cope with him again; perhaps where we are meeting each other, he will entirely devour me. I make thee a present of the Goat,[2]) catch him for me." Therefore the Leopard is now catching the Goat; the Elephant he made formerly a present of him to the Leopard. The Elephant

---

1) Tkat is „he is grazing even while he sleeps".
2 That is „I deliver him up to thee" or: „into thy hand."

o náne ho ro ńa gbánnẹ gbo, Pā W'ir o tra poń ko sọm; tšíań o nésa, tšíań ọ sọń-kọ ka Pā Sip-ań.

Ańúmp V.

Pā Nēs-ań, ńa Pā Bō-ań, ńa Pā Trạk-ań, ńa Pā K'ạ́lma, ńa Pā Páńkal, ńa Pā W'ọr-ań.

Pā Nēs-ań o kánẹ Pā Bō: „Mań kérẹ-mi kạ-sọ́kanẹ!" Pā Bō ọ pā họ: „I šélọ." Kérẹ Pā Nēs ọ bótra-kọ a-tọ́ntọ. Ma Pā Nēs ọ kọ bạp a-sar ro-kant, ńa lọ́kọ k'ek-e, ọ pā họ: „O gbo, i-sar ńa lọ́kọ k'ek-e!" Mo ọ pā yań, ọ fúmpọ, ọ piára ri páli, o tạ́mẹ to ra-foī. Tšíań ọ bótra ań-ńań a-yáńfa trạ́ka sọm-ńa: tšíań ọ kọ tšéla Pā Bō: „Mań kónẹ sọ́kanẹ." Ńa kọ́nẹ, ńa Pā Bō. Ma ńa bēk ka ań-sar-e, Pā Nēs-a ọ kánẹ Pā Bō: „Kọ kar-mi ka ań-sar; I kọ bọm." Pa Bō ọ kọ yíra ka k'ạntr, ọ kạ́li ań-sar, ańá ba k'ek-e; kérẹ Pā Nēs ọ kọ hẹ tra bọm, ọ kọ trạ́ma gbo; kama Pā Bō ọ mọt-kọ bēk ka ań-sar. Mọ ọ der-e, ọ pā họ: „Pā Bō, mań kọ́nẹ." Kérẹ Pá Bō o pā họ: „Kạ́li, ma ań-sar ńa lọ́kọ k'ek-e!" Ma Pa Bō ọ pá yań-e, ọ fúmpọ ri; ka Pa Nēs ọ yóka-kọ, ọ kérẹ-kọ roń'ọ́ń, ọ kọ poń kọ di, kọn' dẹ ań-wut-ń'ọń.¹) Mọ ọ poń di Pā Bō-ań-e, ọ tšéla Pā Trạk, ọ pā họ: „Mań kérẹ-mi ka ka-sọ́kanẹ." Ńa kọ́nẹ, ńa Pa Trạk-ań. Ma ńa fatr ka ań-sar-e, Pā Nēs ọ kánẹ Pā Trạk: „Tas rodí, mína, I tši sọ́tẹ."

---

1) That is the Spider and his children consumed him.

thought that where they would but meet, the Goat will entirely devour him; therefore he was afraid; therefore he gave him to the Leopard.¹)

Fable V.

The Spider, and the Bush-goat, and the Deer, and the Antelope, and the Bushcow, and the Fillentamba.

The Spider said to the Bushgoat: „Come now with me for a hunting!"²) The Bushgoat said: „I will." But the Spider put a snare for him. When the Spider went and met a stone in the bush,³) which grew a beard,⁴) he said: „Oh strange, a stone grew a beard!" When he had said thus,⁵) he fell down, and was there all day, and awoke in the evening. This is the reason that he dealt deceitfully towards his companions in order to devour them; therefore he went and called the Bushgoat, (saying): „Let us go hunt." They went, he and the Bushgoat. When they came near to the stone, the Spider told the Bushgoat: „Go and wait me at the stone; I go to ease myself." The Bushgoat went and sat upon a log of timber, and looked at the stone, which had a beard; but the Spider did not go in order to ease himself, he only went and stood; that the Bushgoat might reach the stone before him. When he came, he said: „Mr. Bushgoat, let us go." But the Bushgoat said: „Look how the stone grew a beard!" When the Bushgoat had said thus, he fell down there, and the Spider took him up, and carried him to his place, and went and ate him entirely, he and his children. When he had eaten the Bushgoat, he called the Deer, and said: „Come with me to the hunting." They went, he and the Deer. When they came near to the stone, the Spider said to the Deer: „Go on before, as for me I shall make water."

---

1) Or: „he gave him into the hand of the Leopard."
2) Or: „Come now, carry me to a hunting!"
3) Or: „wood."
4) That is „a spider's web".
5) The Aorist for the Pluperfect, which is sometimes the case.

Pā Trak o tas, o ko trama o tra káli añ-sar. Pā Nēs o der, o pā ho: "Mañ kónę." Kére Pā Trak o pā ho: "Pā Nēs, káli, ma añ-sar ña lóko k'ek-e!" Ma Pā Trak o pā yañ-e, o fúmpo ri; ka Pā Nēs o yóka-ko, o kére-ko roñ'óñ, o ko di-ko, kon' de añ-wut-ñ'oñ.

Lóko lom Pā Nēs o tséla Pā K'álma, o pā roñ'óñ: "Mañ kónę sókanę." Ña kónę, ña Pā K'álma. Ma ña bēk ka añ-sar-e, Pā Nēs o kánę Pā K'álma: "Tráma kadí, 1 ko gbak a-rása." Pā K'álma o ko trama, o tra káli añ-sar. Pā Nēs o bēk, o pā roñ'óñ: "Mañ kónę." Pā K'álma o pā ho: "Káli, ma añ-sar ña lóko k'ek-e!" Mo o pā yañ-e, o fúmpo ri. Pā Nēs, mo o káli o tána he yóka Pā K'álma, mo o yi o-bána, o kónę ka gbúkę o ko tséla añ-wut-ñ'oñ. Ña der, ña re bañ-ko, ña ko poñ ko di. Pā Nēs o kal tséla Pā Páñkal, o:[1]) "Mañ kónę sókanę." Pā W'or o pā ho: "Atr'ei atšé tra kéta!" Añ-ñañ ña pā: "Ko ñe-e?" Pā W'or o pā ho: "Ka-sókanę aké, ma 'a tšē kal so!" Pa Páñkal o pa ho: "Mañ kónę, Pa Nēs!" Ña kónę. Pā W'or o trañ-ña; kérę ña nam fę ko. Ma ña bēk ka añ-sar-e, Pā Nēs o pā ka Pā Páñkal: "Ko kar-mi ka ak'áutr ka-bána, 1 ko bom." Kérę Pā W'or o máñknę ro-kant, o tra káli-ña. Pā Páñkal o ko trama, o káli añ-sar trañn. Ma Pā Nēs o bēk-e, o:[1]) "Mañ kónę, Pa Páñkal! Ko ma ma káli-e?"[2]) Pā Páñkal o pā ho: "Káli, ma añ-sar ña bā k'ek-a!" Mo o pā yañ, o fúmpo ri. Pā Nēs o kónę lemp, o ko tséla añ-wut-ñ'oñ;

---

1) This is for: o pā, or for: o pā ho: "he said:"
2) Or: Ko mañ káli-e?

The Deer passed on, and went and stood,¹) and was looking at the stone. The Spider came, and said: „Let us go." But the Deer said: „Mr. Spider, see, how the stone grew a beard!" When the Deer had spoken thus, he fell down there; and the Spider took him up, and carried him to his place, and ate him, he and his children.

Another time the Spider called the Antelope, and said to him: „Let us go hunt." They went, he and the Antelope. When they came near to the stone, the Spider said to the Antelope: „Go on before, I go to cut a rassa branch." ²) The Antelope went and stood, and was looking at the stone. The Spider arrived, and said to him: „Let us go." The Antelope said: „Look, how the stone grew a beard!" When he had spoken thus, he fell down there. The Spider, as he saw that he was not able to take the Antelope, because he was large, went away running, and went and called his children. They came, they fetched him, and went and ate him altogether. The Spider called again the Bushcow, he (said): „Let us go hunt." The Fillentamba said: „This matter is puzzling!" His companions said. „Why?"³) The Fillentamba said: „This hunting, because⁴) they do not return again!" The Bushcow said: „Let us go, Mr. Spider!" They departed. The Fillentamba followed them; but they did not see him. When they came near to the stone, the Spider said to the Bushcow: „Go and wait me at the large log of timber, I go to ease myself." But the Fillentamba hid himself in the bush, and was looking at them. The Bushcow went and stood,¹) and looked steadily at the stone. When the Spider arrived, he (said): „Let us go, Mr. Bushcow! What art thou looking at?" The Bushcow said: „Look, how the stone has a beard!" When he had said thus, he fell down there. The Spider departed quickly, and went and called his children:

---

1) Or: „stopped".
2) See the word rása in the Vocabulary.
3) Or „What is the matter?"
4) Or „— when they do not etc.!"

ka ma 'a re bań Pā Páṅkạl, ńa kọ sọm-kọ. Ma Pā W'ọr-a ọ nạṅk yań-e, ọ kọ́nẹ, ọ kọ káne aṅ-ńaṅ be.

Lọ́kọ lọm sọ Pā Nēs ọ kọ kánẹ Pā W'ọr-a, ọ pā họ: „Maṅ kọ́nẹ sọ́kanẹ." Pā W'ọr ọ pā họ. „I šélọ, maṅ kọ́nẹ." Ńa kọ́nẹ. Ma ńa bēk ka aṅ-sar-e, Pā Nēs ọ pā họ: „Pā W'ọr, kọ kar-mi ka ak'ạ̄ntr kạ-bána, I kọ bọm." Ma Pā W'ọr ọ bēk ri, ọ tas, ọ kọ trạ́ma rodí ka aṅ-sar. Ma Pā Nēs ọ bēk, ọ pā ka Pā W'ọr-a: „Rí-a I pā naṅ họ mạ kar-mi-i?" Pā W'ọr ọ pā họ: „Ar'óṅ' táhọ-i?" Pā Nēs ọ pā sọ: „Der ba." Pā W'ọr ọ der; ńa trạ́ma ka aṅ-sar. Pā Nēs o pā họ: „Ma mạ traṅka?" Pa W'ọr ọ pā họ: „Tro mẹ pā-e?" Pā Nēs ọ pā sọ: „Múnọ, mạ nạṅk fẹ-i?" Pā W'ọr ọ pā: „I nạṅk fẹ r'áka." Pā Nēs ọ pā sọ: „Múno, mạ tšẹmp hẹ." Pā W'ọr ọ pā: „I tšémpi." Pā Nēs ọ pā sọ: „A, Pā W'ọr!" Kọn' ọ pā họ: „A, Pa Nēs!" Pā Nēs ọ pā sọ: „Kạ́li ba tọṅ-a!" Pā W'ọr ọ pā sọ: „Kạ́li ba tọṅ-a!" Pā Nēs-a ọ pā sọ: „Pa yéńeu." Tšiaṅ Pā W'ọr ọ pā: „Tro mẹ pā-e?" Pā Nēs ọ pā tọ: „R'áka ra lọ́kọ r'áka." Pā W'ọr ọ pā: „R'áka ra lọ́kọ r'áka." Pā Nēs ọ pā họ: „Pā ba tọṅ-a!" Pā W'ọr ọ pā: „Pā ba tọṅ-a!" Pā Nēs ọ pā họ: „A, Pā W'ọr, múnọ, mạ kẹ́ta! Pā yéṅen tọ́kọṅ!" Pā W'ọr ọ pā: „Tro mẹ pā-e?" Pā Nēs ọ pā họ: „Pā ba: Sar-lọ-."[1]) Pā W'ọr ọ pā yi. Pā Nēs ọ pā sọ: „Pā ba: A-sar ńa lọ́kọ k'ek." Pā W'ọr ọ pā yi; ka ńa ńa-rạṅ ńa fúmpọ ri. Pạ yi aka-bạt, ma ńa ńa-rạṅ ńa fúmpọ ri, ka ar'étr ra yéma wọṅ, ma ńa kal yókanẹ. Ma ńa yókanẹ, Pā Nēs ọ pā họ: „Pā W'ọr, kọ ńẹ ba-e?"

---

1) These two words, as will be seen, form an imperfect beginning of the phrase: „A-sar ńa lọ́kọ k'ek-e!"

and they came to fetch the Bushcow, and went and devoured him. When the Fillentamba saw this, he departed, and went and told (it) to all his companions.

Another time again the Spider went and told the Fillentamba saying: „Let us go hunt." The Fillentamba said: „I am willing, let us go." They went. When they came near to the stone, the Spider said: „Mr. Fillentamba, go and wait me at the large log of timber, I go to ease myself." When the Fillentamba reached there, he went on, and went and stood beyond the stone. When the Spider arrived, he said to the Fillentamba: „Is it there I told thee to wait me?" The Fillentamba said: „Is not this the road?"¹) The Spider said again: „Come here." The Fillentamba came; they stood at the stone. The Spider said: „Why art thou silent?" The Fillentamba said: „What shall I say?" The Spider said again: „Thou, doest thou not see?" The Fillentamba said: „I see nothing." The Spider said again: „As for thee, thou hast no sense." The Fillentamba said: „I have sense." The Spider said again: „Ah, Mr. Fillentamba!" He said: „Ah, Mr. Spider!" The Spider said again: „Look here now!" The Fillentamba said again: „Look here now!" The Spider said again: „Speak now." Therefore the Fillentamba said: „What shall I say?" The Spider said now: „Something grew something?" The Fillentamba said: „Something grew something." The Spider said: „Speak then now!" The Fillentamba said: „Speak then now!" The Spider said: „Ah, Mr. Fillentamba, as for thee, thou art puzzling! Speak then now!" The Fillentamba said: „What shall I say?" The Spider said: „Say now: Sar-lo-." The Fillentamba said it.²) The Spider said again: „Say now: A stone grew a beard." The Fillentamba said it; and they both fell down there. It was in the morning, when they both fell down there, and the sun was about to set, when they rose up again. When they had got up, the Spider said: „Mr. Fillentamba, what is the matter now?"

---

1) Or: „Is not here the road?" Lit. „The road not (it)?"
2) Lit. „thus" or „so".

Pa W'or o pa: „Tr'ei tra yi he ri." Pa Nēs o pā ho: „Tro me pā-e?" Tšíań Pa W'or o pā: „Tro me pā-e?" Pā Nēs o pā: „Pā: Añ-sar ña lóko k'ek." Ma Pā Nēs o pā yañ-e, o fúmpo ri; kére Pa W'or o pā he yi so; o kóne, o ko káne añ-fam-ñ'oń be, o pā ho: „W'úni ó w'úni, be Pa Nēs o ba-mu ka ka-sókane, o poń mu som. Be ma ko ro-kant-e, ma nańk a-sar, ña ba k'ek-e, mam pā fe ho:[1] „A-sar ña lóko k'ek!" Be ma pā yi, ma tra fúmpo ri. Pā Nēs o tra poń mu som."

Añ'ûmp VI.
Pā Nēs-a, ña Pā Bō-ań, ña Pā Trańk-ań, ña Pā Sip-ań.

Pā Nēs kóno mo ko ka lásar tr'ei-ań; tšíań 'a ma yō-ko o-báki, 'a bun ko dif; tšíań o tra káne Pā Bō lóko ó lóko: „'A bun mi dif!" Pā Bō o yif-ko: „Ko yi ka-bun fi-e?" Pā Nēs o pā: „Ma tr'a he ka-bun fi-i?" A-lóko lom Pā Nēs o kóne, o ko keía ka o-baī; 'a wop-ko ri, 'a pā: „Tr' 'a dif-ko." O-bai o pā: „Tr' 'a tšer-ko, tšē ko dif." Pā Nēs o kálane, o ko bap Pā Bō roń'óń. Pā Bō o pā ho: „O gbo, Pā Nēs! Ko yō-mu yań-e?" Pā Nēs o pā: „I bun fi." Pā Bō o pā so: „Ko yi ba ka-bun fi-e?" Kon' o pā ho: „Kar-mi, I tši tróri-mu anína ka-bun fi." Ña díra. Ka ka-bat Pā Nēs o pā ka Pā Bō: „Mań kóne, I ko tróri-mu ka-bun fi; mań kóne ba ro-lal ka añ-wul-a." Pā Bō o tr'a he tši, fo Pā Nēs o kére[2] añ-wut-ñ'oń

---

1) For: ma ma pā fe ho etc.
2) The Aorist for the Pluperfect.

The Fillentamba said: „There is nothing the matter." The Spider said: „How shall I say?" Therefore the Fillentamba said: „How shall I say?" The Spider said: „Say: The stone grew a beard." When the Spider had spoken thus, he fell down there; but the Fillentamba did not say so again; he left, and went and told (the matter) to all his people, he said: „Any one (of you), if the Spider has thee at the hunting, he will entirely devour thee. If thou doest go into the bush, and thou seest a stone, which has a beard, thou must not say; ‚A stone grew a beard!' If thou doest say so, thou wilt fall down there, and the Spider will devour thee altogether."

Fable VI.

The Spider, and the Bushgoat, and the Ant-Eater, and the Leopard.

The Spider he was going about spoiling a thing; therefore they dealt hardly with him, and almost killed him; therefore he was always telling the Bushgoat: „They almost killed me!" The Bushgoat asked him: „What does almost dying mean?"[1]) The Spider said: „Doest thou not know (what) almost dying (means)?" Once the Spider departed, and went to steal at the king's place: they took hold of him there, and said: „Let them kill him." The king said: „Let them set him at liberty, do not kill him." The Spider returned, and went and met the Bushgoat at his place.[2]) The Bushgoat said: „Oh dear, Mr. Spider! What did hurt thee thus?" The Spider said: „I almost died." The Bushgoat said again: „What is now (the meaning of) almost dying?" He he said: „Wait me, I will show thee to morrow (what) almost dying is." They slept. In the morning the Spider said to the Bushgoat: „Let us go, I go to show thee (what) almost dying is; let us now go to the grass-field to the trap."[3]) The Bushgoat did not know, that the Spider had carried his children

---

1) Lit. „What is almost dying?"
2) That is at the Bushgoat's place.
3) Or „noose".

ro-lal, ọ kọ wọ́ńa-ńa ro-bi, ńa ba ẹ-tís. Ań-wul ńa Pā Nēs, o-báki, ań'és-ń'ọń: „Gbánnẹ-Yọń-a;"[1]) ań'és ńa ọ-lọm: „Nant-e Fuk-ań;"[2]) dẹ ań'és ńa ọ-fẹt: „Gbápnẹ Nant ro-Kos."[3]) Ńa kọ́nẹ, ńa Pā Bō; ńa bạp tọń kạ-lọ́mẹ ka ọ-baɩ ọ yi ro-bi, ọ wúra gbo ara-bomp-r'ọń; ań-fẹt ńa Pā Nēs ńa wop-kọ rorála; rí-ań ọ kérẹ Pa Bō-ań. Pā Nēs ọ bēk gbo, ọ pā: „Mań kọ́nẹ !rámạ rodí." O pā: „O gbo, Pā Bō! Kạ́li, mạ kạ-lọ́mẹ ka ọ-baɩ ọ mọ wọń ro-bi-a!" Ka Pā Bō ọ wop ara-bomp, ka Pā Nēs ọ pā: „Kar-mi, I tšı kọ gbạk k'ạntr." Pā Bō ọ tr'a hẹ, fọ ań-wut ńa Pā Nēs ńa yi ro-bi. Ma Pā Nēs ọ mọ gbak k'ạntr yań-e. ań-wut-ń'ọń ńa lıń aka-lọ́mẹ ro-bi. Pā Bō o wop ara-bomp, ań-wut ńa Pā Nēs ńa gbak aka-lim ka ka-lọ́mẹ. Pā Bō o lıń. o wúra 'ra-bomp ra ka-lọ́mẹ fas. Ań-fẹt ńa kọ́nẹ ka gbúkẹ, ńa ko wur ka am-bi; a-lọm[4]) ńa kọ́nẹ rọńáń ro-k'or. Pā Bō ọ tra tšéla: „Pā Nēs-e! Pā Nēs-e. dér-ō!" Pā Nēs ọ bēk, o pā: „Ko ńẹ-e?" O pā họ: „I gbọ́ti ara-bomp ra ka-lọ́mẹ!" Pā Nēs ọ pā: „A w'an! I kánẹ-mu nań họ: kar-mi!" Pa Nēs ọ sǫm ọw'ahẹ́t-k'ọń o-lọm ro-petr. ọ kọ kánẹ ọ-baī, fọ Pā Bō ọ gbọ́ti ka-lọ́mẹ-k'ọń 'ra-bomp. O-baɩ ọ der dẹ ań-fam-ń'ọń, ọ pā họ: „Ko ńẹ-e?" Pā Nēs ọ pā: „Pā Bō ọ gbọ́ti aka-lọ́mẹ 'ra-bomp." Pā Nēs ọ kal kánẹ Pā Bō sọɩ: „'A trạ́ma trạ́ka wop-mu; be ńa yéma wop-mu. gbúkẹ, mạ wọń ka am-bi ńa Pā Trańk." O-baɩ o pā: „Tr' 'a wop-kọ." Pā Bō ọ gbúkẹ, ọ kọ́nẹ; 'a bal-bal-kọ, ọ

---

1) Or: Gbánnẹ kạ-Yọń, lit. „Carry a Yọń." See Yọń, kạ- in the Vocabulary behind.

2) Lit. „Remove Chaff."

3) Lit. „Apply oneself Snot to the Cheeks." The prefix is dropped with the nouns.

4) Or: ńa-rań ńa kọ́nẹ etc., „two went to etc."

to the grass-field, and put them into the hole, having knives."¹)
As to the children of the Spider, the oldest, his name (was):
„Gbánne You-a;" the name of the second (was): „Nant-e Fukan;" and the name of the youngest (was): „Gbápne Nant roKos." They went, he and the Bushgoat; they then met one of
the king's sheep in the hole, it only stretched out its head; the
children of the Spider took hold of it below; thither he led the
Bushgoat. As soon as the Spider came, he said: „Let us go
and stand before."²) He said: „Oh dear, Mr. Bushgoat! Look,
how one of the sheep of the king was going³) into the hole!"
Then the Bushgoat took hold of the head, and the Spider said:
„Wait me, I shall go and cut a stick." The Bushgoat did not
know, that the children of the Spider were in the hole. While
the Spider was thus cutting a stick, his children pulled the
sheep into the hole, the Bushgoat held the head, the children
of the Spider cut the throat of the sheep. The Bushgoat pulled,
and all at once pulled out the head of the sheep. The children
went away running, they came out from the hole, some went
to their own place in the farm. The Bushgoat was calling:
„Mr. Spider! Mr. Spider, pray come!"⁴) The Spider came
and said: „What is the matter?" He said: „I plucked off the
head of the sheep!" The Spider said: „Ah friend! I told thee:
wait me!" The Spider sent his other child into the town, he
went and told the king, that the Bushgoat had plucked off the
head of one of his sheep. The king came with his people, and
said: „What is the matter?" The Spider said: „The Bushgoat
plucked off the sheep's head." The Spider returned and told
the Bushgoat softly: „They are about apprehending thee; if they
want to apprehend thee, run,⁵) and go into the hole of the
Ant-Eater." The king said: „Let them apprehend him." The
Bushgoat fled, and went away; they pursued after him, and he

1) Lit. „they had knives."
2) Or: „Let us go before."
3) Or: „was getting into etc.!"
4) Like the Germ. „komm doch!"
5 Or: „flee."

woñ ka am-bi. 'A ko tra tens-ko; kẹrẹ añ-fạm ña tr'a he fo o woñ ro-bi. Pa Nēs o kọ́nẹ, o ko sánnẹ ro-bi, o pä ho: „Pä Bō, mạ yi rẹ-i?" Pa Bō o wósa: „I yi rẹ anọ́." Pä Nēs o wúra a-fok ña m'ẹr, o soñ Pä Bō, o kánẹ-ko fo: „Bẹ ña yéma nu gbip tẹ́noñ-ẹ, añá ma der wop-mu-ẹ, fẹñ-ña am'ẹr ro-fọr." Mo o poñ pa yañ-ẹ, o pä ka añ-fạm: „Kạ́li-ko anọ́!" O kal sánnẹ, o kánẹ Pä Bō ho: „Bẹ mạ fẹñ¹) am'ẹr ro-fọr-ẹ, bẹ 'a bal-bal ow'úni ka-tši; wur, mạ kónẹ romí ro-k'ọr." Añ-fạm bẹ ña poñ bēk ro-bi, w'úni ó w'úni o tr'a hẹ ma 'a ma yọ̄-ẹ, ña tr'a hẹ bẹs tra wúra Pä Bō-añ. 'A pä: „Pä Nēs, tro sạ ma yọ̄-ẹ?" O pä ho: „Ma sạ yi bẹ, sạ tr'a hẹ bẹs; tr' 'a ko tšéla Pä Trañk-a." Ña sōm o-láñba, o ko tšéla Pä Trañk, ko o bēk. O-baī ẹ pä ho: „W'an-ka-mi, Pä Trañk, bẹ́sa-mi anọ́, mạ wúra-mi Pä Bō!" Pä Trañk o šélo; ko o trap aka-bẹs. Ma Pä Trañk-añ o mo bẹs-ẹ. Pa Nēs o sōm an-wut-ñ'oñ, ña wúra aka-lómẹ, ña kérẹ-ko ro-k'ọr; o-baī o tr'a hẹ tši. Pä Trañk o bẹs hañ o ko bap Pa Bō. Pä Bō o yóka m'ẹr ma-laī, o botr ka ka-sạñ-k'ọñ, o fẹñ Pä Trañk am'ẹr ka ẹ-fọr-y'oñ. Pä Trañk-a o pä: „E-tọf ẹ woñ-mi ro-fọr." O-bai o pa ho: „Fẹñ-ko nạñ, na wúra-ko ẹ-tọf ro-fọr" O-láñba o fẹñ ẹ-fọr-y'oñ; ẹ-kant ẹ wur, ẹ woñ o-láñba ro-sạñ. O-láñba o pä: „A, Pa Trañk o bä ẹ-kant ẹ-bọ́ti gbä!" Ka Pä Nēs o pä ho: „Trạ́ka ẹ-kant tšīañ

---

1) The Aorist for the Perfect tense.

went into the hole. They went to look for him; but the people did not know that he had gone into the hole. The Spider left, and went and bowed himself down at the hole, and said: „Mr. Bushgoat, art thou here?" The Bushgoat answered: „I am here." The Spider took out a parcel of salt, and gave (it) to the Bushgoat, and said to him: „When they want to catch thee to day, as to those who come to apprehend thee, blow them the salt into the eyes." When he had spoken thus, he said to the people: „Look him here!" He bowed himself down again, and said to the Bushgoat: „When thou hast blown the salt into the eyes, (and) when they pursue after that person;[1]) come out, and go to my place in the farm." All the people had arrived at the hole, (but) none knew how they must do, they did not understand to dig to bring out the Bushgoat. They said: „Mr. Spider, how must we do?" He said: „As for us all,[2]) we do not know to dig; let them call the Ant-Eater." They sent a young man, he went and called the Ant-Eater, and he arrived. The king said: „My friend, Mr. Ant-Eater, dig me here, and take me out the Bushgoat!" The Ant-Eater was willing; and he began with the digging. While the Ant-Eater was digging, the Spider sent his children, and they took out the sheep, and carried it into the farm; the king did not know it. The Ant-Eater digged till he came and met the Bushgoat. The Bushgoat took much salt, and put (it) into his mouth, and blew the salt into the eyes of the Ant-Eater. The Ant-Eater said: „Earth got into my eyes." The king said: „Blow ye on him, and take out the earth from his eyes." The young man blew into his eyes, some gum of the eye came out, and got into the young man's mouth. The young man said: „Ah, the Ant-Eater has a very sweet[3]) gum of the eye!" And the Spider said: „About the gum of the eye, about this (only)

---

1) That is the Ant-Eater, the owner of the hole.

2) Or: „As for us individually, we etc." Lit. „As we are all, we etc."

3) Or: „delicious."

mạ trára-i?" Ọ-bai ọ pā: „Mam pā yań-a?" Pā Nēs ọ pā sọ: „Ma nạ nạńk e-kant e-bọ́ti, Pā Trańk kọ́nọ kŏnọne kọ́nọ ta bọt." Ọ-baī ọ pā: „Pā Trańk, der ba, l mẹ́mạr-a!" Pā Trańk ọ pẹ́nša, ọ der he. Ọ-bai ọ kọ ri, ọ kọ feń-kọ ro-fọr, e-kant e wọń ọ-baī ro-sạń, ọ pā: „A w'an, mun' bọ́ti gbā!" Pa Trańk o wur ka ka-bes, ọ kọ trạ́ma ro. Ọ-baī ọ pā: „W'an, der ba!" Pā Trańk ọ pā: „l der he sọ; ma mạ pā min' bọ́ti." Ọ-baī ọ kọ ri; Pā Trańk ọ gbúke, ńa bal-bal-kọ de ka-bor-k'ọń be, ńa poń ań-lal, ńa bạtr Pā Trańk. Pā Nēs ọ pā: „Tr' 'a dif-kọ, káma nạ trára, mọ ọ yi kạ-bọt-e." Ńa dif Pā Trańk. Ma ńa ma tšen-kọ-e, Pā Nēs ọ pā: „l kọ́ne, l kọ bań ka-mọ́te-ka-mi." Ọ kọ́ne, ọ kọ bạp Pā Bō, ọ yi ro-bi (ro Pā Trańk ọ la nań bes-e); ọ káne-kọ: „Wur, mạ kọ́ne ro-k'ọr." Pā Bō ọ kọ́ne. Pā Nēs ọ kálane, ọ kọ bạp 'a poń tšen Pā Trańk-a. Ọ-baī ọ pā: „Pā Nēs, de yer ọ-šem, múnọ sōm-a sạ sọ́tọ ọ-šem ọwé." Pā Nēs ọ pā: „A, ọ-baī ọ mọ yíra he, ọ-láńba ọ yer ọ-šem!" Ọ-baī ọ pā: „l šélọ." 'A wúra a-lạńk, ńa sọń Pā Nēs, de a-fi, de aka-léńa, ńa sọn-kọ. Ńa poń yer ọ-šem seńk. Ọ-baī ọ pā: „Mań kal nạń trań ro, káma sạ kọ wúra Pā Bō." Pā Nēs ọ pā: „Áwa, mań kọ́ne nạń!" Ńa kọ bēk ri. Ọ-baī ọ kọ kạ́li ro-bi, ọ pā họ: „Pā Nēs, der ba, kạ́li-a! Kạ́li ba, mọ w'úni ọ kọt anọ-bi-a!" Pā Nēs ọ pā: „Ọ gbo! Pā Bō kọ́nọń;

thou knowest (something to say)?" The king said: „Why doest thou say so?" The Spider said again: „As ye find the gum of the eye to be sweet, the Ant-Eater himself he is (still) sweeter." The king said: „Mr. Ant-Eater, come here, that I may try!" The Ant-Eater refused, he did not come. The king went there, he went and blew into his eyes, some gum of the eye got into the king's mouth, and he said: „Ah friend, thou art very sweet!" The Ant-Eater came out from the digging,[1]) and went and stood at some distance. The king said: „Friend, come here!" The Ant-Eater said: „I do not come again; because thou saidst that I was sweet." The king went there; the Ant-Eater fled, they pursued after him with all his people,[2]) they went all over the grass-field, and seized the Ant-Eater. The Spider said: „Let them kill him, that ye may know how sweet he is."[3]) They killed the Ant-Eater. When they were cutting him up, the Spider said: „I go away, I go to fetch my basket." He left, and went and met the Bushgoat, he was in the hole (where the Ant-Eater used to dig); he said to him: „Come out, and go to the farm." The Bushgoat went. The Spider returned, he went and found that they had done with cutting up the Ant-Eater. The king said: „Mr. Spider, come share the meat, thou wast the cause that we got this meat." The Spider said: „Ah, the king is not sitting down, and a young man shares the meat!" The king said: „I am willing." They took out a leg, and gave (it) to the Spider, and one of the loins, and the tail, they gave (them) to him. They had done with sharing the whole of the meat. The king said: „Let us (now again) follow yonder, that we may go and take out the Bushgoat." The Spider said: „Well, let us go!" They went and reached there. The king went and looked into the hole, and said: „Mr. Spider, come now, look! Look now, how somebody walked here in the hole!" The Spider said: „Oh dear! It is the Bushgoat;

---

1) That is from the place where he dug.
2) That is with all the kings people; lit. „all his domestics etc."
3) Lit. „how he is sweetnees."

o kọ́nẹ!" Ọ-baī o tr'a hẹ tši, fo kọ́nọ o kọ kánẹ Pā Bō họ: „Kọ́nẹ rọmí ro-k'ọr." Ọ-baī o pā: „Man kal nan ro-pelr." Na kọ bēk ro-petr. Pā Nēs ọ kọ́nẹ ro-k'ọr, ọ kọ ban Pā Bō, ọ kára-kọ, ọ rẹ mank-kọ ka an-kant rorárạn. Ọ-baī ọ kal tšéla Pā Nēs-an, o pā ronọ́n: „Man tẹ́nsa-mi Pā Bō, múnọ trára ma-sọt!" Pā Bō, kọ́nọn 'a ma tẹn¹) bẹ, 'a nạm fẹ kọ. Pā Bō o trạl mọ ọ-baī ọ mọ bánsa ro-petr, ọ mínta hẹ sọ wur ro-petr. Pā Nēs ọ kọ pā ka Pā Bō: „Tro pẹ-e? Tro pẹ-e?" Pā Bō ọ pā: „A, I bun fi ro-bi, Pā Nēs!" Kọ́nọ pā: „Mạ trára tẹ́nọn kạ-bun fi-i?" Kọ ọ pā: „An, I trára." Pā Nēs ọ pā sọ: „Mạ ta tr'a hẹ kạ-bun fi." Pā Bō o mínta hẹ sọ wur ro-petr. Pā Nēs ọ pā: „Kar-mi, I tši trọ́ri-mu kạ-bun fi, kar gbo!" Pā Nēs ọ kọ́nẹ ro-kant, ọ kọ nank an-wut na Pā Sip-a. Ọ kálanẹ, ọ bēk ka Pā Bō, ọ pā họ: „Ra-bomp-ra-mi ra ban; Pā Bō, main paía-mi, I kọ wọnt a-trọl" Na kọ bạp an-wut na Pa Sip-a, na na-rạn, na fạ́nta. Pā Nēs-a o kánẹ Pā Bō: „Kọ fọ́kia-mi an'ạ́ntr anán, (ro tra-sip na-rạn na fạ́nta)." Pā Bō ọ kọ nank-na, ọ tšéla Pā Nēs-a. Pā Nēs ọ bēk, ọ pā: „O gbo! Ko ẹ-šẹm na nē-e?" Pā Bō ọ pā: „Mam ba-na." Pā Nēs o pā sọ: „Mam ba-na." Na yóka-na. Ma na kọ́nẹ ọ-tan-e, Pā Nēs ọ pā: „Man dif-na." Na dif-na. Pā Nēs ọ kal kánẹ Pā Bō, ọ pā họ: „Kọ́nẹ rọmú ro-k'ọr, I tši bạp-mu téte." Pā Bō

---

1) Or: kọn' 'a ma tẹn etc., „him they were seeking etc."

he is gone!" The king did not know, that he had gone and told the Bushgoat: „Go to my place in the farm." The king said: „Let us return to town." They went and came into the town. The Spider went into the farm, he went and fetched the Bushgoat, he brought him, and came and hid him in the wood behind. The king called the Spider again, and said to him: „Come now, seek the Bushgoat for me, thou art acquainted with artifices!" As to the Bushgoat, him they were seeking all about; (but) they did not see him. The Bushgoat heard how angry the king was in town, and dared not to come out again into the town. The Spider went and said to the Bushgoat: „How doest thou do? How doest thou do?"¹) The Bushgoat said: „Ah, I almost died in the hole, Mr. Spider!" He said: „Doest thou understand now (what) almost dying (is)?"²) And he said: „Yes, I understand (it)." The Spider said: „Thou doest not yet know (what) almost dying (is)." The Bushgoat did not venture again to come out into town. The Spider said: „Wait me, I will show thee (what) almost dying (is), only wait!" The Spider went away into the wood, and went and saw the children of the Leopard. He returned, and came to the Bushgoat and said: „My head aches; Mr. Bushgoat, come, go with me,³) I go to look for medicine." They went and met the children of the Leopard, they were two, they lay down. The Spider said to the Bushgoat: „Go bark me that tree,⁴) (where the two leopards lay)." The Bushgoat went and saw them, (and) he called the Spider. The Spider came and said: „Oh dear! What beasts are these?" The Bushgoat said: „Let us have them." The Spider said also: „Let us have them." They took them. When they had gone a little (way), the Spider said: „Let us kill them." They killed them. The Spider told the Bushgoat again, saying:³) „Go to thy place in the farm, I shall meet thee presently." The Bushgoat

---

1) Lit. „How is it? How is it?"
2) Lit. „Doest thou know to day almost dying?"
3) Lit. „he said etc."
4)

o kóne ro-k'or. Pä Sip-a o bēk ro o botr añ-wut-ñ'oñ, o nañk fe ña so; ko mo o tráñane am-bontr ro 'a kére-ña, o ko bēk ro-k'or ka Pä Bō; o bap Pä Bō o tra lap an'ántr. Pä Nēs o der, o máñkne, o tra káli Pä Bō; mo o poñ trára, fo Pä Sip o tra der tra ten añ-wut-ñ'oñ. Pä Sip o der ten añ-wut-ñ'oñ, o pä ho: „Pä Bō, káne kára añ-wut-'a-mi anǵ-e?" O ko yúka-ña, 'a poñ fi toñ. O pä so: „Pä Bō, múno dif añ-wut-'a-mi-i?" Pä Bō o gbúke. Pä Sip o piára ko bal-bal páli. Pä Bō o ko máñkne ka o-baī ra-foī. Pä Sip o bēk, o pä ka o-baī: „Pä Bō o bēk anǵ-i?" O-baī o pä: „O yi re." O yif so Pä Sip: „Ko ñe-e?" Pä Sip o pä so: „O poñ dif añ-wut-'a-mi." O-baī o pä ho: „Káli-ko roráreñ; o dif lo ñoñ ka-lóme-ka-mi." Pä Sip o ko ri roráreñ. Pä Bō o gbúke, o trañ-ko tra ka-bal-bal-ko, häñ o ko máñkne ka Pä Nēs; Pä Sip o nañk fe ko so. Pä Sip o kal kóne ka o-baī, o yif-ko so ho: „Pä Bō o bēk anǵ-i?" O pä: „I nañk fe ko." Pä Nēs o kóne, o ko yóka añ-wut ña Pä Sip, o ko kal-ña, o patr-ña; o treī añ-fatr ro-k'áreñ, o kóne ro-petr, o bap Pä Sip-a, ña tra pä re o-baī-añ tráka añ-wut. Pä Nēs o pä roñáñ: „Ko tr'ei tra ua ma pä anǵ-e?" Pä Sip o pä so: „Pä Bō o poñ dif añ-wut-'a-mi." Pä Nēs o pä: „A, Pä Bō! Yo o yi gbo táñkañ; o dif lo ñoñ añ-wut-'a-mi!" O-baī o pä ka Pä Sip:

went to the farm. The Leopard came to the place where he[1]) had put his children, (and) he did not see them again; and as he followed up the scent (in the way), where they carried them, he went and arrived at the farm of the Bushgoat, he met the Bushgoat stirring up the fire. The Spider came, he hid himself, and was looking at the Bushgoat; as he had learned, that the Leopard was coming to look for[2]) his children. The Leopard came in order to seek his children, and said: „Mr. Bushgoat, who carried my children to this place?" He went and took them up, they were dead then.[3]) He said again: „Mr. Bushgoat, didst thou kill my children?" The Bushgoat fled. The Leopard spent the whole day in pursuing after him. The Bushgoat went and hid himself with the king[4]) in the evening. The Leopard came, and said to the king: „Did the Bushgoat arrive here?" The king said: „He is here." He asked the Leopard again: „What is the matter?" The Leopard said: „He has killed my children." The king said: „See him behind (the yard); he killed the other day a sheep of mine." The Leopard went there behind. The Bushgoat fled, he followed him in order to pursue after him, till he went and hid himself at the Spider's place; (and) the Leopard did not see him again. The Leopard went back again to the king, and asked him again: „Did the Bushgoat come here?" He said: „I did not see him." The Spider left, and went and took the children of the Leopard, and went and broiled them, and cooked them; he left the iron pot on the fire-place, and went into the town, and met the Leopard, they were talking with the king about the children. The Spider said to them: „What matter are ye talking about here?" The Leopard said again: „The Bushgoat has killed my children." The Spider said: „Ah, the Bushgoat, thus he is but always: he killed my children the other day!" The king said to the Leopard:

---

1) Lit. „The Leopard arrived where he etc."
2) Or „to seek etc."
3) Or „already."
4) Or „at the king's place etc."

"Tens-ko." Pä Sip o wur, o kọ́ne trạ́ka kạ-teu Pä Bō; o ko gbánne-ko ro-r'oṅ; o bal-bal-ko. Pa Bō o ko máṅkne so rokant, Pä Sip o naṅk fẹ ko sọ; kérẹ Pa Bō o ko maṅkne roráraṅ ka Pä Nēs. Pä Nēs o trạ́la-ko ri, o ko naṅ'-ko ri, o pā: "Maṅ kọ́ne di, I poṅ patr." Pä Bo o pā: "I mínta he, o-baï o poṅ mi wáṅki." Pä Nēs o pā sọ: "I kára-mu e-nak aṇ́-i?" Pa Bō o pā: "Yáo, kára aṇ́." Pa Nēs o kérẹ-ko e-nak; ṅa yíra gbo, ṅa di. Pa Nēs o pä sọ: "Tro pẹ-mu-e, Pä Bō?" Pa Bō o pä: "I bun fi; ṅa bun mi dif" Pä Nēs o pä sọ: "Mạ trára ténọṅ kạ-bun fi-i?" O pā: "I trára-ki ténọṅ." Pä Nēs o pä ho: "Ma mạ pa naṅ fo mạ tr'a he ki naṅ-a." Pä Bō o pä sọ: "Kérẹ I trára-ki ténoṅ." Pä Nēs o pä sọ: "Man di lemp lemp, káma mạ gbúkẹ. Be Pä Sip o trạ́la am-bontr-'a-mu-e, ro mạ ko be, o trạ traṅ-mu; kọ́ne o-bọ́li." Pä Bō o gbúke sọ (ma ṅa poṅ di), o kọ́ne o-bóli. Pä Sip o tensko, häṅ o támrọ; o kọ́ne sọ ka o-baï. Pä Nēs sọ, mọ o trára, fo Pa Sip o kọ́ne ka o-baï, o ko ri sọ. O bap Pä Sip, o trạ pa-tsi sọ trạ́ka Pä Bō. O-baï o pä ka Pä Sip: "Ro mạ naṅ'-ko be, bạtr-ko, mạ kára-ko romí." Pä Nēs o pä sọ: "Ro mạ naṅ'-ko be, gbip-ko, mạ kára." Kọn' sọ o kọ́ne, o ko baṅ Pä Bō; o káne-ko, fo ka-trạk ka poṅ. Ma ṅa bēk ro-petr-e, Pä Nēs o káne Pä Bō: "Traṅ aṇ́, káma mạ ko wur roráraṅ ka o-baï." Kọn' o kal kọ́ne ka Pä Sip-aṅ, o pä ho: "Kọ́ne roráraṅ ka o-baï, mạ ko máṅkne ro-r'oṅ; Pä Bō, I poṅ kára-ko."

"Seek him." The Leopard went out, and went away in order to seek the Bushgoat; he went and met him in the road; he pursued after him. The Bushgoat went and hid himself again in the bush, (and) the Leopard did not see him again; but the Bushgoat went and hid himself at the back-part of the Spider's place. The Spider heard him there, and went to see him there, and said: "Let us go to eat, I have cooked." The Bushgoat said: "I do not dare, the king has outlawed me." The Spider said again: "Shall I bring thee the rice here?" The Bushgoat said: "Yes, bring (it) here." The Spider carried the rice to him; they just sat down, and ate. The Spider said again: "How art thou, Mr. Bushgoat?" The Bushgoat said: "I almost died; they almost killed me." The Spider said again: "Doest thou know now (what) almost dying (is)?" He said: "I know it now." The Spider said: "Because thou saidst before that thou didst not know it." The Bushgoat said again: "But I know it now." The Spider said again: "Let us eat very quickly, that thou mayest flee. If the Leopard gets the scent of thee, wherever thou goest, he will follow thee; go far away." The Bushgoat fled again (when they had eaten), and went far away. The Leopard sought him, till he was tired;[1]) and he went again to the king's place. The Spider also, when he knew, that the Leopard had gone to the king's place, went there too. He met the Leopard, he was talking over again the matter about the Bushgoat.[2]) The King said to the Leopard: "Wherever thou seest him, seize him, and bring him to me." The Spider also said: "Wherever thou seest him, catch him, and bring (him)." He also left, and went to fetch the Bushgoat; he told him, that the palaver was done." When they came to the town, the Spider said to the Bushgoat: "Follow here, that thou mayest come out behind the king's place." He went again to the Leopard, and said: "Go behind the king's place, and go and hide thyself in the road; as to the Bushgoat, I have brought him."

---

1) Lit. "till he was overcome."
2) Lit. "he was talking it over again about etc."

Pa Sip o ko mańkne ri; Pä Bō o bēk; Pä Sip o wop-ko. Pä Bō o kúlo. O-baı o pä ho: „Ko ńe-e? Káne mo kúlo roráráńe?" Pä Sip o pä: „I sóto Pä Bō." O-baı o pä: „Kára-ko." Pä Sip o kára-ko, 'a dif-ko. Ma ńa poń dif Pä Bō-e, Pä Nēs o bēk. O-baı o pä: „Tro są ma yō-ko-e?" Pä Sip o pä: „Tr' 'a tšen-ko; mo o poń som ań-wut-'a-mi, mína, I tši somko." Ńa poń-ko tšen seńk. Pä Sip o pä ho: „Tr' 'a yer Pä Nēs-a o-laī, kóno sōm I sóto-ko." O-baī o pä ka Pä Sip so: „Ro mą nąńk a-bō be, gbip-ko."

Tšíań Pä Sip o tra gbip tra-bō, ńa ma nąńkane he so tańkań; ro o nąń'-ko, o gbip-ko. Tšíań so ań-wut ńa Pä Bō, ńa tróri Pä Yári fo: „Be mą nańk Pä Nēs-ań, gbip-ko, w'úni las woń." Tšíań so o-sip o nańk gbo a-bō-e, o gbip-ko, o poń ko som; de a-yári, be o nańk gbo a-nēs-e o som-ko.

Ań'úmp VII.

O-Baī re O'wán-k'oń o-béra, de Pä Támba.

O-baī o-lom o kōm tápań w'ahét béra, ko o yi o-fíno tánka be, ko o rúasm-ko, hań o poń bak; ka a-fam a-rúni ńa yémako. Ko o-yóla o re ten-ko, o pä: „O-ráni-ka-mi woń." Ko o soń a-kála a-gbáti ka o-baī, o-kas ka ō-béra; ko o-kas-k'oń o pä ho: „Botr ań-kála-'a-mu; be mą bontr ar'áka, ará yi ka ańsébe rok'ór-e, o-béra mą nántra-ko." Kére o tr'a he ar'áka,

The Leopard went and hid himself there; the Bushgoat came, (and) the Leopard took hold of him. The Bushgoat cried. The king said: "What is the matter? Who is crying behind?" The Leopard said: "I have got the Bushgoat." The king said: "Bring him." The Leopard brought him, (and) they killed him. When they had killed the Bushgoat, the Spider arrived. The king said: "What shall we do with him?" The Leopard said: "Let them cut him up; as he has devoured my children, I shall devour him." They had cut up the whole. The Leopard said: "Let them give much to the Spider, he caused me to get him." The king said to the Leopard again: "Wherever thou seest a bushgoat, catch him."

This is the reason that the Leopard is catching bushgoats, they never meet each other again face to face; where he sees him, he catches him. This is also the reason that the children of the Bushgoat told[1]) the Cat: "When thou doest see the Spider, catch him, he is a bad person."[2]) This is also the reason that as soon as a leopard sees a bushgoat, he catches it, and entirely devours it; and a cat, as soon as it sees a spider, it devours it.

Fable VII.

The King and his Daughter, and Mr. Tamba.

A certain king begat once a girl, and she was exceedingly fair, and he brought her up, till she was grown up; and men wanted her. And a gentleman came and tried to get her,[3]) he said: "She is my wife."[4]) And he offered much money to the king, the father of the woman; and her father said: "Put down thy money; if thou doest name the thing, which is within the amulet, thou shalt marry the woman."[5]) But he did not know the thing,

---

1) Lit. "informed."
2) Lit. "a bad person that."
3) Lit. "came to seek" or "came to obtain her."
4) Lit. "My wife that one."
5) " as for) the woman, thou marriest her."

ará yi ka aṅ-sébẹ rok'ór-e; kọ ọ-kas ka ọ-béra ọ pā: „Mạ támrọ, kálanẹ." Kọ ọ-yóla ọ-lọm o der sọ, ọ re tẹn ọ-bọ́rkọ, kọ̀ ọ sọṅ sọ a-kála a-gbáti. O-kas ka o-béra ọ pā sọ: „Botr aṅ-kála-'a-mu; be mạ bontr ar'áka, ará yi ka aṅ-sébẹ rok'ór-e, mạ nántra ọ-béra." Kẹ́rẹ ọ-láṅba ọ támrọ, ọ tr'a hẹ ar'áka, ará yi ka aṅ-sébẹ rok'ór, kọ ọ-kas ọ pa: „Kálanẹ." Ka aṅ-fạm bẹ ka an-tọſ ṅa der mẹ́mạr, ka ṅa támrọ; ṅa tr'a hẹ ar'áka, ará yi ka aṅ-sébẹ rok'ór. Kọ Támba ọ yéfa ro-tọ́rọṅ ọ-bọ́li, ọ re tẹn ọ-bọ́rkọ, ọ pā họ: „I tši sọ́tọ-kọ, ọ-ráni-ka-mi wọṅ." Ka aṅ-fạm ṅa pā họ: „Támba, mạ yéma, mạ tạ́na hẹ kọ sọ́tọ, ma a yóla bẹ ṅa poṅ támrọ." Kọ mọ ọ kọ́nẹ, ọ bā e-trọ́kọ, ọ ba pạ-lā pạ-fẹ́ra, de pạ-lā pa wóma; ko ọ bā w'ir, ọ bā ma-yántẹ, de m'áro, de e-tuk ya pạ-lā. Ko mọ ọ kọ́nẹ, ọ bạp Pā Rabem-aṅ,[1]) d'or ra báki-ṅa; ọ yif-ṅa: „Ko ṅe-e?" Ṅa pā: „D'or ra báki-su." Kọ ọ sọṅ-ṅa e-tuk. Ma ṅa poṅ di-yi, ọ tas, ọ kọ bạp Pā Kwī-aṅ, ọ pā: „Ko ṅe-e?" Kọn' ọ pā: „D'or ra báki-mi." O wúra ọw'ír,- ko ọ sọṅ-kọ. O tas, ọ kọ bạp Pā R'ọf-aṅ, ọ pā: „Ko ṅe-e mạ fạ́nta anọ́-e?" Pā R'ọf ọ pā: „D'or ra báki-mi." Támba ọ wúra e-trọ́kọ ṅa-rạṅ, ọ sọṅ-kọ. Ma Pā R'ọf-aṅ ọ poṅ di e-trọ́kọ, ọ wúra a-trọl, ọ sọṅ Pā Támba. An-trọl, aṅ'és-ṅa-tši ṅía yi: kạ-wóso. Q pā họ: „Be a-bōk ọ ṅaṅ w'úmi, an-trọl aṅé ṅía ma yọ̄, ṅía w'úmi mọ mun;

---

[1] The Singular is here used for the Plural, or for the whole species; hence the plur. form of the pron. in the following sentences.

which was within the amulet; and the father of the woman said:
„Thou art disappointed, return." Then another gentleman came
again, he came and tried to get¹) the damsel, and he offered
also much money. The father of the woman said again: „Put
down thy money; if thou doest name the thing, which is within
the amulet, thou doest marry the woman." But the young man
was disappointed, he did not know the thing, which was within
the amulet; and the father said: „Return." And all the people
in the country came to try, and they were disappointed; they
did not know the thing, which was within the amulet. And
Tamba came from the east a far way off, he came and tried to
get¹) the damsel, and said: „I shall get her, she is my wife."²)
And the people said: „Tamba, thou doest tell a lie, thou art not
able to get her; when³) all gentlemen have been disappointed."
And as he went along, he had fowls, he had clean rice, and
rice in the husk; and he had a goat, he had penne seed,⁴) and
palm-oil, and rice-straw. And as he went, he met the Hedge-
hog,⁵) hunger was heavy upon them; he asked them: „What is
the matter?" They said. „Hunger is heavy upon us." And
he gave them straw. When they had eaten it, he passed on,
and went and met the Alligator, and said (to him): „What is
the matter?" He said: „Hunger is heavy upon me." He took
out the goat, and gave (it) to him. He passed on, and went
and met the Cerastes, and said (to him). „What is the matter
that thou doest lie here?" The Cerastes said: „Hunger is
heavy upon me." Tamba took out two fowls, and gave (them)
to him. When the Cerastes had eaten the fowls, he took out
a medicine, and gave (it) to Mr. Tamba. As to the medicine,
the name of it is: ka̱-wóso. He said: „If a snake bites a person, this medicine they must make, this one must drink;

---

1) Or: „to obtain."
2) Lit. „my wife that one."
3) Or: „because all etc."
4) A kind of millet.
5) Or: „Grass-cutter." See the word in the Vocabulary.

káma pạ tọ́f'lọ-kọ." Pä K'ọf-an̄ ọ pä sọ: „Tr' 'a kọ ten mafit[1]) ma w'úni yán̄fa, tr' 'a botr-n̄a ka an-trọl." Támba ọ tas, ọ kọ bap Pa Tr'ak-n̄a, ọ pä rọn̄ọ́n̄:[2]) „Ko n̄e̩-e?" O pä:[3]) „D'or ra ban̄-su." O wúra ma-yánte̩, de m'áro, ọ son̄ ka Pä Tr'ak-n̄a, n̄a di. O tas, ọ kọ́ne̩, ọ kọ bēk ro ka ọ-baī, ọ-kas ka ọw'ahé̩t bé̩ra, ọ pä rọn̄ọ́ū fọ: „I der ten ow'ahé̩t bé̩ra trạ́ka nántra-kọ. O-sántki ka ọ-bai ọ pä họ: „A Támba, múnọ yaī ọwé mạ der ten ọ-bé̩ra ọwé̩-i?" Támba ọ pä: „I tši nántrakọ, ọ-ráni-ka-mi wọn̄." D'or ra báki ka a-boī n̄a ọ-baī, kọ Támba ọ wúra pạ-lā, ọ son̄-kọ. Ma am-boī ọ pon̄ di-e̩, ọ kọ́ne̩ ro ka Pä Támba, ọ kọ bóntra-kọ e̩y'é̩tr, e̩yé̩ yi ka an̄-sé̩be̩ rok'ór-e̩; n̄a kọ díra. Ka-bạt 'a kọ yira trạ́ka pä tra ka-náutra. O-kas ka ọ-bé̩ra ọ yif Támba họ: „Mạ yé̩ma ọ-bọ́rkọ-i? Bontr ar'áka, ará yi ka an̄-sé̩be̩ rok'ór." Támba ọ pä: „I trara-tši; ké̩re̩ I mínta he̩." O-kas ọ pä sọ: „Bontr-yi, trạ bā he̩ tr'eī." O pä: „I šélọ." Támba ọ pä họ: „An̄-fon n̄a Pä, mọ ọ yi ọfe̩t-e̩ tạ́pan̄, de aka-bont-k'ọn̄, de e̩-sáutrạk-y'ọn̄, yían̄ yi rok'ór ka an̄-sé̩be̩." Ma Támba ọ pä yan̄-e̩, ọ-sántki ọ pä: „Mạ yé̩ma." Kọ ọ yóka-kọ, kọ ọ tránd-kọ. Kọ ọ-bai ọ pä: „Yáo, ka-sū-ka-mi ka dínne̩ tạ́pan̄ ro-lal; bo mạ wúra-ki, mạ nántra

---

1) The indefinite form for the definite one, as it cannot be misunderstood.

2) Or: ron̄án̄, „to them." See the word k'ak, which is the Sing. of tr'ak in the Vocabulary behind.

3) Or: Na pä: „they said:"

that it may get better with him.¹) The Cerastes said again: „Let them go look for the brains of a deceitful person, (and) let them put them into the medicine." Tamba passed on, and went and met the Ants,²) and said to him:³) „What is the matter?" He said:³) „Hunger troubles us." He took out penne seed, and palm-oil, and gave (them) to the Ants, (and) they ate. He passed on, and left, and went and came to the king, the father of the girl, and said to him: „I come to look for⁴) the girl in order to marry her." A minister of the king said: „Ah Tamba! Thou, such a worthless fellow,⁵) thou doest come to look for this woman?" Tamba said: „I shall marry her, she is my wife."⁶) Hunger was heavy upon a servant of the king, and Tamba took out rice, and gave (it) to him. When the servant had eaten, he went to Mr. Tamba, and went and named to him the things, which were within the amulet; (and) they went to sleep. In the morning they went and sat down to talk about the marriage. The father of the woman asked Tamba: „Doest thou want the damsel?⁷) Name the thing, which is within the amulet." Tamba said: „I know it; but I do not dare (to name it)." The father said again: „Name them, it is of no consequence." He said: „I will." Tamba said: „The hair of the Master, when he was a young child formerly, and his navel-string, and his nails.⁸) these (things) are within the amulet." As Tamba spoke thus, the minister said: „Thou doest tell a lie." And he took him, and chained him. And the king said: „Well, my pipe was once lost on the grass-field; if thou doest find it out, thou shalt marry

---

1) Lit. „that it may get easy with him," = „that he may become easy," or „get out of danger."

2) Lit „implying the whole species."

3) The Singular for the Plural.

4) Or: „to obtain."

5) Lit. „Thou, this worthless one, thou etc."

6) Lit. „my wife that."

7) Here is an ellipsis of a few words, as: „Doest thou want the damsel? If so, name the thing etc."

8) That is ‚cuttings of them'.

o-béra." Támba o pä: „Yáo, I tši wúra-ki." Ko mo o kóne rolal, o ko bap Pä Ra-bem-añ, o yif-ko: „Re mañ ko-e, Támba?" O pä: „I ko ten aka-sū ka o-bai, ka dínne tápañ-e." Pä Rabem-a o pä ho: „Kar-mi, I ko báña-mu-ki." O ko bañ-ki, o soñ Támba. Támba o kére ka-sū ka o-baī. Kére o-sántki o pä ho: „Ma yéma, ki táho." Ko o wop-ko, o yō-ña 'a sapko. Ko o-bai o pä: „Tšer-ko ngñ." Na tšer-ko. Ko o-baī o pä so: „Ak'ónte-ka-mi ka dínne tápañ ro-bañ; be ma wúra-ki, I tši soñ-mu o-béra." Támba o pä: „I tši wúra-ki." Támba o kóne, o ko bap Pä Kwī-añ; kon' o pä ho: „Támba, ko ñe-e?" O pä: „I ko wúra ak'ónte ka o-baī, aká dínne tápañ robañ." Pä Kwī-a o kóne téte, o ko wúra-ki, o soñ Támba. Támba o kára-ki ka o-baī, o re soñ-ko. O-sántki o pä ho: „A, w'úni las! Tr' 'a bal-ko!" O-bai o pä: „De, I bal he ko." O-baī o pä so: „Támba, apa-lä-pa-mi añ-fet ña poñ pántrane-pi de ma-yánte; be ma poñ wúra ama-yánte ka pa-lä, ma tra nántra o-bórko." Támba o pä: „I šélo, I tši wúra-ña." Támba o pä: „Tr' 'a kára apa-la." Na kára-pi. O yíra ro-set, o tra wúra apa-lä ka ama-yánte. Mo o mo yō ama-pant amé, Pä Tr'ak¹) o bēk, ña gbáti, ña yif Támba: „Ko ma yō anó-e?" Támba o pä ho: „O-baī o soñ-mi ama-pant amé, káma I wúra

---

1) Here Pa is in the Sing., and Tr'ak in the Plur.; the following pron. is governed by Pā, and therefore in the Singular. See the word k'ak in the Vocab. behind.

the woman."¹) Tamba said: „Yes, I shall find it out." And as he went to the grass-field, he happened²) to meet the Grass-cutter, who³) asked him: „Where art thou going to, Tamba?" He said: „I go to look for⁴) the pipe of the king, it was once lost." The Grass-cutter said, „Wait me, I shall fetch it for thee." He went and fetched it, and gave (it) to Tamba. Tamba carried the pipe to the king. But the minister said: „Thou doest tell a lie, it is not this." And he seized him, and caused them to beat him. The king said: „Let him go." They let him go. And the king said again: „My cymbal⁵) was once lost in the sea;⁶) if thou doest find it out, I shall give thee the woman." Tamba said: „I shall find it out." Tamba left, and happened to meet the Alligator; he said: „Tamba, what is the matter?" He said: „I go to find out the cymbal of the king, which was formerly lost in the sea."⁶) The Alligator departed directly, and went and found it out,⁷) and gave (it) to Tamba. Tamba brought it to the king, and came and gave (it) to him. The minister said: „Ah, a bad person! Let them drive him away!" The king said: „No, I do not drive him away." The king said again: „Tamba, as regards my rice the children have mixed it with penne-seed; when thou hast taken out the penne-seed from the rice, thou shalt marry the damsel." Tamba said: „I will, I shall take it out." Tamba said, „Let them bring the rice." They brought it. He sat down in the house, and was taking out the rice from the penne-seed. As he was doing this work, the Ants⁸) came, they were numerous, (and) they asked Tamba: „What doest thou do here?" Tamba said: „The king gave me this work, that I might take out

---

1) Lit. „thou marriest the woman."
2) Lit. „he went (and) met etc."
3) Lit. „he asked etc."
4) Or: „to seek."
5) See the word k'ónte in the Vocabulary.
6) Or: „in the water."
7) Or: „took it out."
8) The wole species is implied.

apa-lā ka ama-yánțe amé." Pā Tr'ak o pā: "Yíra, kar-su."
Téte ña poň wúra apa-lā ka ma-yánțe be; apa-lā pa-féra ra kabalaí k'in, ama-yánțe ra ka-balaí ka-lom. Támba o yóka atrabalaí tra-rạň atšé, o ko trạmạr-tši ka o-baí, o pā: "I poň."
Q-sántki o pā ho: "Támba o yi w'úni las, tr' 'a faı-ko." Ňa yóka-ko, ňa sap-ko, 'a tránd-ko. Q-baī o káne aň-ráni-ň'oň ň'áňle, o pa: "Kóne, na ko kúta-mi m'antr, I yema búko." Ňa kóne, de w'ahét béra o-lom, o béka tramát. Ma ňa ko-e, Pā R'of o gbatr-ňa[1]) be, támbe ow'ahét béra o gbatr[1]) he ko. Qw'ahét o gbúke, o de káne o-baí ho: "Pā R'of o gbatr[1]) ambórko be ro-bat." 'A kóne, 'a ko baň-ňa, 'a kára.[2]) W'úni ó w'úni o tr'a he an-trol tráka yéňkas-ňa ma-der; ňa poň píka be, ňa fánta. Q-baī o pā: "Tr' 'a tšéla Támba, kóno trára tr'eī."
Ňa tšéla Támba; o der, o-baī o pā roňóň: "Támba, káli aň-ráni-'a-mi, ňa tra fi; Pā R'of o gbatr-ňa;[1]) ma trára an-trol ňa-tši-i?" Támba o pā ho: "I trára." Q-baī o pā so: "Yóna-mi an-trol-e." Támba o pā: "Tr' 'a ko ten ma-fit[3]) ma w'úni yáňfa; míaň me yóna-ňi; téte ňa tra yókane." Q-baı o pā: "I málane."
Q yóka a-bar, o sut-ňi o-sántki ra-bomp, ma-fit[3]) ma wur; ňa yóka-ňa, ňa-soň Támba; kon' o yóka-ňa, o rúňkatr-ňa ka antrol. O soň-ňi ka o-béra o-kin, o yókane. Q-baī o pā: "Básara-mi, w'an-ka-mi!" Támba o pa so: "Téna-n i ma-fit[3]) ma w'úni yáňfa, amé ma poň." Q-baı o yō 'a sut o-sántki o-lom ka 'ra-bomp so; ma-fit[3]) ma wur, ňa soň-ňa ka Támba; o yóka, o botr ka an-trol tráka o-béra o-lom; o yókane so. Q-baī o pā so: "W'an-ka-mi, rámara-mi to lemp aň-ráni-'a-mi ňa-raň,

---

1) Or: ňaň, "bit."
2 The Object is dropped here.
3) The indefinite form for the definite one, as it cannot be misunderstood.

the rice from this penne-seed." The Ants said: „Sit down. (and) wait us." Presently they had taken out the rice from all the penne-seed; the clean rice in one basket, (and) the penne-seed into another basket. Tamba took these two baskets, and went and put them before the king,¹) and said: „I have done." The minister said: „Tamba is a bad man, let them cut his throat." They took him, and beat him, and chained him. The king told his four wives, and said: „Depart ye, and go and scoop water for me, I want to bathe." They went, and another girl, making five. When they went, the Cerastes knocked (stung) all of them, except the girl he did not knock (sting) her. The girl ran, and came and told the king (saying): „The Cerastes has knocked (stung) all the young women at the brook." They left, and went to fetch them, and brought (them). No one knew the medicine to cure them; they had all fainted, and lay down. The king said: „Let them call Tamba, he is clever."²) They called Tamba; he came, (and) the king said to him: „Tamba, look at my wives, they are dying; the Cerastes knocked (stung) them; doest thou know the medicine for it?" Tamba said: „I know." The king said again: „Make me the medicine." Tamba said: „Let them go and look for the brains of a deceitful person; with them I must make it: (and) directly they will get up again." The king said: „I agree (to it)." He took an iron bar, and knocked a minister on the head with it; the brains came out, they took them, and gave (them) to Tamba; he took them, and mixed them with the medicine. He gave it to one woman, (and) she got up. The king said: „Go on for me, my friend!" Tamba said again: „Get me the brains of a deceitful person, these are finished." The king made them knock again another minister on his head; the brains came out, they gave them to Tamba; he took (them), and put (them) into the medicine for another woman; (and) she got up also. The king said again: „My friend, heal me now quickly my two wives,

---

1) Lit. „placed them before etc."
2) Lit. „he knows something."

aná tšía." Támba o pā so: „Tr' 'a kára ma-fit ma w'úni yáñfa." O kal sut o-sántki o-lom, 'a wúra ma-fit-m'oñ, 'a soñ Támba; kon' o yóka-ña, o botr ka an-trol, o soñ am-béra ña-rañ, aná tšía; ña yeñk téte ma-der, ña yókane. Kére añ-sántki a-lom ña o-baī, aná tšía, ña gbúke, ña kóne. Ma añ-sántki, aná tšía, ña gbúke, ña poñ kóne; o-baī o wúra y'etr e-lópra, o soñ Támba; o soñ-ko so o-bórko, owó o der tápañ tra re ten-e. O-baī o wúra so ka-léñken ka-lom ka ka-petr-k'oñ, o soñ-ki ka Támba. O wúra so tra-petr tra a-trar tra-rañ, de an-trar be, o soñ-tši Támba; kon' o sáke so o-yóla o-bána. Ko o-baī o bak; mo o poñ bak yañ-e, o soñ Támba an-tof-ñ'oñ, o pā ho: „Be I fi-e, Támba, kóno na ma pólo o-baī." Mo o-baī o re fi-e, ña wúra 'ra-baī, ña soñ Támba; kon' o kal so sóto a-fósa, de a-kála, o tas o-baī tápañ.

who are left."[1] Tamba said again: „Let them bring the brains of a deceitful person." He knocked again another minister, they took out his brains, they gave (them) to Tamba; (and) he took them, and put them into the medicine, and gave (it) to the two women, who were left;[1] they got well directly, and got up. But the other ministers of the king, who were left,[1] fled, and went away. When the ministers, who were left,[1] had fled, and gone away; the king took out[2] clothing, and gave (it) to Tamba; he gave him also the damsel, for whom he came formerly to obtain her. The king also took out[2] some neigbouring yard in his town, and gave it to Tamba. He also took out[2] two slave-towns, with all the slaves, and gave them to Tamba; (and) he also became a great gentleman. And the king got old; when he had grown old thus, he gave Tamba his country, and said (to his people): „When I am dead, Tamba, him ye must make king." When the king came to die, they took the kingdom, and gave (it) to Tamba; (and) he also got again power, and property, more than the former king.[3]

---

1) Or: „who remained."
2) Or: „took," or „picked out."
3) Lit. „he surpassed the king before."

Chapter V.

Proverbs.

The following ones were met with by the author: —

1. As'ạni tra wop kọ, lit. „The state of having set the teeth on edge holds him," := „One's teeth are set on edge." Sense: „A burned child dreads the fire." Or somewhat like: „Bought wit is best." Or: „One learned wit." Or like the Germ. proverb: „Durch Schaden wird man klug." Thus if for instance one goes to a place, of which he was told before that some evil will befall him there; but still goes, and the evil, which he before scorned at, comes upon him, on his return he may say: as'ạni tra wop-mi; and if asked to go to such a place again, he will refuse to do so by saying: I kọ he ri, as'ạni tra wop-mi, „I do not go there, I learned wit."

2. Mer, pạ rónkạt, pạ wósi; lit. „Swallow, it is bitter, it is dry." Sense: Take a thing patiently, however trying it may be." Or like the Germ. proverb: „Was ich nicht ändern kann, nehm' ich geduldig an."

> Note. The pronominal form pạ, as used with the verb wósi, which is the long form of wos, „get dry, be dry," and which, therefore, according to analogy ought to be ọ; can only be accounted for on the ground that it is used with a proverb; where greater liberty is allowed with regard to the form of words, than in other common language. Another reason for which this form seems to be used, is to make it agree with the form of the preceding pronoun. The short form of wosi could not have been used here, because it is a positive proposition; but wos has the sense of „get dry"; only in negative propositions it has also the sense of „be dry". See the Note after wos, v. n. in the Vocabulary.
>
> For the better understanding of this proverb it may be observed, that rónkạt has reference to the acerb taste, which unripe fruit has (as unripe limes), which makes it very unpleasant to swallow; and wósi refers to dry food (as dry rice), which will not go down the throat so easily, as when

moistened with palaver-sauce, as this is made lubricous by a vegetable called ocra by the Liberated Africans in Sierra-Leone, which forms one of its ingredients.

3. Séṅe Tšémpi o tas am-baī kạ-tšemp; lit. „Senge the Wise exceeded kings in wisdom." Sense: „Thou art wiser than I, I will not contend with thee."

Note. Senge is a fabulous person, said to have lived in the first world, and to have been greatly renowned on account of his wisdom. (Cf. the word tšémpi, adj. in the Vocab.).

4. Ak'ór kạ-fot ka tạ́na he aṅ-kạ́patr; lit. „The empty belly (stomach) is no match for the chest." Sense: „A man cannot work well without eating."

5. Télma Mọ́du[1] o bentr a-tšik kạ-tas; lit. „A loquacious person (a babbler) hinders strangers from going on;" i. e. „he must talk to them before they go on."

6. Fạr-fạr o yi he kótšine; lit. „Making far-far does not loose itself," or: „One making far-far does not loose himself," or: „does not make himself free." Or: „The fạr-fạr does not loose himself."

Note 1. This proverb is taken from the catching of a bird in a trap. It often happens that a bird is caught by one of its feet only; if so, it will struggle hard to get loose; but the more it struggles, the more it will be entangled. While thus struggling it makes a noise by the flapping of its wings resembling the sound of far-far, whence this word is taken; the sense of which is that a man will not free himself from a difficulty by much struggling.

Thus if one has a palaver at the court, and then wants to talk again and again without being called upon to do so, thinking that by so doing he will extricate himself from his difficulty; one of the old men at the court, or the king, may say to him: „Fạr-fạr o yi he kótšine."

Note 2. As to the form of this word, it is either an adjective, when w'úmi, „a person" is to be understood; or it might be a name for an individual of that class of persons, who behave in this way as stated above. If it is taken as

---

[1]) See the word Mọ́du in the Vocabulary, as also Télma.

an abstr. noun in o-, we must suppose the prefix to be dropped; but it may be observed here, that the term far-far was otherwise only met with as an adverb in connection with the verb yọ, „make," used in reference to a bird caught in a trap, which struggles to get loose. (Cf. the Note at the 8th. the proverb below.)

7. Mạ bar gbo tsímne, mạ trạ bar sap: lit. „The more thou strugglest, the more thou wilt be caught." The sense of this is much the same with the preceding one. The more a person struggles to extricate himself from a palaver at the Barc, or Court-house, by talking much and passionately; the more he will get entangled in it, by his incautions and unguarded expressions.

8. Trạ́ma kạdí ọ gbịp hẹ bom-añ; lit. „To stand ahead does not catch a woman;" or: „The being first does not etc.;" or: „One being first does not catch a woman;" or: „A being first does not catch a woman," that is the one who asks first for a woman to marry her, does not always get her. Sense: „He who hurries for a thing will miss it; but he who takes time, will get it." Or something like: „Nothing good is done in a hurry." Or like: „Hasten slowly fair and softly goes far in a day." Or like the Germ. proverb. „Eile mit Weile."

Note. As regards the form trạ́ma kạdí, the greater part of what has been stated about the form far-far in the 6th. proverb above, applies also to this: Trạ́ma kạdí is either to be taken as an abstr. noun with the prefix ọ-, which, in that case, we must suppose to be dropped here; or it is to be looked upon as a verbal adjective, when w'úni may be understood. The latter supposition seems to be the correct one. The form trạ́ma kạdí might possibly be an Infinitive absolute, in which case the pronoun ọ would be the irrelative or impersonal one. See the Preface § 20.

9. Añ-kil ọ bentr a-méra gbántane; or: Pä Kil ọ bentr a-mera[1]) gbántane;[2]) lit. „The ground-pig prevents a mind spreading itself," that is „hinders an agreement, or „a harmony of mind."

---

1) Or: „plan, design."
2) Or: „making itself known," or: „diffusing itself."

Sense: „He who works in secret (as the ground-pig does under the ground), prevents unity, being intent upon, by secret machinations, to sow the seed of disunity among those, who were likely to become of one mind about a thing or matter."

10. O trand o-póto: o rak-rak, kére o bákar; lit. „He is like a European; he is of a delicate constitution, yet he is strong." This may be spoken in reference to a person, who is of a delicate health, but nevertheless able to do a great deal; because they say that Europeans in Africa are in general of delicate health, but yet able to accomplish a great deal in war and also otherwise.

Part II.

Some Specimens

the Author's own Temne Compositions and Translations.

Chapter I.

Colloquial Phrases.

1. Salutations.

a) On first meeting a person in the forenoon, or about noon, the usual salutations are as follows:

A. Kóri-'u, Pà! (Yà! Wan!)

A. „I salute thee, Sir! (Madam! Child!)"

B. Ambá! Kóri-'u, Pà! (Yà! W'an!)

B. „Very well!¹) I salute thee, Sir! (Madam! Child!)"

A. Tro pe-e?
or:
Tro pa yi-e?
or:
Tro pe-mu-e?

A. „How is it?" or „What news?" or:
„How art thou?"
or:
„How art thou?"

B. Aṅ aṅ! Múno, tro pe-e?

B. „So so! Thou, how art thou?" or:
„Tolerably well! Thou, how etc.?"

or:
Tr'eī ó tr'eī! Múno, tro pe-e?
or:
Q báki gbo! Múno, tro pe-e?"

or:
„Nothing but trouble! Thou, how art thou?"
or:
„It is but hard! Thou, how art thou?" or:
„Only trouble! Thou, how art thou?"

or:
Tr'eī ó tr'eī tra yi he! Múno, tro pe-e?

or:
„Very well!²) Thou, how art thou?"

---

1) Or: „Thank you! I etc.!"
2) Lit. „There is nothing the matter!"

A. An díra-i? or: Mạ díra-i? „Hast thou slept well?"
B. Yáo, I díra. Múnọ, mạ „Yes, I did sleep well.
   díra-i? Thou, didst thou sleep well?"

b) If a person is not well he may say:

B. De. I díra he; ra-trū ra B. „No, I did not sleep; I am
   báki-mi ténọñ. very ill to day."
A. Ko báñsa-mu-e? A. „What hurts thee?" or:
  „What pains thee?"
B Ra-bomp-ra-mi ra bañ. or: B. „My head aches." or:
  Ra-bomp ra bañ-mi. or: „The head pains me." or:
  Ma-der-ma-mi ma bañ be. „My skin hurts me all over."
  or: or:
  I sọkọ wónane. „I had fever all night."
A. Mạ ba tra ten e-trọl. A. „Thou must look for medicine."

B. Yáo, I kọ ten-yi. B. „Yes, I go to look for it."
A. Re mañ kọ-e? A. „Where art thou going to?"
B. I kọ ro-k'ọr. or: B. „I go to the farm." or:
   I kọ ro-petr. „I go to town."

c) On parting they may say:

A. Mam piár'-ó, Pa! (Ya!) A. „Let us live (be) well all
  day, Sir! (Madam!)" or:
  „Good bye,Sir! (Madam!)"
B. Ambá! Mam piár'-ó, Pa! B. „Very well!¹) Let us live
   (Ya!) (be) well all day, Sir!
  (Madam!)" or: „Very well!
  Good bye, Sir! (Madam!)"

———

1) Or: „Thank you! Let us etc.!" or „Thank you! Good bye etc.!"

d) If it is toward evening, one does not say: Mam piár'-ó, etc.! but:

A. Man díra-ó, Pä! (Yä!)

A. „Let us sleep well, Sir! (Madam!)" or: „Good night, Sir! (Madam!)"

B. Ạmbá! Man díra-ó, Pä! (Yä!)

B. „Very well!¹) Good night, Sir! (Madam!)" or: „Very well!¹) Let us sleep well, Sir! (Madam!)"

e) If one has met a person already in the earlier part of the day, and happens to meet him again, he does not use the same salutation: Kóri-'u, etc.! but:

A. Páng-mu, Pä! (Yä!) or:
Páng-mu-ó, Pä! (Ya!)

A. „I have met thee, Sir! (Madam!)"

B. Ạmbá! Páng-mu, Pa! (Ya!)

B. „Very well! I have met thee, Sir! (Madam!)"

A. Am piár'-i? or:
Mạ piár'-i?

A. „Hast thou been well?" or: „Hast thou lived well?"

B. Yáo, I piár' o-tan!

B. „Yes, I have been pretty well!"

f) To one who just returned from a journey, or to a stranger just arrived, the salutation is:

A. Sẹn-ó, Pä! (Yä!) or:
Séng-ŏ, Pä! (Yä!)
or:
Sẹn-ó! Sẹn-ó, Pä! (Ya!) or:
Séng! Séng-ó, Pä! (Ya!)
Ọ-tem, sẹn-ó!

A. „Welcome, Sir! (Madam!)"
or:
„Welcome! Welcome, Sir! (Madam!)"
„Sire, welcome!"

B. Ạmbá! Kóri-'u, Pa! (Ya!)

B. „Very well!¹) I salute thee, Sir! (Madam!)"

A. Ko ma yéfa-i?

A. „Where doest thou come from?"

---

1) Or: „Thank you! etc.!"

B. I yéfa ro-Bâke-Lóko.   B. „I came from Port-Loko."
or: or:
I yéfa ro-Kamp.   „I came from Freetown."

    g) If one sneezes, they say:

A. Sen-e!   A. „God bless thee!" Germ.
                    „Zur Genesung!"
B. Ambá!   B. „Very well!" or: „Thank you!"

    h) If one visits a sick person, he addresses him thus:

Séke-ó! or: ⎫   „I am sorry!" or: ⎫
Séke ó!   ⎭   „I pity thee!"   ⎭
or: or:
Séke-ó! Séke! ⎫   „I am very sorry!" or: ⎫
Séke-ó! Séke! ⎭   „I pity thee very much!" ⎭
or: or:
Woī! Trank gbo,¹) Pa! (Ya!)   „Alas! Be but quiet, Sir! (Madam!)" or:
or:
Woī! Woī! Ma trū ra-trū, Pā! (Yā!) or: „Alas! Alas! Thou art ill indeed, Sir! (Madam!)" or:
Woī! Woī, Pa! (Ya!) Ma trū ra-trū!²)   „Alas! Alas, Sir! (Madam!) Thou art ill indeed!"

    i) If they want to show their sympathy with one, or to condole with one on the death of a near relative, they say:

Trank gbo,¹) Pa! (Ya!)   „Be but quiet, Sir! (Madam!)
or: or:
Trank gbo!¹) Trank gbo, Pa! (Yā!) or: „Be but quiet! Be but quiet, Sir! (Madam!)" or.
Woī! Woī! Trank gbo, Pa! (Yā!)   „Alas! Alas! Be but quiet, Sir! (Madam!)"

---

    1) Lit. „Be but silent, Sir! (Madam!)"
    2) Or: Ma trū tra-tšen! „Thou art ill truly!" or: „in truth!"

j) If one goes on a journey, he may have to tell compliments from others; as one would say to one going to Port-Loko:

Námina Módu ó, (l) kóri-ko; Áli Bóndo ó, (l) kóri-ko.	„Tell Namina Modu and Ali Bondo how do you do for me." [1]) Lit. „As to Namina Modu, salute him; as to Ali Bondo, salute him."

k) One coming from Port-Loko might say to one:

A. Námina Módu o kóri-mu.	A. „Namina Modu salutes thee."
B. Ambá! Ambá!	B. „Very well! Very well!" [2])

l) Or on meeting the messenger one would ask him:

A. Námina Módu o yi ri-i?	A. „Is Namina Modu there?"
B. O yi ri; o kóri-mu.	B. „He is there; he salutes thee."
A. Ambá!	A. „Very well!" Or: „Thank you!"

m) If an aged person, or one of superior rank is addressed, the salutation is:

A. O-tem, kóri-'u! or: Kóri-'u, o-tem! or: O-tem báki, kóri-'u! Kóri-'u, bom! [3]) or: Bom, kóri-'u! [4])	A. „Sir, I salute thee!" or: „Sire, I salute thee!" „I salute thee, Madam!" or: „Madam, I salute thee!"

n) If an aged person, or a superior, speaks to one, and the person addressed does not distinctly hear, what he said, he says:

Tro ma pā-e? or.	„How doest thou say?" or:
Ko r'áka-e? or:	„What is it?" or:

---

1) Or: „Salute N. M. and A. B."
2) Or: „Thank you! Thank you!"
3) Or: Kóri-'u, o-bom!
4) Or. O-bom, kóri-'u!

Pā? or Pā-i?	„Sir?"
Yā? or Yā-i? or Nā?	„Mam?" or „Madam?"

o) In sending one's compliments to a gentleman by his domestics, one may say to them:

Kóri Pā-ṅ! or: Kóri Pà-aṅ!	„Salute the Master!" or: „Remember me to thy Master!"
Kóri Yā-'ṅ! or: Kóri Yā-aṅ!	„Salute the Mistress!" or: „Remember me to thy Mistress!"

p) If the Plural is to be expressed, the forms are as follows:

Kó'i-nu, Pā-ña!	„I salute you, Sirs!"
Kó'i-nu, Yā-ña!	„I salute you, Madams!"
Kó'i-nu, a-fęt!	„I salute you, children!"
Mam piár' ṇan-ó, Pā-ña!	„Good bye, Sirs!"
Mam piár' naṅ-ó, Yā-ña!	„Good bye, Madams!"
Man díra naṅ-ó,¹) Pā-ña!	„Good night, Sirs!"
Man díra naṅ-ó, Yā-ña!	„Good night, Madams!"
Tro pe ṇaṅ-e?	„How are ye?" or „How do ye do?"
Páne-nu, Pā-ña!	„I have met you, Sirs!"
Páne-nu, Yā-ña!	„I have met you, Madams!"
Sęn naṅ-ó!	„Welcome ye!" or „Welcome to you!"
Sékę-naṅ-ó! or: Sékę naṅ-ó!	„I am sorry for you!" or: „I pity you!"
Sęn naṅ!	„God bless you!" Germ. „Zu eurer Genesung!"
Sęn naṅ-ó! Sęn naṅ-ó!	„Ye are very welcome!" Lit. „Welcome ye! Welcome ye!"

2. Of Worship.

A. Man der naṅ rámne K'úru-masába.	A. „Let us pray to God." or: „Let us worship God."

---

1) Lit. „Let us sleep ye, etc.!"

or:
Ma léṅ'sir naṅ K'úrumasäba

B. Maṅ kọ ro-míšidi.
A. Kar-mi, I tši káranẹ aṅ-réka-'a-mi.
B. Tšimonẹ toṅ lemp.
A. Múnọ, ma trára káraṅ-i?
B. I trára k'in k'in.
 or:
 Aṅkó, I trára ọ-tan.
A. Ma trára káraṅ tra-témnẹ-i?
B. Aṅ, I trára ọ-tan.
A. Ma trára ama-leṅ ma-témnẹ-i?
B. Aṅ, I trára-ṅa gbáraṅ.
A. Ma tral atra-rámnẹ rok'ór-i?

B. I tral k'in k'in; kérẹ I tral aka-rámnẹ ka ọ-Rábu gbáraṅ.

A. Aṅ-réka ṅa K'úru, ma bọtar-ṅi-i?
B. Aṅ, I bọtar-ṅi táṅka bẹ; aṅ-réka aṅé ṅa tas ẹ-réka ẹ-lọm bẹ.
A. O-póto ọ gbair-su ka-wándi ka-fíno ténọṅ.
B. Aṅ, ọ trọri-su ar'im ra K'úru tra-tšeṅ.

or.
„Let us praise God by singing."
B. „Let us go to Church."
A. „Wait me, I will bring my book with me."
B. „Make great haste then."
A. „Thou, canst thou read?"
B. „I know single (words)."[1]
 or:
 „Yes, I know a little."
A. „Canst thou read Temne?"[2]
B. „Yes, I can a little."
A. „Doest thou know the Temne hymns?"
B „Yes, I know them well."
A. „Doest thou understand the meaning[3] of the prayers?"
B. „I understand a word now and then;[4] but I understand the Lord's prayer perfectly."[5]
A. „As to the book of God, doest thou like it?"
B. „Yes, I like it very much; this book exceeds all other books."
A. „The white man gave us a good address to day."
B. „Yes, he shows us the word of God in truth."

---

1) Lit. „I know one one."
2) Lit. „Doest thou know to read Temne?"
3) Lit. „Doest thou understand the pr. in the inside (within)?"
4) Lit. „I understand one one, etc."
5) Or: kérẹ ka-rámnẹ ka ọ-Rábu, I tral-ki gbáraṅ; „but as to the Lord's prayer, I perfectly understand it."

A. Ténọñ kía ọ lápsọ gbaía-su ka-wándi; ọ kálanẹ sọ tọñ ka an-tọf, añá 'a kómạrkọ, trạka kal bákạsnẹ mader.

A. „To day he preached the last time to us; he returns now again to his native country,¹) to recruit his health again."

B. Káñkọ K'úru o mar-su tra wop ar'ím, ará ọ poñ trọri-su ẹ-lọ́kọ ẹ-laī; káma sạ tšē yi gbo a-trạl; kẹ́rẹ káma sạ yi sọ a-yọ̄ ña atrá sạ poñ trạl!

B. „May God help us to hold the word, which he has shown us many times; that we may not be hearers only; but that we may also be doers of what we have heard!"

3. Of the School.

A. Ke mañ kọ-ẹ, w'ahẹ́t?

A. „Where art thou going to, child?"

B. I kọ́nẹ ka ọ-káramọko tra tạ́kas kạ-káráñ a-réka.

B. „I go to the schoolmaster to learn to read a book."

A. Trọ́ri-mi añ-réka añá mạ tạ́kas-e.

A. „Show me the book which thou art learning."

B. Kạ́li-ñi; añ-réka añé añ-réka ña K'úru ñañ.

B. „See it; this book is God's book."²)

A. Trọ́ri-mi ọd'ẹ́r, ro ma káraň-e.

A. „Show me the place, where thou doest read."

B Kar-mi, I tši láfti a-bọ́pạr; kạ́li ọd'ẹ́r ọwọ́ I káraň.

B. „Wait me, I will turn over the leaf; see the place where I read."

A. Mạ tạ́kas kạ-gbal-i?

A. „Hast thou learned to write?"

B. De, I ta tạ́kạs hẹ ki ọ-fíno.

B. „No, I did not learn it well yet."

A. Pạ truī he, be mạ mẹ́marki o-fíno.

A. „It will not be hard, if thou doest try it well."

B. I láne-tši; kére I trạp gbo rạs.

B. „I believe it; but I only just began."

---

1 Lit. „to the country where they bare him."
2) Lit. „this book the book of God that."

A. Ma bā k'afri, de d'úba, de k'úpo-i?
B. Añ, I bā ey'étr eyé.
A. Ma tákas ka-leñ ma-leñ ma-témne-i?
B. Añ, I trára ka-leñ-ña.
A. Ma trára ka-lom-i?
B. De, I trap gbo ras tra tákas ka-lom.
A. Básar o-fino, káma ma trára-ki lemp.

A. "Hast thou paper, and ink, and a pen?"
B. "Yes, I have these things."
A. "Hast thou learned to sing Temne hymns?"
B. "Yes, I can sing them."
A. "Doest thou know arithmetic?"¹)
B. "No, I only just began with learning arithmetic."
A. "Continue (persevere) with well, that thou mayest learn it soon."

4. Of the House.

A. Kóri-'u, Pā!
B. Ambá! Kóri-'u! Ma yéma woñ-i?
A. Añ, I tši woñ.
B. De yíra, káli ka-wañ ka yi ri.
A. M'ámo, o-tem; I tši yíra anó ka am-mésa rayér.
B. Tšē yíra ro-rắre rayér, a-fef a-báki ña yi ri.
A. Tra bā he mi tr'eī, o-trañk o gbáli he mi wop.
B. Ma yéma fánta ro-ténta, ta-lóm ka añ-gbáta-i?

A. "I salute thee, Sir!"
B. "Thank you! I salute thee! Wilt thou come in?"
A. "Yes, I shall come in."
B. "Come sit down, look there is a chair."
A. "Thank you, Sir;²) I shall sit down here near the table."
B. "Do not sit near the door, there is a strong draught there."
A. "It is no matter to me, I shall not catch cold."
B. "Doest thou wish to lie down in the hammock, or on the mat?"

---

1 Lit. "Doest thou know counting?"
2) Or: "Much obliged to you, Sir; etc."

A. Dẹ, pa ta léla hẹ mi.
B. Káli a-bíliṅ, be ma yéma fánta o-taṅ.
A. Dẹ, I yéma gbo yíra roghántaṅ.
B. Be mạ yéma r'áka, tṣéla ọw'ahẹ́t.
A. M'ámo, Pā! I tši yọ-tši.

A. „No, I do not yet feel tired."
B. „Look a sofa,¹) if thou doest wish to lie down a little."
A. „No, I only wish to sit down in the piazza."
B. „If thou doest want any thing, call the child."
A „Thank you, Sir! I shall do it."

5. Of Eating and Drinking.

A. De yíra ro-mẹ́sa.
 or:
 Maṅ gbẹtgbẹ́tnẹ ka ka-di.
B. Ma rámnẹ K'úru tra rúba ey'ẹtr-'ẹ-su ẹ-di.
A. Káli r'ā ra-bọ́ti-di, a-nak-ó, a-sáka-ó.

B. I bọ́tar hẹ a-sạ́ka. yer mi o-šẹm o-toīs.
A. Mạ yéma o-šẹm o-nákat-i?
B. Dẹ, I tši di an-troko a-patr.³)
A. Mạ bọ́tar hẹ kạ-di ka-lop-·i?
B. Dẹ, I di hẹ kạ-lop.
A. Mína, d'or ra bā-mi, I tši di o-šẹm o-sálkạr, dẹ malel. or:

A. „Come sit down to the table."
 or:
 „Let us recline to the eating."
B. „Let us pray God to bless our food."
A. „See there is something delicious to eat, rice, and palaver sauce."
B. „I do not like palaver-sauce, give me roast beef."
A. „Doest thou want fried beef?"
B. „No, I shall eat of the stewed fowl."²)
A. „Doest thou not like to eat of the fish?"
B. „No, I do not eat fish."
A. „As for me, I am hungry,⁴) I shall eat salt meat and beans." or:

---

1) That is a sofa made of mud.
2 Or: „boiled fowl."
3) Or: ọwọ́ 'a patr, „which they stewed."
4) Lit. „hunger has me."

Mína, I tši di o-sem o-kal. de ka-lop ka-kul.

„As for me, I shall eat broiled beef, and smoked fish."[1)

B. Yéntra-mi am'ér, de tragbénbe.

B. „Hand me the salt and the pepper."

A. Am bótar e-yóka, de e-kū-i?[2)

A. „Doest thou like cassada, and Mandingo yams?"

B. Añ, I bótar-yi táùka be.

B. „Yes, I like them very much."

A. Káli a-tis a-lom; ma yéma ka-bep-i?

A. „See there is another knife; doest thou want a spoon?"

B. De, I yéma he ka-bep.

B. „No, I do not want a spoon."

A. Ma yéma mun ma-ber-i?

A. „Doest thou wish to drink liquor?"

B. De, I tši mun m'antr.

B. „No, I shall drink water."

Chapter II.

Addresses delivered to the Temnes.

1.

On John 14, 6.

„Yísua o pā ronón: Mine yi ar'óñ, de atra-tšeñ, de añ-ñésam: w'úni ó w'úni o tána he der ka o-kas, támbe ka ka trā-ka-mi." Yōn 14. 6.

I poñ der anó tra tróri-nu ar'óñ' da-fútia r'in, ará K'úru o káne-su ka ar'ím-r'oñ; pakášife K'úru o yéma káma a-fam be d'er ó d'er ña trára ar'óñ aré, ña tra ar'ím-r'oñ. Tša K'úru o botr w'úni ka 'ra-rū aré, káma o leñki-ko, káma o yíkis owó bémpa-ko. Tráka tši K'úrumasába mo o bémpa w'úni, o bémpako o-fíno de o-tot; tr'ei ó tr'ei tra-las tra yi he ronóñ. Kére w'úni o lásar an-toñ ña K'úrumasába, tšía ba-tši ña kánta ar'óñ' da ro-riánna, ka ra-fi ra woñ ka 'ra-rū be; pakášife a-fam be ña yi a-las, ña be ña poñ sáke a-gbéña ña K'úru ro-méra. Kére

---

1) Or: „dried fish."
2) Or: ma-nei-i? „country-yams?"

háli w'úni o lásar an-toṅ ṅa K'úru, K'úru o bótar-ko hálisa, o botar he ka-naṅ'-ko ka aṅ-fósa ṅa ra-fi, de ka aṅ-fósa ṅa Setáni; o bána-ko i-neï, ko o kánti r'on' da-lom ro-riánna. Ka an-toṅ ṅa Músa K'úru o pä ho: Be ma yō at'reí atšé ma tra káli. Kére ka-ráraṅ ka mo w'úni o poṅ lásarne, o bā he so a-fósa tra yo ma-treı ma K'úrumasäba, káma pa tésane-ko; am-méra ṅa w'úni ṅa yi a-las háli; w'úni ó w'úni o yi be owó gbáli wop an-toṅ ṅa K'úru o-fíno. Tráka tši w'úni ó w'úni o gbáli he kísi, o gbáli he ko ro-riánna tráka ra-bomp ra ma-yos-moṅ ma-fíno. Ma-yos-ma-su ma-fíno ma gbáli he kánti riäna tra trássu; K'úru o trára-tši o-fíno. O soṅ-su an-toṅ-ṅoṅ káma sa naṅk gláraṅ ra-yat-ra-su, de ma-las-ma-su; káma sa trára sa bā he a-fósa tra wop an-toṅ-ṅoṅ o-fíno, ma pa bóne-ko, de káma sa naṅk sa gbáli he woṅ ro-riánna tráka 'ma-yos-ma-su; tša a-fam be ṅa poṅ lásar an-toṅ ṅa K'úru e-lóko e-laï. Tšiaṅ o kánti r'on' da-lom tra trássu ka ka-sómpane de ka 'ra-fi ra Yísua ow'án-k'oṅ gbeṅ. Ar'óṅ aré ra yi ar'óṅ' da i-neï. Šya be sa yi a-fam a-las rodí ka K'úrumasäba, w'úni ó w'úni o yi he o-fíno de o-tratšéṅ rodí ka K'úru; kere šya be sa gbáli kísi ka ar'óṅ aré, ará K'úru o poṅ tróri-su ka ar'ím-r'oṅ tšía yi mo ho yē ka ka-láne Yísua. W'úni ó w'úni owó yéma der ka K'úru ka r'on' da-lom, tšía yi ho tráka ama-yos-moṅ ma-fíno gbeṅ, o tána he der roṅóṅ tabána, o tra dúne gbo. W'úni lom o yi he, o-nábi o-lom o yi he, owó tána mar-nu tra ko ro-riánna, támbe Yísua ow'án ka K'úrumasäba. Kóno yi atra-tšéṅ, kóno yéfa ka k'úru tra tróri-su ama-šélo ma K'úru o-kas-k'oṅ, de tráka fi tra trássu.

W'úni ó w'úni, o-nábi ó nábi, owó mo tšē tróri-nu atšé, atrá I poṅ tróri-nu, o tróri-nu ra-yem, ko o pä he tra tšéṅ. W'úni ó w'úni owó tšē láne ow'án ka K'úrumasäba, o béka K'úrumasäba ra-yem, pakášife o láne he at'amasére, atrá K'úru o poṅ soṅ-su tráka ow'án-k'oṅ. K'úru o káne-su ka ar'ím-r'oṅ fo o tra soṅ-su a-ṅésam a-tabána tráka ra-bomp ra Yísua ow'án-k'oṅ gbo sōn. W'úni ó w'úni owó láne ow'án ka K'úrumasäba, o tra sóto a-ṅésam a-tabána; kere w'úni ó w'úni owó tšē láne ow'án ka K'úrumasäba, o gbáli he soto a-ṅésam a-tabána. K'úru, o-kas, o sōm ow'án-k'oṅ, káma o báni ara-rū; pakášife o-maleíka ó maleíka o tấña he su mar, o-nábi ó nábi o tấna he su mar; w'úni ó w'úni o tấna he wop an-toñ ña K'úru o-fíno. Mahámadu kon' so o lásar an-toñ ña K'úru, ma a-fam a-lom ña poñ yō; Yísua kon' sōn o bā he tr'eī ó tr'eī tra-las. Añ-nábi be, añá K'úru o poñ sōm ka a-fam tápañ ña-ñáne so ña bā ka-kísi tráka ra-bomp ra Yísua, ña ba ka-sóto ka-lápar ka ma treī-ma-ñañ ma-las ka ma-tšir ma Yísua; pakášife w'úni ó w'úni o ba ma-treī ma-las rodí ka K'úru Mahámadu o bā ka-kísi tráka ra-bomp ra Yísua gbo sōn. Yísua koñ' sōn o bā he tr'eī ó tr'eī tra-las, pakášife o yi ow'án ka K'úrumasāba.

Mo K'úru kóno-kónone o poñ botr ar'óñ aré tra trássu, sa bā ka-láne fo ar'óñ aré ra béki-su, sa bā ka-wop ar'óñ' da-tši, ka sa gbáli trára tra-tšeñ, fo K'úru o péñša he w'úni ó w'úni, owó der roñóñ ka ar'óñ aré, pakášife K'úru o tána he yéma. W'úni ó w'úni owó láne fo Yísua o yi ow'án ka K'úru, K'úru o tra bótar-ko; kére w'úni ó w'úni owó péñša, fo Yísua o yi ow'án ka K'úrumasāba, owó péñša, fo Yísua o poñ de ka 'ra-rū tra báni-su, ow'úni owó o gbéña K'úru, ko K'úru o báñsar-ko, o tra sóm'ra-ko ro-yahánnama. Kére w'úni ó w'úni owó láne Yísua, o bā ka-wop so an-toñ-ñoñ, añá o poñ tróri-su ka ar'ím-r'oñ, kía yi ho ka am-beíbal; pakášife ak'áfa aké gbo son kía yi gbo ak'áfa ka K'úru.

Yísua o káne-su fo sa bā ka-bótar K'úru ka am-méra-'a su be, de ka añ-fósa-'a-su be; fo sa bā tra mémar, káma sa yérane atr'eī tra-fíno, atrá Yísua o sótona-su ka ra-fi-r'oñ. W'úni ó w'úni owó yéma K'úru tra ba-ko i-nei, o gbáli ñi sóto tráka ra-bomp ra Yísua gbo sōn. K'úru o tra málane aka-rấene-ka-nu ka añ'és ña Yísua gbo; be na rámne he K'úru ka añ'és ña Yísua, K'úru o šélo he tra trála-nu, na rámne gbo ka-tšiñ tral.

A-fam ña poñ wúra s'on' tra-laī tráka der ka K'úru. A-lom ña tens w'úni, talóm o-nábi tráka kása-ña ratróñ; a-lom so ña náne ña gbáli der ka K'úru tra 'ma-yos-ma-ñañ ma-fíno, de tra ka-wop-ka-ñañ a-sum. Kére ar'óñ' d'in ra yi ri gbo; Yísua kóno yi ar'óñ' da-tratšéñ, ará ma gbáli kére a-fam ro-riánna. Kóno-kónone o pa ho: W'úni ó w'úni o gbáli he der ka K'úru.

o-kas, támbe ka ka-trā ka-mi. Šya bẹ sạ bā tra náši ama-treī-ma-su ma-lạs ka ma-tšir ma Yísua; sạ bā tra lánẹ-kọ trạka kalápar ama-treī-ma-su ma-lạs bẹ. O-ráhu¹) ka Kúru ọ bā tra sạki ẹ-méra-'ẹ-su. W'úni lọm ọ yi hẹ ọwọ́ tạ́ua yọ́na-su amatreī amé támbe Yísua. Trạ́ka tši ń'ēs a-lọm ńa yi hẹ, a-fọ́sa a-lọm ńa yi hẹ, ańá gbạ́li fútia-su, támbe Yísua sōn. R'áka ó r'áka ra tạ́ua hẹ kérẹ-nu ro-riánna ka-rárạń ka ra-fi, támbe ama-tšir ma Yísua, amá ọ poń loń trạ́ka 'ma-treī-ma-su ma-lạs. Šya bẹ sạ bā ma-treī ma-lạs ma-laī; kérẹ K'úru ọ šélọ tra lápạrsu trạ́ka ra-bomp ra Yísua, bẹ sạ némtẹnẹ-kọ trạ́ka tši. Be sạ yéma hẹ K'úru tra lápạr-su trạ́ka ra-bomp ra Yísua, ọ gbạ́li hẹ tšera-su ama-treī-ma-su ma-lạs kókō, sạ gbạ́li hẹ wọń ro-riánna táńkań.

A-máne-'a-mi! I némtẹnẹ-nu, tšē nạ lánẹ ama-yọs-ma-nu trạ́ka ka-fútia-nu; tšē na lánẹ o-nábi trạ́ka ka-fútia-nu, ńa gbạ́li hẹ fútia-nu kī ó kī! Kérẹ lánẹ nań Yísua sōn trạ́ka ka-fútia-nu. I trạ́ra fo nạ ta lánẹ hẹ Yísua trạ́ka ka-fútia-nu; kerẹ trạp nạń tenọń tra yō-tši; tróńkạr nạń rońọń lemp, táni ań-lọ́kọ a-fíno²) ńa tas tra tránnu, táni na fi ka 'ma-treī-ma-nu ma-las, nạ dínnẹ tabána. Bẹ Yísua ọ náši ama-trei-ma-nu ma-lạs ka ma-tšir-m'ọń, na trạ bā ma-tọ́fal ka ẹ-méra-'ẹ-nu, pạ trạ foī-nu tr'eī, nạ trạ yi ma a-fam, ańá poń wur n'ímisa na-bána, nạ gbạ́li hẹ sọ nésa ra-fi. Háli nạ trára nań nạ trạ fi anínań, nạ gbạ́li hẹ nésa, pakášife nạ trára, nạ trạ bā ma-bọ́nẹ ma-bána³) ro-riánna karáraṅ ka ra-fi. Kérẹ be na lánẹ hẹ Yísua, be nạ lánẹ Mahámadu, bẹ na rámnẹ-ko, nạ gbạ́li hẹ fúti, nạ trạ nésa ra-fi; pakášife K'úru ọ poń trọ́ri-su fọ r'on' d'in día yi ri gbo trạ́ka a-fam bẹ. O-póto ó, w'úni bi ó, ọ-yóla ó, ọ-mọ́nẹ ó, ńa bẹ ńa bā kạ-fú!i trạ́ka Yísua ọw'án ka K'úrumasába sōn; kọ w'úni ó w'úni ọwọ́ tšē lánẹ Yísua gbo sōn trạ́ka fútia-kọ, ọ gbạ́li hẹ fúti tabána, ọ bā gbo tra kọ ro-yahánnama.

---

1) Or: Ań'úmpạl ńa K'úru ńa bā etc.
2) Or: a-foī-tr'eı, „convenient, seasonable."
3) Or: bā ma-trạ́ma ma-fíno, „be in a happy state" = „be well off."

Mẹ l yéfa nọ ka-lápsọ. I náne he fo l tši der so ka an-tof
añé, pakášifẹ ra-trū ra-báki ra wop-mi. Kérẹ pa tésane K'úru
tra kára-mi sọ anọ́. dẹ tra trọ́ri-nu so ar'ím ra K'úru! I ṣi anọ́
trạ-reṅ trạ-lai, l trọ́ri-nu ar'óṅ' da K'úru ẹ-lọ́ko ẹ-lai; kẹ́rẹ nạ
wop he ri, pạkášifẹ nạ bótrạr he ẹ-méra-'ẹ-nu ka 'ma-trei ma
K'úru nạ bótrạr ẹ-méra-'ẹ-nu tra ẹy'étr ya no-rū. Tšía ba-tši
pạ báṅ'sanẹ añ-fạm, aṅa poñ sōm-su anọ́ tra trọ́ri-nu ar'ím ra
K'úru, ka ña šélọ he káma ọ-pólo ọ ṣíra sọ re; kẹ́rẹ ña ṣéma
he nu noi ar'ím ra K'úru be, ña trạ trei ras w'úni k'in anọ́ tra
gbaīr-nu kạ-wạndi, be pạ ṣi họ nyaṅ tšémpi tra trạl ar'ím ra
K'úru, dẹ tra wop-ri sọ. Ke mínẹ sọ l tši der win win tra
gbaía-nu kạ-wándi. Kẹ́rẹ l tši ṣíra d'ẹr ó-lom tra kạ́li, he pạ
ṣi añ-fam, añá ṣi ri, ña šélọ tra málanẹ ar'ím ra K'úru, ará mẹ
kọ trọ́ri-ña; tša K'úru o ṣéma káma a-f m be d'ẹr ó d'ẹr ña
trạl ar'ím-r'oñ.

A-mánẹ-'a-mi! I némtẹnẹ-nu, be na bótar am'úmpal-ma-nu,
lánẹ nạñ Yísua, wópnẹ-ko nañ tráka fútia-nu! Káṅko K'úru o
mar-nu tra ṣō atr'ei atšé I kanẹ-nu lemp; táni na fi ka 'ma-trei-
ma-nu ma-las, nạ poñ fẹ tši ṣọ, táni na dínnẹ tabána. Ra-fi
ra ma der-añ tra trássu be, ko be nạ poñ he sọ́tọ ka-lápar ka
'ma-treī-ma-nu ma-lạs ka ka-tra ka Yísua, bañ ma na ṣi ano-rū,
nạ gbạ́li he fúti, na bā ka-dínnẹ tabána! Kẹ́rẹ be Yísua o poñ
tšéra-nu ama-treī-ma-nu ma-las, nạ gbáli he nésa ra-fi, na gbáli
he nésa ka-rọk an-tọ́ñka ka añ-rḗi a-lápsọ, na trạ fi mo ho na
kọ díra, ka nạ trára fo na tra wur so ka tra-bóma-tra-nu ka an-
rḗi a-lápsọ, nạ trạ kọ ro-riáma tra ṣíra ri ka ma-bọ́nẹ ma-bána,
amá gbạ́li he poñ táñkañ ó táñkañ.

2.

On 2 Cor. 5, 19. 20.

E-méra-'ẹ-su dẹ ar'ím ra K'úru ra trọ́ri-su fọ K'úrumasába
kọ́nọ mọ soñ-su ẹy'étr ẹ-fíno be. Ka ka-trạp K'úru o bémpana
w'úni ẹ-tọf, kọ kọ́no mọ soñ-ras w'úni ó w'úni a-ñésam. K'úru
o botr añ-lọ ña ka-kōm-ka-su, dẹ ọd'ẹr ro 'a kómạr-su; kọ́no
mọ soñ-su r'áka ó r'áka ará sạ bā. Kọ́no mọ bénẹ-su ra-tr'ei
ó tr'ei.

Ka-báni-ka-su ka 'ra-trar ra setáni ka yi ama-pant ma K'ŏru.
Kọ́nọ wúra as'ádka tra báni-su. Ọ sōm ọw'án-k'ọń, ọ reń-kọ
ama-treī-ma-su ma-las bẹ: kọ K'úru ọ málanẹ as'ádka, atrá Yísua
ọ kára tra trássu. Yísua ọ káne ẹ-tétu-y'ọń tra trámạs ar'ím
ra-tọt aré ka a-fạm bẹ. Ań lọ ńa-tśi K'úru ọ bémpa w'úni,
w'úni ọ yi ọ-mánẹ ka K'úrumasäba: kẹ́rẹ w'úni ọ lásạr an-tọń
ńa K'úru. Tśía bā-tśi K'úru ọ báń'sạr-kọ. kọ w'úni ọ nésa K'úru.
Ama-lás ma w'úni ma lásạr ama-máne ka-trọ́ń ka K'úru dẹ ka-
trọ́ń ka w'úni. E-méra-'e-su ẹ lā ma-gbéńa tráka K'úru, kọ
K'úru ọ báń'sạr-su tráka 'ma-treī-ma-su ma-lạs. A-fạm bẹ 'a
gbéńa K'úru ka ẹ-méra-'ẹ-ńań. ńa yọ̄ ma-treī ma-lạs ma-laī.
Kẹ́rẹ K'úru ọ wúra s'ádka. káma kọn' dẹ śyań sa mánẹ sọ.
Śya sa gbáli hẹ yọ̄ káma K'úru dẹ Śyań sa kal mánẹ; kẹ́rẹ
K'úru kọnọ gbáli yọ-tśi. Ọ bā-su i-neī. ọ sōm Yísua ọw'án-
k'ọń owọ́ yokanẹ ma-dẹr. ọwọ́ kása-su ratrọ́ń. dẹ ọwọ́ wop an-
tọn ńa K'úru ọ-fino tra trássu. ka ka-bélań-ka-su; pạkáśifẹ śya
sa lásạr-ńi lọ́kọ ó lọ́kọ. K'úru ọ sōm ọw'án-k'ọń káma ọ sọ́mpanẹ,
káma ọ fi; káma K'úru ọ gbáli su tśéra 'ma-treī-ma-su ma-lạs.
Yísua kọ́ń' ọ bā hẹ tr'eī ó treī tra-las, kọn' ọ sọ́mpane gbo ka
ka-bélán-ka-su. Yań K'úru ọ kála ma-mánẹ ka-trọ́ń ka a-fạm
dẹ ka-trọ́ń-k'ọń. Ọ yéma hẹ su sọ reń ama-treī-ma-su ma-lạs,
bẹ sa wópnẹ-kọ. bẹ sa wop ar'ím-r'ọń. K'úru ọ Śélọ tra lápạr
ama-treī -ma-su ma-las tráka ra-bomp ra Yísua, be sạ lánẹ Yísua,
be sa wópne ọw'án ka K'úru.

K'úru ọ yéma káma kọn' dẹ śyań sa kal máne; ọ tśéla a-
fam bẹ ka ka-sań ka ẹ-tétu-y'ọń. ọ némtẹnẹ-su ka ka-sań-ka-ńań
káma sa málanẹ ama-mánẹ-m'ọń. káma sa lánẹ Yísua. Yísua
kọ́nọ gbáli fútia-su kọn' sōn.

I pọń dẹr rọnú. K'úru ọ sōm-mi rọnú, káma I trọ́ri-nu ar'ím-
r'ọń. Na gbáli hẹ katr k'ẹ́rẹ, be na wop hẹ ri, pạkáśifẹ nạ
trára-ri; na gbáli hẹ káne K'úru ka an-réï a-lápsọ: „I tr'a hẹ
nań ar'ím-ra-mu-ẹ." K'úru ọ tra tọ́ńkas-nu ka ar'ím, ará I trọ́ri-
nu lọ́kọ ó lọ́kọ: I trọ́ri-nu atrá na bā ka-yọ̄, káma na kísi; be
na kísi hẹ. nyań nya bā-tśi. Śya bẹ sa yi a-fạm a-lạs rodí ka
K'úrumasába; w'úni ó w'úni ka-trọ́ń-ka-nu ọ pọń lásạr an-tọń

ña K'úru e-lóko e-laī: w'úni ó w'úni ka-tróń-ka-nu o yō ma-treī ma-las ma-laī.

A-máne-'a-mi! Bótrár nań am-inéra, na bā ra-beī ra-bána ka K'úru, na gbáli he ram-ko-e r'áka ó r'áka! Kére Yisua kóno wop ara-beī-ra-nu, kóno gbáli ram-ri, be na láne-ko. K'úru o šélo tra lápar ama-treī-ma-nu ma-las tráka ra-bomp ra Yisua. I der ronú ka ań'és ña Yisua de ka ka-bélań-k'oń. I némtene nu káma na málane ama-máne-m'oń. Be na láne Yisua, be na málane ka-fúti-k'oń mo ho a-bóya, be na yéma fúti ka 'ma-tšir ma Yisua gbo, amá o loń tra trannu be: K'úru o šélo tra lápar-nu. K'úru o gbáli he málane w'úni ó w'úni, támbe owó mo der rońóń ka ań'és ña Yisua ow'án k'oń. K'úru o pā ho: „Kóne nań ka 'ra-rū be, trámas nań ar'ím ra-to' ka a-fám be. W'úni ó w'úni owó láne, 'a mátas-ko,[1] o tra fúti: kére w'úni ó w'úni owó tšē láne, o tra dínne." Be na básar ka-tšē-wop ar'ím ra K'úru, na láne be Yisua: K'úru o tra sómpa-nu ka-sómpa ka-bána: be na málane he ka-sōm-ka-mi, na fárki ka-sōm ka K'úrumasāba, ko K'úru o tra sōm-nu ro-yahánnama tra sómpane ri tabána táńkań. Na bā tra wop ar'ím ra K'úru ano-rū: pakášife be na poń fi, na gbáli he wop-ri so. K'úru o soń-su a-lóko ano-rū gbo tráka bénene tra riánna.

Be o-baī o-lom o yéma mar w'úni móne; kére ow'úni ka-tši o péńsa, o málane fe ar'ím ra o-baī, o fárki ama-tot ma o-baī: o-baī ka-tši mo bań'sar he ko-i? Kére K'úrumasaba o yéma soń-nu ará tas r'áka ó r'áka ará o-baī o gbáli soń-nu. W'úni ó w'úni o gbáli he lápar ama-treī-ma-nu ma-las: kére K'úru o šélo tra lápar-nu, be na láne Yisua; kére o gbáli he läpar-nu támbe na láne Yisua ow'án ka K'úrumasāba.

Pakašife K'úru o pā: „Kóne nań ka 'ra-rū be, trámas nań ar'ím ra-tot ka a-fam be;" I poń der ronú, I poń treī o-kas-ka-mi, de ań-máne-'a-mi, de an-tof añá 'a kómar-mi, I poń der ka an-tof-'a-nu, ro tra-trū-tra-laī tra wop-mi, ro a-póto a-gbáti ña fi ka der-ka-ñań gbo ka an-tof añe: kére tr'eī ó tr'eī tra gbali

---

1 Or: pátar-ko m'antr . „baptize him (with water by sprinkling;" mátas is: „baptize by immersion."

he mi bentr; pąkášife I yéma tróri-nu ar'ón' da K'úru, káma ną trára-ri, káma na wop-ri, káma na sóto ma-bóne ma-bána ro-riánna.

Be ną wop ar'ím ra K'úru, ará I tróri-nu, pą bóne-mi báli, I tši mútši K'úru m'ámo trąka tši. Kére be ną wop he ar'ím ra K'úrumasäba, ará I tróri-nu lóko ó lóko, nyań nya bā-tši, uyań nya bā ka-wósa-tši, K'úru o trą sómpa-nu trąka tši.

R'on' d'in ra yi ri gbo trąka fúti; r'on' d'in ra yi gbo, ará ko ro-riánna; a-fąm be na bā tra kot ka ar'óń aré, am-póto de ań-fam a-bi. K'úru o tróri-su ar'óń aré ka ar'ím-r'ońl, ará l trámąs-nu. K'úru o sońl fe w'úni tr'áfa trą-rań, kére k'áfa k'in gbo; ka a-fam be 'a bā tra wop ak'áfa aké; w'úni ó w'úni owó mo tšē wop ak'áfa aké, o gbáli he ko ro-riánna, o trá dínne gbo, K'úru o tra sōm-ko ro-yahánnama tra sómpane ri tańkan tabána. A-laī ka-trón-ka-nu ńa ma pa ho: „Ań-réka, ańá są bā, ńa yi ho alukrána, ńa yi a-tíno tra trássu, ńa béki ań-fam a-bi; ka ak'áfa ką-póto kía yi ką-fino tra am-póto, ka béki am-póto." Pą yi he yań. Ań-réka-'a-nu ńa yi ho alukrána, de ań-réka a-póto e-yi fe win; kére e péskiane. Alukrána ńa tróri-nu ar'ím ra w'úni gbo; kére ań-réka ańá I kára-nu, ńa tróri-nu ar'ím ra K'úru tra-tšeń. K'úru o gbáli he sońl a-fąm e-réka ye-rań e-péskiane, ar'ím ra K'úru ra yi trą-tšeń tańkań tabána. W'úni ó w'úni owó kárań ań-réka a-póto de ań-réka ńa Mahámadu a-méra fino, o gbáli trára fo ań-réka a-póto ńa tási alukrána; ań-réka a-póto ńa yi gbo ar'ím ra K'úru.

A-máne-'a-mi! Bótrar nań am-méra! Yísua kóno mo tóńkas-nu ka ań-réï a-lápso, be na wop ar'ím-r'ońl ó, be ną wop he ri ó, o tra tóńkas-nu! Háli ną wop he ar'ím-r'ońl ano-rū, ną bā tra trąma rodí ka Yísua, káma o tóńkas w'úni ó w'úni ka-trón-ka-nu. Ak'áfa-ka-nu ka tróri he nu atr'eï atšé; kére ak'áfa ka K'úru ka káne-su-tši, ka káne-su fo Yísua ow'áń ka K'úrumasäba o trą tóńkas-nu ka[1]) ań-réka-ńońl, ńa yi ho ka[1]) am-beibǫl; pą yi he ka ań-réka-'a-nu, ńa yi ka[1]) alukrána. Alukrána ńa káne he nu fo Yísua o yi ow'áń ka K'úrumasäba. Mahámadu o pā fo kon'

---

1) Or: mo etc.

bána o tas Yísua; kẹ́rẹ o kólonẹ gbo ka-tšiṅ, o yéma gbo; K'úru
o sōm hẹ ko kókō. N'ēs a-lom ňa yi hẹ ri, aňá gbáli fútia-su,
támbe aṅ'és ňa Yísua; ko w'úni ó w'úni owọ́ mo pẹ́nša-ko, o
trạ̄ dínnẹ gbo.

Mahámadu o líṅkạr a-fạm trạ́ka wop ar'ím-r'oṅ, o dif-ňa bẹ,
aňá tšē šélo tra wop-ri. Kẹ́rẹ K'úru o gbẹ́ňa atr'ei atšé, o yéma
hẹ sạ líṅkạr a-fạm tra wop ar'ím-r'oṅ; o kánẹ-su gbo: Be nạ̄
wop ar'ím-ra-mi, be nạ̄ lánẹ Yísua, nạ̄ trạ sọ́to ma-bọ́nẹ ma-
bána ro-riánna; kẹ́rẹ be nạ̄ wop hẹ ar'ím-ra-mi, be nạ̄ lánẹ hẹ
Yísua; nạ̄ trạ dínnẹ gbo, nạ̄ tra sọ́mpanẹ ka an'ántr táṅkaṅ
tabána. Yo o pá, kẹ́rẹ o líṅkạr hẹ w'úni ó w'úni, mo Mahámadu o poṅ yọ́ tạ́paṅ.

Káṅko K'úru o mar-nu, káma nạ̄ tšē gbo tral ar'ím-r'oṅ ka-
tšiṅ, ará I tróri-nu; kẹ́rẹ káma na yō-ri so; káma na woṅ ro-
riánna, dẹ káma na sọ́to ri ma-tráma ma-fíno táṅkaṅ ó táṅkaṅ.

3.

On Jude v. 14. 15.

Fo a lọ́ko ňa trạ der mo K'úru o tra tọ́ṅkas a-fạm bẹ mo
ama-yos-ma-ňaṅ, K'úru o poṅ gbal-tši ka am-méra ňa a-fạm bẹ,
Sạ nạṅk a-fạm a-laí aňá ma yo ma-trei ma-las ma-laí, talóm ma-
trei ma-fíno, ňa sọ́to hẹ a-ram trạ́ka tši ano-rū; kẹ́rẹ ňa tra
sọ́to-ňi ka 'ra-rū ará ma der-e. O-nábi Énok, owọ́ káli pa won
hẹ ka-ráraṅ ka 'ra-fi ra Ádam, dẹ aṅ-fạm aňá yi ka 'ma-réï
ma-tši, ňa trára, fo K'úru o tra rok e-tọ́ṅka ya a-fạm ka aṅ-réï
a-lạ́p'so. Énok kọ́no trámas-tši, o pa ho: „Káli, o Rábu o mo
der-e rẹ e-wul e-laí ya am-maleika-ňoṅ tra rok e-tọ́ṅka ya a-
fạm a-las bẹ trạ́ka 'ma-treï-ma-ňaṅ ma-las, amá ňa yō:" ko o
maṅ aṅ-fạm, aňá yi ka 'ma-réï ma-tši, káma ňa túbi. Énok o
kánẹ-su fo Yísua o tra der so ka aṅ-réï a-lạ́p'so. O tróri-su
fo Yísua o tra tšéla a-fạm bẹ tráka tráma roňóṅ rodí, fo o tra
ram a-fạm a-las bẹ mo am'ólo ma ama-yos-ma-ňaṅ. E-tétu ya
Yísua bẹ ňa pa r'im r'in, ňa kánẹ-su fo šya hẹ sa ba tra tráma
ka Yísua rodí, káma o róka-su e-tọ́ṅka. Na kánẹ-su fo Yísua
kọ́no mo rok an-tọ́ṅka ňa aṅ-káli dẹ aṅ-fi. K'úru o yentr ka-

rok aṅ-tǫ́ṅka ka aṅ-réï a-láp'so ka Yísua; pą́kášifę ǫ yi ǫw'án ka w'úni. Kǫ́nǫ fi trą́ka a-fąm bę, ko ǫ trą der sǫ mǫ ǫw'án ka w'úni ka ę-bunt ya k'úru. Énok ǫ ká̀nę-su fǫ ǫ trą der rę am-maleika-ṅǫṅ, aṅá ma paía-kǫ ka ę-bunt ya k'úru. E-wul ę-lai ṅa trą tor ka k'úru dę kǫn' tra búndąs aṅ-yíki ṅa aṅ-réï ṅa-tši, dę tra yíkis-kǫ ǫwǫ́ trą́pi-ṅa. Ka-der ka Yísua aṅ-lǫ ṅa-tši ka trą tas ka-der-k'ǫṅ ką-trǫ́trǫkǫ, mǫ ǫ der tra są́kę ma-der, dę tra sǫ́mpanę tra trássu.

Są bä tra bótrąr am-méra, káma są bénęnę trą́ka aṅ-réï ṅa-tši, káma są bap-ko ǫ fíno. Yísua ǫ trą der tra tǫ́ṅkas a-fąm bę, pą yi hę tra trǫ́ri aṅ-yíki-ṅoṅ gben; kę́rę tra rǫk an-tǫ́ṅka ṅa a-fąm ka an-tof bę. Aṅ-fąm bę aṅá poṅ ką́li ka 'ra-rū aré, dę w'úni ó w'úni owǫ́ 'a tšē ta kōm ka 'ra-rū aré. Yísua o tra tšéla-ṅa roṅǫ́ṅ rodí. Am-báki dę aṅ-fęl, aṅ-yóla dę am-mǫ́nę, ṅa bę ṅa tra wur ka tra-bóma-tra-ṅaṅ, dę aṅá yi a-ką́li aṅ-lǫ ṅa-tši ka an-tof, ṅa bę ṅa bā tra trą́ma ka Yísua rodí. O trą gbéṅgbeṅ w'úni ó w'úni, ǫ trą tunt ama-yǫs-m'ǫṅ, ǫ trą ṅaíbi ę-nánę ę-máṅknę ya am-méra-ṅ'ǫṅ bę. Aṅ-lǫ́kǫ ṅa-tši aṅá Yísua ǫ mǫ fétąr am-méra,¹) ṅa trą kǫ ro-riáuna; kę́rę aṅá Yísua ǫ mǫ ṅap,²) ṅa trą bal-ṅa, káma ṅa yéfa ro-d'er-k'ǫṅ kądí. Yísua ǫ trą ṅátra aṅ-fam-ṅoṅ ro-riáuna; kę́rę aṅá tšē lánę-kǫ, ǫ trą fíta-ṅa ka an'ántr na-tabána. Yísua ǫ trą tǫ́ṅkas a-fąm trą-tšeṅ. Be są fófąr a-fąm trą́ka 'ma-treī-ma-ṅaṅ ma-lą̄s ṅa kátrnę tr'érę. Kę́rę Yísua kǫ́nǫ-kǫ́nǫnę ǫ trą wópa-ṅa t'amasérę, o trą trǫ́ri-ṅa ara-yai ra atr'érę-tra-ṅaṅ. ǫ tra ṅaíbi ama-yǫs ma-lǫs, amá ṅa yō-ę, as'ím tra-las atrá ṅa fǫf-ę, dę ę-nánę ę-las ęyę́ yi ka ę-méra-'e-ṅaṅ ka t'amasérę tra tra-tšeṅ. hā ṅa gbą́li hę pénša. E-tétu ya Yísua sǫ, aṅá trámar-ṅa ar'ím ra K'úru, ṅa trą wúra t'amasérę traka traṅṅáṅ. Yísua ǫwǫ́ mǫ tǫ́ṅkas-su, ǫ trára od'ér ro a-fam ṅa yo ama-trei-ma-ṅaṅ ma-ląs ma-máṅknę bę, kǫ ǫ trą líṅkar-ṅa tra wósa atra-tšeṅ tra ka-rǫk-k'ǫṅ an-tǫ́ṅka, aká sōm-ṅa ka an'ántr na-tabána.

Ka aṅ-réï ṅa ka-rǫk ę-tǫ́ṅka ya a-fąm Yísua ǫ trą botr ama-

---

1) Or: ǫ mǫ sǫṅ ma-mári, ṅa etc.
2) Or: ǫ mǫ sǫṅ ma-téri, ṅa etc.

trạma ma-tabána ma w'úni ó w'úni. A-tan ńa yi ri gbo, aṅá ma náne atr'eï atšē. A-fạm a-laī ńa kạ́li mọ họ ńa bā tra kạ́li tabána ano-rū. Be w'úni ọ fi ra-fi ra-šimtar, ńa náne họ atšē tra gbạ́li he yọ́ne roṅáṅ. Nạ mar tra béneṇe trạ́ka 'ra-fi lọ́kọ ó lọ́ko; káma be ara-fi ra der, nạ tšē ri nésa, káma ra tšē der rọnú, ma nạ tšē ri náne. Kére be nạ wópne he Yísua, be nạ yéma he fúti ka 'ma-tšir-m'ọṅ gbo, nạ poṅ he béneṇe trạka ra-fi; pakášife K'úru ọ ta poṅ he lápar ama-treï-ma-nu ma-lạs; kọ be K'úru ọ poṅ fe tšéra-nu ama-treï-ma-nu ma-lạs, ra-fi ra trạ yentr-nu ka aṅ'ántr na-tabána ro-yahánnama. Ya sạ bā tra kạ́li, de tra bótrne lọ́kọ ó lọ́kọ, mọ họ sạ kar ka-der ka Yísua a-réï ó a-réï, káma sạ gbạ́li bā ma-bọ́ne ka ka-der-k'ọṅ. Ya sạ bā tra kạ́li a-réï ó a-réï, mọ họ ma sạ ma yéma tra poṅ kạ́li, ma ra-fi ra fátrar.

A-máne-'a-mi! Pa mar-nu tra trap kạ-béneṇe trạ́ka aṅ-réï ńa-tši lẹmp. Tra-reṅ e-wul tramát tra poṅ tas, mo Énok o fof as'ím tra-tši trạ́ka ka-der ka Yísua, ke e-tétu ya Yísua be ńa pā r'im r'in; ńa káne-su fọ Yísua, ọwọ́ yi tra tóṅkas-su, o fátrar lẹmp. O tra der tšentšene, be aṅ-lọ́ko, aṅá K'úru o poṅ botr, ńa bek. Kére Yísua ọ fatr w'úni ó w'úni, pakášife ma 'ra-fi ra bap-su, yaṅ ka-rọk an-tọ́ṅka ka ma bap-su so. Be nạ kạ́li ka-túbi-ka-nu, a-pạṅk ńaṅ; pakášife nạ tr'a he a-lọ́kọ réke ra-fi ra ma der tra tránnu; be pạ yi ka ka-reṅ kạ-lọm, talọ́m ka aṅ-réï a-lọm, talọ́m ka aṅ-gbéleṅ a-lọm, nạ tr'a he tši. Trạ́ka tši béneṇe naṅ trạ́ka ra-fi, fạ́le naṅ ka ar'óṅ'-da-nu ra-lạs; kọ́ne naṅ ka Yísua ka e-méra-'e-nu be, káma nạ gbạ́li bā ma-bọ́ne rọṅọ́ṅ rodí, be ọ der-e. Rámne naṅ K'úru, káma o sạ́ki e-méra-'e-nu, de káma nạ sạ́ke a-wut ńa K'úru.

Šya be sạ poṅ lạ́sar an-tọṅ ńa K'úru ka e-náne-'e-su, ka as'ím-tra-su, de ka 'ma-yos-ma-su. Káne gbạ́li lápar ama-trei-ma-su ma-las-ẹ? Káne gbạ́li náši ama-trei-ma-su ma-lạs ka aṅ-réka, aṅá K'úru ọ gbal trạ́ka tr'ei ó tr'ei sạ yō-e? Am'ántrar-ma-su ma gbạ́li he yō-tši, r'áka ó r'áka ra gbạ́li he yō-tši, támbe ama-tšir ma Yísua; kọ́no gbạ́li yak-su ka 'ma-trei-ma-su ma-las be, kọ́no gbạ́li lápar ama-yos-ma-su ma-lạs be; be kọn' ọ yak fe su, sạ tra fi ka 'ma-treï-ma-su ma-las, ka sa bä tra sǫmpane ara-ban' da K'úru ro-yahánnama táṅkaṅ ó táṅkaṅ.

Ten's naṅ a-ni ṅa ka-fúti, aká Yísua o poṅ waía-su ka 'matšir-m'oṅ; tšē na mémar tra botr ama-yos-ma-nu ma-fíno ka kabélaṅ ka 'ma-tšir ma Yísua, K'úru o gbáli he málane-ṅa. Kére aṅá ma láne Yísua, ṅa gbáli kar aṅ-réï ṅa ka-der ka Yísua re ma-bóne; pakášife kon', owó mo tóṅkas-ṅa, o waía-ṅa 'ma-tširm'oṅ gbeṅ; pa yi kon' owó ṅa láne, owó ṅa wópne, owó poṅ nášia ma-treï-ma-ṅaṅ ma-las ama-tšir-m'oṅ. Yísua kóno-kǫnone, owó mo tóṅkas-ṅa, o tra tráma-ṅa ráraṅ, o tra pa roṅáṅ: „Der naṅ. aṅá o-kas-ka-mi o poṅ rúba, sóto nan ak'e ka 'ra-baī, ará ṅa poṅ bénene tráka tránnu!" Aṅá láne Yísua ṅa tra tráma roṅóṅ rodí re ma-bóne; kére aṅá tšē láue-ko, aṅá tšē trála-ko, ṅa gbáli he tráma roṅóṅ rodí, o-nímis o-bána o tra wop-ṅa, pakášife Yísua o tra sōm-ṅa ka an'ántr na-tabána.

W'úni owó tšē bénene tráka ra-fi, o bä tra nésa ra-fi, pakášife ra-fi ra tra yentr-ko ka ka-sǫmpane ka-bána ro-yahánnama. Kére w'úni owó poṅ bénene tráka ra-fi, kóno yi o-foi-tr'ei; pakášife be o fi, o tra fúti ka-sǫmpane ka 'ra-rū aré be táṅkaṅ tabána, ko o tra yíra ka K'úru rokóm táṅkaṅ ó táṅkaṅ.

Téte ma na bä a-ṅésam, trap naṅ ka-bénene tráka ra-fi; be na poṅ he bénene, be ra-fi ra bēk-e, na bä he so a-lóko tráka bénene ka-ráraṅ ka ra-fi; na gbáli he so yō ma-pant, na gbáli he so túbi ka-ráraṅ ka ra-fi. Sa sak e-santr ka 'ra-rū aré, kére ka ra-rū ará ma der-e sa tra rok eyé sa poṅ sak.

A-máne-'a-mi! Bótrar naṅ am-méra, káma na sak e-santr e-fíno tráka 'ra-rū ará ma der-e, káma na gbáli so rok a-yíki a-tabána ro-riánna rokóm, káma na gbáli bä ma-bóne, be Yísua o der so ka aṅ-réï a-láp'so tra tóṅkas a-fam be. Be na bótar am'úmpal-ma-nu, bénene naṅ tráka ra-fi; aṅ-ṅésam-'a-nu ano-rū ṅa yi a-búrap; kére aṅ-ṅésam aṅá sa bä ka 'ra-rū ará ma der-e, ṅa bä he o-tálane, ṅa tra won táṅkaṅ tabána; ko w'úni ó w'úni owó tšē poṅ láne Yísua, o tra ko ro-yahánnama tra sǫmpane ri tabána; kére w'úni ó w'úni, owó poṅ wópne Yísua tráka kafúti, o tra ko ro-riánna tra sóto ri ma-bóne ma-tabána. Be ra-fi

ra bap-nu, na poṅ he bénene. na tra tůbi tráka tši ka-ráraṅ
ka ra-fi; kére aṅ-lo ṅa-tši na tra tůbi gbo ka-tšiṅ.

Aṅ-fam aṅá poṅ bénene téte tráka ra-fi, a-fam a-tšémpi de
a-mári-tr'eï ṅaṅ; pakášife be ra-fi ra bēk, am-maleíka ṅa K'úru
ṅa tra kére am'ůmpal-ma-ṅaṅ ro riáuna tra yíra ri táṅkaṅ ó
táṅkaṅ; kére aṅ-fam aṅa tšē poṅ bénene, a-fam a-paṅk ṅaṅ;
pakášife be ṅa fi, setáni o tra kére am'ůmpal-ma-ṅaṅ ro-
yabánnama tra sómpane ri ka-sómpane ka-bána táṅkaṅ tabána.

K'aṅko K'úru káma na fi ar'óṅ' da-fíno, de káma šya be
sa gbánne-so ka ka-trā ka-dío ka K'úrumasāba rokóm ka aṅ-réï
a-láp'so tráka yíra roṅóṅ ro-riánna táṅkaṅ ó táṅkaṅ!

4.
On Luke 10, 10—16.

Yísua o pā ka aṅ-karándi-ṅoṅ, mo o sōm-ṅa tra gbaī ka-
wándi: „Be na woṅ ra ka-petr, ka ṅa málane he nu; wur ṅaṅ
ka as'óṅ tra ka-petr ka-tši, ka pā ṅaṅ: Háli ka-bof ka ka-petr-
ka-nu so, aká gbáp'sa-su, sa kóṅkoṅ-ki ronú; kére trára ṅaṅ
atsé fo ara-baī[1]) ra K'úru ra poṅ fátrar-nu. Ke I káne-nu, fo
atr'eí tra aṅ-fam ṅa ro-Sódom tra tra yi físa ka aṅ-réï ṅa ka-
rok an-tóṅka, pa tas atr'eí tra ka-petr ka-tši. Owó mo trála-
nu o trála-mi; ko owó trála-mi, o trála owó sōm-mi; ko owó
fárki-nu, o fárki owó sōm-mi.“

Kóta mo Yísua o yö ma-yos ma-kabáne ma-laī ka-tróṅ ka
aṅ-fam ṅa aṅ-Yéhudi, kóta mo o ták'sa-ṅa ka-tšemp ka-bána, de
a-fósa a-bána; aṅá láne-ko mo ho ow'áṅ ka K'úrumasāba, ṅa yi
gbo a-tan. Yísua o trára-tši o móta trap ka-ták'sa-ṅa. Tráka
tši o káne aṅ-karándi-ṅoṅ, fo a-fam ṅa tra yo-ṅa, ma ṅa yö-
ko; ko o káne-ṅa atrá ṅa ba ka-yo tráka ka-petr, aká tšē ṅa
málane; o káne-ṅa fo ṅa ba tra tróri aṅ-fam ṅa ka-petr ka-tši
fo ara-baṅ' da K'úru ra rénsa-ṅa; pakášife ṅa málane fe ar'ům
ra K'úru. Ko Yísua kóno-könone o tróri-su ka-sómpa, aká ma
der-e ka tra-petr be, atrá tšē wop ar'ím-r'oṅ. Yísua o káne-

---

1. Or: ka-gbáka ka K-, „the reign of etc.“

su w'úni ó w'úni owó tšē wop ar'ím-r'oṅ, o tra sómpane royahánnama tabána. Sódom ka yi ka-petr ka-bána tápaṅ; ko pakášife aṅ-fam ńa ro-Sódom ńa yō ma-treī ma-las ma-laī, K'úru o dim-ńa ka an'ántr, aná tor ka k'úru. K'úru o sōm fe ar'ím-r'oṅ ka aṅ-fam ńa ro-Sódom, o maṅ fe ńa tra fále ka ar'óń'-da-ńaṅ ra-las; kére pakášife ńa yō ma-treī ma-las ma-laī, o dim-ńa. Kére ronú K'úru o poṅ sōm ar'ím-r'oṅ ka ka-saṅ-ka-mi; 1 poṅ der ronú, ko K'úru o maṅ-nu ka ka-saṅ-ka-mi, káma na wop ar'ím-r'oṅ; o trori-nu atrá o poṅ yóna-nu, o trori-nu fo o poṅ sōm Yísua ow'án-k'oṅ tra fútia-nu ka ka sómpane-k'oṅ, de ka 'ra-fi-r'oṅ. Ak'áfa ka K'úru, kía yi ho am-beíbal ka káne-su fo: „Ya K'úru o bótar ara-rū, bā o sond ow'án-k'oṅ kōm ro-k'or sōn; káma w'úni ó w'úni owó láne-ko, o tšē dínne, kére káma o sóto a-ńésam a-tabána." Yísua o fi tra tránnu mo ho s'ádka tráka ra-bomp ra ama-treī-ma-nu ma-las. Ama-treī amé be aṅ-fam ńa ro-Sódom ńa tr'a he na tápaṅ; tráka tši be nyaṅ na wop fe ar'ím ra K'úru, ará o sōm ronú ka ka-trá-ka-mi, o tra sómpa-nu, pa tas aṅ-fam ńa ro-Sódom. Yísua o káne aṅ-karándi-ńoṅ tra kóṅkoṅ ka-bof ka tr'átrak-tra-ńaṅ ka aṅ-fam, aṅá tšē wop ka-sōm-k'oṅ; o káne-ńa tra trori-ńa, fo K'úru o báṅ'sar-ńa háli. Yísua, mo o ńatr ro-riánna, o káne aṅ-karándi-ń'oṅ, káma ńa ko ka 'ra-rū be, tra trámas ar'ím-r'oṅ ra-tot ka a-fam be, tra sáki a-fam be a-karándi-ń'oṅ. O káne-ńa, fo w'úni ó w'úni owó láne-ko, o tra fúti; kére w'úni ó w'úni owó tšē láne-ko mo ow'án ka K'úrumasába, de owó tšē wop-ko mo o-fútia ka a-fam, o tra dínne gbo. Be K'úru o sómpa aṅ-fam ńa ro-Sódom o-baṅ, pakášife ńa yō ma-treī ma-las, háli ma ńa tšē bā ar'ím-r'oṅ; o tra sómpa-nu pa tas-ńa, be na fárki ka-sōm ka Yísua, ow'án ka K'úrumasába, de be na káši tra wop-ki. Be o-bai o-lom o sōm a-tétu ka aṅ-fam-ń'oṅ tra kére r'im roṅáṅ, aṅ-fam ńa-tši ńa bā tra wop ar'ím ra an-tétu mo ar'ím ra o-baī; ko be ńa fárki ar'ím ra an-tétu, ńa fárki ar'ím ra o-bai, owó sōm-ko. Ye pa yi so, be a-fam ńa wop he ar'ím ará e-tétu ya Yísua ńa trámar-ńa ka aṅ'és ńa Yísua, ńa fárki Yísua kóno-kónone, owó sōm e-tétu tra trámas ar'ím-r'oṅ; ko owó fárki ar'ím ra Yísua, o fárki ar'ím ra K'úrumasába, pakášife kọ́nọ sọm Yísua ọw'án-k'oṅ tra fútia-su ka ka-sómpaṇe-k'oṅ, de ka 'ra-fi-r'oṅ. Be a-fam ña fárki an-tétu ña o-baī, o-baı ọwóṅ ọ tra sọ́mpa aṅ-fam ña-tši tráka tši. Ye pa yi sọ. K'úru ọ tra sọ́mpa w'úni ó w'úni, ọwọ́ tšē wop ar'ím ra Yísua, ọw'án-k'oṅ, ọwọ́ tšē kọ lane, de ọwọ́ fárki ar'ím-r'oṅ; ọ tra sọ́mpa-kọ, pa las aṅ-fam ña ro-Sódom, añá K'úru ọ dim ka an'ántr, aná tor ka k'úru. Háli ma a-fam a-laī ña tšē láne Yísua, ọ tra lásar ar'ím-r'oṅ. ará ọ pa: „W'úni ó w'úni ọwọ́ mọ láne, ọ tra kisi; kere w'úni ó w'úni ọwọ́ n.o tšē láne, ọ tra dínne." Ar'ím ra K'úru ra yi tra-tšeṅ, háli ma a-fam be ña tšē ri láne. Pa bē' he tra tral ar'ím ra Yísua gbo, tra náneri ra-fíno de ra-tratšéṅ, na bä tra yo-ri sọ. Be w'úni, ọwọ́ ba ra-trū, ọ sọ́tọ e-trọl, ọ bä tra di-yi, be ọ yéma sọ́tọ ka-yeṅk ma-der. Ye pa yi sọ, be sa yéma sọ́tọ ma-treı ma-fíno ka ar'ím ra K'úru, sa bä tra yo atrá ọ trórı-su ka ar'ím-r'oṅ. Be na gbáli na naṅk ama-yi ma aṅ-fam, añá yi ro-Sódom tápaṅ, be na gbáli na naṅk ka-kúlo-ka-ñaṅ, de ka-ñák-ñak-e-šek-ke-ñaṅ, na tra ñáṅka naṅ aṅ-fam ña-tši i-neı. Kére kóta ka-sọ́mpane-ka-ñaṅ ka yi ka-baṅ; ka-sómpane ka añá ma fárki, añá ma tšē wop ar'ím ra Yísua, ará l poṅ trámar-nu e-lóko e-laı tápaṅ, ka tra las o-bána. Be na wop ar'ím, ará l trámar-nu, na wop he ar'ím-ra-mi gbeṅ; kere na wop ar'ím ra K'úru, ọwọ́ sōm-mi rọnú; ka be na wop he ar'ím, ará l trórı-nu, na wop he ar'ím ra K'úru; ka trára naṅ, be na yō yaṅ-e, na tra ba k'áši ka-bána rodí ka K'úru. E-lóko e-laī l poṅ der rọnú tápaṅ, l poṅ der ka aṅ'és ña Yísua tra trámar-nu ar'ím ra-tot, tra maṅ-nu, káma na málane ka-fúti-k'oṅ. aká o poṅ's tra tránnu sọ, de káma na tórane rodí ka K'úru tráka 'ma-treı-ma-nu ma-las; káma Yísua ọ gbáli tšéra-nu-ña. Míne yi a-tétu ña Yísua, kọnọ sōm-mi rọnú tra tšéla-nu ka ka-béIaṅ-k'oṅ; káma na láne-kọ, káma na wop ar'ím-r'oṅ ka tra-tšeṅ. Be na trála fe mi. na trála he Yísua, ọwọ́ sōm-mi rọnú, na fárki ọwọ́ tana kísia-nu sōn; na fárki ọwọ́ mo re tóṅkas-nu ka aṅ-réï a-láp'sọ; na fárki ọwọ́ mo re gbak ama-treı-ma-nu ka-ráraṅ ka ra-fi. W'úni ó w'úni ọwọ́ tšē tral ar'ím ra Yísna, Yísua ọ tra trámar-kọ ka ka-tra-k'oṅ ka-méro ka aṅ-réï a-láp'sọ: ka añá ma tráma ka ka-méro-k'oṅ be, o tra sōm-ṅa ro-yahánnama, ka an'ántr na-tabána. Be a-fam ṅa fárki an-tétu ṅa o-baī, ṅa fárki o-baī; pakášife antétu o yi ka-saṅ ka o-baī. Ye pa yi so, be a-tétu ṅa Yísua o tramar-nu ar'ím ra K'úru, Yísua kóno kónone kóno fófar-nu ka ka-saṅ-k'oṅ. Tráka tši be a-tetu ṅa Yísua o tróri-nu ka-sōm ka Yísua, pa yi mo ho Yísua kóno-kónone o tor ka k'úru tra tróri-nu-ki. Tra yi tr'eï tra-bána tra-fíno tra tral ar'ím ra K'úrumasába. E-wul e-laī ya a-fam ṅa gbáli he tral-ri, pakášife etétu ya Yísua ṅa der he roṅáṅ. A-laï ṅa tra šélo naṅ tra wopri lemp de ma-bóne, be pa yi ṅa gbáli tral-ri gbo. Be aṅ-fam ṅa ro-Sódom 'a poṅ' naṅ tral tápaṅ, atrá nyaṅ na poṅ tral, ṅa tra pon' na túbi tšéntšene. Tráka tši atr'eï tra aṅ-fam ṅa ro-Sódom tra tra yi físa ka aṅ-ŕéï a-láp'so, pa tas atr'eï tra aṅá ma tral ar'ím ra K'úru; kére ṅa yō fe atrá ṅa poṅ tral. Nyaṅ na poṅ tral ar'ím ra K'úru; kére na yō fe atrá na poṅ tral. E-wul e-laï ya a-fam, aṅá yi ro-krífi, ṅa túbi báli; pakášife ṅa poṅ fárki ar'ím ra K'úru ano-rū; ke be pa gbáli na yi ṅa tra kal so ano-rū, ṅa tra wop naṅ ar'ím aŕé lemp de ma-bóne; kére ṅa gbáli he so kal.

A-máne-'a-mi! Bótrar naṅ am-méra ka 'ma-treï amé! Téte na ba a-lóko a-foī-tr'eī tra túbi, de tra ko ka Yísua tráka sóto ka-lápar ka 'ma-treī-ma-nu ma-las. Lánsa na bā he so a-lóko tráka tši ninaṅ. W'úmi ó w'úmi owó fárki an-toṅ ṅa Músa, ṅa dit-ko, ṅa bā he ko i-neī. Kére ka-sómpane ka aṅá ma fárki Yísua, ow'áṅ ka K'úrumasába, de aṅá ma fárki ama-tšir ma Yísua, amá o loṅ tráka traṅṅáṅ, amá gbáli fetar-ṅa sōn; — kasómpane ka aṅ-fam ṅa-tši ka tra tas o-bána. Pa yi he tr'eï tra-lol tra fárki ama-tšir ma Yísua, owó yíra téte ka ka-dío ka K'úrumasába rokóm, owó mo kal der tra tóṅkas a-fam be, de owó bā ara-gbáka téte ro-riáṅna de ka an-tof, bā o botr aṅa gbéṅa-ko be ka ma-nī-m'oṅ ráta.

A-fam a-mári-tr'eī ṅaṅ, aṅá ma tral ar'ím ra K'úru, de aṅá ma wop-ri so! A-fam a-mári-tr'eī ṅaṅ, aṅá ma sóna Yísua tra-wu ano-rū re ma-bóne; káma ṅa tšē bā tra sóna-ko tra-wu ka aṅ-ŕéï a-láp'so de o-nínis ro-yahánnama!

Ténoṅ kía I láp'so gbaïa-nu ka-wándi, pakášife I tši kálane

ka an-tọf a-póto, kẹ I tši lémne-nu ténoñ. Tra-reñ trofátr tra-
rạñ tra poñ tas, mẹ I mó'a der ka an-tọf 'a-nu tra trámar-nu
ar'ím ra K'úru, kẹ I poñ gbaïr-nu ka-wándi e-lókọ e-laï. Kẹ́rẹ
háli I poñ gbaía-nu kạ-wándi e-lókọ e-laï, w'úni k'in o yi hẹ
ka ka-trọñ-ka-nu, ọwọ́ wop as'ím-tra-mi trạ́ka tésạs am-méra-mi.
Nạ poñ trạl ar'ím ra K'úru e-lókọ e-laï; kẹ́rẹ nạ tral-ri gbo, na
poñ fẹ wop-ri. Nyañ na bä atr'eí atšē, nyañ na ba tra wósa
ka K'úrumasäba trạ́ka ka-tšē-wop ar'ím-r'ọñ, ko o tra sómpa-na
trạ́ka tši. Nạ gbạ́li hẹ kátr k'ẹ́rẹ, na gbáli hẹ pa ka K'úru ka
añ-rḗï a-láp'sọ fọ yē: „Sa tral hẹ nañ ar'ím-ra-nu, sa tr'a hẹ
nañ ama-šélọ-ma-nu;" pakášifẹ na poñ tral ar'ím-r'ọñ, na poñ
trára ama-šélọ-m'ọñ; e-tétu ya Yísua ña poñ trọ́ri-nu ar'ím-r'ọñ
de ama-šélọ-m'ọñ; kẹ́rẹ na yéma hẹ ri wop. I káne-nu fo
K'úru ọ poñ sōm ọw'án-k'ọñ gbeñ ka 'ra-rū aré tra fi trạ́ka a-
fạm, káma ña tšē ba ka-dínne; kẹ́rẹ káma ña gbáli sótọ ka-
lápạr ka 'ma-treï-ma-ñañ ma-las, de káma ña gbáli kọ ro-riánna.
Be nạ láne Yísua, be ua séline-kọ, be na wop ar'ím-r'ọñ, be
na treï kạ-yō ma-treï ma-las; K'úru o trạ tšéra-nu ama-treï-ma-
nu ma-lạs, o trạ sọñ-nu a-ñésam a-tabána ro-riánna.
 A-máne-'a-mi! Bótrar nañ am-méra, trap nañ ténoñ tra
wop ar'ím ra K'úru, ará I poñ trọ́ri-nu; káma na tšẹ dínne
tabána; kẹ́rẹ káma na fúti ka 'ra-ban' da K'úrumasäba. Ne̥m-
te̥nẹ nạñ K'úru, káma ọ mar-nu tra láne-kọ, tra wọp ar'ím-
r'ọñ, de tra yo tr'eï ó tr'eï, atrá o poñ káne-nu ka ar'ím r'ọñ.
Ne̥mte̥nẹ-kọ nañ tra fútia am'úmpal-ma-nu, de tra bä-nu i-nei,
de tra tạ́nạs-nu, káma na gbáli sákẹ rọñóñ; tša pa yi hẹ ka
añ-tọ́sa ña nyañ na gbáli sákẹ ka K'úru: kọ́no bä tra mar-nu
trạ́ka yō-tši.
 Káñkọ K'úru na sákẹ ka Yísua tra-tšeñ, káma ọ sákẹ ronú,
de káma nạ sótọ ma-trạ́ma ma-fíno ro-riánna. Riánna o yi
ọd'ér ọ-ma-bónẹ; kạ-sọ́mpanẹ ó kạ-sọ́mpanẹ ka yi hẹ ri, ra-trū
ó ra-trū ra yi hẹ ri, m'ọ́nẹ ó m'ọ́nẹ ma yi hẹ ri; kẹ́rẹ ma-
bónẹ gbo táñkañ ó táñkañ.

Chapter III.

The ten Commandments.

(E-toṅ trofátr.)

K'úrumasäba ọ fọf as'ím atré bẹ, ọ pā họ:

1. Míuẹ yi Yehófa Ok'úru-ka-mu, ọwọ́ wúra-mu ka an-tọf ña Mísra, ka añ-set ña ra-trar. Tšē bā tr'úru tra-lọm támbe mínañ.¹)

2. Tšē bémpanẹ a-rọñ ó a-roñ a-fos, talọ́m ra-bálanẹ ó ra-bálanẹ ra r'áka ó r'áka ará yi ka ak'úru rokọ́m, talọ́m ará yi ka an-tọf rokọ́m, talọ́m ará yi ro-m'antr ka an-tọf roráta. Tšē sọ́na-yi tra-wu, dẹ tšē léñki-yi: tša mínẹ Yehófa Ok'úru-ka-mu I yi K'úru ọwọ́ bā kạ-trutr, ọwọ́ ram ama-treï ma-lạs ma añ-kas ka tra-bomp tra añ-wut ba ka 'ra-kómra, ará béka tra-sas dẹ ará béka tr'áñlẹ ka añá gbéña-mi; dẹ ọwọ́ bā i-neï trạka e-wul ya añá bọ́tạr-mi, dẹ añá wop ẹ-toñ-'ẹ-mi.

3. Tšē bontr añ'és ña Yehófa Ok'úru-ka-mu kạ-tšiñ; tša Yehófa o gbáli he nạñk w'úni, ọwọ́ bontr añ'és-ñọñ kạ-tšiñ, mọ w'úni páñi-tr'eï.

4. Nánẹ añ-réï ña añ-Sábat tra wop-ñi a-sạm. Ma-réï tramát ro kin mạ yi tra yọ̄ ma-pant, dẹ mạ yi tra yọ̄ ama-pant-ma-mu bẹ; kérẹ añ-réï, añá béka tramát dẹ rạñ, ña yi añ-Sábat ña Yehófa Ok'úru-ka-mu: ka añ-réï añé mạ gbáli hẹ yọ̄ ma-pant ó ma-pant, pa yi hẹ múnọ, pạ yi hẹ ọw'áñ-ka-mu ọ-rúni, pạ yi hẹ ọw'áñ-ka-mu ọ-béra, pa yi hẹ am-boï-'a-mu a-rúni, pạ yi hẹ am-boï-'a-mu a-béra, pạ yi hẹ tra-šem-tra-mu tra ka-petr, pạ yi hẹ o-tšik, ọwọ́ yira ka tra-petr-tra-mu: tša ka ma-réï tramát ro kin Yehófa ọ bémpa atr'úru dẹ an-tọf, dẹ ka-bañ, dẹ r'áka ó r'áka ará yi ri rok'ór, kọ o fótanẹ ka añ-réï añá béka tramát dẹ rạñ: tšíañ Yehófa ọ rúba añ-réï ña añ-Sábat, kọ o sámas-ñi.²)

---

¹) Or: tr'úru tra-tšel rayér-ka-mi; „strange gods beside me."
²) Or: o yo-ñi a-sạm; „he made it sacred."

5. Nésa o-kas-ka ınu dẹ o-kára-ka-mu; káma ma boḷ añ-ńésạm-'a-mu ka an-tọf, aňá Yehófa Ọk'úru-ka-mu o soň-mu.

6. Tšē dif.

7. Tšē yọ kạ-rạp.

8. Tšē keía.

9. Tšē soň t'amasére tra ra-yem trạ́ka o-fátranẹ-ka-mu.

10. Tšē bā a-féla trạ́ka aň-set ňa o-fátranẹ-ka-mu; tšē bā a-féla trạ́ka o-ráni ka o-fátranẹ-ka-mu, pạ yi hẹ trạ́ka am-bọī-ň'oň a-rúni, pạ yi hẹ trạ́ka am-bọī-ň'oň a-bẹ́ra, pạ yi hẹ trạ́ka o-nā-k'oň, pạ yi hẹ trạ́ka aň-sofali-ň'oň, pạ yi hẹ trạ́ka r'áka ó r'áka, ará o-fátranẹ-ka-mu o bā.

Chapter IV.

Translation of some Psalms.

Aň-Sálma 1.

1. W'úni mári-tr'ei woň, owọ́ tšē kọt ka ka-maň ka aň-fạm a-lạs, dẹ owọ́ tšē trạ́ma ka ar'óu' da aň-fạm aňá yö o-lạs, dẹ owọ́ tšē yíra ka ka-waň ka aň-fam a-šel-tr'ei.

2. Kẹ́rẹ owọ́ tésa trạ́ka an-tọň ňa Yehófa, dẹ owọ́ tramtrámnẹ an-tọň-ň'oň ra-yaň dẹ tratrák-aň.

3. Ọ bálanẹ mo ň'ạntr aňá 'a tšẹp ka trạ-bat trạ m'antr rayẹ́r, aňá soň ama-kómi-ma-tši ka aň-lóko-ňa-tši; dẹ ẹ-bóparya-tši ẹ gbạ́li hẹ yímra, dẹ tr'ei ó tr'ei atrá o yo o náfas-tši.

4. Pạ yi hẹ yaň trạ́ka aň-fạm a-lạs; kẹ́rẹ (ňa yi) mo ẹ-fuk, ẹyẹ́ aň-fef ňa fálira.

5. Tšiaň aň-fạm a-lạs ňa gbạ́li hẹ trạ́ma ka ka-rok antọ́ňka, pạ yi hẹ aň-fam aňá yö o-lạs ka aň-gbánnẹ ňa aň-fạm a-trạtšéň.[1])

6. Tša Yehófa o trára ar'on' da aň-fạm a-tratšéň;[2]) kẹ́rẹ ar'on' da aň-fạm a-lạs ra dínnẹ.

---

1) Or: ňa an-trạtšéň; „of the righteous."
2) Or: da an-trạtšéň; „of the righteous."

Añ-Sálma 23.

1. Yehófa ǫ yi ǫ-trǫl-ka-mi; I gbạ́li hẹ pań r'áka.

2. O yǭ-mi I fạ́nta rạ trạ-lal trạ k'éreń kạ-fíno; ǫ kérẹ-mi¹) ka am'ántr ma o-fótanẹ rayẹ́r.

3. O kal bákas añ'úmpạl-'a-mi;²) ǫ kérẹ-mi ka as'óń' tra ma-lómpi trạ́ka ra-bomp ra añ'és-ń'ǫń.

4. Ańkó, kóta mẹ I kǫt³) ka ka-gbóńkạl ka añ-fǫīr ńa rań, I gbạ́li hẹ nésa tr'eī ó tr'eī trạ-lạs: pakášifẹ⁴) múnǫ mạ yi rǫmí; ka-sétẹ-ka-mu⁵) dẹ ka-trạk-ka-mu tra béfạt-mi.

5. Ma béncna-mi a-mésa trạ́ka ka-di rod'ér ka añ-gbéńa-'a-mi kạdí;⁶) am-pǫ́ti-'a-mi ńa la paī.⁷)

6. Ma-tǫt dẹ ma-bǫ́ńa ma tra tram-mi gbo ama-réī ma añ-ńésạm-'a-mi bẹ; kẹ I tši yíra ka añ-set ńa Yehófa tabána.

Añ-Sálma 126.

A-leń ńa tra-tšik.

1. Mǫ Yehófa ǫ kála e-fúnti ya Sion, sạ yi mǫ hǫ ańá ma wǫ́rap.

2. Ań-lǫ ńa-tši tra-sań-tra-su tra lásanẹ ma-šel, dẹ tra-mer-tra-su (tra lásanẹ) ma-leń: ań-lǫ ńa-tši ńa pā ka-trǫ́ń ka añ-káfri: Yehófa ǫ pońyǫ́na-ńa ma-trei ma-bána.

3. Yehófa ǫ pońyǫ́na-su ma-trei ma-bána; pạ bóṇẹ-su.⁸)

---

1) Or: ǫ bótrar-mi am-méra ka etc., „he takes care of me at etc."

2) Or: añ-ńésam-'a-mi.

3) Or better: Yẹ pạ yi sǫ, mẹ I kǫt etc.; „thus it is also when I walk etc."

4) Or: tša etc.

5) Or: ak'ántr-ka-mu.

6) Or: rod'ér ka ańá gbéńa-mi kạdí.

7) Or: ńa la ha ńa lóńa.

8) Or: sǫ bā ma-bóńe. Or: tšía sõm pạ bóṇẹ-su.

4. Kála sọ, o Yehófa, ẹ-fúnti-'ẹ-su, mọ¹) atra-bat tra antọf ña ka-díọ!

5. Añá sáka ẹ-santr m'ántrar, ña tra re róka ma-bọ́nẹ.

6. Ña wur ña tas ka bōk-añ, ña bánanẹ ẹ-santr, ña kálanẹ sọ ña der rẹ ma-bọ́nẹ, ña káranẹ ama-gboñ-ma-ñañ.

Note. The first verse, if translated literally is as follows: „When the Lord brought back the captives of Zion etc.;" according to the sense of the common Engl. version. But according to a learned Commentator the Hebr. שׁוּב in Kal is always to be taken intr. in the sense of „return", or „return to", when the place to which one returns follows also often in the Acc. This assertion he founds on the principal passage of Deut. 30, 2. 3. where this expression first occurs, and in the first six verses of which שׁוּב occurs several times, and only once it is given tr. by „turn, bring back"; but even there it will give a better sense in rendering it by „return to", as v. 2.: „And shalt return unto the Lord thy God, and shalt etc." v. 3.: „Then the Lord thy God will return to thy captivity etc." This observation applies also to the other passages where שׁוּב is given tr. in the common version; but where it will give a very good sense when rendered by „return to"; viz. in Ps. 14, 7. 85, 4. and Jes. 52, 8.

When taken intr. the Engl. version of the 1st. verse of the preceding Psalm would be as follows: „When the Lord turned himself to the returning (i. e. conversion) of Zion, etc.;" and in Temne: Mọ Yehófa o sạ́kẹ ka ka-sạ́kẹ ka Sion, etc., or more fully: ka ka sạ́kẹ ka am-méra ka Sion etc.

As שׁוּב has also the sense of „be converted", שִׁיבָה may be given by conversion, hence שׁוּב שִׁיבָה = „return to the returning," or „return (turn oneself) to the conversion;" and שׁוּב שְׁבוּת, „return to the captivity," or fig. „to the misery of etc."

---

1) Or: Kálanẹ sọ, o Yehófah, ka ra-fúnti-ra-su, mọ etc.; „return again, o Jehova, to our captivity, as etc."

Chapter V.

Hymns.

1. Am-Bósnẹ trạ́ka Riánna. (2 Cor. 5, 1.) (C. M.)

1.

Sạ bā a-sel ṅa yi rokọ́m.
Ṅa tas ẹ-sel nọ-rū;
Kẹ be sạ fi sạ kọ́nẹ ri.
Tra yfra ri rokọ́m.

2.

Ṅa yi a-sel a-bákạr gbaṅ.
Ṅa yi hẹ ka aṅ-tọf;
Ṅa teī hẹ ınẹ ẹ-sel ẹ-lọm,
Ṅa yi ri ro rokọ́m.¹)

3.

Yehófa kọ́nọ bẹ́mpa-ṅi,
A-fạm ṅa sal hẹ ṅi;
Aṅ-sel aṅé ṅa yẹ́sẹ hẹ,
A-fam ṅa šim hẹ ṅi.

4.

Aṅ'úmpal-'a-mi ṅa bósnẹ gba,
Tra bēk aṅ-sel ṅa-tši;
Ṅa yéma treī aṅ-sel nọ-rū,
Tra bā aṅá rokọ́m.

5.

Sạ kar ra-fi, pạ bọ́nẹ-su;
Tša ría yọ sạ treī
Aṅ-sel-'a-su a-yaī aṅé,
Tra woṅ aṅ-sel a-fu.²)

1 Or: Ṅa wọn ṅa tas 'ra-rū.
2) Or: Tra woṅ aṅ-sel rokọ́m.

2. Ama-Bótạr de ama-Tọt ma K'úrumasäba.

(P. M. Or like: Though troubles assail etc.[1])

1.

Yehófa rokọ́m,
Ọ yọ̄-mi ọ-tọt;
Ọ dis-mi, ọ muns-mi, o lošir-mi sọ,
Ọ bótrạr-mi 'méra, o nạ̊ṅka-mi 'nei:
Hä r'áka ra gbạ́li he yọ̄-mi ọ-baṅ.

2.

Yehófa rokọ́m,
Ọ bémpa-mi gbetr;
Ọ báni-mi so ka 'ra-trar ra ọ-las:
Ọ yō-mi ow'áṅ ka ọ-kas-k'oṅ rokọ́m:
Ọ tšer-mi l ṅatr ro-riáṅua b' l fi.

3.

Yehófa rokọ́m.
Aṅ-fósa-ṅ'oṅ sön.
Na béne-mi tọt ama-réï-ma-mi be,
Ọ yō-mi l fäṅta, l díra sọ gbes.
Ọ yō-mi l táme, l yókane ras.

4.

Yehófa rokóm,
Ọ kạ́li-mi tọt;
Ọ yóna-mi atr'eí tra-kabáne tra-tši.
Ow'áṅ-k'oṅ ọ fi ka ka-bélaṅ-ka-mi:
I trára toṅ kọ́nọ mọ bótạr-mi gba.[2]

5.

Mọ kọ́nọ mi ba,
I nésa he so;
Tša r'áka ra-sómpa ra gbạ́li he fatr:
O búmar-mi lọ́kọ ó lọ́kọ tra-tšeṅ,
Ka r'áka ra-fíno l gbạ́li he paṅ.

1) Or according to the Germ. tune: „Ob Trübsal uns kränkt, etc."

2) Or: I trára toṅ kọ́nọ mọ téna-mi gba.

6.

Yehófa rokǫ́m
Ka-lápsǫ ka-tši,
Ǫ sōm a-maleíka tra kére̱-mi ro,
Ro Yísua o yíra rokǫ́m ka ka-wań,
Ro m'ǫ́ne̱ ó m'ǫ́ne̱ ma gbáli he̱ wǫń.

3. Doxology. (L M.)

(Praise God from whom etc.)

1.

K'úru o soń e̱-rúba be̱,
Mań léńsir-kǫ, — tšē tši pálne̱.
Tǫk-ko a-fa̱m be̱ ka 'ra-rū,
Nya a-maleíka ńa k'úru.

2.

K'úru o-Kas, mań léńsir-ko;
Léńsir Qw'án-k'ǫń kōm gbo sōn;
K'úru o-Rúhu léńsir na̱ń,
Ka-Sas ra-sa̱m mań léńsir na̱ń.

Chapter VI.

The Lord's Prayer.

(Ka-rámne̱ ka o-Rábu.)

Pa-ka-su, owǫ́ yi ro ka riánna, káńkǫ¹) ań'és-'a-mu ńa yi a-sa̱m; káńkǫ¹) ara-baī-ra-mu ra hēk; káńkǫ¹) ama-šélǫ-ma-mu ma yǫ́ne̱ ka au-tǫf, ma ma yǫ́ne̱ ro ka riánna. Yer-su ténǫń ar'á-ra-su ra-di, ará béki. Tšéra-su ama-trei-ma-su ma-la̱s, ma šyań sa̱ tšer sǫ ańa ma yǫ-su o-la̱s. Tšē su wǫ́ńa ka r'ā ra-gbǫ́sa; kére̱ wúra-su ka ma-treī ma-la̱s. Tša múnǫ bà 'ra-baī, de̱ ań-fósa, de̱ ań-yíki táńkań ó táńkań. Amína.

---

1) Or: tra, „let".

Part III.

Temne - English Vocabulary.

Note. See the Preface § 22.

Abbreviations explained.

a.	active.	log.	logical.
abbr.	abbreviated.	n.	neuter.
abr.	abruptive.	n.	noun.
abs.	absolute.	obj.	objective.
abstr.	abstract.	obs.	obsolete.
adj.	adjective.	onom.	onomatopoetic.
adv.	adverb.	part.	particle.
aux.	auxiliary.	pass.	passive.
caus.	causative	pers.	personal.
cf.	confer.	pl.	plural.
comp	compound.	poss.	possessive.
concr.	concrete.	postp.	postposition.
conj.	conjunction.	pr.	pronoun.
contr.	contracted.	pref.	prefix.
def.	definite.	prep.	preposition.
dem.	demonstrative.	prob.	probably.
dim.	diminutive.	prop.	proper.
doubl.	doubly.	prox.	proximate.
emph.	emphatic.	rad.	radix.
euph.	euphonic.	recipr.	reciprocal.
expl.	expletive.	refl.	reflexive.
fig.	figuratively.	rel.	relative.
freq.	frequentative.	rem.	remote.
inch.	inchoative.	revert.	revertive.
indef.	indefinite.	sing.	singular.
impers.	impersonal.	spec.	specific.
insep.	inseparable.	spont.	spontive.
int.	interjection.	subj.	subjective.
intens.	intensive.	suff.	suffix.
inter.	interrogative.	v.	verb.
irrel.	irrelative.	verb.	verbal.
lit.	literally.	vow.	vowel.
loc.	local.		

A.

A-, pref. indef. „a, an"; e. g. a-set, „a house".

A-, pref. emph. vow. to make compound indef. prefixes, as: ka-, ma-, na-, etc. or k', tr', etc. definite; e. g. ama-bǫ́ne, „the joy", from ma-bǫ́ne, „joy"; ak'ántr. „the stick", from k'antr. „a stick". See Pref. § 22. b.

-A, suff., being a weaker form of -aṅ, used relatively only. It may be affixed to nouns, pronouns and to some local adverbs; e. g. kía. „it". from ki, „it".

-A, suff., often added at the end of a proposition for the purpose to make the last vowel sound agree with a preceding vowel sound a, or to cause a sort of quibble. Sometimes it is used after exclamatory sentences, as: der ba lemp-a! „come here quickly!"

-A? inter. suff., depending on euphony, and used with ma? me? and mọ? when having the sense of „why?" e. g. main bes anǫ́-a? „why doest thou dig here?" — For its other uses see the Grammar.

-A? inter. loc. suff. „where?" implying the subsantive verb „be"; it is affixed to nouns and pronouns like the Hebr. אֵי. — E. g. an-tis-a? „where is the knife?" or: an-tis ṅí-a? lit. „the knife where is it?" = ṅí-a an-tis-a? lit. „where is it the knife;" mún'-a? „where art thou?" = the Hebr. אַיֶּכָּה Gen. 3, 9.; trí-a? or tśí-a? „where are they (spoons, sticks etc.)?" for tría-a? or tśía-a? More particulars about the use of this suff. will be found in the Temne Grammar.

A! int. „ah! oh! now! well!" It is expressive of wonder, dislike, censure, and approval, also of joy or grief, pain and compassion; e. g. a w'an! „oh boy!"

'A, abbrev. form of ṅa, pr. subj. „they, it;" e. g. 'a sap-ko, „they flogged him."

'A-mi, pr. poss. abbr. „my", for: ṅa-mi, lit. „of me;" e. g. aṅ-set-'a-mi, „my house."

'A-mu, pr. poss. abbr. „thy", for: ńa-mu, lit. „of thee;" e. g. ań-set-'a-mu, „thy house."

'A-ńań, pr. poss. abbr. „their", for: ńa-ńań, lit. „of them;" e. g. ań-set-'a-ńań, „their house."

'A-nu, pr. poss. abbr. „your", for: ńa-nu, lit. „of you;" e. g. ań-set-'a-nu, „your house."

'A-su, pr. poss. abbr. „our", for: ńa-su, lit. „of us;" e. g. ań-set-'a-su, „our house."

Aka-, def. pref. = ka-. „the"; e. g. aka-bep, ka-bep, „the spoon;" but ka-bep, „a spoon."

Aká, pr. rel. „which"; e. g. ka-bep aka I wai, „the spoon which I bought."

Aké, pr. dem. prox. „this"; e. g. ak'ántr aké, „this stick."

Alikáli, n. title of the kings of the Port-Loko territory. Lit. „the chief judge." It seems in the first place to be derived from the Mandingo Alkáli, „alcaid", or „alcalde", and ultimately from the Ar. قَاضِي, قَاضٍ, judex, and with the article: summus judex. In Temne the i is inserted after the Arab. article al- for the sake of euphony. The Chiefs of the Sikhs in India are called: akali, which no doubt comes from the same root.

Alukrána, n. „the Koran." From the Ar. اَلْقُرْآنُ, coranus.

Am, euph. form of ma, „thou", used before b, m and p with interrogative propositions; e. g. am poń di-i? „hast thou eaten?" — See ma in loco.

Am-, pref. def. „the", used before the letters b, m and p; e. g. am-bitra, „the bottle."

Ama-, pref. def. „the"; e. g. ama-ber, „the liquor."

Amá, „pr. rel. „which"; e. g. ma-lémre amá I bä, „the limes which I have."

Ambá! int. and adv. „well! thank you!" Cf. for examples Colloquial Phrases. pag. 105 etc.

Amé; pr. dem. prox. sing. and pl. „this, these;" e. g. ama-trei amé, „these things."

Amína,) adv. „amen", „so be it." From the Ar. اٰمِين. amen.
Amíni,) ita sit. The Temnes say amíni, the Mori-men amína.

An-, pref. def. „the", used before the letters d, n and t; e. g. an-tis, „the knife."

An, euph. form of ma, „thou", used before d, n and t with interrogative propositions; e. g. an dira-i? „hast thou slept?"

Añ. pref. def. „the", used before all consonants excepting b. m and p, as also d, n and t; e. g. añ-gbáta, „the mat."

-Añ, suff., indicating with verbs a continuance of the energy of the verb, with which it is used, while one speaks of it, as: ña ma di-añ, „they are eating." It is generally used with participial propositions. If a verb, having more than one syllable, terminates in a, then the vowel of the suff. is cut off, as: kǫ́nǫ me tila-'ñ, „him I am selling."

-Añ, suff., used with pronouns, when it makes them emphatic, or rather absolute. This form may, however, be also used relatively; but the weaker form -a, which see above, is never used absolutely. It is also used with a few local adverbs. When used with nouns or names, it seems to be used as a sort of expletive or euph. particle, or as a sort of inseparable dem. pr., at least it contains the element of it. Añ is sometimes yet followed by the suffix -e, and thus, becomes a compound one, and may be thus used with verbs and nouns; e. g. ñañ, „it", from ñi; as: an-tis-'a-mi ñañ, „this is my knife," lit. „my knife it."

Añ, euph. form of ma, „thou", used before g and k with interrogative propositions; e. g. añ ko ro-pètr-i? „art thou going to town?"

Añ, adv. „yes", used with a nod of the head. It is an almost inarticulate sound; e. g. o-kas-ka-mu o yi ri-i? Añ, o yi ri; „is thy father there?" „Yes, he is there."

Añ añ! int. or adv. „so so! tolerably well! nothing particular! pretty well!" It is an almost inarticulate sound. See Colloq. Phras. p. 105.

Aná, pr. rel. „which"; e. g. na-béña ana I kára, „ropes which I brought."

Aña-, pref. def. „the"; e. g. aña-sel, „the house."

Añá, pr. rel. sing. and pl. „who, they who; which." When referring to a noun of place, it may be given by „where"; e. g. añ-sel añá o̩ sal, „the house which he built."

Añai-, pref. def comp. „the"; as añai-yári, „the cat," = añ-yári.

Ané, pr. dem. prox. „this"; e. g. an'ántr ané, „this fire."

Añé, pr. dem. prox. sing. and pl. „this, these;" e. g. añ-fa̩m añé, „this people."

Añáñ, pr. dem. rem. sing. and pl. „that, those." Sometimes merely ñañ, which see; e. g. „añ-fa̩m añáñ, „those persons."

Anína, } = nína, or nínañ, adv. „to morrow"; e. g. anínañ lóko
Anínañ, } wúno̩ñ I tši kóne̩, „to morrow about this time I shall go." The longer form may be used absolutely.

A̩ñkó, adv. „yes"; e. g. ma̩ kóne̩ ro-k'or-i? A̩ñkó; „doest thou go to the farm?" „Yes."

Ano̩, adv. emph. „here"; e. g. o̩ yi fe̩ ano̩, „he is not here."

Ano̩, prep. prox. „here at, here in, here from, here to." It implies the adv. „here"; e. g. ano̩-petr, „here in this town."

Apa-, pref. def. „the"; e. g. kára pa-lã apa-fíno, „bring the rice the good one."

Apá, pr. rel. „which", e. g. pa̩-lã apá I waĩ, „rice which I bought."

Ara-, pref. def. „the"; e. g. ara-béña, „the rope."

Ará, pr. rel. „which"; e. g. ra-béña ará I gba̩k, „a rope and rope which I cut."

Aré, pr. dem. prox. „this"; e. g. ara-béña aré, „this rope."

Atra-, pref. def. = tra, „the"; e. g. atra-bep, „the spoons," = tra-bep.

Atrá, pr. rel. „which"; e. g. tra-bep atrá dinne̩, „the spoons which are lost."

Atšé, = atré, pr. dem. prox. sing. and pl. „this, these;" e. g. atr'ei atšé, „this matter." See the Note after kótši.

Áwa! int. „well! well now! very well!" Germ. „wohlan!" Lat. age! e. g. áwa, sa̩ kóne̩! „well, we go!"

B.

B', abbr. of be, which see; e. g. b' I fi, „when I die."

Ba, adv. „now, here;" e. g. kạ́li ba! „look here!"

Bā, v. a. „have, possess;" also „have-for-, have-on-" (as pity on one, see the next word); e. g. ọ bā hẹ a-kála, „he has no money." As an aux. v., bā with the long form of the Infinitive of another verb, or also with a verbal noun, expresses duty or obligation to do what is indicated by the Infinitive of the principal verb, as: mạ bā tra gbal, „thou must write," lit. „thou hast to write."

Bā w'úni i-neī, „have mercy" or „pity upon one;" e. g. ọ bāmi i-neī, „he had pity on me."

Bā w'úni tr'eī, „be a matter to one, concern one;" e. g. múnọ trạ bā tr'eī-i? Yáo, mínẹ trạ bā tr'eī; „does it concern thee?" „Yes, it concerns me."

Baf, v. a. „make" (as a farm), „cultivate, clear" (as land for a farm); e. g. ọ kọ baf a-tọ̣f, „he goes to clear land for a farm."

Baī, ọ-, pl. a-, n. „king"; e. g. ọ-baī ka an-tọf, „the king of the country."

Baī, ra-, pl. trạ-, n. „kingdom, government, office of a king;" e. g. ra-baī-r'ọń, „his kingdom."

Bak, v. impers. „be hard, be trying;" e. g. pạ bak hẹ, be mạ mémạr ọ-fíno, „it will not be hard, if thou doest try well." It also serves to express the adv. „hardly", as: pạ bak ri mọ ọ fútia ań-ńẹ́sạm-ń'ọń, „he hardly saved his life there," lit. „it was hard there when he saved his life." It is the short form of báki.

Bak, v. inch. and n. „get" or „be strong; get old, grow up, grow; come to the full time" (as applied to pregnancy); e. g. I bak tọń, „I got old now;" — ọ kási bak, „he will not grow" (as a child).

Bak, ka-, n. „strength, hardness, firmness; age;" e. g. ka-bak-ka-tśi, „its hardness" (as of wood); ka-bak-k'ọń, „his age."

Bak ra-fọr, kạ-, n. comp. „boldness, audacity, impudence, want of modesty;" lit. „strength (as regards, or of) the eye;" e. g. o bā kạ-bak ra-fọr, „he is bold," lit. „he has boldness."

Bak, adj. „lasting"; e. g. ra-rū ra-bak tabána, „a world lasting for ever."

Bak, } v. rel. „be strong for-on-with-, be heavy on-" (as a sick-
Baki, } ness on a person); „be older than-;" e. g. o báki-mi o-tan, he is a little older than I." Short form also: „get strong for-, get heavy upon-, be trying for-."

Báka, o-, pl. a-, n. „one of the Baka nation." See Pref. § 4. d.

Bákạr, adj. „strong, firm, fast;" (rad. bak.) E. g. o fọ́fa r'im rabákạr, „he spoke with a strong voice."

Bákạr, o-, adj. but used adverbially, „fast, firm, firmly, tight." See an ex. under lin, v. a.

Bákạr, v. rel. u. (rad. bak) „be strong, be firm, be fast" (as a post etc.); „be hard" (as wood); e. g. ak'ạntr ka bákạr, „the post is firm." The suffix is rather redundant.

Bákạs, v. caus. (rad. bak), „make strong, strengthen" (as the heart, or body); „make heavy;" e. g. o bákạs ka-but-ka-mi, = o bákạs-mi ka-but, „he strengthened, my heart," = „he encouraged me."

Bákạs an'úmpạl na- ('a-), „strengthen the soul of-, refresh one's soul;" e. g. o bákạs an'úmpạl-'a-mi, „he refreshes my soul."

Bákạsne, v. caus. and refl. (rad. bak), „strengthen oneself, refresh oneself" (as by food etc.); also „encourage oneself" (with or without ka-but, „heart"); e. g. o bákạsne, „he encouraged himself."

Bákạsne ma-der, „refresh one's own body, recruit one's own health;" e. g. o bákạsne ma-der, „he refreshed his body."

Báke, kạ-, pl. trạ-, n. „wharf, landing-place, port." From báke, „go on shore, land."

Báke Lọ́kọ, n. prop. „The town Port Loko." See Pref. § 4. c.

Báki, v. rel. long form of bak, which see above.

Báki, adj. „strong, hard; heavy, serious" (as a palaver); e. g. tr'ei trạ-báki, „a serious matter;" „grievous" (as an illness); „great" (as a battle); „laborious" (as work); e. g. ma-pant ma-baki, „hard work;" „old" (of rational objects).

Báki, o-, adj. but used adverbially, „strongly"; e. g. an-fef na feñ o-báki, „the wind blows strongly."
Báki, v. impers. „be hard, be trying;" e. g. o báki, „it is hard."
Báki, v. impers. a. „be hard for-, be trying for-;" e. g. o bákiko tra yō-tši, „it was hard for him to do it."
Báki, v. n. „be strong" (as wood, or tide); „be heavy" (as a load, or palaver); „be hard" or „stale" (as bread); „be old" (of anim. objects only); „be sad, be distressing" (as news); e. g. am'ántr ma báki ténon, „the tide is strong to day."
Báki ra-for, adj. comp. „bold, impudent, wanting modesty;" e. g. w'úni báki ra-for, „an impudent person."
Báki, am-, n. „the old (people);" also „the dead", or „the manes, the shades;" lit. „the old ones." See Pref. § 12, a. and cf. the Hebr. עם עולים Hez. 26, 20.
Bal, v. a. „drive away, expel, drive;" e. g. 'a bal-ko, „they drove him away."
Bal-bal, v. freq. a. (rad. bal), „pursue after, chase, drive all about, drive far away; persecute;" e. g. 'a bal-bal-ko o-ban, „they pursued hotly after him."
Bal-bal, ka-, n. verb. „act of pursuing after, chasing; persecution;" e. g. ka-bal-bal-k'on o-šem, „his chasing the animal."
Bála, v. inch. (rad. bal), „get married, marry" (of females); e. g. o-béra o pon bála, „the woman has got married."
Balaí, ka-, pl. tra-, n. „basket"; e. g. ka-balaí ka-bána, „a large basket."
Bálane, v. prob. caus. and refl., or spont. (rad. bal), „be like." Often followed by: mo- „as"; e. g. ra bálane mo a-bōk, „it is like a snake."
Bálane mo (ho), „be like as, resemble;" e. g. ra bálane mo ho a-bōk, „it resembles a snake."
Bálane, ra-, pl. e-, n. „likeness, representation, picture;" e. g. ra-bálane-r'on, „his likeness."
Bálma, a-, pl. e-, n. „country-knife, dagger;" e. g. o ba a-bálma, „he has a dagger."
Bamp, a-, pl. e-, n. „bird"; e. g. a-bamp a-fíno, „a fine bird."

Bań, v. a. „pain, cause pain to-. hurt;" e. g. ka-sam ka bań-mi, „the sore pains me."

Bań, v. n. „be angry, be cross" (habitually so); „ache, ail;" also „be hot" (as the sun); e. g. ra-bomp-ra-mi ra bań, „my head aches;" — ow'úni owé o bań, „this person is cross."

Bań, adj. „angry, cross; painful, severe;" e. g. w'úni bań, „an angry person."

Bań, o-, adj. but used as an adv. „severely, hotly, sharply, painfully." Cf. yō-w'úni o-bań, under Y.

Bań, v. a. „fetch"; e. g. bań a-tis, „fetch a knife."

Bań, ra-, n. „anger, indignation, wrath;" e. g. ra-ban'-d'oń, „his wrath."

Bań, ka-, n. „the sea, as opposed to dry land;" ro-bań, „at sea."

Bána. v. n. „be large, be big, be great;" e. g. míne bána, „I am great."

Bána, adj. „large, big, great; heavy" (as a tornado); e. g. o-nā o-bána, „a large cow."

Bána, o-, adj. but used adverbially, „greatly, much;" applied to sewing „with large stitches," e. g. o sot o-bána, „he sews with large stitches."

Bána, v. rel. (rad. bā), „have-for-, carry-for-;" e. g. o bána-ko k'óta, „he has cloth for him."

Bána, v. rel. (rad. bań), „fetch for-;" e. g. bána-mi a-tis, „fetch me a knife."

Bánane, v. rel. and refl. „have with oneself, carry with oneself;" e. g. o bánane aù kála, „he carried the money with himself."

Báni, v. a. „redeem, ransom;" e. g. o báni-mi ka 'ra-trar, „he redeemed me from slavery."

Báni, ka-, n. verb. „act of redeeming, redemption;" e. g. ka-báni-k'oń, „his redemption."

Báńka, ka-, pl. tra-, n. „temporary hut in a farm of a conical form, the roof reaching down to the ground." It is used to cook under, and superior to, and higher than the one called a-gbom. Also „any rude round hut in a farm;" and also „the form of an annular eclipse," about which see the Temne Dict.

Báṅ'sa, for báṅqsa, v. caus. and inch. (rad. baṅ), „get angry, be angry" (occasionally so), lit. „get angered," or „get made angry;" e. g. o-baī o báṅ'sa, „the king got angry." Applied to the sea „roar, rage."

Báṅ'sa, v. freq. and caus. (rad. baṅ), „pain, hurt, cause pain to; ail;" e. g. an'ántr na báṅsa he ko, „the fire did not hurt him."

Báṅ'sa, ka-, n. „anger" (occasional); „pain"; e. g. ka-báṅ'sa-k'oṅ, „his anger." Applied to the sea: „roaring, raging," = the Hebr. קצף Jon. 1, 15.

Báṅ'sane, v. impers. freq. or intens. caus. and refl. (rad. baṅ), „grieve, displease to, pain, make angry," lit. „cause pain to oneself;" e. g. pa báṅ'sane-ṅa, „it grieved them."

Báṅ'sar, v. caus. inch. and rel. (rad. baṅ), „get angered at-," or „about-," or „with-, be angry with-, be displeased," or „vexed with-," or „about-;" e. g. Pa Sóri o báṅ'sar-mi, I tsi fófar-ko, „Mr. Sori is angry with me; I shall speak to him."

Bant, ka-, pl. tra-, n. „bone"; e. g. ka-bant ka-loĺ, „a small bone."

Bántra, a-, pl. e-, n. „bow; arch;" also „spring" (of a gunlock); fig. „war". See Tradit. pag. 4.

Bap, ka-, pl. tra-. n. „country axe, hatchet."

Bap, v. a. „meet, meet with, find;" e. g. I bap-ko ro-r'oṅ, „I met him on the road."

Bap o-fíno, „fare well, meet with a happy lot, be well off;" e. g. o bap o-fíno ro-krífi, „he met with a good lot in Hades."

Bápar, v. rel. (rad. bap), „be present;" e. g. o bápar he ténoṅ. „he was not present to day."

Bar, a-, pl. e-, n. „species of hawk white and black living of fish."

Bar, v. a. „add, put more, increase" (as wages); e. g. I tsi bar aṅ-ram-'a-mu, „I shall increase thy wages."

Bar, v. n. and aux. „go on, continue." As an aux. it expresses continuance of the exercise of the energy indicated by the principal verb, or a progress of the same, as: o bar ko sap, „he went on to flog him," = „he flogged him more."

It also expresses the adv. „more;" or also „more and more";
in the latter case it is generally followed by gbo, „but".
When it is repeated and followed by gbo, it serves to express the words: „the more —, the more —." It is generally construed with the short form of the Infinitive, sometimes also with the verb. noun. See Proverb 7, p. 100.

Bar, a-, pl. ẹ-, n. „bar, iron bar; country bar worth about
Bára, 2s." Derived from the Span. bara.

Bári, ka̱-, pl. tra̱-, n. „twin"; e. g. o kōm tra̱-bári, „she brought forth twins."

Básạr, v. rel. a. „continue, continue with-, go on with-, persevere in-, with-;" prob. rel. form of an obs. bas; e. g. básạr akakáraṅ, „go on with the reading."

Básạr, v. rel. n. „continue, persevere;" e. g. o básạr hẹ, „he does not continue."

Básạra, v. rel. (properly doubly rel.), „continue for-, go on with-for-, persevere for-; persevere with-" or „in- for-," i. e. „go on with" (a thing) „for" (another, or) „in behalf of" (another); e. g. básạra-mi ama-pant amé, „go on with this work for me."

Bat, ka̱-, pl. tra̱-, n. „water-brook, brook," e. g. ro-bat, „at the brook."

Ba̱t, adj. „early"; e. g. ka ar'étr ra-ba̱t o der, „at an early sun he came," i. e. soon, when the sun was not up long get.

Ba̱t, adv. „in the morning, early;" also spec. in the sense of „fully" when used with the verb so̱k, „dawn"; e. g. o der ba̱t, „he came early."

Ba̱t, ka̱-, or ra̱-, pl. tra̱-, n. „morning". The pl. is seldom used. E. g. ra-ba̱t ra-fíno, „a fine morning."

Ba̱tr, v. a. „seize, take hold of, apprehend;" e. g. ba̱tr-ko̱, „seize him."

Batr, a-, pl. ẹ-, n. „a small young palm-tree."

Be, adv. „when"; e. g. be I fi-e, „when I die."

Be, conj. „if"; e. g. be o der he etc., „if he does not come etc."

Bē, n. „bey, king" or „chief".

Be, adv. in form, but often used in the sense of an adj. „all, whole, every; all kind, all sort, all sorts;" as applied to place „all over, every where;" e. g. añ-fam bẹ, „all the people;" -- ey'ẹtr bẹ, „all sorts of things."

Bẽ', abbr. of bẽk,¹) v. impers. „be sufficient, be enough, suffice;" e. g. pạ bẽ' hẹ, „it is not enough."

Bẽ', abbr. of bẽk,¹) v. n. „arrive, reach, be sufficient, be enough, suffice;" e. g. ọ ta bẽ' hẹ, „he has not yet arrived."

Béfạt, v. a. „comfort, soothe, make quiet" (as a child); e. g. ọ béfạt-kọ, „he comforted him."

Beĩ, ra-, pl. rạ-, n. „debt" (receivable and payable); e. g. ọ bã hẹ ra-beĩ, „he has no debt" (to pay).

Beíbạl, a-, pl. ẹ-, n. „Bible". From the English.

Bẽk, v. a. „arrive at, come to, reach;" e. g. ar'ạ́fa ra bẽk akapetr, „the army reached the town."

Bẽk, v. n. „reach, arrive, come, come near;" e. g. ọ poñ bẽk, „he has arrived."

Béka, v. a. „amount to, make, be worth;" also „call, hold as;" e. g. añ-gbáta añá béka ẹ-sas, „the 3rd. mat," lit. „the mat which makes three." See next word.

Béka w'úni ra-yem, „call one a liar, give the lie to one;" e. g. ọ béka-mi ra-yem, „he called me a liar."

Béki, v. a. (rad. bẽk), „be fit for-, be proper for-, be suitable for-, suit;" e. g. am'ọ́lọ amé ma béki ama-pant, „this amount suits the work."

Béki, v. n. (rad. bẽk), „be fit, be sufficient, be enough, suffice; e. g. am'ọ́lọ amé ma béki, „this price is sufficient. Long form of bẽk.

Béki, adj. „fit, proper, suitable" (as a person, or as time); sufficient, enough; worthy; due;" e. g. w'úni béki, „a worthy person;" — a-ram a-béki, „a suitable reward;" — ey'ẹtr ẹ-béki, „sufficient materials."

Béla, a-, pl. ẹ, n. „sail" (as of a canoe or ship); e. g. am-béla

---

1) These abbr. forms are used before the negative adv. hẹ „not."

a-bána, „the main sail," lit. „the large sail;" — w'ān, yísa ri am-béla, „boy, hoist the sail there."

Bélaṅ, ka-, pl. tra-, n. „side, part, region" (as of a house, or country); also „place, stead;" e. g. ka ka-bélaṅ-k'oṅ, „in his stead."

Bem, ra-, pl. tra-, n. „hedge-hog, grass-cutter," so called because this animal cuts grass. It is a kind of urchin, resembling the porcupine; but has only strong hairs instead of quills. It lives of rice and groundnuts.

Bémpa, v. a. „make, repair, put in order; perform the usual" or „necessary ceremonies for (a thing);" e. g. o bémpa aka-fantr, „he made the bed."

Bémpa, ka-, n. verb. „act of making, etc.;" e. g. ka-bémpa 'ra-rū, „the making of the world."

Bémpana, v. rel. (rad. bémpa), „make-for-; make-with-, make-of-" (as a table of wood); e. g. o bémpana-mi a-mésa, „he made a table for me."

Bémpane, v. rel. and refl. „make for" or „to oneself;" e. g. o bémpane a-mésa, „he made a table for himself."

Beñ, a-, pl. e-, n. „board"; e. g. a-beñ a-bóli, „a long board."

Béña, ra-, pl. na-, n. „rope" (especially the wooden country one), „any rope, string;" e. g. ra-béña ra-bóli, „a long rope."

Béña ra ka-but, ra-, pl. na-béña na tra-but, „heart-string."

Béne, v. a. „keep, preserve;" e. g. o béne o-sem, „he preserves the meat;" also „bury"; e. g. 'a béne-ko, „they buried him."

Béne w'úni o-tot, } „keep one well;" e. g. o béne-ko o-tot, „he
Béne w'úni tot,   } keeps him well."

Béne w'úni ra-tr'ei, „keep one from harm;" e. g. o béne-mi ra-tr'ei, „he keeps me from harm."

Béne w'úni ra-tr'ei ó tr'ei, „keep one from every harm;" e. g. K'úru o bene-mi ra-treī ó treī, „God keeps me from every harm."

Bénena, v. rel. (rad. bene). „prepare-for-, make-ready for-" (as food for one); e. g. o bénena-mi r'ā ra-di, „he prepared some food for me."

Bénene, v. refl. a. „prepare, make ready," lit. „prepare-for oneself" (as things for a journey); e. g. I bénene ey'étr-'e-mi,

„I made my things ready." Also „prepare oneself for-, make oneself ready for-" (as for a journey); e. g. o bénene ratšik, „he makes himself ready for a journey."

Bénene, v. refl. n. „prepare oneself, make oneself ready;" e. g. I poṅ bénene, „I have made myself ready."

Bénene, ka-, n. verb. „act of making oneself ready, act of preparing oneself, preparation;" e. g. ka-bénene-k'oṅ, „his preparation."

Bentr, v. a. „prevent, hinder;" e. g. o bentr-mi tra ko ro-kamp, „he prevented me from going to Freetown;" also „withhold-from-" (as money from one); e. g. o bentr-mi aṅ-k'ála-'a-mi, „he withholds my money from me."

Bep, ka-, pl. tra-, n. „spoon"; e. g. ka-bep ka-bána, „a large spoon."

Ber, ma-, n. „intoxicating liquor of any kind;" also „palmwine"; e. g. ma-ber ma-fíno, „good palmwine."

Béra, adj. „female"; e. g. w'an béra, „a girl," lit. „female child."

Béra, o-, pl. a-, n. „woman, female;" e. g. o-béra o-fíno, „a fine woman."

Béra o-bi, o-, pl. a-béra a-bi, n. „black female."

Béra o-féra, o-, pl. a-béra a-féra, n. „white female."

Bes, v. a. „dig"; e. g. bes a-bi, „dig a pit."

Bes, v. n. „dig, make a hole," or „grave"; e. g. tšē ri bes, „do not dig there."

Bes, ka-, n. verb. „act of digging, etc.;" e. g. ka-bes-k'oṅ, „his digging."

Bésa, v. rel. (rad. bes), „dig for-, dig-for-; dig with-, dig-with-;" e. g. bésa-mi a-bi, „dig a hole for me."

Bésa, adj. „belonging to digging," as: y'etr e-bésa, „digging tools."

Bi, adj. „black, dark;" e. g. k'óta ka-bi, „black cloth."

Bi, a-, pl. e-, or tra-, n. „pit, hole;" e. g. a-bi a-bólon, „a deep pit."

Bía, v. inch. (rad. bi), „get dark, get black;" e. g. ka-rintr ka bía, „the sky gets dark."

Bía, v. impers. inch. „get dark"; e. g. pa bía, „it gets dark."

Bil, a-, pl. e-, or tra-, n. „canoe"; a-bil a-pólo, „a ship," lit. „a white man's canoe."

Biliṅ, a-, pl. e-, n. „mud-sofa, joined to a wall at the inside of a house, any sofa;" e. g. a-bíliṅ a-bána, „a large mud-sofa."

Bítiṅ, a-, pl. e-, n. „drum"; e. g. o fer am-bítiṅ, „he beats the drum."

Bítra, a-, pl. e-, n. „bottle"; e. g. a-bítra a-tšiṅ, „an empty bottle."

Bō, ka-, pl. tra-, n. „cake, country bread" (as made of rice flour and honey; e. g. ka-bō ka-fíno, „fine country-bread."

Bō, a-, pl. e-, or tra-, or also o- in the sing. and tra- in the pl., n. „a species of antelope of the size of a goat, black, and having long retroverted horns," also called: „bushgoat." Between its horns it has long red hairs.

Bof, ka-, n. „dust" (as in the street); e. g. ka-bof ka-laī, „much dust."

Boī, a-, pl. e-, n. „servant"; e. g. a-boī a-béra, „a maid-servant."

Boīs, adj. „fattened"; e. g. o-nā o-fel o-boīs, „a fattened calf."

Bōk, v. n. „weep, cry, lament;" e. g. ow'ahét o tra bōk, „the child is crying."

Bōk, v. a. „weep for-, bemoan, bewail, lament;" e. g. tra ña ko bōk-ko, „let them go and bewail him."

Bōk, a-, pl. e-, n. „snake, serpent;" e. g. a-bōk a-las, „a bad snake."

Bóka, a-, pl. e-, n. „bill-hook"; e. g. a-bóka a-bána, „a large bill-hook."

Bol, a-, pl. e-, n. „country made pot, earthen pot" (for cooking); e. g. a-bol a-fíno, „a fine earthen pot."

Bol, v. a. „prolong" (as life). See the next word.

Bol aṅ-ñésam, „prolong life, have long life;" e. g. káṅko ma bol aṅ-ñésam! „mayest thou have long life!"

Bólam, o-, pl. a-, n. „one of the Bolom nation, Bolom."

Bóli, adj. „long"; e. g. ra-béña ra-bóli, „a long rope."

Bóli. o-, adj. but used adverbially, „long, a long time; a long way, a far way off, far away;" e. g. o kóne o-bóli, „he went far away."

Bólo, a-, pl. ę-, n. „throat"; e. g. o wop-kọ ro-bólo, „he held him by the throat."

Bom, adj. „female"; e. g. aṅ-fạm a-bom. „the women, the females."

Bom, ọ-, pl. a-, n. „woman, female;" also „mother, madam." For the pl. form a-bom they also use: bom-ńa, placing the prefix behind the noun, which is sometimes done with a few nouns.

Bom, a-, pl. ę-, n. „sheath, scabbard;" e. g. am-bom ńa aṅ-gbáto, „the sheath of the cutlass."

Bọm, v. n. „ease nature, ease oneself; dung;" e. g. o kọ bọm, „he went to ease nature."

Bóma, kạ-, pl. trạ-, n. „grave"; e. g. 'a bęs kạ-bóma, „they dig a grave."

Bomp, ra-, pl. trạ-, n. „head"; also „chapter"; e. g. ra-bomp-r'ọṅ, „his head."

Boṅ, ra-, pl. trạ-, n. „river"; e. g. ra-boṅ' da-bána, „a great river;" for ra-boṅ ra-bána.

Bóna, a-, pl. ę-, or tra-, n. „nation;" e. g. a-bona a-bána, „a great nation."

Bóndo, am-, n. „the Bondo institution;" also „the ceremonies connected with it." See Pref. § 17.

Bọ́ńa, a-, pl. ma-, n. „kindness, favour" (shown and received): „benevolence, grace, mercy;" e. g. o sọ́to ma-bọ́ńa, „he received kindness."

Bọ́nę, v. impers. a. „gladden, rejoice, cheer;" as: pa bọ́nę-kọ, „he is glad." lit. „it gladdens him."

Bọ́nę, v. n. „move"; e. g. ara-rū be ra bọ́nę, „the whole world moves."

Bọ́nę; ma-, n. „joy, gladness, happiness;" e. g. ma-bọ́nę-m'ọṅ, „his gladness."

Bọ́nę-tr'eī, ka-, n. comp. „haughtiness, presumption;" e. g. ka-bọ́nę-tr'eī-k'ọṅ, „his haughtiness."

Bont, ka-, pl. trạ-, n. „navel, navel-string."

Bontr, v. a. „call, name, mention;" e. g. bontr am'ọlọ-ma-tśi, „mention the price of it."

Bontr añ'és ña-, v. comp. „guess", lit. „call the name of-;" e. g. be ɪnạ bontr añ'és ña ar'áka ará yi etc. „if thou doest guess the thing, which is etc."

Bontr w'úni añ'és, „call one by name, call one's name;" e. g. ọ bontr-kọ añ'és, „he called him by his name."

Bọntr, a-, or i-, pl. ma-, n. „smell, scent, odour" (good or bad); e. g. i-bọntr i-fíno, „a good scent."

Bóntra, v. rel. (rad. bontr), „call-for-, mention-," or „name-to-, name-for-" (as the name of an object to one); e. g. bontra-mi añ'és-ñ'ọñ, „mention me his name."

Bóntrạs, v. freq. a. (rad. bontr), „call over" (as names), „name; praise;" e. g. ña bóntrạs am'és-ma-ñañ, „they called over their names."

Bópạr, a-, pl. ẹ-, n. „leaf"; e. g. ẹ-bópạr ẹyé, „these leaves."

Bor, kạ-, pl. trạ-, n. „domestics, people who live under one's control; company;" also „crew" (as of a boat); e. g. ka-bor ka am-bil, „the crew of the canoe." The pl. is used of the domestics of a plurality of masters.

Bọ́rkọ, ọ-, pl. a-, n. „damsel; a young woman" (married or not); e. g. ọ-bọ́rkọ ọ-fíno, „a fair damsel."

Bósne, v. n. „long, have a great desire." Prob. a refl. form of an obs. bos; e. g. ọ bósne tráka ọw'án-k'ọñ, „he longs for his son."

Bósne, a-, pl. e, n. „longing, anxious desire;" e. g. am-bósne-ñ'ọñ, „his longing,"

Bọt, v. n. „get sweet, be sweet, be delicious, be savoury." Short form of bọ́ti. E. g. añ-sạ́ka añé ña bọt he, „this palaver sauce is not savoury." See the Note after wos, v. n.

Bọt, kạ-, n. „sweetness, deliciousness;" e. g. ka-bọt ka ẹ-nak, „the deliciousness of the rice."

Bot, kạ-, pl. trạ-, n. „ball, lump" (as of soap); „pill" (as of medicine); e. g. trạ-bot trạ-sas, „three pills."

Bọ́tạr, v. rel. (rad. bọt), „love, like," lit. „be sweet toward-;" e. g. ọ bọtạr-kọ, „he loves him."

Bọ́tạr, ma-, n. „love"; e. g ma-bọ́tạr ma K'úru, „the love of God."

Bóti, v. n. (rad. bọt), „be sweet, be savoury, be delicious" (as food); e. g. aṅ-sạka añé ña bóti, „this palaver sauce is delicious."

Bóti-di, adj. comp. „delicious to eat;" e. g. y'etr e-bóti-di, „delicious food."

Bóti-sọm, adj. comp. „delicious to devour;" e. g. r'ā ra-bóti-sọm, „something delicious to devour."

Bóti-trạl, ọ-, adj. but used adverbially, „sweetly", lit. „sweet to hear" (applied to singing or music); e. g. aṅ-fẹt añé ña leṅ ọ-bóti-trạl, „these children sing sweetly." See rạ̈mi below.

Botr, v. a. „put, put down, place, set; fix" (as time); e. g. botrñi rayér, „put it aside."

Bótra, v. rel. (rad. botr), „put-for-, place-for-;" e. g. bótra-mi-ri ro-k'úma, „put it in the box for me."

Bótra w'úni a-tónto, „put an allurement" or „enticement for one, put a snare for one;" e. g. 'a bótra-kọ a-tónto, „they put a snare for him."

Bótra w'úni yáñfa, „act deceitfully against one," lit. „put deceitfulness" or „a trick for one;" e. g. o bótra-mi yaṅfa', „he acted deceitfully against me."

Bótrạr, v. rel. (rad. botr), „put-to-, put-at-, set-to-" (as the mind to a person or thing); e. g. bótrạr-ñi am-méra, „set the mind to it," = „take care of it."

Bótrạr am-méra ka—,) „set the mind to-, take care of-, mind,
Bótrạr' am-méra ro-,) set the heart to-;" e. g. ọ bótrạr am-méra rọñóñ, „he takes care of him."

Bótrạr w'úni am-méra, „put the mind to one, take care of one;" e. g. ọ bótrar-mi am-méra: „he takes care of me."

Bóya, v. a. „make a present to-with- or of-, present-with-, make a present with- or of-," as: I bóya-mu-tśi, „I make thee a present of it;" — ọ bóya-mi ọw'ír, „he made me a present with the goat;" — ọ bóya-kọ ka Pā Sip, „he made the Leopard a present of him."

Bóya, a-, pl. e-, n. „present, gift;" e. g. a-bóya a-fíno, „a fine present."

Búkọ, v. n. „bathe, wash oneself;" e. g. I kọ búkọ, „I go to bathe."

Búma, a-, pl. ẹ-, n. „young tender shoots," or „leaves" (as from roots left in the ground), „verdure, herb, green;" e. g. ẹ-búma ẹ-laī ẹ yi ri, „there is much green there."

Búmar. v. rel. (rad. bum), „watch over, mind, guard, take care of;" e. g. ọ búmar ak'ọ́r, „he watches over the farm."

Bun, v. n. and aux. „miss, make a mistake." As an aux. it serves to express the adv. „almost, nearly," as: o bun kọ dif, „he almost killed him."

Bun, kạ-, n. verb. „act of missing, mistake;" kạ-bun fi, „almost dying."

Búndạs, v. caus. (rad. búnda), „make large, enlarge, make great;" fig. „magnify, glorify;" e. g ọ búndạs an-set-ň'ọň, „he enlarged his house."

Bunt, a-, pl. ẹ-, n. „cloud"; e. g. a-bunt a-bi, „a dark cloud."

Búrạp, adj. „short"; e. g k'ạntr kạ-búrạp, „a short stick."

But, kạ-, pl. trạ-, n. „heart" (as the organ; also used figuratively as the seat of courage, etc.); e. g. ka-but-k'ọň, „his heart."

Bútu, a-, pl. ẹ-, n. „bag"; also „pillow"; e. g. a-bútu a-yọ́fạt, „a soft pillow."

D.

D', pref. insep. and indef. „a, an;" e. g. d'im, „a word," for da-im.

Da, prep. poss. „of"; it is a euph. form of: ra; e. g. ar'ón'-dasu, „our road;" -ar'ón' da K'úru, „the way of God." See the Note at the end of this letter.

Da, pref. indef., euph. form of ra, „a an;" e. g. r'on' da-fíno, „a good road."

Da-tši, pr. dem. log. „that", being a euph. form of: ra-tši; e. g. ar'ón' da-tši, „that road."

Dáta, postp. „below, beneath," being a euph. form of. ráta; e. g. ro-tạn' dáta, „under the root," for ro-tạnk ráta. This form is used after nouns terminating in ň, or ňk, when the g or gk is cut off.

Datróṅ, postp., euph. form of ratróṅ, „in the middle, amongst."
It is used after nouns terminating in ṅ, when the g is cut
off. E. g. ọ tráma ka ar'óṅ' datróṅ, „he stood in the middle
of the road;" — ka tra-tšen' datróṅ, „amongst the hills."

Dayér, postp., euph. form of rayér, „near, close to, at" or „by
the side;" e. g. ọ tas ka 'ra-bon' dayér, -- ọ tas ro-bon'
dayér, „he passed close to the river;" — ọ tas ro-r'on' dayér,
„he passed by the side of the road." It is used after nouns
terminating in ṅ, when the g is cut off. See the Note at
the end of this letter.

De, or re, = der, v. n. and aux. „come"; e. g. ọ de he naṅ,
„he did not come." As an aux. it is construed with the
long and with the short form of the Infinitive. De is a euph.
form of: re, which see; e. g. ọ de tra gbal, „he comes in
order to write." See more under the form re; what has
been stated there, applies also here.

De, adv. „no". It is pronounced with a strong impetus. E. g.
de, 1 naṅk fẹ ko, „no, I did not see him."

De, conj. „and"; e. g. pa-lā de e-yóka, „rice and cassadas."

Der, v. n. and aux. = de, or: re, „come"; e. g. o der romí,
„he came to me." It is construed in the same way as:
de, which see.

Der, ka-, n. verb. „act of coming, coming;" e. g. ka-der-k'oṅ,
„his coming."

D'er, pl. s'er, n. „face"; ro-d'er, „at the face."

Der, a-, or i-, pl. ma-, n. „body, skin." The sing. is seldom
used, the pl. being used for it; e. g. ma-der-m'oṅ, „his body."

D'er, n. „place"; def. form: od'ér, „the place;" e. g. d'er ọ-
fíno, „a good place."

D'er ó d'er, „everywhere, anywhere;" e. g. K'úru o yi d'er
ó d'er, „God is everywhere."

Di, v. a. „eat", also „take" (as medicine); „wear away, wear
off" (as a cutlass a grinding-stone); e. g. ọ di e-trol, „he
took medicine."

Di, v. n. „eat"; e. g. di ri, „eat of it," lit. „eat there;" di ka-,
„eat out of-."

Di, adj. „eating"; e. g. r'a ra-di, „something to eat."

Di, kạ-, n. verb. „act of eating, an eating, meal;" e. g. kạ-di kạ-bạl, „a breakfast."

Di, pr. obj. = ri, of which it is a euph. form, „it"; e. g. tśē gbon'-di, „do not touch it." See the Note at the end of this letter.

Di, adv. loc. „there". It is a euph. form of ri, used before n and before ñ, when the g is dropped. E. g o wọn di, „he was long there."

Día, pr. emph. „it, this," being a euph. form of: ría; e. g. ar'ón' da ro-Ma-lal día-rē, „this is the road to Malal."

Dí-a, adv. loc. emph. „there"; e. g. ro añ-gbálañ ña gbópẹ, dí-a o botr ara-bomp-r'ọñ, „where the rock was rugged, there he put his head;" — dí-a o sọ́tọ-ñi, „there he got it."

Dí-añ, adv. loc. abs. „there, at that place." it is a euph. form of: rí-añ; e. g. dí-añ I sọ́tọ-ñi, „there I got it." (Cf. -ñ under N.)

Dif, v. n. „kill, commit murder;" also „kill beef; be fatal" (as an illness); e. g. o poñ dif-i? „has he killed beef?"

Dif, v. a. „kill, execute, murder;" also „prove fatal to" (as a sickness); e. g. 'a dif-kọ, „they killed him."

Difa, v. rel. „kill-to-, kill-for-; kill-with-;" e. g. o dífa-mi añtrọ́kọ, „he killed the fowl to me," = „he killed me the fowl."

Dim, v. a. „destroy, ruin;" e. g. 'a dim aka-petr, „they destroyed the town."

D'im, pl. s'im, n. „word, voice;" e. g. ad'ím-r'ọñ, „his word;" D'im is a euph. form of: r'im.

Dímśẹ, v. n. „go out" (as fire); e. g. an'ántr na dímśẹ, „the fire went out."

D'in, adj. num. „one", being a euph. form of r'in; e. g. r'on' d'in, „one way."

Dinnẹ, v. refl. (rad. dim) „perish, get lost," lit. „destroy oneself;" e. g. ka-lómẹ o dinnẹ, „the sheep got lost."

Dinnẹ, kạ-, n. verb. „act of perishing, perishing; destruction, ruin, perdition;" e. g. ka-dinnẹ-k'ọñ, „his perdition."

Dío, adj. „right" (in opposition to left); e. g. ka-trä ka̱-dío, „the right hand."

Dío, ka-, n. „the right" (hand); also „the South."

Dir, ka-, pl. tra̱-, n. „mortar" (as to beat rice in); e. g. ka̱-dir ka̱-bána, „a large mortar."

Díra, v. n. „sleep, go asleep;" e. g. ña ko̱ díra, „they went to sleep."

Dis, adv. „yesterday": e. g. o der dis, „he came yesterday."

Dís, v. caus. (rad. di), „give-to eat, feed;" e. g. e-bamp ña dis añ-fet-'a-ñañ, „the birds feed their young ones."

Dis ra-foi, „yesterday evening, last evening;" e. g. o bĕk dis ra-foi, „he arrived last evening."

Dis tratrák, „yesterday night," e. g. ña der dis tratrák, „they came yesterday night."

Do-, prep. „into, in, at, to, from;" e. g. o won' do-set, „he went into the house." It is a euph. form of ro-, which see.

Dokóm, postp., euph. form of rokóm, „on the top, upon;" e. g. o yi ro-tšen' dokóm, „he is on the top of the hill;" — o yíra ka añ-ron' dokóm, „he lives on the top of the mountain." See the Note at the end of this letter.

D'oñ, pr. poss. „his, her." It is a euph. form of r'oñ; e. g. ra-ban'-d'oñ, „his anger."

D'or, n. „hunger"; def. form ad'ór, „the hunger." It is a noun in ra-; e. g. d'or ra bā-mi, „I am hungry;" lit. „hunger has me."

D'úba, n. „ink", = r'úba; e. g. d'úba ra-lai, „much ink;" def. form: ad'úba, „the ink "

Dúni, adj. „male", it is a euph. form of: r'úni; e. g. w'an dúni, „a boy," lit. „a male child."

Note. The euph. forms with d under the preceding letter are used after words terminating in ñ, when the g is dropped, as: r'oñ' da-fíno, „a good road," for: r'oñ ra-fíno; — ar'óñ' da-tši, „that road," for: ar'óñ ra-tši.

E.

E-, pref. def. and indef. „the"; e. g. e-tis, „knives", or „the knives."

E, pr. subj. „it; they;" e. g. ey'étr-'e-mi e dínne, my things are lost."

E-, pref. emph. vow. to make nouns with the inseparable pref. y' definite, as: ey'étr. „the things," from: y'etr, „things". Cf. Pref. § 22. b.

-E? suff. indirect inter. used at the end of a proposition, if already an inter. adverb precedes; e. g. re mań ko-e? „where art thou going to?"

-E, part. expl. often used at the end of conditional propositions. It is of a mere expl. nature, used with sentences depending on the conj. be, „if", and on the adv. ma, me, mo, „when", and on: be, „when"; e. g. be o-béra o nésa he o-wosk'oń-e etc., „if the woman does not respect her husband etc." But it is also used with nouns not only in the Voc. case, but also otherwise. Sometimes it is added to the suffix-ań in addition. (Cf. the suff. -ań in loco.) It is also sometimes affixed to adverbs, or at the end of exclamatory pro positions depending on: tro! „how!" or ko! „what!" or after the calling of names, when it serves to indicate the Vocative. They also often use it with obligative and participial propositions.

-E, this form is sometimes used for the preceding one in the capacity of an expletive particle.

'E, prep. poss. „of"; e. g. ey'étr-'e-mi, „my things," lit. „the things of me."

'E-mi, pr. poss. „my", lit. „of me." See the preceding word.

'E-ńań, pr. poss. „their", lit. „of them;" e. g. ey'étr-'e-ńań, „their things."

Eyáń, pr. dem. rem. „those"; e. g. ey'étr eyáń, „those things."

Eyé, pr. rel „which"; e. g. ey'étr eyé I sóto, „the things which I got."

Eyë, pr. dem. prox. „these"; e. g. ey'étr eyé, „these things."

F.

Fai, v. n. „be hot, have a burn, be burned;" e. g. I fai ro-trä, „I have a burn on the hand."

Fai, adj. „hot" (as water); „burnt" (as a farm); e. g. m'antr ma-fai, „hot water."

Fai, v. a. „cut one's throat, kill, slaughter, butcher;" e. g. 'a fai-ko, „they cut his throat."

Fak, a-, pl. e-, n. „skate" (fish).

Fak, v. a. „throw down; fell" (as a tree); also „set up" (as a krifi for worship); e. g. o fak an-tis-'a-mi, „he threw down my knife."

Fáka, v. rel. „throw-to-, throw-unto-, throw-for-, let drop-" or „fall-for-" (as a child, or a thing to one); e. g. fáka-mi ka-bō, „throw the bread to me."

Fálañ, v. n. „escape from the grave by a sort of transmigration." (see Pref. § 10. b.). Also „apostatize" (from a religion), „err from the right way" (in the Mohammedan sense of the word); fig. „be utterly disappointed in obtaining one's object;" e. g. o fálañ ka 'ra-móri, „he apostatized from Islamism."

Fále, v. n. (rad. fal), „turn, turn away; be turned away;" e. g. o fále roñgñ, „he turned away from him."

Fáli, v. a. „turn, move away, turn aside, remove, shove aside;" e. g. fáli ak'án'r, „turn the stick aside."

Fálir, v. n. „fly"; e. g. am-bamp o fálir o-bóli rokóm, „the bird soars high up."

Fálira, v. caus. „make to fly about, waft about, drive about" (as the wind chaff); e. g. añ-fef na fálira e-fuk, „the wind wafts the chaff about."

Fam, a-, n. the pl. of w'úni, „person", which see. The sing. form o-fam, is not much used; e. g. añ-fam añé, „these persons," = „this people."

Fam a-rúni, a-, n. pl. „males, men;" lit. „male persons."

Fam a-bom, a-, n. pl. „females, women," lit. „female persons."

Fánta, v. n. „lie down;" e. g. o ko fánta, „he went to lie down."

Fant'r (for fántar), ka-, pl. tra-, n. „bed"; e. g. ka-fant'r-k'oñ, „his bed."

Far-far, prob. adj. onom. „making far-far." See Proverb. 6, pag. 99 about this word.

Fárki, v. a. „despise, slight, set at nought; degrade;" e. g. o fárki-ko, „he slighted him."

Fas, adv. spec. „on a sudden, suddenly, all at once, at once" (as if a thing, on which one pulls, gives way at once, or is torn off). It indicates quickness or suddenness of separation, and is used with wúra, „take" or „pull out," and with gbǫ́ti, „tear off;" e. g. o wúra-ki ka ka-trā-k'ǫṅ fas, „he pulled it (cloth) out of his hand on a sudden."

Fatr, a-, pl. e-, n. „iron"; also „an iron cooking pot."

Fatr, v. n. „be near, be close; come near, go near;" e. g. tsē ri fatr. „do not go near there."

Fatr, v. a. „go near to, come near to, approach, be close" or „near to;" e. g. o fatr-mi, „he is close to me."

Fátrane, v. recipr. „come near together, come close to each other, approach each other;" e. g. ma fátrane naṅ, „let us come near together."

Fátrane, o-, pl. a-, n. „neighbour, one living close to another;" e. g. o-fátrane-ka-mi, „my neighbour."

Fátrar, v. rel. n. „draw near;" e. g. ra-fi ra fátrar, „death draws near." The suff. is rather redundant here.

Fátrar, v. rel. a. „draw near to, approach, be near to;" e. g. fátrar-mi, „draw near to me."

Fe, = he, adv. „not"; e. g. w'úni ó w'úni o naṃ fe tši, „no one saw it." This form is generally used after or before the letter m. Fe is to be considered as a euph. form of: he, which see below.

Fef, a-, pl. e-, n. „wind, breeze;" e. g. aṅ-fef ṅa feṅ o-báki ténoṅ, „the wind blows strongly to day."

Féla, a-, pl. e-, n. „desire, longing, lust;" also „sexual desire" or „desire for sexual commerce;" e. g. a-féla ṅa e-lop ṅa wop-mi, „I have a desire for fish," lit. „a desire of fish holds me."

Feṅ, v. a. „blow, play" (as a wind-instrument); blow-on-, blow-into-;" e. g. o feṅ aka-sū, „he blew the trumpet;" — 'a feṅ-ko e-kul, „they blew into his nostrils."

Feṅ, v. n. „blow" (as the wind, or into some thing); e. g. o feṅ ka e-kul-y'ǫń, „he blew into his nostrils. Cf. also the ex. under a-fef above.

Fer, v. n. „play on a stringed instrument, make music;" e. g. o-láńba o trạ fer, „the young man is playing on a stringed instrument."

Fer, v. a. „play, strike" (as a stringed instrument); „beat" (as the drum); e. g. ọ-yéli owé o fer am-páńkal ọ-fino, „this minstrel plays the cithern well;" — o-láńba o fer am-bítiń, „the young man beats the drum."

Féra, adj. „white, clean;" as applied to rice „deprived of the husks;" e. g. pa-la pạ-féra, „clean rice."

Fet, v. n. „be young; be tender" (as roots); „be fresh" (as palm-wine); „be new" (as the moon); e. g. o fet rạs, „he is still young."

Fet, adj. „young; tender" (as plants); e. g. e-yóka e-fet, „tender" or „young cassadas."

Fet, a-, pl. of w'ahét, which see. The sing. o-fet, is sometimes used.

Fétạr, v. rel. (rad. fet), „make white, make clean" (as rice, or clothes); „clear up, make plain" (as a palaver); „cleanse, whitewash" (as a wall); „make to blush." (The natives being of a dark colour get a whitish appearance when made to blush. Thus if one is convinced of his guilt, after having denied it, by clear facts, and if those present scold him for it, he will blush). With am-méra, „clear one of a charge, justify." (Cf. next word). E. g. o fétar am-pa, „he cleared up the matter;" — 'a fétar-ko ténoń, „they made him blush to day."

Fétạr am-méra ńa w'úni, } „clear one of a charge, declare one's
Fétạr w'úni am-méra,   } innocence, acquit one, justify one."
lit. „make clean one's heart;" e. g. 'a fétar-ko am-méra ténoń, „they cleared him of the charge to day."

Fi, v. n. „die, be dead;" as applied to the phases of the moon, „be done" or „over, die away, be in the last quarter"; hence also „be new"; e. g. o fi ar'óń' da-fino, „he died happily," lit. „he died the good road;" — be ań'óf ńa fi, „when the moon is over."

Fi o-tot, „die happily, „lit. „die well."

Fi. adj. „dead", as applied to the moon „dying away, being in the last quarter. new;" e. g. w'úni fi, „a dead person."

Fi, ka-, n. verb. „act of dying"; also „mortality"; e. g. ka-fi ka w'úni, „the mortality of man."

Fi, ra-, pl. tra-, n. „death"; sometimes the abstract stands for the concrete „a dead one)"; e. g. ra-fi-r'oṅ, „his death."

Fi, a-, pl. e-, n. „loin, hip" (also used of the meat of an animal slaughtered); e. g. 'a soṅ-ko a-fi, „they gave him one of the loins."

Fino, v. n. „be good" (morally and physically); „be fair, be beautiful, be lovely, be fine" (as a child); „be kind, be pious; be even, be smooth" (as a rock); e. g. aṅ-yal ańé ṅa fíno. „this boat is fine."

Fino, adj. „good" (morally and physically); „fair, beautiful, fine; pious; smooth" (as a rock or stone); applied to condition „happy"; also „kind" (as a word, or a person); e. g. a-fam a-fino, „good people;" — r'im ra-fíno, „a kind word."

Fino, o-, adj. but used adverbially „well, kindly;" e. g. o yó-mi o-fíno, „he treated me well."

Firdaus, n „paradise". From the Ar. فِرْدَوْس, beatorum sedes, paradisus.

Fisa. adj. „better". See an ex. pag. 127.

Fit, ma-, n. „brains, brain;" also „marrow" (of bones).

Fita, v. a. „cast away, throw away, throw, fling;" e. g. w'an, tsè ri fíta, „boy, do not throw it away."

Fita, v. rel. „throw-away for-;" e. g. fíta-mi am-bítra ańé, „throw this bottle away for me," == „throw me this bottle away."

Fo, conj. „that", == ho; often used before direct and indirect speech, and frequently answering to the Gr. ὅτι. It may often be given by „saying" in direct speech, and by „that" with indirect speech. It is probably the verb. adjective from fo, „say". E. g. ma yéma fo I ták'sa-mu-i? „doest thou want me to teach thee?" lit. „doest thou want that I teach thee?"

Fǫ, v. n. „say," = hǫ. It is generally followed by yē, which seems to be the dem. pr. for eyē, „these" (words); in the 1st. person sing. the pers. verbal pronoun is often, or generally dropped. When followed by yē, it is generally used as an introductory phrase to arrest the attention of the one, to whom one wants to say something. E. g. fǫ yē, mań kǫnę ro-Kamp anínań, „I say, let us go to Sierra-Leone to morrow," for: I fǫ yē etc., lit. „I say these (words) etc.;" — I fǫ yē, w'an etc., „I say, boy etc.;" — o fǫ yē, o gbáli he der, „he says he cannot come." Fǫ alone, or also: fǫ yē may be used with direct and indirect speech, as: o fǫ: Mań kǫnę nína bat, „he said: Let us go to morrow morning." or: o fǫ yē: Mań kǫnę etc., „he said: Let us go etc.," lit. „he said these (words): etc."

Fǫ, adj. verb. — hǫ, „saying". See fǫ, conj.

Fǫ yē, = hǫ yē, see fǫ. v. n.

Fǫf, v. n. „speak, talk;" e. g. I kǫ fǫf rońáń, „I go speak to them;" — o gbáli he fǫf, „he cannot speak."

Fǫf, ka-, pl. tra-, n. „speech, word;" in the sing. „act of speaking;" e. g. ka-fǫf-k'oń, „his speaking."

Fǫf d'im r'in, „make an agreement" or „treaty," lit. „speak one word;" e. g. ńa fǫf d'im r'in tráka tši, „they made an agreement about it."

Fǫ́far, v. rel. (rad. fǫf), „speak to, address, speak with, reason with, warn;" e. g. I tši fǫ́far-ko, „I shall speak to him."

Fǫ́far, ka-, pl. tra-, n. verb. „act of addressing (one); address;" e. g. ka-fǫ́far-k'oń ań-fam, „his addressing the people."

Foi, ra-, pl. tra-, n. „evening"; e. g. ra-foi ra poń bēk, „evening has arrived."

Foi-kára, v. n. comp. „be easy to bring" or „to bring away;" e. g. ow'úni owé o foi-he-kára, „this person is not easy to bring away."

Foi-tas, v. impers. comp. „be easy to pass;" e. g. pa foi ri tas, „it will be easy to pass there;" — o foi ri tas, „it is (was) easy to pass there."

Foi-tr'ei, v. n. comp. „be of such a character as to be easy to deal with, be of a sociable character. be good-natured; be well off;" also „make joke" or „jest of a thing, jest," or „joke about a thing;" as: mạ foῑ he tr'eῑ. „thou doest not joke about a thing;" also „be convenient" (as time).

Foῑ-tr'eῑ, adj. „sociable, good-natured; convenient, seasonable" (as time); „easy, happy;" e. g. a-lókọ a-foῑ-tr'eῑ, „a convenient time;" — w'úni foῑ-tr'eῑ, „a person well off."

Foῑ w'úni tr'eῑ, v impers. a. „be easy for-, be well with-" = „be comfortable, be happy, be well off;" e. g. pạ foῑ-kọ-tr'eῑ, „it is getting better with him," = „he is getting well off;" — ọ foῑ-ko-tr'eῑ, „he is comfortable," lit. „it is well with him."

Foir, a-, pl. ẹ-, or trạ-, n. „shadow, shade, shelter" (as of a tree); e. g. ań'ạntr ńa yer-su a-foῑr, „the tree gives us shelter."

Fọk, a-, pl. ẹ-, n. „parcel, any thing wrapped up in the form of a parcel;" e. g. a-fọk ńa m'er, „a parcel of salt."

Fókia, v. revert. and rel. (rad. fọk), „unwrap-for-; bark-for-, take off-for-" (as the cover of a parcel for another); e. g. fókia-mi ań'ạntr ańé, „bark this tree for me."

Fon. ra-, pl. a-, n. „hair"; e. g. ań-fon-ń'ọń, „his hair."

Fọr, ra-, pl. ẹ-, n. „eye"; e. g. ẹ-fọr 'ẹ-su, „our eyes."

Fósa, a-, n. „power, influence, might, ability;" e. g. ọ bā he ri a-fósa, „he has no influence there." = „he is not able to do any thing there."

Fot. adj. „addle, barren" (as an egg); „empty" (as a box, or as the stomach); e. g. ra-mẹs ra-fot, „an addle egg."

Fótane, v. refl. „rest oneself, rest, repose;" e. g. I kọ fótane ọ-tan, „I go to rest a little." Prob. from an obs. fóta.

Fótane, ọ-, n. loc. „resting place, place of repose;" e. g. ọ-fótane-'ọ-mi, „my resting-place."

Fu, adj. „new"; e. g. k'óta kạ-fu, „new cloth."

Fuk, ẹ-, n. „chaff" (as of rough rice when beaten in a mortar). That which comes off in threshing or flogging rice (as they say) is called: ẹ-gbáfta.

Fúmpọ, v. n. „fall down, fall;" e. g. ọ fúmpọ ri, „he fell down there."

Fúmpọ káši, „become liable to a fine or penalty, become guilty of a breach of the country law."

Fuṅk, a-, pl. ẹ-, or trạ-, n. „store-house" (for grain or for agricultural productions). „barn"; e. g. a-fuṅk a-bána, „a large store-house."

Fúnti, a-, pl. ẹ-, n. „prisoner of war, captive."

Fúnti, ra-, n. „captivity"; e. g. ra-fúnti-ra-ñaṅ, „their captivity."

Fúti, v. n. „escape, be saved;" e. g. ọ fúti ri, „he was saved there."

Fúti, kạ-, n. verb. „act of escaping, escape, deliverance, salvation;" e. g. ka-fúti-ka-su, „our salvation."

Fútia, v. caus. „make to escape, save;" e. g. kọ́no fútia-mi, „he saved me."

Fútia, adj. „saving"; e. g. ar'óṅ' da-fútia, „the saving way," i. e. „the way by which one is saved."

Fútia, ọ-, pl. a-, n. „saviour"; e. g. ọ-fútia-ka-mi, „my Saviour."

Fútia, kạ-, n. verb. „act of saving, a saving;" e. g. ka-fútia-ko, „the act of saving him," = „his deliverance."

G.

Gba, adv. „very, indeed, much, well;" e. g. pa bóne-mi ténọñ gba, „I am very glad to day;" — a, K'úru o bọ́tar-su gba! „oh, God loves us much!"

Gbā, kạ-, pl. trạ-, n. „score, twenty;" e. g. trạ-gba tra-rañ, „two scores," = „forty"; — tra-gbā tra-sas, „three scores," = „sixty."

Gbaī, v. a. „split" (as wood); „burst, open" (as a nut); „tear" (as cloth); fig. „impart" (as instruction); „interpret" (as dreams); e. g. o gbai ak'óta, „he tore the cloth."

Gbaía, v. rel. „split-for-; tear-to- or for-; open-for-;" fig. „impart-to-;" o gbaía-mi ak'óta, „he tore the cloth to me," = „he tore me the cloth."

Gbaīr, v. rel. (rad. gbaı), „impart-to-, give-to-" (as instruction), lit. as it were „tear off-towards-." See the next word.

Gbaía w'úni kạ-wándi, ⎱ „impart instruction to one, preach to
Gbaīr w'úni ka-wándi, ⎰ one;" e. g. o gbaīr-ko kạ-wándi, „he gave him instruction."

Gbak, ma-, n. „rust"; e. g. añ-faĩr ña bã ma-gbak, „the iron is rusty," lit. „the iron has rust."

Gbak, v. a. „cut" (as wood); cut off, decide, settle" (as a matter), „determine"; e. g. ọ gbak ak'ạ̃ntr, „he cut the stick."

Gbak, v. n. „cut; judge, give an opinion."

Gbạ́ka, v. a. „cut; decide, judge" (as a matter); „rule over, govern;" e. g. kánẹ mọ gbạ́ka an-tọ́f añé-e? „who is governing this country?"

Gbạ́ka, ka-, n. verb. „act of governing" or „of ruling, reign, government;" e. g. kánẹ bã ka-gbạ́ka ka an-tọ́f-e? „who has the government of the country?"

Gbáka, ra-, n. „office of governing (a country); government;" e. g. kánẹ bã 'ra-gbạ́ka ra an-tọ́f-e? „who has the government of the country now?"

Gbákanẹ, v. recipr. „vie" or „contend with each other;" e. g. 'a gbákanẹ ka ka-lạm ma-sar, „they vied with each other in throwing stones;" — 'a gbákanẹ ka gbúkẹ, „they vie with each other in running," = „they ran a race."

Gbal, v. a. „write; make a sketch of, sketch;" e. g. ọ gbal a-réka, „he wrote a letter."

Gbal, v. n. „write; make a sketch; e. g. ọ gbal ọ-fíno, „he writes well."

Gbal, ka-, n. verb. „act of writing, writing;" e. g. I nạñk ka-gbal-k'ọñ añ-réka, „I saw his writing the letter," = „I saw him writing the letter."

Gbal, a-, or i-, pl. ma-, n. „line, letter, character" (as of a book): pl. also „writing"; e. g. ma-gbal ma-fíno, „good writing." Also „sketch; mark."

Gbála, adj. rel. „belonging to writing;" e. g. k'úpọ kạ-gbála, „a pen," lit. „a feather to write with."

Gbálañ, a-, pl. ẹ-, n. „rock, rocky place;" e. g. a-gbálañ a-bána, „a large rock."

Gbálap, v. n. „twinkle with the eyes, twinkle;" e. g. ọ́ trạ gbálap, „he is twinkling with the eyes."

Gbạ́li, v. n. „be able, can." Often used as an aux. to express an ability for the exercise of the energy, indicated by the principal verb, as: o gbáli he yō-tŝi, = o gbáli he tŝi yō, „he cannot do it." It is generally construed with the short form of the Infinitive, sometimes also with the long one.

Gbáli, v. a. „be able for-;" e. g. o gbáli-tŝi, „he is able for it."

Gbam, v. a. „beat, pound, bruise to powder" (as in a mortar); e. g. gbam apa-la, „pound the rice."

Gbań, a-, pl. tra-, n. „dry land" (as opposed to the sea); „country;" e. g. ro-gbań, „in the country" (in opposition to the city).

Gbań, adv. spec. „very, well, closely;" it is used with bákar, „firm, strong, fast," and with wópane, „hold together, be united together;" e. g. ak'ántr ka tráma bákar gbań, „the post stands very fast."

Gbań, v. a. „lay across" (as a bridge); „meet; oppose, prevent, obstruct" (as a road); „waylay"; e. g. 'a gbań-ko ro-r'oń, „they waylaid him in the road."

Gbáńane, v. recipr. „meet each other;" e. g. I tr'a he ro sa ma gbáńane, „I d'ont know where me may meet each other."

Gbánne, v. refl. a. (rad. gbań), „meet with, meet;" also „lay across oneself," hence „carry on the shoulder;" e. g. o gbánne ak'ántr, „he carried the stick on the shoulder;" — o gbánne-ko ro-r'oń, „he met with him in the road."

Gbánne, v. refl. n. „meet, meet together, assemble;" e. g. 'a gbanne ro-r'oń, „they meet in the road."

Gbánne, a-, pl. e-, n. „meeting, assembly;" e. g. ań-gbanne ńa ań-fam, „the meeting of the people."

Gbań's, v. caus. „go to meet;" e. g. o gbań's Pa Sóri, „he went to meet Mr. Sori."

Gbáń'sane, v. caus. rel. and recipr., „surround, enclose, besiege" (as a town, or army). lit. „make to meet each other around-," or „for-", or „against-"; e. g. mań gbáń'sane-ko nań, „let us surround him."

Gbánta, v. a. „slap, strike, knock; flog, whip; toss" (as waves a canoe); e. g. o gbánta-mi ka a-kos-'a-mi, „he slapped me on one of my cheeks."

Gbántań, a-, pl. e-, n. „porch, piazza;" e. g. o tráma ro-gbántań, „he stood in the piazza."

Gbántaṇe, adj. refl. „spreading itself, making itself known, diffusing itself;" also „making known, advertising;" e. g. w'úni gbántaṇe tr'eï, „a person advertising a matter," or „a person making known a matter." Prob. from an obs. gbant.

Gbánṭe, adj. „different, various, diverse;" e. g. ẹ-bamp ẹ-gbánṭe, „various birds."

Gbántrani, a-, pl. e-, n. „outskirts" or „boundary of a farm where it borders on the bush" or „forest"; e. g. ọ yọ̄ ma-mant ro-gbántrani, „he does work at the outskirts of the farm."

Gbápṇe, v. refl. (rad. gbap), „fasten itself, fix itself, adhere;" e. g. ma-kíma ma gbápṇe ka ẹ-kos-y'oṅ, „soot adheres to his cheeks."

Gbáp'sa, v. freq. and inch. a. „get fastened to, adhere to, stick to; keep close to, attend to;" e. g. w'an, gbáp'sa-mi rayẹr, „boy, keep close to my side."

Gbáraṅ, adv. „clearly, plainly, well, fully;" e. g. ọ káṇe-kọ-tši gbáraṅ, „he told it plainly to him."

Gbáski, v. a. „separate, part, divorce; divide; distinguish;" e. g. gbáski atra-lómẹ ka atš'ír, „separate the sheep from the goats."

Gbáta, a-, pl. e, n. „mat"; e. g. a-gbáta a-lọl, „a small mat."

Gbáti, v. n. „be numerous, be many, be plentiful; e. g. pạ-lä pạ gbáti ri, „rice is plentiful there."

Gbáti, adj. „many, numerus, much;" e. g. ẹ-lop ẹ-gbáti, „many fish."

Gbátọ, a-, pl. ẹ-, n. „cutlass, sword;" e. g. aṅ-gbátọ-ṅ'oṅ, „his cutlass."

Gbạtr, v. a. „set" (as a trap); „waylay, lie in ambush for-, set a trap for-;" e. g. ọ gbạtr ọ-šem, „he set a trap for the animal;" — ọ gbạtr-mi ro-r'oṅ, „he lay in ambush for me in the road."

Gbatr, v. a. „knock, tap sharply" (as on a door, or on one's head); „strike" (as a bell); „sting" (used of the cerastes); e. g. ọ gbatr-mi, „he knocked me;" — ọ gbatr aka-rárẹ, „he knocked on the door."

Gbạ́trọ, v. n. „be round about;" e. g. ña gbạ́trọ ro-pẹtr bẹ, „they were all round the town."

Gbéleṅ, a-, pl. ẹ, n. „bell; hour;" e. g. pạ yi gbo aṅ-gbéleṅ ña aṅ-réï aṅá béka ẹ-sas, „it is but the 3d. hour of the day."

Gbeṅ, adv. „indeed, very, verily, just, exactly." It has often the sense of the adj. „own" without a prefix. E. g. o lópra to gbeṅ, „he is now dressed indeed;" — aṅ-lo ṅa-tśi gbeṅ, „that very time;" — ow'áṅ-ka-mi gbeṅ, „my own child."

Gbéṅa, v. a. „hate"; e. g. o gbéṅa-mi, „he hates me."

Gbéṅa, ką-, n. verb. „act of hating, hatred;" e. g. o gbéṅa-ko ką-gbéṅa ką-bána, „he hates him very much," lit. „he hates him (with) a great hatred."

Gbéṅa, ma-, n. „hatred;" e. g. ma-gbéṅa amá o gbéṅa-mi, ma etc., „the hatred with which he hates me, it etc."

Gbéṅbe, ką-, pl. tra-, n. „pepper of any kind;" e. g. ką-gbéṅbe ką-yim, „red pepper, cayenne."

Gbéṅgbeṅ, v. a. „question, examine by questioning, inquire into by questioning, examine;" e. g. I tśi gbéṅgbeṅ-ko tráka tśi, „I shall question him about it."

Gbépar, v. rel. n. (rad. gbep), „rise, go up on the top, reach the top" or „zenith, reach the highest point, reach the meridian", (as the sun); e. g. ar'étr ra poṅ gbépar, „the sun has reached the meridian;" — ra-yóla-r'oṅ ra gbépar, „his gentleman-ship has reached the highest point (its zenith);" — ka-bóne-tr'ei-k'oṅ ka pon' to gbépar, „his presumption had now reached the highest degree." It is sometimes followed by rokóm, „on top," as: o poṅ gbépar rokóm, „he has reached the top."

Gbépar, v. rel. a. (rad. gbep), go on the top of-;" fig. „reach" or „rise to the rank of-;" e. g. o gbépar ra-yóla, „he rose to the rank of a gentleman;" — o gbépar aṅ-set, „he went on the top of the house."

Gbépar 'ra-bomp ratróṅ, „rise to" or „reach the zenith" or „meridian" (as the sun at noon), lit. „rise to the very middle of the head;" e. g. ma ar'étr ra gbépar 'ra-bomp ratróṅ etc., „when the sun reached the meridian etc."

Gbép'trane, v. recipr. (rad. gbep), „join together, be close together, be near to each other;" e. g. ma yíra są gbép'trane, „let us sit close together," lit. „let us sit we are close together."

Gbéra, a-, n. „flour" (as made of rice); e. g. a-gbéra a-laī, „much rice-flour."

Gbes, adv. „all night, the whole night;" e. g nánañ gbes, „all last night."

Gbétgbëtne, v. refl. „recline" or „sit down with the legs close together" (as the Temnes do at their meals), „sit down with legs put on each other," = the Gr. ἀνακλίνομαι or ἀνάκειμαι; or = the Lat. accumbere; hence „sit down" or „recline to a meal." This form is used of old people and of women. Gbátgbätne, or gbátigbätine is „to recline" or „sit down in an improper" or „indecent manner, with the legs stretched out far from each other" or „astride, so as to offend chastity." Those who do so are said not to like others to eat with them. This latter form is used of men only. E. g. o-baī o woñ tráka kǫ́li aná poñ gbétgbëtne ka añ-fánta ńa ka-nántra, „the king went in to see those who had sat down to the marriage feast;" — but: w'an, tšē gbátgbätne, „boy, do not sit down astride."

Gbetr, adv. „middlingly, just right, just, good, well; quite, fully; accurately, minutely;" e. g. o wañ gbo gbetr ténon, „it is but partially clear to day;" — I yif-kǫ-tši gbetr, „I asked him minutely about it."

Gbetr, adj. „middling, right, just right, good, accurate; e. g. mapant ma-gbetr, „accurate work;" r'ä ra-gbetr, „a thing just right."

Gbip, v. a. „catch, capture, make-prisoner;" e. g. o gbip antrǫ́ko, „he caught the fowl."

Gbípa, v. rel. „catch-for-, capture-for-;" e. g. gbípa-mi an-trǫ́ko, „catch the fowl for me," = „catch me the fowl."

Gbo, adv. „only, but, just; quite; then." With a verb it often expresses the words „as soon as." E. g. I ngń'-ko gbo win, „I saw him but once;" — be I poñ gbo-e, I tši der, „as soon as I have done, I shall come," lit. „when I have but done etc."; — mo o yéfa gbo ro-petr, ńa kǫ́ne, „as soon as he came from town, they went away." Cf. also the aux. v. bar in loco.

Gbo gbe̱tr, „just exactly, but just;" e. g. ar'étr ra putr gbo gbetr. mo̱ o̱ kóne̱, „the sun was but just risen above the horizon, when he left."

Gbo ra̱s, „but just, only just," lit. „only yet," Ger. „eben erst;" e. g. o̱ trap gbo ra̱s tra yō ma-pant, „he only just began to do work."

Gbo to̱ṅ, „then now, now;" e. g. maṅ kóne̱ gbo to̱ṅ, sa̱ sóto ey'e̱tr-'e̱-su, „let us then go now, we have got our things."

Gbóṅ, a-, or i-, pl. ma-, n. „bundle" (as of rice cut), „a handful, a sheave;" e. g. a-gboṅ ṅa pa-la, „a sheave of rice."

Gbóṅkal, ka̱-, pl. tra̱-, n. „dale, valley."

Ghóṅko̱, a-, pl. e-, or tra̱-, n. „old forest, forest" (where the timber trees have not yet been cut out); e. g. o yi ro-gbóṅko̱, „he is in the forest."

Gbóṅkto, a-, pl. e-, n. „kitchen"; e. g. o yi ro-gbóṅkto, „he is in the kitchen."

Gbópe̱, v. n. „be rugged, be uneven, be rough" (as ground or a stone); e. g. an-to̱f ṅa gbópe̱ ri, „the ground is rugged there."

Gbópe̱-gbópe̱, v. freq. or intens. n. „be very rugged, be very uneven, be very rough;" e. g. an-to̱f ṅa gbópe̱-gbópe̱ ri, „the ground is very uneven there."

Gbórka, o-, pl. a-, n. „one not initiated into the secret society of the Bondos" or „of the Porros; one ceremoniously unclean." Cf. Pref. § 18. a.

Gbósa, adj. „belonging to tempting" or „alluring" or „seducing, tempting;" e. g. r'a ra-gbo̱sa ra yi ri, „there is a temptation there," lit. „a tempting thing is there;" from the v. rel. gbósa, „tempt-with-," (rad. gbos, „tempt.")

Gbo̱ti, v. a. „pluck-off, tear-off, pull-off, pluck" (as fruit from a tree, or a rope); e. g. o̱ gbóti ma-lémre, „he plucked limes."

Gbúke, v. n. „run, run away, flee;" e. g. aṅ-fam be ṅa gbúke, „all the people ran away."

Gbúke, v. a. „run away from, flee from;" e. g. o gbúke-mi, „he ran away from me;" — ọ gbúkẹ am-bōk, „he fled from the snake."

Gbutr, v. n. „be short;" e. g. ak'ạntr ka gbutr, „the stick is short."

Gbútrạs, v. caus. „shorten, make short;" passively „be shortened;" e. g. gbútrạs-ki, „shorten it;" — ak'ạntr ka rẹ gbútrạs, „the stick will be shortened."

H.

Ha, conj. = hañ „so that, in somuch that;" e. g. ña káne-su fo ow'úni ọwé ọ sạkẹ; kére ọ sạkẹ sọī, hā a-fam ña gbạli he tši trára, „they told us that this person turns himself; but he turns himself softly, so that people are not aware of it."

Hā, adv. = hañ „till, until;" e. g. I kar-ko, hā pạ léla-mi, „I waited for him, till I was tired," lit. „till it tired me."

Háli, conj. „though, although;" e. g. be nạ nánẹ gbo trạka keía, háli na keía he etc., „if ye only think of stealing, although ye do not steal etc."

Háli, adv. „very, much;" e. g. ak'óta aké I gbạli bẹ ki sọnd, I yéma-ki háli, „as for this cloth I cannot part with it, I am much in need of it."

Hálisa, adv. „moreover, yet, still, still yet, yet still;" e. g. ña yō ma-pant hálisa," = hálisa ña yō ma-pant, „they still do work;" — kóno mo soñ-su rạs ey'étr bẹ, „he is yet giving us all things still."

Hañ, conj. = ha, which see.

Hañ, adv. = hā, which see.

Hẹ, adv. „not". = fe which see; e. g. ọ ta der hẹ, „he did not yet come." It is only used with verbs like fe, and both forms might be considered as negative suffixes to form negative verbs.

Họ, conj. = fọ, which see.

Họ, v. n. „say", = fọ, which see.

Họ, adj. participial „saying", = fọ, which see.

Họ yē, = fọ yē, which see.

I.

-i? direct inter. suff. placed at the end of the proposition; e. g. I der royáṅ-i? „shall I come yonder?" — I trei toṅ-i? „shall I leave off now?"

'i, abbr. form of ṅi, pr. obj. „it", used after the letter ṅ. See an ex. in Temn. Trad. p. 6.

Iyóō, adv. „yes"; e. g. kǫ ǫw'ahét ǫ pā hǫ: Yā, toísa-mi ambamp. O-kára-k'ǫṅ ǫ pā hǫ: Iyóō; „and the child said: Mother, broil me the bird. His mother said: Yes."

K.

K', pref. indef. and insep. „a, an;" e. g. k'antr. „a stick," for ka-ą́ntr.

Ka, prep. „in, into; to; at; from; for; with; according; while;" e. g. ǫ wur ka aṅ-set, „he came out from the house." The sense is indicated by the verb with which it is used.

Ka-, pref. def. = aka-, „the"; as ka-bep, „the spoon." It is the def. form of ka-.

Ka, prep. poss. „of". It is the def. form of ka; e. g. o-kas ka o-baī, „the father of the king."

Ka, conj. „and", = kǫ and ko; this form is used before words with or before the vowel a; e. g. ka ṅa pā hǫ: etc., „and they said: etc."

Ka, adv. „then; when," — kǫ and ko; this form is used before words with or before the vowel a; and in the minor proposition. If any time is indicated in the antecedent, or if the adv. ma in the sense of „when" precedes; then ka has the sense of „then"; otherwise it has the sense of „when"; e. g. ǫ poṅ gbo der-e, ka ṅa móta kóne, „as soon as he had come, then only they left," — „he had just come, before they went away;" — ǫ yi ka der, ka aṅ-tsik ṅa bĕk, „he was just coming, when the strangers arrived." See the Note after kǫ, adv.

Ka, pr. subj.-def. „it"; e. g. ka-bep ka dínne, „the spoon is lost."

Kạ-, pref. indef. „a, an;" e. g. kạ-bep, „a spoon." With verb.

nouns it may often be given by „to" with a following Infinitive, for which the verb. noun often stands. Verb. nouns derived from transitive verbs may still take an object in the Acc.

Ka, prep. poss. „of". It is the indef. form of ka; e. g. ka-bep ka Sóri. „a spoon of Sori."

Ka, pr. subj. indef. „it"; as: ka-bep-ka-mi ka dinne, „a spoon of mine is lost."

Ka a-lókọ lom, „at a certain time, once;" = lókọ lom.

Ka-mi, pr. poss. def. „my", lit. „of me;" e. g. ka-bep-ka-mi, „my spoon."

Ka-mi, pr. poss. indef. „my", lit. „of me;" e. g. ka-bep-ka-mi, lit. „a spoon of me," = „a spoon of mine" or „my spoon."

Ka-mu, pr. poss. def. „thy", lit. „of thee"; e. g. ka-bep-ka-mu, „thy spoon."

Ka-mu, pr. poss. indef. „thy", lit. „of thee;" e. g. ka-bep-ka-mu, lit. „a spoon of thee" = „a spoon of thine" or „thy spoon."

Ka-ñañ, pr. poss. def. „their", lit. „of them"; e. g. ka-bep-ka-ñañ, „their spoon."

Ka-ñañ, pr. poss. indef. „their," lit. „of them;" e. g. ka-bep-ka-ñañ, „a spoon of them," = „a spoon of theirs" or „their spoon."

Ka-nu, pr. poss. def. „your", lit. „of you;" e. g. ka-bep-ka-nu, „your spoon."

Ka-nu, pr. poss. indef. „your", lit. „of you;" e. g. ka-bep-ka-nu, „a spoon of you," = „a spoon of yours" or „your spoon;" — ka-bep-ka-nu kiañ, „this (is) a spoon of yours," lit. „a spoon of yours this (it)."

Ka ka láp'sọ, ⎫ „at last," lit. „at the end;" e. g. ọ der ka ka-
Ka ka-láp'sa, ⎭ láp'so, „at last he came," or „he came at last."

Ka-láp'sọ, ⎫ n. but used adverbially, „the last time," lit. „the
Ka-láp'sa, ⎭ end;" for which they more generally use the aux. v. lápso, „be last." E. g. me I kọ ri ka-lápsọ, „when I went there the last time."

Ka-láp'sọ-ka-tši, ⎫ „at last, afterwards," lit. „at the end of it;"
Ka-láp'sa-ka-tši, ⎭ e. g. ka-láp'so-ka-tši ọ soñ-mi ey'étr-'e-mi, „at last he gave me my things."

Ka ka-ráraṅ-ka-tši, ⎫ „afterwards, after this," lit. „at its back"
Ka-ráraṅ-ka-tši, ⎭ or „at the back of it;" e. g. ka ka-ráraṅ-ka-tši I tši der, „afterwards I shall come."

Ka ka-ráraṅ aké, ⎫ „after this," lit. „at the back (of) this;" e. g.
Ka-ráraṅ aké, ⎭ ka ka-ráraṅ aké o tšē tši so yō, (or: o tšē so yō tši), „after this he did not do it again."

Ka-ráraṅ, n. but used as a prep. „after", lit. „the back;" e. g. ka-ráraṅ ka ka-tšim, „after the war." The preposition ka, „at" is dropped before the noun.

Ka-su, pr. poss. def. „our", lit. „of us;" e. g. ka-bep-ka-su, „our spoon."

Ka-su, pr. poss. indef. „our", lit. „of us;" e. g. ka-bep-ka-su, „a spoon of us." „a spoon of ours." — „our spoon."

Ka-troṅ, n. but used as a prep. „between, amongst, among." lit. „the middle;" e. g. ka-troṅ ka aṅ-fam, „amongst the people." See the observation at the n. ka-ráraṅ above.

Ka-tši, pr. dem. log. „that"; e. g. ak'áṅtr ka-tši, „that log of timber" (spoken of)

Ka-tši, pr. poss. neut. „its", lit. „of it;" e. g. ka-ra-ka-tši, „its branch," lit. „the branch of it."

Kabáne, adj. „wonderful, astonishing, extraordinary;" e. g. tr'ei tra-kabáne, „a wonderful thing."

Kábi, o-, pl. a-, n. „blacksmith".

Kadi, adv. „before, ahead, forwards, onward;" e. g. o ko kadí, „he went forwards;" — tráma kadi, „stand ahead."

K'áfa, pl. tr'áfa, n. „book". This word is used by the Mórimen, and by those who speak deep Temne, as they call it; the common word for it is a-réka, which see.

Káfri, o-, pl. a-, n. „infidel, unbeliever, hea'hen." From the Ar. كَافِرْ, infidelis; Mand. kafir.

K'aídi, ⎫ pl. tr'aíri, n. „paper". From the Ar. كَاغِدْ, charta;
K'aíri, ⎭ e. g. k'aíri ka-fíno, „good paper."

K'ak, pl. tr'ak, n. „ant in general;" also: „small black ant, sugar-ant." As regards the form Pa Tr'ak-ṅa, the prefix ṅa belonging to Pa is here put behind Tr'ak instead of behind Pa, as it would not do to say Pa-ña Tr'ak; because Tr'ak is here taken as a name to which Pa-ña, „Messrs." is applied. Pa belongs to those nouns which may take the indef. pl. pref. behind instead of before the noun, as will be seen from the Temne Grammar. The pr. may follow in the sing., though the noun is in the pl., and vice versa; as all of them are taken as one whole, or the sing. for the whole species. See Fables p. 90.

Kal, v. n. „return". As an aux. it serves to express the adv. „again"; e. g. I tši kal sǫń-mu-tši, „I shall give it to thee again;" — kal kánta ka-ráre, „shut the door again."

Kal, v. a. „scorch" (as fire the leaves of a tree etc.; see the adj. below); „broil"; e. g. an'ántr na kal e-bópar be, „the fire scorched all the leaves;" — kal ǫ-šem, „broil the meat."

Kal, adj. „scorched" (as the leaves of a tree by a fire, or as the feathers of a fowl, or the hairs of a skin on a fire); „broiled"; e. g. e-bópar e-kal, „scorched leaves;" — ǫ-šem ǫ-kal, „broiled meat."

Kála, a-, n. „goods" (as used for bartering and valued by the bar, as they call it, from a bar of iron, the first circulating medium introduced here), hence „property, money;" e. g. a-kála a-féra, „cash". lit. „white money," = „silver coin;" a-kála a-bánia, „ransom". See the word bar, a- in loco. The word is also used of money in the sing. without any adjunct; as: ǫ bā a-kála a-gbáti, „he has much money."

Kála, v. caus. (rad. kal), „bring back, return, restore, give back, repay." lit. „cause to return;" also „revenge oneself on-for-;" e. g. kǫno kála ma-máne-ma-ñań, „he effected their reconciliation." lit. „he restored their friendship;" — I tši kála-ko-tši, „I shall revenge myself on him for it," lit. „I shall give it back to him;" — ǫ kála-mi-tši, „he returned it to me."

Kálane, v. spont., or caus. and refl. (rad. kal), „return"; lit. „return of one's own accord" or „bring back oneself;" e. g. mań kálane, „let us return;" — ǫ kálane so ro-Báke Lǫkǫ, „he returned again to Port-Loko."

Káli, v. n. „look, look about; be awake; live;" — e. g. ǫ káli o-fino, „he looks well about;" — ko ma ma káli-e? „what art thou looking at?"

Káli, v. a. „look at;" e. g. o káli-mi, „he looked at me."

Káli, adj. „waking, awake, alive;" e. g. w'úni káli, „a person awake."

Káli, v. a. „postpone, defer, put off; detain;" e. g. káli ka-kóneka-mu ro-kamp, „postpone thy going to Freetown;" — o káli o-tšik, „he detained the stranger."

Káli-káli, v. freq. or intens. n. „look all about, look out" (as one on a watch, or as a spy).

Káli w'úni o-nósi-neī, „look with pity (compassion) on one;" e. g. o káli-mi o-nósi-nei, „he looked with pity on me."

Káli w'úni o-tot, } „look well upon one, look with favour upon
Káli w'úni tot, } one, take good care of one;" e. g. o káli-mi tot, „he takes good care of me."

K'álma, pl. tr'álma, n. „a large black antelope with white lips and long retroverted horns, about the size of a year old calf, and of great strength, so as to fight with a leopard." Its meat has a strong disagreeable smell.

Káma, conj. „that"; e. g. káne-ko káma o der, „tell him that he may come."

Kámu, a-, pl. e-, or tra; or o-, pl. tra-, n. „an iguana, guana."

Kamp, ro-, „Freetown (in Sierra-Leone)," so called, because the settlers, when they arrived there, made a camp near the shore, lit. „at the camp." From the Engl.

Káne? pr. rel. inter. „who"? e. g. káne yo atr'ei atšé-e? „who did this thing?"

Káne, v. a. „tell, command; say to, relate;" o káne-ko-tši, „he told it to him."

Káne, a-, or i-, pl. ma-, n. „saying; history, narration; news;" e. g. I ko tral ań-káne ńa an-tšik, „I go to hear the news from the strangers."

Káńka, v. a. „confine" (as water by a dam); „obstruct one's progress; surround, besiege "(as a town); „detain by force;" e. g. 'a káńka ań-sel, „they surrounded the house."

K'ánkąl, pl. tr'ąnkąl, n. „tornado, thunderstorm;" e. g. k'ąnkąl ką-bána ką trą der, „there is a heavy tornado coming."

Káŋko! int. expressing the Optative, „may! grant that! o that!" e. g. káŋko K'úru o mar-mi! „may God help me!" It is constr. with the def. verb.

Kant, e-, n. „gum of the eyes;" Ger. „Augenbutter"; Lat. pituita crassa, gramia.

Kant, a-, pl. trą-, n. „wood, bush, wood lands, young forest;" e. g. o yi ro-kant, „he is in the bush."

Kánta, v. a. „shut" (as a door); e. g. k'ánta ka-ráre, „shut the door."

Kánti, v. revert. a. (rad. kánta), „open" (as a door); e. g. kánti karáre, „open the door."

K'antr, pl. tr'antr, n. „stick, log of timber" (felled); „timbertree" (standing); e. g. k'antr ka-bóli, „a long stick."

Kápatr, a-, pl. e, n. „breast, chest; bosom;" e. g. o yi ka añkápatr-ń'oń, „he was in his bosom."

K'ar, pl tr'ar, n. „louse:" e. g. o bá tr'ar trą-laī, „he has many lice."

Kar, v. a. „wait, wait for, await, expect;" e. g. tšŏ ko ri kar, „do not wait for him there;" -— kar-mi ba, w'an! „wait me here, boy!"

Kára, o-, pl. a-, n. „mother; mistress;" e. g. o-kára-k'oń, „his mother." This form is not used when addressing a mother.

Kára, v. a. „bring, bring away;" e. g. 'a kára-ko, „they brought him."

Kára, v. rel. „bring-for-, bring-to-;" e. g. kára-mi n'antr, „bring me fire," = „bring fire for me."

Káramǫko, o-, pl. a-, n. „teacher, schoolmaster," lit. „reading master." Prob. from the Mand. karamo, „schoolmaster".

Káraŋ, v. n. „read"; also „learn"; e. g. o káraŋ o-fíno, „he reads well." See the next word.

Káraŋ, v. a. „read; learn;" also „teach"; e. g ko káraŋ añ-réka ańé, „go read this letter." In the first place from the Mand. karań, but ultimately from the Ar. اقْرَأ, legit.

K'áraṅ, pl. tr'áraṅ, n. „fire-place, hearth;" e. g ro-káraṅ, „at the fire-place."

Karándi, o-, pl. a-, n. „scholar, disciple." Mand. karandiño. E. g. aṅ-karándi-ñ'oṅ, „his disciples."

Kárane, v. rel. and refl. (rad. kára), „bring with" or „for oneself;" e. g. o kárane a-gbáta, „he brought a mat with himself."

Karmǫ́kǫ, o-, pl. a-, n. = káramǫkǫ, o-, which see.

K'áro, pl. tr'áro, n. „wooden bowl, bowl;" e. g. k'áro ka-bána, „a large bowl."

Kas, o-, pl. a-, n. „father; master;" in the pl. also „ancestors, forefathers;" e. g. o-kas-ka-mi, „my father." This form is not used for addressing a father.

Kása, v. n. „intercede, mediate;" also „be of a middling quality" or „stature" (as goods, or people); e. g. Pa Sóri o Sélo he kása, „Mr. Sori will not intercede."

Kása, v. a. „intercede for-, interpose between-, interfere between-, interpose in behalf of-; be" or „stand between-;" also „make peace between-, effect a reconciliation between-." It is always followed by ratróṅ, „between"; e. g. kóno kása-su ratróṅ, „he intercedes for us;" — a-kuṅk ña kása-su ratróṅ, „there is a fence between us."

K'áši, pl. tr'áši, n. „breach of the law which subjects the offender to penalty, guilt, trespass;" also „penalty itself." Cf. fúmpo káši, under F.

Káši, v. n. „refuse, be not willing, will not; be saucy, be unrelenting;" I káne-kǫ tra yǫ ma-pant, kǫ o káši, „I told him to do work, and he refused." Also used as an aux., when it is construed with the short form of the Infinitive. See bak, v. inch.

Kásra, adj. „violent"; e. g. w'úni kásra, „a violent person." From the Ar. نَسّ, violentia.

Katr, v. a. „put" (as a word, or excuse); „fasten; make" (as a heap). See the next word.

Katr k'ére, „make an excuse, make an apology;" e. g. o katr k'ére, „he made an excuse."

K'átrạk, pl. tr'átrạk, n. „foot"; e. g. ak'átrạk-k'oṅ, „his foot."

Kátrnẹ, v. refl. n. (rad. katr), lit. „put oneself, fasten oneself;" hence „mix oneself in a matter, interfere, meddle;" e. g. tšẹ kátrnẹ ka kọ ri, „do not meddle by going there."

Kátrnẹ, v. refl. a. „put-oneself, make-oneself" (as an excuse). See next word.

Kátrnẹ k'ẹrẹ, „excuse oneself, make an excuse for oneself;" e. g. ọ kátrnẹ k'ẹrẹ, „he excused himself."

Kẹ, conj. „and", = ka and kọ; this form is used before words with or before the vowels ẹ, e and i; e. g. kẹ mẹ l ṅaṅ'-kọ, etc., „and when I saw him, etc."

Kẹ, adv. „then; when," = ka and kọ; this form is used before words with or before the vowels ẹ, e and i, and in the minor proposition. If any time is indicated in the antecedent, or if the adv. mẹ „when" precedes; then kẹ has the sense of „then"; otherwise it has the sense of „when"; e. g. ọ yi gbo ka kọ ro-Kamp, kẹ l der, „he was just about going to Freetown, when I came;" - mẹ l bọ na bes ro-kuṅk-e, kẹ l fir aṅ-kála aṅé, „when I was engaged in digging in the yard, then I found this money."

Note. When ma, or me, or mọ, „when" occurs in the antecedent; then the ka, or kẹ, or kọ is generally left untranslated in English. The form ma corresponds with ka, me with kẹ, and mọ with kọ. The forms ka, kẹ and kọ in the sense of „then, when" are only used in the minor proposition; but ka ma, kẹ me, and kọ mọ, may be used in the antecedent in the sense of „and when", and in the minor in the sense of „then when", or „then" or „when" simply. Sometimes ka, kẹ and kọ may be given by „before". See kọ, adv. below.

K'ẹ, pl. tr'ẹ, = k'eṅ, pl. tšeṅ, n. „property inherited," hence „inheritance, property;" e. g. ak'ẹ-k'oṅ, „his inheritance;" — o-kas-ka-mi ọ tšia-mi k'ẹ ka-bána, „my father left me a large inheritance."

Kē-ó-kē, = kī-ó-kī, or = kō-kó, adv. „at all, by all means, at all events, however;" with a negation „not at all," or „by no means;" e. g. yo-tši kē-ó-kē, „do it by all means;" —

pa back kĕ-ó-kē, tšĕ pal m'ántr, „however hard it may be, do not forget water."

Keï, ra, pl. tra̤-, n. „theft, thievery;" e. g. ra-keï-r'oṅ, „his theft."

Keía, v. n. „steal, practise theft;" e. g. o keia ro-petr, „he stole in the town."

Keía, v. a. „steal;" e. g. o keía e-yóka ro-k'or, „he stole cassadas in the farm."

Keía, ka̤-, n. verb. „act of stealing, theft;" e. g. ka-keía-k'oṅ, „his theft."

K'ek, pl. tš'ek, or tr'ek, n. „beard"; also fig. „a spider's web;" e. g. o ba k'ek ka-bóli, „he has a long beard." See the Note after kótši.

Kel, ro-, thus they call an arm of the Sierra Leone river, and that part of the Temne country which is contiguous to it.

Kélfa, o-, pl. a-, n. „captain of an army, war-officer, hero, warrior;" e. g. o-kélfa o-bána, „a great hero."

Kélfa, ra-, n. „office" or „rank of a captain of an army; bravery, heroism;" e. g. ra-kélfa-r'oṅ, „his bravery."

K'éme, pl. tr'éme, n. „hundred"; e. g. tr'éme tra-rañ, „two hundred."

K'éṅke, pl. tr'éṅke, n. „a sort of cymbal worn on the thumb, and struck by a thimble on the middle finger," or „by several fingers, to accompany the drum." It is made of iron or brass, and resembling a large thimble.

Kére, conj. „but"; e. g. o yénia der, kére tr'ei tra bentr-ko, „he wished to come, but something prevented him."

Kére, adv. „even, yea." See an ex. in Tradit. p. 28.

Kére, v. a. „carry, lead, carry away;" e. g. w'an, kére ey'étr eyé, „boy, carry these things away;" also „carry-to-, carry-for-," as: kére-mi ey'étr eyé, „carry these things away for me."

K'ére, pl. tr'ére, n. „excuse, apology." See the word katr, above.

K'éreṅ, pl. tš'éreṅ, or tr'éreṅ, n. „grass"; e. g. k'éreṅ ka-laï, „much grass." See the Note after kótši.

Kéta, v. a. „puzzle, perplex, embarrass;" e. g. atr'eí atšé tra kéta-mi, „this thing puzzles me."

Kéta, v. n. „be puzzling, be perplexing;" e. g. atr'eí atšé tra kéta, „this thing is perplexing."

K'etr, pl. tr'etr, or tš'etr, n. „a whip". See the Note after kótši.

Ki, pr. obj. „it"; e. g. o wai-ki ro-petr, „he bought it in town."

Kí', pr. emph. abbr. „it, this" for kía; e. g. ka-lápso-ka-tši kí' táho aké, „this is not the end of it," lit. „the end of it (its end) it not this."

Kī-ó-kī, adv. = kē-ó-kē, or kō-kō. See kē-ó-kē.

Kía, pr. emph. „it, this." Sometimes it refers to the noun k'a, „time", when it may be given by „this time," in which case it is sometimes preceded by ténoń, „to day." E. g. ka-bep-ka-mi kía yi tši, „this is my spoon."

Kía-kē, pr. dem. prox. comp. „this" or „it (is) this" or „this it (is)," lit. „it this;" e. g. ka-bep-ka-mi kía-kē, „this is my spoon," lit. „my spoon it (is) this."

Kía yi,   \
Kía yi ho, } „namely, that is, that is to say," lit. „it is;" e. g. ak'áfa ka K'úru, kía yi (ho) am-beíbal, „the book of God, that is the Bible."

Kil, a-, pl. e, or tra; or o-, pl. tra-, n. „ground-pig."

K'íma, pl. tš'íma, \
K'ímo, pl. tš'ímo, } n. „smoke"; e. g. k'íma ka-bána, „a great smoke."

Kíma, ma-, n. „soot"; e. g. ma-kíma ma-laī, „much soot."

K'in, adj. num. „one"; e. g. ka-bep k'in, „one spoon."

Kíńa, v. rel. = kóńa, which see.

Kira, v. a. „agitate, disturb, trouble" (as people, or water); e. g. w'an, tšē kira am'ántr, „boy, do not disturb the water."

Kísi, v. n. „escape, be saved;" e. g. o kísi ri, „he was saved there."

Kísi, ka-, n. verb. „act of being saved" or „of escaping, salvation."

Kísia, v. caus. „cause to escape, save;" e. g. kóno kísia-mi ri, „he saved me there."

Ko, v. n. „go". When used as an aux. it may sometimes be given by „come, happen." E. g. sa ko rok pa-la, „we go to reap (cut) rice;" — ña ko ro-Kamp, „they go to Freetown."

Ko, conj. „and", = ka and ke; this form is used before words with or before the vowels o, ǫ and u; e. g. ka ma ña der etc.. „and when they came etc."

Kǫ, adv. „then, when," = ka and ke; this form is used before words with or before the vowels o, ǫ and u in the minor proposition. If any time is indicated in the antecedent, or if the adv. mo, „when" precedes; then ko has the sense of „then"; otherwise it has the sense of „when"; e. g. o yi ka kǫ ro-Kamp, kǫ ǫ-tšik o der, „he was about to go to Freetown, when the stranger came;" — mo ǫ yi ka ko ro-Kamp, ǫ tšik o der, „when (as) he was about to go to Freetown, (then) the stranger came;" — I poñ gbo gbal añ-réka, ko ǫ der, „I had just written the letter, when (then) he came," = „I had just written the letter before he came." See the Note after ke, adv.

Ko, pr. obj. „him, her;" e. g. I nañ-ko, „I saw him."

Ko? pr. inter. „what?" e. g. ko ma ma yo-e? „what art thou doing?"

K'ǫ, abbr. of k'oñ, „his, her;" this form is used if it comes to stand between the two constituent parts of a comp. noun; as: ka-mar-k'ǫ-tr'ei, for ka-mar-tr'ei-k'oñ, „his luckiness."

Kō-kō, adv. = ki-ó-ki, or = kē ó ke, which see.

Ko ñe-e? „what is the matter? why?" for: ko ña yi e? lit. „what is it?"

Ko ñe — e? „what is the matter that —? why —?" E. g. ko ñe ma fánta anó-e? „why doest thou lie down here?"

Ko ñe ba-e? „what is the matter now?" lit. „what is it now?" for: ko ña yi ba-e?

Ko tr'ei-e? „how is this?" „how comes this?" lit. „what thing?"

Ko tr'ei tra — e? „why —?" „what is the matter that —?" E. g. ko tr'ei tra ma der-e? „why doest thou come?"

Ko'i, for kóri, v. a. „salute; visit." This form is used in salutations before the obj. pr. of the 2d. pers. plur., as: ko'i-nu, pa-ña! „I salute you, Sirs!"

K'ólọ, pl. tr'ólọ, n. „hollow" (as in a tree); „cavity" (as of a bowl); e. g. k'ólọ ka-bána, „a large hollow."

Kólonẹ, v. refl. (rad. kólo), „commend oneself, boast;" e. g. ọ kólonẹ gbo kạ-tšiṅ, „he boasts but in vain."

Kōm, v. a. „bring forth, bear, produce" (as a woman a child, or a tree fruit); e. g. ọ-kára owọ́ kōm-mi, „the mother who bare me."

Kōm, v. n. „bring forth, bear, be fruitful, bear fruit; bring forth children, be delivered of a child;" e. g. aṅ'ạ́ntr aṅé ṅa kōm he, „this tree does not bear;" — o-ráni-ka-mi ọ kōm he, „my wife does not bring forth children" = „is barren."

Kōm, adj. „bringing forth; born, brought forth;" e. g. aṅ'ạ́ntr a-kōm ma-kómi ma-fíno, „a tree bringing forth good fruit."

Kōm, kạ-, n. verb. „act of bringing forth, birth, parturition, delivery; act of being born;" e. g. ka-kōm-k'ọṅ, „her parturition," or also „his being born;" — aṅ-lo ṅa ka-kōm-ka-mi, I tr'a he ṅi, „as to the time of my delivery, I do not know it;" — ka-kōm-kọ, „the act of bringing him forth," = „his birth."

Kómanẹ, v. rel. and refl. „bear with-" (as a child with a natural spot, or with four fingers on one hand), lit. „bring forth with" or „on oneself;" e. g. am-méra-ṅ'oṅ aṅá 'a kómanẹ-kọ ṅa tófạl, „he is of a natural mild temper," or „his temper is naturally mild," lit. „his temper with which they bare him is mild." Also simply „bear"; e. g. ya 'a kómanẹ-kọ gbo, „thus he was born," lit. „thus they just bare him."

Kómanẹ, adj. „innate, inborn, natural, hereditary;" e. g. am-méra ṅ'oṅ a-kómanẹ, „his natural temper;" — r'ä ra-kómanẹ raṅ, „that is a hereditary thing."

Kómạr, v. rel. „bear, bring forth," lit. „bear-at-," but the suff. is here redundant; e. g. ro 'a kómạr-kọ, „where he was born," lit. „where they brought him forth."

Kómi, n-, or i-, pl. ma-, n. „fruit"; e. g. ma-kómi ma-fíno, „good fruit."

Kóm'ra, ọ-, pl. a-, n. „a woman in childbed," for kómạra.

Kóm'ra, ra-, pl. trạ-, n. „generation, offspring, descendants, posterity;" also „one's domestics, those under one's control," or „under the head of a family." The plur. is used of a plurality of families, the sing. being already a collective noun; e. g. 'ra-kómra-ra-mi, „my posterity."

Koṅ', pr. emph. abbr. for kóno, „he, she; him, her;" e. g. koṅ' táho yō tši, „it is not he who did it," or „not he did it;" — koṅ' sōn, „he alone."

K'oṅ, pr. poss. „his, her," for ka ko „of him, of her," with the euph. ṅ added; e. g. ka-bep-k'oṅ, „his spoon."

K'oṅ, pr. obj. „him, her." This form is used if it follows a comp. loc. prep., which is followed by the prep. ka, k'oṅ being a contraction of ka ko like the preceding pr. poss.; e. g. ka-troṅ ka Sóri de ka-troṅ-k'oṅ, „between Sori and between him."

Kón'a? for kóno-a? pr. inter. „where is he?" = the Hebr. אַיִן; e. g. kón'a Sóri? „where is Sori?" The subst. verb „be" is always implied. Cf. the suff. -A? above.

Kóṅa, = kíṅa, v. rel. (rad. kiṅ, or koṅ), „make-to fall down" or „drop off for-" (as the wind, or a person, fruit from a tree for one); e. g. aṅ-fef ṅa kóṅa-mi ma-lémre, „the wind made limes to fall down for me."

Kóne, v. refl. (rad. ko), „go away, go, depart, leave, start," lit. „go oneself;" as applied to the water „flow"; e. g. o kóne dis ra-foi, „he left yesterday evening"

⁕Kóṅkoṅ, v. a. „shake, shake off" (as dust from cloth), „shake out, knock out" (as dirt from the inside of a box by knocking on it), „knock on;" e. g. kóṅkoṅ ak'úma, káma e-di e wur, „knock on the box that the dirt may come out."

Kóno, pr. emph. „he, she; him, her;" e. g. kóno yō-tši, „he did it."

K'óno, pl. tr'óno, n. „turkish sabre, scimitar, curvated cutlass."

Kóno-könone, pr. refl. „he himself, she herself; himself, herself;" e. g. kóno-könone o yō-tši, „he himself did it."

Kónoṅ, pr. abs. „he, she; him, her;" e. g. w'úni las kónoṅ, „he is a bad person," lit. „a bad (wicked) person he."

K'ónte, pl. tr'ónte,
K'ónteṅ, pl. tr'ónteṅ, } n. „an instrument resembling a bell with some rings on it to hold it with the

fingers, while it is struck with some fingers of the other hand." It is made of iron or brass, and used by Chiefs, when they wish to pause, or stop a little in speaking or in their address to the court, and to give a sign to their women to applaud him by clapping their hands.

K'or, pl. tr'or, n. „belly, abdomen; bowels;" also sometimes applied to the „womb", though they have the word. ka-fantr ka am-pórn for it, which signifies „the bed of the foetus;" hence it is also used of the „menses", or the „menstruation" of women (cf. trū k'or), and of „pregnancy"; fig. „the inside" (of a thing); e. g. ak'ór-k'oṅ ka súle, „his bowels are loose," = „he has diarrhoea," = o bā k'or ka-súle; — ak'ór-kami ka baṅ, „my belly aches," = „I have griping pains;" — ak'ór ka am-pǫ́ti, „the inside of the cup." With ro- it is also used as a preposition and postposition; see rok'ór.

K'or, pl. tr'or, n. „farm"; e. g. o yi ro-k'or, „he is in the farm."

Kóri, v. a. „go to see, visit; salute;" e. g. o ko kóri owóntrk'oṅ, „he went to see his brother;" — kóri 'u, Pā! „I salute thee, Sir!"

Kos, a-, pl. e-, n. „cheek"; e. g. e-kos-y'oṅ, „his cheeks."

Kǫt, v. n. „walk, go about;" e. g. kǫ́li-ko o trạ kǫt ri, „look him. he is walking there;" - aṅ-yal aṅé ṅa kǫt o-fíno, „this boat walks well."

K'óta, pl. tr'ōta, n. „cloth"; e. g. k'óta ka-fíno, „fine cloth."

Kóta, conj. = háli, „though, although, even if;" e. g. kóta w'úni k'in ka aṅ-fi-e o trạ der na roṅáṅ etc., „although one of the dead would come to them etc."

Kótar, v. rel. (rad. kǫt), „tie on, tie" (as a cow); e. g. kótar o-nä ka ak'ạ́ntr, „tie on the cow to the post;" — kótar ambil ro-kantr, „tie the canoe to the post."

Kótši, = kót'ri, for kótari, v. rel. and revert. „untie, loose, let loose" (as a cow, or a bird from a trap); e. g. kótši ambamp, „let the bird loose;" — kótši aṅ-soī, „loose the horse." From kǫt, „tie."

Note. The r is frequently changed into s, and vice versa after t, as tšē, for trē, adv. „do not, not;" or as a pr. dem. „this, these."

Kótšine, v. rel. revert. and refl. for kótarine, „loose oneself, make oneself free, untie oneself" (as a cow, or horse, or a bird from a trap, or a person from some difficulty); e. g. añ-soi o kótšine, „the horse made himself loose." See the preceding Note.

Krífi, o-, pl. a-, n. „krifi, spirit," i. e. „demon, tutelary spirit, genius, a being of an intermediate order between God and men, a sort of demigod, and in the opinion of the Temnes an object worthy of adoration." It answers to the Gr. δαιμόνιον or δαίμων. See Pref. §§. 11—13 and δαίμων in Passow's Gr. Lexicon. The religion of the Temnes consists properly in the worship of these krifis.

Krífi, adj. „belonging to a krifi." or „produced by a krifi," hence „superior, extraordinary;" e. g. pa-la pa-krífi, „krifi's rice" (as they believe that it is not planted by men, but by krifis), also called: pa-yáka. Krifi is used here to indicate the excellency of a thing like the Hebr. אֱלֹהִים in Jon. 3, 3. or in Gen. 10, 9.

Krífi, ro-, „the residence" or „abode of krifis and of departed spirits, the invisible" or „future world, hades," answering to the Gr. ᾅδης, and to the Hebr. שְׁאוֹל. See Pref. § 10; and Tradit. p. 36—40.

Kū, a-, pl. e-. n. „Mandingo yam" (which is white).

Kul, adj. „smoked, dried" (as meat); e. g. o-šem o-kul, „smoked beef."

Kúlo, v. n. „cry, lament;" also „low" (as a cow); „howl"; e. g. 'a kúlo tráka troń, „they lamented for him."

Kúlo, ka-, n. verb. „act of crying" or „lamenting" or „lowing; lamentation, crying;" e. g. ka-kúlo-ka-ñań, „their lamentation."

K'úma, pl. tr'úma, n. „box"; also „coffin"; e. g. ar'úma-ra-mu ra yi ro-k'úma, „thy shirt is in the box."

Kuńk, a-, pl. e-, or tra-, n. „fence, barrier, hinderance;" also „yard", or „the place fenced in;" also „the metal handle on a gun, because it is, as it were, a fence to protect the trigger"; fig. „protection"; e. g. o-kára-ka-mi o yi ro-kuńk, „my mother is in the yard;" — a-kuńk ńa yi-su ratróń,

„there is a fence between us;" — o̩ yi-mi a-kuṅk, „he is a protection to me."

K'úpo̩, pl. tr'úpo̩, ⎫ n. „feather, pen, quill;" e. g. ak'úpo̩-ka-mi,
K'úpa, pl. tr'úpa, ⎭ „my pen." The full form for a writing pen is k'úpo̩ ka̩-gbála, lit. „a feather to write with."

Kur, adj. „old, ancient" (not applied to rational beings, for which they use báki; but to inanimate things, and to irrational beings); e. g. e̩-lópra e̩-kur, „old wearing apparel," or „old clothes;" — o̩-nā o̩-kur, „an old cow."

K'úru, pl. tr'úru, n. „heaven, sky; deity, God." Though the verb. pr. for this noun according to analogy is ka̩; yet when applied to God we have employed the general form as used for nouns animate, i. e. o̩; but when used of „heaven", the form ka̩. This word may also be used of false gods. E. g. ak'úru ka wáraṅ ténoṅ, „the sky is bright to day; — K'úru o̩ bápa̩r d'er ó d'er, „God is everywhere present." It seems to be cognate to the Gr. ὁ κύριος, „lord."

K'úrumasába, n. „God, the supreme Being." This is the most solemn name of the Deity. Cf. Pref. § 11. a.

Kus, v. a. „empty" (as a box); „pour out" (as liquids); also „close by a public procession and festival" (as the great fast, or the Ramadan of the Mohammedans; or the initiatory course of instruction of the Bondo Institution, after which the Bondo girls or women are discharged); hence also: „discharge; keep, hold" (as a feast); e. g. kus ak'úma, „empty the box;" — 'a kus aṅ-sūm ténoṅ, „they closed the fast to day by a public procession;" — aṅ-rígba o̩ kus am-bóndo ténoṅ, lit. „the headwoman of the Bondo Institution closed the Bondo ceremonies to day by a public procession," = „the headwoman of the Bondo Institution discharged the Bondo girls to day."

Kut, n. n. „scoop water, lade water, draw water;" o̩ ko̩ kut, „he goes to scoop water."

Kut, v. a. scoop, draw, lade" (as water); e. g. sa̩ ko̩ kut m'antr, „we go to draw water."

Kúta, v. rel. „scoop-for-, lade-for-, draw-for-" (as water); e. g. o̩ kúta-mi m'antr, „he scooped water for me."

Kúta, v. a. „plant, sow" (as rice). lit. „cover over" (the rice sown); e. g. sa ko kúta pa-lā, „we go to plant rice."

Kwéa, o-, pl. a-, n. „one of the Quea people, a Quea Temne." See Pref. § 4. a.

Kwi, o-, or a-, pl. tra-, n. „alligator."

L.

Lā, v. n. „be full, increase, be numerous, be plentiful, be abundant;" e. g. ak'áro ka lā, „the bowl is full;" — an-fam na lā ri, „the people are numerous there."

Lā, v. rel. „be full of, be full with, be filled with;" e. g. ak'áro ka lā m'antr, „the bowl is full of water;" — o lā ka-tšemp, „he was full of wisdom."

Lā, ka-, pl. pa-, n. „rice". The sing. is hardly ever used. E. g. pa-lā pa-fíno, „fine rice."

Lā, v. aux. „use, be used;" it indicates habit of exercising the energy, denoted by the verb, and often serves to express the adverbs „habitually, usually, always," and is construed with the short form of the Infinitive; e. g. mo o lā yō, „as he used to do;" — mo mo la yō, „as he is used to do;" — o lā ko ri, „he used to go there;" — me me lā yō, „as I usually do." It answers to the Lat. soleo.

Láfti, v. a. „turn upside down, reverse, turn over" (as a leaf, or as a fish on a grate), „turn up; shift" (as a sail); „turn" (as a canoe its proper course); e. g. láfti am-bil, „turn the canoe upside down;" — láfti am-béla, „shift the sail."

Laī, v. n. „be many, be numerous, be plentiful, be great;" applied to the sun „be" or „stand still high (above the horizon);" e. g. ma-lémre ma laī ri, „limes are plentiful there."

Laī, adj. „many, numerous, great;" e. g. a-fam a-laī, „many persons;" r'únia ra-laī, „a great multitude."

Laī, o-, adj. but used adverbially „much"; e. g. o fof o-laī trąka tron, „he spoke much about him."

Lakat, a-, pl. e-, n. „stump of a tree, trunk of a tree, after its head," or „branches have been cut off;" e. g. o boɪr-ñi ka aṅ-lạ̈kạl, „he put it on the stump."

Lákte, v. n. „look up, lift up the eyes, look upwards;" e. g. o lákte, „he looked up."

Lal, a-, pl. e-, or tra-, n. „grass-field, pasture-field;" e. g. o yi ro-lal, „he is on the grass-field."

Láma, a-, pl. e-, n. „locust"; e. g. e-láma e-laī, „many locusts."

Lámbe, a-, pl. e-, n. „present in token of respect" or „homage, homage, present; e. g. 'a kére-ko a-lámbe, „they carried a present to him in token of respect" (as to a king); — ña yō-ko a-lambe, „they did homage to him."

Láne, v. a. „believe, believe in, trust in, confide in;" e. g. o láne he tši, „he does not believe it;" — o láne Yísua, „he believes in Jesus."

Láne, v. n. „believe, confide;" e. g. o láne he, „he does not believe."

Lane, ka-, n. verb. „act of believing" or „of trusting in; believing, faith, confidence;" e. g. ka-láne-k'oñ, „his faith;" — ka-láne-ko, „the act of believing in him."

Láñba, o-, pl. a-, n. „a young man, a man," espec. „a young man dressed in a showy manner to attract the attention of females;" e. g. kạli o-láñba o-fíno, „look a fine young man."

Lạ̈ñk, a-, pl. e, n. „thigh; leg" (as of meat); in the pl. „the lap;" e. g. ow'ahét o fạ̈nta ka e-lạ̈nk ya o-kára-k'oñ, „the little child lies in the lap of its mother."

Lạ̈ñka, v. a. „swing" (as in a hammock); „stir up" (as rice in a bowl of water, so that the stones may settle down, when washing it); e. g. 'a lạ̈ñka-ko ro-tẹ̈nta, „they swung him in the hammock."

Lánsa, adv. „perhaps; e. g. lánsa o der, „perhaps he comes."

Lap, v. a. „stir up, keep up, poke" (as fire by putting its fuel in order or together); e. g. lap an'ántr, „stir up the fire."

Lap, v. n. „be ashamed, be modest;" e. g. ña lap tra yō-tši, „they are ashamed to do it."

Lap, a-, or i-, pl. ma-, n. „shame, modesty;" e. g. o bā ma-lap, or: o bā i-lap, „he is ashamed," lit. „he has shame;"

— o woṅ ma-lap, „he got ashamed," lit. „he entered (into) shame." The sing. is seldom used.

Lápar, v. rel. „be ashamed of-;" also „forgive"; e. g. o w'an, I lápar-mu gbo! „oh boy, I am but ashamed of thee!" o lápar-mi, „he forgave me."

Lápar, ka-, n. verb. „act of being ashamed of, act of forgiving, forgiveness;" e. g. ka-lápar-k'oṅ, „his forgiveness."

Lápatr, ka-, pl. tra-, n. „a burning stick, a fire-brand, torch;" e. g. fil aka-lápatr, „turn the torch to and fro" or „round" (to keep it burning).

Lápra, a-, pl. e-, n. „a skull-cap, cap;" e. g. a-lápra a-fíno, „a fine cap."

Láp'ro, } v. doubl. rel. for lápara, (rad. lap), „forgive-to-," lit.
Láp'ra, } „be ashamed of (one) for" or „on account of" (a thing); e. g. o láp'ro-mi-tši, „he forgave it to me."

Láp'ro, } ka-, n. verb. „act of forgiving-to-, forgiving, forgive-
Láp'ra, } ness; e. g. ka-láp'ro-k'oṅ, „his forgiveness."

Láp'so, } v. caus. and inch. lit. „get made late, get made last,
Láp'sa, } get finished," hence „be last." As an aux. it serves to express the adv. „last", or „the last time;" e. g. kóno láp'so der, „he came last;" — me I láp'so naṅ'-ko, „when I last saw him." It is construed with the short form of the Infinitive, and is derived from the obs. root lap, „be late," for which they now use the inch. form lápo, „get late, be late."

Láp'so, } adj. „last, hindmost;" e. g. ka aṅ-réï a-láp'so, „on
Láp'sa, } the last day;" — aṅá yi a-láp'so, „they who are last."

Láp'so, } ka-, n. verb. „state of being last, end; e. g. I yéma
Láp'sa, } naṅk ka-láp'so ka ka-trak, „I want to see the end of the palaver." The def. form is sometimes used to express the adv. „the last time," for which see ka-láp'so under k; as also for: ka ka-láp'so in the sense of „at last."

Láp'so ka-, ka-, see ka-lápso ka- under k.

Las, v. caus. pass. (rad. la), „be filled," hence also „be full" (as bottles, or as the moon); e. g. aṅ'óf ṅa yéma las, „the moon wants to get full," = „is about to be full."

Las, adj. „filled, full;" e. g. añ'óf a-las, „the full-moon."

Lạs, v. n. „be bad" (morally and physically); „be wicked, be evil; be ugly" (as a person); e. g. ọw'úni owé ọ lạs gba, „this person is very wicked."

Lạs, adj. „bad; wicked, evil; ugly;" e. g. ọ-bẹ́ra ọ-lạs, „an ugly woman."

Lạs, ọ-, adj. but used adverbially „badly, amiss, wrong;" e. g. 'a rúsạm-kọ ọ-lạs, „they brought him up badly;" — ọ yọ̄-mi ọ-lạs; „he treated me badly;" — ọ yọ̄-tši ọ-lạs, „he did it amiss." Cf. also yọ̄ ọ-lạs, under Y.

Lạs, a-, or i-, pl. ma-, n. „badness, wickedness, iniquity, bad character, evil; e. g. ọ bā ma-lạs, „he is of a bad character," lit. „he has a bad ch." or „badness"; — añai-lạs-ñóñ, = ma-lạs-m'ọñ, „his wickedness." The sing. is but seldom used.

Lạ́sa, v. inch. (rad. lạ́s), „get bad, get spoiled" or „corrupted" (as rice); „get ugly" (as one's face by age or sickness); as applied to the womb, or to the embryo „abort"; e. g. apa-lā pa lạ́sa, „the rice got spoiled;" — ak'ór-k'ọñ ka lạ́sa, „she aborted," = „she had an abortion," lit. „her womb got spoiled." See also pọ́ru.

Lásanẹ, v. caus. rel. and refl. (rad. lā), „fill for oneself" (as a vessel); also „be filled with-, be full with-" (as a sail with wind); lit. „fill itself with-;" e. g. am-bẹ́la ña lásanẹ a-fef, „the sail is full with wind;" — ọ lásanẹ ak'áro, „he filled the bowl for himself."

Lásạr, v. caus. and rel. (rad. lā), „fill up, fill, make full" (as a vessel, or as wind a sail); „fulfil" (as one's word or promise); e. g. añ-fef ña lásạr am-bẹ́la, „the wind fills the sail;" — am'ántr ma lásạr ak'áro, „the water fills the bowl;" — ọ lásạr ar'ím ará ọ trañ-ña, „he fulfilled the word, which he promised to them."

Lásạr, caus. rel. and pass. „be filled up, be full" (as a vessel, or sail); „be fulfilled" (as a promise); fig. „be complete" (as a number); e. g. ak'áro ka lásạr, „the bowl is filled up" = „is full;" — am-bẹ́la ña lásạr, „the sail is full;" — am'ántr ma trạ lásạr, „the tide is getting full."

Lạsạr, v. caus. (rad. lạs), „make bad, spoil, corrupt;" also „transgress, violate" (as a law); lit. „act badly towards;" — ọ lạsạr apa-la, „he spoiled the rice;" also „profane" (as a sacred place).

Lạsạrnẹ, v. caus. and refl. „spoil" or „corrupt oneself, make oneself offensive; offend, sin;" e. g. ọ lạsạrnẹ ka K'ūrū, „he sinned against God;" — lit. „act badly towards oneself" = „make oneself bad."

Lẹ́kanẹ, v. recipr. (rad. lẹk), „lie with each other, have sexual commerce with each other" (as man and wife; but also used of an unlawful sexual commerce); hence „commit impurity with each other;" e. g. 'a ta lẹ́kanẹ hẹ, „they had no sexual commerce with each other as yet."

Lel, a-, or i-, pl. ma-; or sing. a-, pl. ẹ-, n. „country-bean;" e. g. ña di gbo ma-lel, „they ate only country-beans."

Léla, v. impers. caus. (rad. lel), „make tired, tire;" e. g. pa ta léla he mi, „I have not yet got tired," lit. „it did not yet tire me," (the inch. sense is implied in the form of the verb. pr.; — ọ léla-mi, „I am tired," lit. „it tired me." The object becomes the subject with such impers. verbs in an Eng. translation.

Lẹmp, adv. „quickly, straightways; fast; abruptly;" e. g. der ba lẹmp-a, „come here quickly;" — ọ gbúkẹ lẹmp, „he ran fast."

Lẹmp-lẹmp, adv. intens. or emph. „very quickly; very fast;" e. g. an'eí na lólạs apa-la lẹmp-lẹmp, „the sun ripens the rice very fast."

Lémnẹ, v. a. „bid farewell to;" e. g. ọ lémnẹ-mi ténọn, „he bid farewell to me to day."

Lémre, a-, or i-, pl. ma-, n. „lime, species of lemon;" e. g. ma-lémre ma-lai, „many limes."

Leñ, v. n. „sing"; añ-fẹt añé ña leñ ọ-fíno, „these children sing well." Also „blossom, get blossoms."

Leñ, v. a. „sing"; e. g. ña leñ i-leñ, „they sung a hymn."

Leñ, kạ-, n. verb. „act of singing, singing;" e. g. ka-leñ-k'ọñ, „his singing."

Leñ, a-, or i-, pl. ma-, n. „song, hymn, poem;" also „air, tune;" e. g. añ-leñ añé ña rạ́mi ọ-bọ́ti-tral, „this song sounds sweetly," lit. „this song sounds sweet to hear;" — i-leṅ i-tọ́fạl, „a soft tune."

Léña, kạ-, pl. trạ-, n. „tail"; e. g. wop ọ-nä ka ka-léña, „hold the cow by the tail;" — kạ-léña kạ-bọ́li, „a long tail."

Léñi, a-, or i-, pl. ma-, n. „flower; blossom;" e. g. ma-léñi ma-fíno, „fine flowers."

Léṅken, kạ-, pl. trạ-, n. „neighbouring yard." With ro- it becomes a prep. or a postp., as also an adv. See rolẹ́ṅken.

Léṅki, v. a. „serve" (as God); „wait upon, attend to, attend" (as a servant his master); also „treat well;" e. g. ọ léṅki-mi ọ-fíno, „he serves me well;" — ọ léṅki ọ-tšik, „he treated the stranger well."

Léñ'sir, } v. freq. or intens. and rel. (rad. leñ), „praise" or „cele-
Len'sir, } brate by singing," lit. „sing about-;" e. g. 'a léñ'sir-kọ téngñ, „they celebrated him by singing to day;" also „mock by a satirical song."

Lim, kạ-, pl. trạ-, n. „neck" (as of a person, or of a bottle); e. g. ka-lim ka am-bítra, „the neck of the bottle."

Límba, ọ-, pl. a-, n. „one of the Limba nation, a Limba." See Pref. § 4. c.

Límba, adj. „belonging to the Limba nation" or „country, limba;" e. g. an-tọf a-límba, „the Limba country."

Liñ, v. a. „draw close" (as a person); „draw, pull, haul; draw up" (as an anchor); e. g. liñ ara-béña ọ-bákạr, „draw the rope tight;" — liñ añ-fatr, „draw up the anchor."

Liñ, v. n. „draw, pull;" e. g. w'an, liñ ọ-fíno! „boy, pull well!"

Lọ, a-, n. „time"; also „turn"; e. g. me I káne-mu añ-lọ ña-tši, „as I told thee that time;" — añ-lọ ña-tši gbeñ, „that very time;" — añ-lọ-'a-mi ña-né, „this is my turn."

Lọ ña-tši, añ-, „at that time, then;" e. g. añ-lọ ña-tši ra-fi ra yi he, „at that time there was no death."

Lọ ñoñ, } „the other day, lately, a short time ago;" e. g. 'a
Lọ ñañ. } yéma dif-kọ lọ ñoñ, „they wanted to kill him the other day."

Lọ́kọ, v. n. „germinate, grow, sprout, come" or „shoot forth" (as seed sown); e. g. pa-la pa lọ́kọ, „rice shoots forth."

Lọ́kọ, v. a. „grow, bring forth, produce;" e. g. an-tọf ańé ńa lọ́kọ pạ-la pạ-fíno, „this ground produces good rice."

Lọ́kọ, a-, or i-, pl. ẹ-, or ma-, n. „time"; also „day"; e. g. ań-lọ́kọ ańé, „this time;" — ma-lọ́kọ ma-sas, „three times;" — a-lọ́kọ a-foi-tr'ei, „a convenient time;" — I kọ he ri, háli a-lọ́kọ ń'iń, „I did not go there even once;" — ań-lọ́kọ ńa-tši táhọ ténọń, „that time (is) not to day;" — a-lọ́kọ a-béki tra kọ́ne ńa-ńē, „this is a fit time to go," lit. „a fit time to go it this." Cf. the pref. i- under the „Addenda" behind.

Lọ́kọ, ọ-, pl. a-, n. „one of the Lọ́kọ nation, a Loko." See Pref. § 4. c.

Lọ́kọ, adj. „belonging to the Lọ́kọ country" or „nation"; e. g. ań-tọf a-lọ́kọ, „the Loko country."

Lọ́kọ lọm, \
Lọ́kọ lọm, a- / = ka a-lọ́kọ lọm, „at a certain time, some time, once, one day, some day, by and by;" e. g. I tši der kóri-mu lọ́kọ lọm, „I shall come to see thee some day."

Lọ́kọ lọm, a-, „another time, another day, some other day;" e. g. I tši ko ro-Kamp a-lọ́kọ lọm, „I shall go to Freetown some other day."

Lọ́kọ ó lọ́kọ, „always; from time to time, now and then," lit. „time and time;" e. g. ye I me yọ lọ́kọ ó lọ́kọ, „thus I always do;" — ọ der rọmí lọ́kọ ó lọ́kọ, „he comes to me now and then."

Lọl, v. n. „get ripe" (as fruit), „be ripe;" e. g. ma-lémre ma tra lọl, „limes are getting ripe." Also „get red hot, get fit for the hammer" (as iron). It is the short form of lóli, „be ripe." See the Note after wos, v. n. below.

Lọl, v. n. „be small, be little," e. g. ọ-na ọwé ọ lọl, „this cow is small."

Lọl, adj. „small, little;" e. g. w'úni lọl, „a little person."

Lọm, v. n. „count, reckon;" e. g. ọ gbáli lọm ọ-fíno, „he can count well."

Lọm, v. a. „count, reckon;" also „tell, relate;" e. g. lọm ań-kála ańé a-féra, „count this cash;" — mọ ọ lọm am-pa, „when he related the matter."

Lọm, kạ-, n. verb. „act of counting" or „of reckoning;" e. g. ka-lọm-ña, „the act of counting them;" — a-fạm a-lai ña yi ri, ña tási kạ-lọm, „many persons are there, they are not to count," lit. „— — they exceed counting."

Lọm, adj. „other, another, some, certain; such and such; next;" e. g. w'úni lọm, „a certain person;" — a-fạm a-lọm ña der romí tẹ́nọń, „some persons came to me to day."

Lọ́me, kạ-, pl. trạ-, n. „sheep"; e. g. kạ-lọ́me kạ-bána, „a large sheep."

Lomp, v. impers. „be right, be proper, be fit;" e. g. ọ lomp he nañ-i? „was it not right?" — pạ lomp fẹ tra yọ̄ atr'ei atšé, „it will not be right to do this thing." It is the short form of the impers. v. lómpi, which see below.

Lómpạr, v. caus. (rad. lomp), „load" (as a gun); „set" (as a trap); lit. prob. „make fit at;" e. g. tšḗ sọ lómpạr am-pínkar, „do not load the gun again."

Lómpi, v. impers. „be right, be proper;" e. g. ọ-lómpi, „it is right."

Lómpi, adj. „proper, right; righteous; fit, exact;" e. g. ma-pant ma-lómpi, „exact work;" — w'úni lómpi, „a righteous person."

Lómpi, ma-, n. „righteousness, justice, propriety; fitness, exactness;" ma-lómpi-m'ọń, „his righteousness;" — ọ bā ma-lómpi, „he is righteous;" — ma-lómpi-ma-tši, „the propriety of it."

Lōń, v. a. „pour out, shed, spill" (as liquids); „upset" (as a vessel with liquid, or as a storm a canoe); e. g. lōń am'ántr, „pour out the water."

Lóña, } v. inch. „get spilled; run over, overflow" (as water);
Lóñọ, } „capsize, upset, sink, perish" (as a canoe, or people at sea); e. g. am'ántr ma lóña, „the water ran over;" — ambil ña lóña ro-bań, „the canoe upset at sea;" — ań-fạm ña lóñọ ro-m'antr, „the people perished in the water."

Lop, kạ-, pl. ẹ-, n. „fish"; e. g. kạ́li, kạ-lop kạ-bána! „look, a large fish!"

Lópra, adj. „belonging to dressing" or „clothing"; also „dressed;" e. g. y'ẹtr ẹ-lópra, „clothes" or „wearing apparel."

Lóšir, v. a. „clothe, dress, give clothes to;" e. g. ọ lóšir-mi, „he clothed me." Also „wrap in" (as a corpse in cloth).

M.

M', pref. indef. and insep. „a, an;" e. g. m'antr, „water; tide," for ma-ántr.

Ma-, pref. indef. „a, an;" e. g. ma-bọ́ne ma-bána, „a great joy."

Ma, adv. „how, as," = mẹ and mọ; this form is used before words with, or before the vowel a; e. g. ar'ím ra K'úru ra trọ́ri-su, ma sạ ba tra rámne K'úru, „the word of God tells us, how we are to worship God."

Ma, adv. „when, after; while, as," = mẹ and mọ; this form is used before words with, or before the vowel a; e. g. ka ma ńa nạń--kọ, ńa tšéla-kọ, „and when they saw him, they called him;" — ma ńa díra, „while they slept;" — ma ńa ma gbal-e, „while they were writing."

Ma, prep. poss. „of"; e. g. ma-tọt ma K'úru, „the goodness of God."

Ma, conj. „as, because," = mẹ and mọ; this form is used before words with, or before the vowel a; e. g. ma ań-fam ańé ńa keía e-trọ́kọ, tšía sōm ọ-bai ọ sọ́mpa-ńa, „because these people stole fowls, therefore the king punished them."

Ma—? adv. „why?" = mẹ and mọ; this form is used before words with, or before the vowel a, and this sense the forms ma, me and mo have, if they are followed by the inter. suff. -a? at the end of the proposition. The verb. pronouns of the 2d. pers. sing. and pl. are sometimes contracted with this adv., the vowel of the pr. being cut off; and in the 3d. pers. plur. they may use 'a after ma? instead of ńa. The form ma? is used with the 2d. pers. sing. and with all three persons in the pl.; the 2d. pers. sing takes the form mań, before g and k, which is for: ma ań, or also mam, before b, m and p, which is for: ma mạ, or for ma am; and in the 2d. pers. pl. they may use the form man, for ma na. E. g. ma mạ trańk-a? „why art thou silent?" — mań yọ yań-a? or: ma mạ yọ yań-a? „why doest thou do so?" — mam bes anǫ́-a? "why doest thou dig here?" — ma mam bes anǫ́-a? "why art thou digging here?" — man bes anǫ́-a? "why do ye dig here?" — ma nạ ma bes ano-a? "why are ye digging here?" — ma 'a bes anǫ́-a? "why do they dig here?" for ma ńa bes anǫ́-a?

Ma, part. = me and ma, used for various purposes:
1) for to express the Participle, and the Present, and sometimes also the Future tenses, in the 2d. pers. sing., and in all three pers. of the pl.; if the form mina "I" is used for the 1st. pers. sing., they may also employ it for this person; otherwise they use the form me, which see below. E. g. be mạ poń ań-gbálań, ko mạ ma sọm-e? "if thou hast done with the rock, what wilt thou eat?" — ma ńa ma gbal-e, "while they were writing;" — re mań kọ-e? "where art thou going to?" — See more examples in the Traditions. The 2d. pers. sing. may also take the forms mań, and mam. What has been stated about these two contracted or euph. forms under the preceding word ma? applies also here. Cf. also the part. trạ under T, as used to form the Future.
2) for the Obligative Mood in the sense of "must, were, had." Sometimes ma alone stands for ńa ma- or for 'a ma-, "they must, they were, they had," in this Mood. For the 2d. pers. sing. they may also here use the contr. or euph. forms mań and mam, about which see under ma? above, and sometimes ma alone. E. g. mạ ma pä he họ I kọne, = mam pä he họ I kǫ́ne, "thou must not say that I am gone;" — ńa ma pä he họ o kǫ́ne, "they must not say that he is gone away." The form ma is used with this Mood for the 2d. pers. sing., and for all three pers. in the pl., as also for the 1st. pers. sing., if the pr. mína is used. It may be observed here with regard to the contr. forms, that the part. and the verb. pr. are sometimes transposed without affecting the sense.
3) for the Hortative Mood in the sense of "let", and "let us".
a) If ma is used in the sense of "let", the verb. pr. follows,

as: ma ma pā hẹ ho I kọ́nẹ, „let thee not say that I am gone." But also here, instead of ma ma, they may use the contr. or euph. forms mań or mam, according as euphony may require it. (Cf. about these forms the adv. ma? above.)

b) If ma is used in the sense of „let us," it is not followed by the verb. pr.; except if more than two persons are spoken of, in which case the pr. nań „ye" follows the verb. When ma has this sense, it takes the euph. forms mam, man and mań; viz. mam before b, m and p; man before d, n and t; and mań before g and k. E. g. man di nań, „let us eat," lit. „let us eat ye;" — ma fą́nta, „let us lie down;" — mań kọ́nẹ, „let us go." When used in the sense of „let" ma is used for the 2d. pers. sing., and for all three persons in the plural.

Note. When the particles ma, mam, man and mań are followed by a verb with a pers. object, they may be given by „come now!" as: mam paía-mi! „come now accompany me!" = „come now with me!"

More particulars about the particles ma, mẹ and mọ will be found in the Grammar.

Ma, pr. subj. „thou"; e. g. ma gbą́li hẹ yọ̄-tśi. „thou canst not do it."

Ma-mi, pr. poss. „my", lit. „of me;" e. g. ma-lémre-ma-mi, „my lemons."

Ma mu, pr. poss. „thy", lit. „of thee;" e. g. am'áro-ma-mu, „thy palmoil."

Ma-nań, pr. poss. „their", lit. „of them;" e. g. ma-lémre-ma-nań, „their lemons."

Ma-nu, pr. poss. „your", lit. „of you;" e. g. ma-yi-ma-nu, „your state."

Ma-tśi, pr. poss. neut. „its, their;" e. g. ma-kómi-ma-tśi, „its fruit."

Ma-tśi, pr. dem. log. „that, those;" e. g. ma-yọs ma-tśi, „those deeds."

Málanẹ, v. refl. n. „agree, consent to, agree to, assent;" e. g. ọ málanẹ hẹ, „he did not agree to."

Málanę, v. refl. a. „accept, receive, agree to" (as to an opinion, etc.); „approve of, consent to; embrace, welcome, receive with pleasure" (as a stranger); e. g. sa málanę-tši, „we agree to it;" — ǫ malanę ǫ-tšik, „he received the stranger with pleasure."

Maleika, ǫ-, pl. a-, n. „angel"; Mand. maleika. From the Ar. مَلَاكَ, angelus.

Mam — ? „why doest thou — ?" for: ma ma, or for: ma am. See the adv. ma? above.

Mam, for: ma ma, or for: ma ma; see the part. ma, 1. 2. and 3. a above.

Mam, euph. form of ma, for which see the part. ma, 3. b. above.

M'ámo, n. „thanks". It is often used as an int. in the sense of „thank you!" or „have thanks!" lit. „thanks!" E. g. m'ámo, pā! „thank thee, Sir!" In order to express emphasis it is repeated, as m'ámo! m'ámo! „thank you! thank you!" It is also used as a sign of approbation by a master to his people, when working well; and as a sign of congratulation to parents at the birth of a child; in both these cases it is generally repeated, as: m'ámo naṅ ó! m'ámo naṅ ó! „thank you! thank you!" or „that's right! that's right!" or like the Ger. „bravo! bravo!" — m'ámo naṅ ó, nyaṅ a-baf! „that is right, ye farmers!" Cf. also: mútši w'úni m'ámo below.

Man, euph. form of ma, for which see the part. ma, 3. b. above.

Maṅ — ? „why doest thou — ?" for: ma aṅ. See the adv. ma?

Maṅ, for: ma aṅ, or for: ma ma, or ma ma; see the part. ma, 1. 2. and 3. a.

Maṅ, cuph. form of ma, for which see the part ma, 3. b.

Maṅ, v. a. „admonish, exhort, advise; bid; warn, chastise;" e. g. ǫ maṅ-kǫ tra yō-tši, „he exhorted him to do it;" — ǫ-kas-k'oṅ ǫ tra maṅ-kǫ, „his father will chastise him." Before m the ṅ is also changed into m for the sake of euphony.

Maṅ, ka-, or a-, pl. ę-, n. „exhortation, admonition; counsel, advice; warning, chastisement;" e. g. a-maṅ a-ninis, „an awful warning;" — ka-maṅ ka-fíno, „a good counsel."

Máne, o̱-, pl. a-, n. „friend"; e. g. o̱-máne-ka-mi, „my friend."

Máne, ma-, n. „friendship, agreement, concord;" e. g. ma-máne ma-ñañ, „their friendship."

Mañk, ka̱-, pl. tra̱-, n. „maize, indian corn."

Mañk, v. a. „hide, conceal; disguise;" also „bury"; e. g. o̱ mañk an-tis, „he hid the knife;" — o̱ mañk e-náne-y'oñ, „he disguised his thoughts;" — 'a bę́ne-ko ro-tof, „they buried him in the ground." Also „keep-from-, hide-before-" or „from-", as tšē mi tši mañk, „do not hide it from me."

Mañk, adj. „hiding, concealing;" pass. „hidden, concealed;" e. g. r'à ra-mañk, „a hidden thing."

Máñkne, v. refl. a. „hide oneself for-, waylay, lie in ambush for-;" also „hide oneself from-" or „before —; hide-with" or „on oneself;" e. g. 'a máñkne-mi ro-r'oñ, „they lay in ambush for me in the road;" — o̱ máñkne-ña, „he hid himself from them;" — o̱ máñkne a-bálma, „he concealed a dagger on his person (body)."

Máñkne, v. refl. n. „hide" or „conceal oneself;" e. g. ña máñkne ro-set, „they hid themselves in the house."

Máñkne, adj. „hidden, concealed, secret;" e. g. tr'ei tra̱ máñkne, „a hidden thing" or „matter".

M'áñle,
M'ánle, } adj. num. „four"; e. g. ma-lémre m'ánle, „four limes."

M'antr, n. „water"; also „soup" or „beef-tea; tide;" e. g. m'antr ma-bóti, „good water," lit. „sweet water." i. e. not salt, but fit to drink; — m'antr ma-báki, „a strong tide."

M'ántra̱r, pl. of ñ'ántra̱r, which see.

Mar, v. a. „help, assist;" e. g. o̱ mar-mi, „he assisted me."

Mar, v. impers. a. „be right" or „proper for, befit, behove, become;" e. g. pa̱ mar-ko̱ tra yo̱-tši, „it behoves him" or „it will become him to do it."

Mar, v. aux. indicating duty and propriety, and expressing the Engl. „ought". It is constr. with the long and with the short form of the Infinitive. E. g. ma̱ mar tra yo-tši, „thou oughtest to do it;" — o̱ mar tši yo̱, „he ought to do it."

Mar-tr'eī, kạ-, n. „luckiness, happiness;" e. g. ka-mar-tr'eī-k'oṅ or ka-mar-k'ọ-tr'eī, „his luckiness."

Mára, v. n. „burn, flame" (as fire). See n'antr, „fire".

Mą́rạt-mą́rạt, adv. onom. „making mą́rạt-mą́rạt." This word cannot be given otherwise; it is always used with trọm, „ruminate", indicating the sound which ruminating or chewing the cud causes. See Fables p. 62.

Mári, ma-, n. „right, propriety, justice;" e. g. kọ́no bā ma-mári, „he is in the right;" it is the contrary of ma-téri, „wrong".

Mári-tr'ei, v. n. „be lucky, be fortunate, have good luck, be happy;" e. g. kọn' mári-tr'eī, „he is lucky."

Mári-tr'eī, adj. „lucky, fortunate, happy;" e. g. w'úni mári-tr'eī, „a lucky person."

M'áro, n. „fat; palmoil;" e. g. m'áro ma-lạs, „bad palmoil."

Mą́tạs, v. a. freq. (rad. mat), „immerse repeatedly, dip repeatedly, baptize;" e. g. 'a mą́tạs-kọ ro-m'antr, „they dipped him into the water repeatedly."

Me, adv. „how, as," = ma and mo; this form is used before words with, or before the vowels e and i; e. g. ọ trọ́ri-mi, me I bā tra yō-tši, „he showed me how I am to do it;" — me me lā yọ̄, „as I use to do."

Me, adv. „when, after; while, as," = ma and mo; this form is used before words with, or before the vowels e and i; e. g. me me gbal-e, „while I was writing;" — ke me I nạṅ'-kọ, I tšéla-kọ, „and when I saw him, I called him."

Mē, pr. dem. prox. for amé, used for the comp. dem. pr. mīamé, which see.

Me, conj. „because, as," = ma and mo; this form is used before words with, or before the vowels e and i; e. g. míne, me I tšē yọ̄ ma-pant, I sọ́tọ he a-ram, „I, because I did no work, (I) got no pay."

Me —? adv. „why?" = ma and mọ; this form is used before words with, or before the vowels e and i, and this sense me has, if it is followed by the inter. suff. -a? at the end of the proposition, with which it is used. This form is only used for the 1st. pers. sing., and the verb. pr. I is generally dropped after me, if another me as the sign of the participle follows. E. g. mẹ I bes anǵ-a? „why do I dig here?" — mẹ me bes anǵ-a? „why am I digging here?" for: mẹ I me bes etc.?

Mẹ, part. = ma and mọ, used for various purposes:

1) for to express the Participle, and the Present, and sometimes also the Future tenses. This form is only used in the 1st. pers. sing.; the verb. pr. I is then generally dropped, so that mẹ stands for: I mẹ; e. g. kónọ mẹ tíla-'n̄. „him I am selling;" — mína mẹ der-an̄. „I am coming;" — yẹ mẹ la yọ, „thus I am always doing," for: yẹ I me la yọ. Cf. also the part. tsi under T, as used to form the Future.

2) for the Obligative Mood in the sense of „must, was, had;" but mẹ alone often stands for: I mẹ, „I must, I am, I was, I had," as is also the case when used for the participle etc., as stated under 1. above. The form mẹ expresses the Oblig. Mood in the 1st. pers. sing. only. E. g. mẹ pa he họ ọ kónẹ, = I mẹ pa he họ ọ kónẹ, „I must not say that he is gone."

3) for the Hortative Mood in the sense of „let", and „let me". Also with this Mood mẹ is only used for the 1st. pers. sing.
   a) If mẹ is used in the sense of „let", the verb. pr. I may follow; but it is also often, or generally, dropped, so that mẹ stands for: mẹ I, „let me," lit. „let I;" e. g. mẹ I pa he họ ọ kónẹ, or: mẹ pa he họ ọ kónẹ, „let me not say that he is gone."
   b) If mẹ is used in the sense of „let me," the verb. pr. I is of course dropped, as: mẹ pa he họ ọ kónẹ, „let me not say that he is gone," and thus may coincide with the form under a, above.

Mémar, v. rel. (rad. mem), „try, attempt, endeavour; prove, put to the test," lit. „make an attempt at-;" e. g. o mémar ka-gbal, „he tried to write," lit. „he attempted writing."

Mer, v. a. „swallow;" e. g. tsē trọm-n̄i, mer-n̄i gbo, „do not chew it, swallow it only."

Mer, ra-, pl. tra̯-, sometimes na-, n. „tongue"; e. g. ra-mer-r'oṅ, „his tongue."

M'er, n. „salt", e. g. m'er ma-laī, „much salt."

Méra, a-, pl. e̯-, n. „mind, heart (as the seat of understanding, not the organ), understanding, sense; conscience; temper; it is properly the intellectual part of man;" e. g. o bā he a-méra, „he has no sense;" — am-méra-ñ'oṅ ña kíra-ko, „his mind (conscience) troubles him;" — am-méra añá 'a kómane-ko, „his natural temper," lit. „the mind they bear him with."

Méro, adj. „left" (in opposition to „right"); e. g. ka-trā ka̯-méro, „the right hand."

Méro, ka-, n. „the right hand" (where ka-trā, „hand" is to be understood).

Mésa, a-, pl. e̯-, n. „table". From the Span. mesa; e. g. a-mésa a-lol, „a small table."

M'etr, pl. of ñ'etr, n. „a fixed time, time, period; festival." The sing. is hardly ever used. E. g. m'etr ma-bóli, „a long period;" — ña yō̯ m'etr ma-bána, „they hold a great festival."

Mi, pr. obj. „me"; e. g. o sap-mi, „he flogged me."

Mía, pr. emph. „it, this; they, them, these;" e. g. am'áro-ma-mi mía yi tši, „this is my palm-oil."

Mía-mē, pr. dem. comp. „this, these," lit. „it (is) this, they (are) these." See an ex. under ñ'ēs, „name" below.

Míañ, pr. abs. „it, this; they, them, these;" e. g. am'és-ma-ñañ míañ, „these are their names," lit. „their names (are) these." (Cf. -ñ under N.)

M'im, n. „liver"; e. g. m'im ma-bána, „a large liver."

Min', pr. emph. abbr. „I; me;" e. g. min' táho yō̯-tši, „it is not I who did it."

Mína, } pr. emph. „I; me;" e. g. mína yō̯ atr'eí atšé, „I did
Míne, } this thing."

Mínañ, pr. abs. „I; me;" e. g. mínañ-i? „is it I?"

Mínta, v. n. „be bold, venture, dare;" e. g. o mínta tra fof, „he ventures to speak."

Mínta, v. a „dare, venture, face, dare to face, dare to go near to-, dare to vie with-, dare to compete with-, be a match for-;" e. g. ọ mínta he kọ, „he does not dare to face him" or also „he is no match for him."

Mísidi,) a-, pl. e-, n. „mosque, church;" Mand. misero. From
Míšidi, } the Ar. مَسْجِدِ, oratorium, templum Muhammedis as-
Mísiri,) sectarum.

Mísra, n. „Egypt". From the Ar. مِصْر, Egyptus.

Mọ, adv. „how, as," = ma and me; this form is used before words with, or before the vowels o and u; e. g. ma trára mọ ọ yọ-tši-i? „doest thou know how he did it?" — mọ mọ la yọ, „as he uses to do."

Mọ, adv. „when, after; while, as," ma and me; this form is used before words with, or before the vowels o and u; e. g. mọ ọ lápsọ mu nank, „when he last saw thee;" — mọ ọ poṅ kọ́ne, ṅa yíra tráka di, „after he had left, they sat down to eat;" — mọ mọ díra-e, „while he was sleeping."

Mọ, conj. „because, as," = ma and me; this form is used before words with, or before the vowels o and u; e. g. kọ́nọ, mọ ọ tšē yọ ma-paut, ọ sólọ he a-ram, „he, because he did no work, got no pay."

Mọ —? adv. „why?" — ma and me; this form is used before words with, or before the vowels o and u; and this sense mọ has, if it is followed by the inter. suff. -a? at the end of the proposition, with which it is used. This form is only used for the 3d. pers. sing., and the verb. pr. o is generally dropped after mọ, if another mọ, as the sign of the participle follows. E. g. mọ o bes anó-a? „why does he dig here?" — mọ mọ bes anó-a? „why is he digging here?" for: mọ ọ mọ bes anó-a?

Mọ, prep. „according to;" e. g. o yo mọ ar'ím ra o-kas-k'oṅ, „he did according to the command of his father." This form does not change its vowel for the sake of euphony.

Mọ, part. = ma and me, used for various purposes:
1) for to express the Participle, and the Present, and sometimes also the Future tenses. This form is only used in

the 3d. pers. sing.; the verb. pr. is then generally dropped, so that mǫ stands for: ǫ mǫ; e. g, yǫ mǫ la yǭ, „thus he is always doing," for: yǫ o mǫ la yǭ; — mǫ mǫ gbal-e, „while he was writing;" — kǫ́nǫ mǫ der-añ, „he is coming." Cf. also the part. tra under T, as used to form the Future.

2) for the Obligative Mood in the sense of „must, was, had;" but mǫ alone often stands for ǫ mǫ, „he must, he is, he was, he had;" as is also the case when it is used for the participle etc., as stated under 1. above. The form mǫ is only used for the 3d. pers. sing. — E. g. mǫ pā he hǫ I kone, = ǫ mǫ pa he hǫ I kone, „he must not say that I am gone."

3) for the Hortative Mood in the sense of „let, let him," lit. „let he." Also with this Mood mǫ is only used for the 3d. pers. sing. —

  a) If mǫ is used in the sense of „let", the verb. pr. ǫ may follow; but it is also often, or generally, dropped, so that mǫ stands for: mǫ ǫ, „let him;" e. g. mǫ ǫ pā he hǫ I kǫ́ne, = mǫ pa he hǫ I kǫ́ne, „let him not say that I am gone."

  b) If mǫ is used in the sense of „let him," the verb. pr. is of course dropped, as: mǫ pā he hǫ I kǫ́ne, „let him not say that I am gone;" and thus the form may be the same with the one under a, above.

Mǫ am'ǫ́lǫ ma-. „according to," lit. „according to the value of—", = mǫ; e. g. I yǭ mǫ am'ǫ́lǫ ma ad'ím-ra-mu, „I did according to thy word."

Mǫ hǫ, „as, like;" also „as if;" e. g. w'úni ó w'úni mǫ yǭ he ma-pant mǫ hǫ K'úru, „no man works like God;" — yǭ mǫ hǫ ma 'a mam-mu; kére tšē yǭ o-las, „do as they bid thee; but do not do wrong."

Mǫ hǫ ma, ⎱ „according as, as;" e. g. mǫ hǫ mǫ mǫ yéma tra
Mǫ hǫ me, ⎰ poñ yǭ, „as he will wish to have done." The
Mǫ hǫ mo,   use of the different forms depends on euphony; the first being used for the 2d. pers. sing., and for all three

pers. in the pl., the second for the 1st. pers. sing., and the third for the 3d. pers. sing.

Módu, n. This word is derived from the Susu. The proper sense of the term is „son (of), possessor (of)," like the Hebr. בַּעַל; for it is also used with common names, not only with proper ones, as Télma Módu, „a prater, a loquacious person," lit. „a son of prating." Télma is here, no doubt, the abstr. noun ka-télma, „prating, loquaciousness," the prefix being dropped. In the Susu (and sometimes in the Temne also), this word is frequently joined with the name of the mother to form patronymics of males, or the names of sons. Thus Námina Módu, as used in Temne, was the proper name of the Alikáli of the Port-Loko territory in the author's time. Námina was the name of one of his father's wives. As polygamy is common among the Temnes, it is rather a convenient mode of distinguishing the names of the various children of the different wives, who had one common husband. Námina Módu is therefore lit. „the son of Namina." The word Módu is, however, not so frequently used among the Temnes as among the Susus; because the Temnes may express the same thing also in their own way. See Proverb 5, p. 99. (Cf. also Tem. Grammar §. 37, 1. Note 2.)

M'ólo, n. „amount, value, price;" e. g. am'ólo ma ak'óta, „the price of the cloth;" — ak'óta ka ba m'ólo ma-báki, „the cloth is valuable," lit. „the cloth has a high price."

M'oṅ, pr. poss. „his, her," lit. „of him;" e. g. ma-bóṅe-m'oṅ, „his joy."

M'óṅe, n. „poverty; trouble, misery, distress;" e. g. o bā m'óṅe, „he is in trouble," lit. „he has trouble;" = m'óṅe ma wopko, lit. „trouble holds him."

Móṅe, adj. „poor, miserable;" e. g. w'úni móṅe, „a miserable person."

Móri, o-, pl. a-, n. „a Mohammedan, a mori-man;" derived from móri, „teach, show" (as a road, and in the Mohammedan sense of the word „show the right way," as they pretend to do; for they often set themselves up as teachers). Vei móre; Mand. morolu „religious people." The Hebr. מֹרֶה „teacher" presents itself.

Móri, adj. „belonging to a mori-man" or „to a Mohammedan;" e. g. w'úni móri, „a Mohammedan" or „mori-man."

Móri, ra-, n. „the Mohammedan religion, Islamism, Mohammedanism;" e. g. o woṅ' da-móri, „he embraced Islamism," = o woṅ ka ra-móri, lit. „he entered Islamism."

Mórka, a-, pl. e-, n. „white ant, termite;" Lat. termes fatale; e. g. e-mórka e-laï, „many termites."

Mot, v. aux. „be first; be before, anticipate." As an aux. it
Mó'a, serves to express the adverbs „first, before;" e. g. kọ́no mọt bĕk, „he arrived first;" — mọt naṅ kọ rováṅ, „go ye first yonder;" — der romí l mọta di, „come to me before I eat;" — o mọ́ta mi woṅ, „he entered before me." In the two last senses it is used transitively.

Móta, adj. „first"; e. g. aṅ-réï a-móta, „the first day."

Móte, ka-, pl. tra-, n. „bag, basket (to hang on one's shoulder, made of a kind of cane); e. g. ka-móte ka-bána, „a large bag."

Mótra, v. n. „sink, go down to the bottom, sink down, go down" (as a stone in the water, or the sun below the horizon); also „dive" (as a duck); „be drowned;" e. g. aṅ-fatr ṅa motra ro-m'antr, „the iron sank in the water;" — ar'etr ra mótra, „the sun went down." Cf. the Lat. mergi, and the Gr. δύω.

Mu, pr. obj. „thee"; e. g. o tra dif-mu, „he will kill thee."

Mun', pr. emph. abbr. „thou; thee;" e. g. mun' táho, „it is not thou."

Mun. v. a. „drink; lap" (as a dog); e. g. o mun m'antr, „he drank water."

Mun, v. n. „drink"; e. g. o mun he, „he did not drink;" — o mun ri, „he drank of it," lit. „he drank there."

Múno, pr. emph. „thou; thee;" e. g. múno ma lásar an-tis, „thou didst spoil the knife," = „it was thou who spoiled etc."

Múnoṅ, pr. abs. „thou, (it is) thou; thee;" e. g. w'úni las múnoṅ! „thou art a bad person!" lit. „a bad person thou!"

Mun's. v. caus. (rad. mun), „give-to drink, make-to drink." Ger. „tränken", = the Gr. ποτίζω; e. g. I mun's-ko. „I gave him to drink." Also „cool-in water" (as redhot iron).

Mut. ka-, pl. tra-, n. „back; outside;" e. g. ka ka-mut-k'oṅ, „on his back;" — ka-mut ka am-póti, „the outside of the cup;" — o kála ka-mut, „he returned the back," = „he returned." With the prep. ro-it becomes also a prep. or postp., for which see romút.

Mútši, v. a. „call, call to, bid, express" (as thanks to one, see the two next words); „invite"; e. g. I mútši-ko, „I called him."

Mútši m'ámo, „give thanks, be thankful," lit. „call thanks."

Mútši w'úni m'ámo, „give thanks to one, be thankful to one;" also „congratulate one;" as: I mútši-nu m'ámo, „I thank thee;" o mútši-ko m'ámo tráka o-kómra, „he congratulated him on the birth of a child," lit. „— — — on account of the woman in child-bed."

Mútši w'úni šéke, „sympathize with one, express one's sympathy to one;" e. g. I mútši-ko šéke, „I sympathized with him." Lit. „I called pity to him."

Mútši w'úni sen'-ó, „bid one welcome, welcome one;" e. g. o mútši-mi sen'-ó, „he bid me welcome." Lit. „he called welcome to me."

N.

N', pref. indef. and insep. „a, an;" e. g. n'antr, „a fire," for: na-antr.

'N-, abbr. of an-. See an ex. under šya.

-'N, suff abbr. form of -aṅ. See the suff. -aṅ under A.

Ṅ-, pref. indef. and insep. „a, an;" e. g. ṅ'antr, „a tree," for: ṅa-ántr.

-Ṅ, a euph. letter added to some Adverbs and Pronouns terminating in a vowel, as toṅ, „now, for: to; yaṅ, „thus", for: ya; kónoṅ, „he", for: kóno; etc. This letter corresponds with the Gr. ν ἐφελκυστικόν. These forms are always used at the end of a proposition, though not exclusively; but the short forms are never used at the end. See more about this in the Grammar.

Na-, pref. indef. "a, an," but generally used for the pl.; e. g. n'antr na-bána, "a large fire;" — na-béña na-bóli, "long ropes."

Na, pr. subj. "it, they;" e. g. an'ántr na dímše, "the fire is gone out."

Nä, o̯-, pl. ra̯-, n. "ox"; also "cow"; e. g. o̯-nä o̯-bána, "a large cow."

Na, part. = nañ, which see.

Ña-, pref. indef. "a. an" (sing. and pl.); e. g. a-fa̯m ña-ra̯ñ, "two persons;" — ña-set, = a-set, "a house."

Ña, pr. subj. "it; they;" e. g. a-bil ña yi he ri, "there is no canoe there," lit. "a canoe it is not there;" — añ-fa̯m ña kóne, "the people have left."

Ña, pr. obj. "it; them" (also used for nouns in ma-); e. g. o̯ bal-ña, "he drove them away;" — am'ántr loñ-ña, "as for the water pour it out."

Ña, prep. poss. "of"; e. g. añ-set ña Sóri, "Sori's house," lit. "the house of Sori."

Ña, o̯-, pl. a-, n. "companion, man, one of a company;" e. g. o̯-ña-mu, "thy companion," lit. "one of thee (thine)," = o̯-ñañ, which see below.

Ña, pr. emph. "they; them;" but often used for the sing. "he" when joined with other emph. pronouns, or with proper names, implying the copula "and"; e. g. ña Pä Kámu-e, "he and the Iguana."

Na̯, pr. subj. "ye, you;" e. g. na̯ dífa-mi o̯-nä, "ye did kill me the cow." = "ye killed me the cow."

Ña-tši, pr. dem. log. "that, those;" e. g. añ-fa̯m ña-tši, "those persons" (spoken of before).

Ña-tši, pr. poss. neut. "its, their," lit. "of it; e. g. añ-fon-ña-tši, "its hair," lit. "the hair (hairs) of it."

Nábi, o-, pl. a-, n. "prophet". From the Ar. نَبِي, propheta.

Náfas, v caus. (rad. náfa). "make to thrive, make to be well off; execute" or "carry out luckily; make prosperous, help forward; be of use to-;" e. g. o náfas ka-tšim, „he carried on the war luckily;" — o náfas atr'eí atšé, „he carried this thing out luckily;" — ar'á aré ra náfas-mi, „this thing helps me forward" or „is of advantage to me."

Ńaíbi, v. a. „reveal, make known" (as a secret); „prove, make clear" (as one's guilt); e. g. ńaíbi ka-keía-k'oń, „prove his theft."

Nak, a-, pl. e-, n. „rice boiled" or „cooked"; e. g. e-nak e-bóti-di, „delicious rice."

Ńak-ńak, ka-, n. verb. „act of gnashing" or „of striking together" (as the teeth); „act of making a chattering noise with- (the teeth). See the next word."

Ńak-ńak e-šek, ka-, n. „act of gnashing the teeth;" e. g. ka-ńak-ńak-k'oń e-šek, „his gnashing of teeth."

Nákat, adj. „fried" (as meat in a pot); e. g. o-šem o-nákat, „fried beef," = u-šem u-nákat.

Nal, v. a. „abuse, use abusive language against; challenge;" e. g. o nal-mi, „he abused me."

Nam, v. a. „see"; it is a euph. form of nańk, used before b. f. m and p; e. g. mo o nam-mi etc., „when he saw me etc."

Nám'ra, v. rel. and inch. „get satisfied" or „satiated with food;" e. g. o-ná o nám'ra he, „the cow does not get satisfied." Probably from an obs. nam.

Nań', v. a. euph. form of nańk, used before g and k; e. g. „I nań'-ko ro-petr, „I saw him in town."

Nań, part. and adv. = na, used to express the Conjunctive, and a recently past time, or the Imperfect tense, in which latter case it may be given by the adverbs „to day, before" or „already", or by the aux. verb „did"; e. g. be šya yi nań-e, na bap-mi ka ro-k'or ka o-ná, „if it had been I, ye would have met me in the inside of the cow;" — I poń gbal nań, = I pon' na gbal, „I have written to day;" — I káne-mu nań ho; tšē ko, „I told thee before; do not go." — I yo-tši nań, „I did it already;" — káli ań-sot, owó I wat nań, „see the horse, which I bought to day;" — ńa-der na ro-i? „did they come yonder?" The form nań is used more absolutely than na; but the latter is often connected with, or prefixed to nouns indicating time, to make that time more definite, when it may be given by „last" or by „this", according to the nature of the noun, with which it is used; e. g. ọ der na ra-yań, „he came to day at noon;" — na tratrák, „last night;" — na-bạt, „this morning." This particle or adv. is always used of a recently past time, or of events having taken place the same day they are spoken of. Cf. also the longer forms nána and nánań below.

Nạń, pr. subj. „ye", a euph. and stronger form of na, generally used behind the verb with the Imperative; e. g. dif-kọ nạń, „kill ye him;" — der nań anọ́, „come ye here."

Nań, v. a „bite"; e. g. an-tran o nań-mi, „the dog bit me."

Nań, = ańáń, pr. dem rem. „that, those;" used if it is the subject of a proposition without the noun; e. g. a-gbáta ńań, „that is a mat," lit. „a mat that;" but: ań-gbáta ańáń, „that mat."

Nań, pr. obj. „them", generally used for to express the poss. pr. of the 3d. pers, pl. in connection with the poss. prep., as: am'áro-ma-ńań, „their palm-oil," lit. „the palm-oil of them."

Nań, pr. abs. „they; them;" e. g. ńań na yọ̄-tsi, „they did it," = „it is they who did it."

Nań, ọ, pl. a-, n. = ọ-ña, „one of one's family" or „kindred" or „household, companion, one of one's company;" e. g. ọ-ńań kọ́nọń, „this (he) is one of their company," lit. „one of their company he;" — owọ́ ka a-ńań, „he who is of their company;" kạ̈li ọ-ńań, „look one of their company." The form ọ-ńań is used more absolutely than ọ-ña, which latter form is used with poss. pronouns.

Nána, } adv. „to day." They are stronger forms than na and
Nánań, } nań, and as to the form nánań it may be used quite absolutely; while nána may be used with nouns indicating time like na, to make this time more definite, as: nána bạt, „this morning;" — ọ-der nána ra-yań, „he came to day at noon;" — ọ der nánań, „he came to day;" — a-lọ réke mạ der-e? Nánań, or: l der nánań; „what time didst thou

come?" „To day," or „I came to day;" nána ra-foi, „last evening;" — ña fer a-bítiñ nána gbes. „they beat drum all last night." Also these forms like na and nañ are always used of a recently past time. Cf. na and nañ above.

Náne, v. n. „think, suppose;" e. g. tro ma náne-e? „how" or „what doest thou think?" — I náne ho Sóri kónoñ, „I think it is Sori," lit. „I think that Sori he."

Náne, v. a. „think of, remember, consider, account;" e. g. I náne-tši, „I remember it;" — I náne-ko ho w'úni fíno, „I account him as a good person; — tra sa náne-tši lóko ó lóko, „let us always remember it."

Náne, a-, or i-, pl. e-, or ma-, n. „thought; meaning, sense;" e. g. K'úru o trára e-náne-'e-su, „God knows our thoughts." Cf. the pref. i- under 1 above.

Naṅk, v. n. „see"; fig. „understand;" e. g. ma naṅk-i? „doest thou understand?" or „doest thou see?"

Naṅk, v. a. „see, find; look upon, account;" e. g. sa gbáli he naṅk K'úru, kére K'úru o gbáli naṅk tr'ei ó tr'ei atrá sa yo, „we cannot see God, but God can see every thing which we do." Fig. „perceive, understand."

Náṅka, v. rel. „look with-on-." See the next word.

Náṅka w'úni i-nei, „look with pity" or „compassion on one;" e. g. o náṅka-mi i-nei, „he looks with pity on me."

Náṅkane, v. recipr. „see each other face to face, meet each other face to face;" hence also „hold a council, consult together;" e. g. na naṅkane ténoñ, „they held a council to day."

N'áṅle, N'ánle, } adj. num. „four"; e. g. a-fam ň'áṅle, „four persons."

Nant, ka-, pl. tra-, n. „mucus of the nose, snot, snivel."

Nant, v. a. „remove, carry away;" e. g. nant ey'étr-'e-mi, „carry my things away;" — sa nant ey'étr eyé a-lo ñ'in, „we carry these things away at one time."

N'antr, n. „fire"; def. an'ántr, „the fire," = „hell"; e. g. an'ántr na mára par-par, „the fire burns briskly;" — an'ántr na yo he ko o-bañ, „the fire did not hurt him."

N'antr, pl. y'intr, n „tree"; e. g. ń'antr a-bána, „a large tree;" — y'intr e-lai, „many trees."

Nántra, v. a. „marry" (of the male); e. g. o-lánba o nántra ow'án béra ka Pā Sóri, „the man married the daughter of Mr. Sori."

N'antrar, pl. m'ántrar, n. „tear"; e. g. m'ántrar ma gbáro-ko, „he sheds tears," lit. „tears flow down from him," or more fully: m'ántrar ma gbáro-ko e-for, lit. „tears flow down from his eyes;" or: am'ántrar ma gbáro, „the tears flow;" or: e-for-y'oń e gbáro m'ántrar, lit. „his eyes flow with tears," = „he sheds tears." The sing. is hardly ever used.

Nap, v. a. „knock, strike, beat; knock-with-;" ań-ṭam ńa yéma ko nap, „the people wanted to beat him;" — o nap-ko i-sar, „he knocked him with a stone."

Nap, v. a. „condemn, find guilty, convince one of his guilt;" e. g. 'a ńap-ko trákа ra-keī, „they condemned him for theft."

Náši, v. a. „wipe off, wipe out, blot out" (as the writing on a slate); e. g. O K'úru, náši ama-treī-ma-mi ma-las! „O God, blot out my sins!"

Nášia, v. rel. „wipe off-for-; wipe off-with-; e. g. nášia-mi amagbal, „wipe out the letters for me;" — nášia ama-gbal k'óta, „wipe off the letters with a cloth."

Natr, v. n. ascend, go up, rise, rise up;" also „go up the country;" e. g. ak'íma ka natr, „the smoke rises up;" — o ńatr ro-gbań, or also simply: o ńatr, „he went up the country."

Natr, v. a. „go up at-, go up along- or on-; ascend" (as a tree); e. g. o ńatr aka-bal, „he went up at the brook."

Nátra, v. caus. „make-to rise up, raise, make to ascend, take up, lift up" (as an oar); e. g. ńátra ka-trá-ka-mu, „lift up thy hand."

Ně, pr. dem. prox. „this, these," for: ańé. This form is used for the comp. dem. pr., as ńía-ňě, „this," lit. „it this;" e. g. ań-gbáta-ń'oń ńía-ňě, „this is his mat," lit. „his mat it this."

Ňe, contr. form for: ńa yi, as: ko ńe-e? „what is the matter?" lit. „what is it?"

Nei, i-, n. „pity, compassion, mercy;" also „pitiable state"; e. g. o bā-ko i-nei, „he had pity on him."

Neī, a-, or i-, pl. ma-. n. „country yam, common yam" (very white); e. g. ma-neī ma-lai, „many yams."

N'eī, n. „sun" (as the source of heat); e. g. anei na bañ ténoñ, „the sun is hot to day;" as the source of light the sun is called ar'étr which see.

N'émi, n. „kind of hammock said to have been sent by God." See Tradit. p. 32.

Némtene, prob. a refl. form of an obs. némte, „beseech, beg, intreat, implore, beg for pardon, beg pardon from;" e. g. o némtene-mi, „he begged my pardon."

Népal, a-, pl. e-, n. „the long grass used for thatching;" e. g. e-népal e-fíno, „fine grass."

Népal, adj. „made of grass, thatched with grass;" e. g. a-set a-népal, „a grass-house," or „a house thatched with grass."

Nēs, ra-, n. „fear, dread;" e. g. ra-nēs-r'oñ, „his dread."

Nēs, a-, pl. e-, n. „spider"; e. g. a-nēs a-bana, „a large spider."

N'ēs, pl. m'ēs, n. „name"; also „character; fame;" e. g. am'ēs-ma-ñañ mía-mē, „these are their names," lit. „their names they these."

Nésa, v. n. „fear, be afraid;" e. g. o nésa, „he is afraid;" — tšē nésa, „do not be afraid."

Nésa, v. a. „fear, dread, be afraid of-; respect, honour;" e. g. o nésa-mu, „he is afraid of thee."

Nésam, a-, pl. e-, n. „breath, life, animal life," = ἡ ψυχή; e. g. o ba he so a-nésam, „he is dead," lit. „he has no life again."

Nésam, adj. „living, alive;" e. g. r'a ra-ñésam, „a living creature."

Ni, pr. obj. „it; them;" e.g. ana-béña, kára-ni, „as to the ropes, bring them."

Ni, a-, pl. e-, n. „portion, share; e. g. kára añ-ni-'a-mi, „bring my share."

Ni, a-, pl. e-; or a-, or i-, pl. ma-, n. „sole of the foot, foot; footstep;" e. g. kot ka 'ma-ni-ma-mi, „walk in my footsteps."

Ni, pr. obj. „it; them;" e. g. añ-gbáta, o tíla-ñi, „as to the mat, he sold it."

Nía, pr. emph. „it, this; they, them, these;" e. g. an-tis, ñia yi-tši, „this is the knife," lit. „the knife it is it," or „as for the knife, this is it."

Nía-n̂é, pr. dem. comp. „this, these," lit. „it (is) this, they (are) these;" e. g. añ-set-'a-mi, ńia-ńē, „this is my house," lit. „my house it (is) this."

Nía yi, } „namely, that is, that is to say," lit „it is-;"
Nía yi ho, } e. g. I ko bañ añ-réka-'a-mi, ńia yi ho am-beíbal, „I go to fetch my book, that is the Bible."

N'ímisa, n. „trouble of any kind, distress;" e. g. o wọń n'ímisa. „he got into trouble."

Nin, e-, n. „dung, excrements" (of men and beasts; that of infants they call e-sóro); e. g. e-nin ya tra-nā, „cow-dung."

N'in, adj. num. „one"; e. g. a-set ń'in, „one house."

Nína, } adv. „to morrow;" the longer form may be used absoNínań, } lutely; and the shorter may be joined with nouns of time, to make this time more definite; e. g. I tši yọ-tši nínań, „I shall do it to morrow;" — o tra kal so nína rafoī, „he will return again to morrow evening;" — nína bạt, „to morrow morning;" — nína tratrák, „to morrow night."
Cf. also anína, and anínań, under A.

Nínis, o-, n. „terror; fierceness; awfulness, frightfulness;" e. g. o-nínis o wop-ko, „he feels terrified," lit. „terror holds him" or „took hold of him."

Nínis, adj. „terrible; fierce; awful; frightful;" e. g. o-šem o-nínis, „a fierce animal;" — r'ā ra-nínis, „a terrible thing."

No, adv. „here, hither;" e. g. o yíra no, „he lives here." Cf. also anó under A.

No, prep. „here in, here at, here to;" the adv. „here" is implied; e. g. o yi no-petr, „he is here in this town." Cf. anó, prep. under A.

N'of, pl. y'of, n. „moon; month; e. g. y'of e-sas, „three months."

Noï, v. a. „take, take away-from-, dismiss-from, take away;" „tšē noï ey'etr-'e-mi, „do not take away my things;" — 'a noï-ko a-kála, „they took money away from him."

Nọń, pr. dem. rem. for: ńań, used with lọ, „time"; see: lọ ńọń under L.

N'oṅ, pr. poss. „his, her," lit. „of him, of her," being a contraction of ña ko, with the euph. ñ affixed; e. g. aṅ-trar-ñ'oṅ, „his slaves;" — aṅ-sel-ñoṅ, „his house."

Nọ́si-neī, o-, n. „pitiable condition;" also „pity, compassion;" e. g. o-nọ́si-neī o wop-ko, „he is in a pitiable condition." lit. „a p. c. holds him;" — K'úru o ṅáñka-su o-nọ́si-nei, „God looked with pity on us."

Nu, pr. obj. „you"; e. g. sa tra bap-nu re-petr, „we shall meet you in town."

N'ump, pl. m'ump, n. „fable, tale, story;" e. g. man tram m'ump, „let us tell stories."

N'úmpal, pl m'úmpal, sometimes also y'úmpal, n. „shadow of a person" (when standing in the sun ; „shade, soul" or „spirit (of man)," = the Lat. umbra. It is also used of the spirit of God. The animal life is called a-ñésạm, which see. Cf. Pref. § 12, b. where more particulars will be found about ñ'úmpal.

Nyā, pr. emph. „ye; you;" but also used for the sing. „thou" when joined with other emph. pronouns, or with proper names, implying the copula „and"; e. g. nyā yō atr'ei atšé, „ye did this thing," — nyā kāne der tra dif o-šem-e? „thou and who came to kill the beast?"

Nyāṅ, pr. abs. „ye; you;" e. g. nyāṅ, nyā lásạr am-bil añé, „ye, ye spoiled this canoe."

O.

O-, pref. def. and indef. „a, an; the;" e. g. o-baī, „the king" or „a king."

O-, pref. emph. vow. to make nouns with the inseparable pref. w', and one with d' definite; as: ow'úni, „the person," from w'úni, „a person;" — ow'ān, „the child," from w'an, „child"; etc.; od'ér, „the place," from d'er, „a place."

O! int. „oh! o!" denoting wonder, surprise, also grief and compassion. E. g. o, o-póto! „Oh, a white man!" — o Pā, I trára alrá I pa! „oh Sir, I know what I say!"

Ó! int. or expl. part. It is placed at the end of saluting or of exclamatory propositions, when like -e it serves to indicate the Vocative. It is always used with such words, which are addressed directly to another. If it has any sense with such propositions, it is that of „now" or of the Ger. „doch". Also the Liberated Africans at Sierra-Leone are fond of affixing the vowel sound o at the end of a proposition, or of a word, especially when calling to another; they may often be heard to say — „come-o!" == „come now!" or „come then!" E. g. sen'-ó, Pa! „welcome, Sir!" See more ex. in the Colloq. Phras. p. 106 – 110. Cf. also the Grammar about this particle.

Ǫ, pr. subj. „he, she;" e. g. ǫ fi dis, „he died yesterday."

Ǫ, pr. impers. or irrel. „it"; e. g. ǫ lómpi, „it is right."

Ǫ, for: ǫ pa; or: ǫ pa hǫ, „he said." See Tradit. p. 68.

Ó, conj. or copulative part. „and"; when it is used to join several nouns or names, then the ó behind the last is to be given by „also", or it may be left untranslated; and when it occurs twice, or behind two nouns, it may be given by" — as well as —", or by „both —, and —." E. g. d'er-ó-d'er, „every place," lit. „place and place;" — Bási ó Sori ó, „Basi as well as Sori;" — k'óta ó, ǫ-yúka ó, a-taba ó, „cloth and cassadas and tobacco also."

-'Ǫ-mi, pr. poss. „my", lit. „of me;" e. g. ǫd'ér-'ǫ-mi, „my place;" — ǫ-šem-'ǫ-mi, „my meat."

'Ǫ-mu, pr. poss. „thy", lit. „of thee;" e. g. ǫ-šem-'ǫ-mu, „thy meat."

'Ǫ, prep. poss. „of" for: wǫ. See the two preceding words.

Ǫ gbo! „oh dear! what is that! oh strange!" e. g. ǫ gbo, i-sar na lókǫ k'ek-e! „oh strange, a stone brought forth a beard!"

Ǫwé, pr. dem. prox. „this"; e. g. ǫ-trar ǫwé, „this slave."

Ǫwǫ́, pr. rel. „who, he who; which;" e. g. ǫ-bai ǫwǫ́ fi, „the king who died."

Ǫwǫ́n, pr. dem. rem. „that, that one;" e. g. ǫ-lánba ǫwǫ́n, „that young man."

P.

P', pref. indef. and insep pl.; e g. p'in, „one"; — p'ánle, „four"; — pa-la p'in, „one sort of rice."

Pā, v. n. „say, speak, talk about a matter;" e. g. o pā gbo rosan, „he speaks only at the mouth" (not according to what is in his heart); — 'a pā rokín, „they converse together."

Pā, v. a. „say; state, talk over" (as a ma'ter); „tell; pronounce;" e. g. pā-tśi ronón, „tell it to him;" o pā am-pā, „he stated the matter."

Pā, a-, pl. e-, or ma-, n. „saying, word; matter, palaver; statement, subject of inquiry, affair about which one speaks; story;" e. g. o tra pā am-pā ninan, „he will talk over the matter to morrow;" — mine ba 'ma-pa ma-tśi, „I have to talk those matters."

Pā, o-, pl. a-pā, or pa-ña, n. „Sir, Master, Mr.;" also „father" (when addressing one, otherwise o-kas is used). When applied to irrational beings it may be given by the def. article „the" in English, as: Pa Nēs, „the Spider," lit. „Mr. Spider;" — kóri 'u, Pa! „I salute thee, Sir!" Cf. the word k'ak in this Vocab. about the form Pa-ña.

Pa-, pref. def. = apa-, „the"; e. g. pa-la, = apa-la, „the rice;" — pa-yáka, „the krifi rice." Cf. krifi, adj. in this Vocab.

Pa-, pref. indef. pl. e. g. pa-la pa-fíno, „good rice."

Pa, pr. impers. or irrel. „it"; e. g. pa bóne-ko, „he is glad."

Pa, pr. sub. indef. „it"; e. g. pa-la pa bak lemp, „rice grows fast."

Pa, pr. subj. def. „it"; e. g. apa-la pa lása, „the rice got spoiled."

Pa-mi, pr. poss. def. „my". lit. „of me;" e. g. pa-la-pa-mi, „my rice."

Pa-mi, pr. poss. indef. „my", lit „of me;" e. g. pa-la-pa-mi, „rice of mine," = „my rice."

Pai, v. n. „jump, leap;" e. g. o pai ro tof, „he jumped down on the ground;" — o pai ka ka-bat, „he leaped over the brook."

Pai, v. n. „be ready" (as for a journey); e. g. ma pai-i? „are thou ready?" — I paī, mañ kǫnẹ, „I am ready, let us go;" — I ta paī hẹ, „I am not yet ready."

Paī, adv. spec. „very, quite, up to the brim; altogether," used with lā, „be full, be numerous;" with lásạr, „fill, make full;" and with káši, „refuse, will not." E. g. atr'ák ña lā ri paī, „the ants are very numerous there;" — lásạr am-pǫti paī, „fill the cup up to the brim." or „make the cup quite full;" — ǫ káši bak paī, „he will not grow at all."

Paía, v. a. „accompany"; e. g. Sóri ǫ trạ paía-mu ri, „Sori will accompany thee there."

Pạkášifẹ, conj. „because"; e. g. ǫ gbạ́li hẹ tši poñ yō, pạkášifẹ ǫ yi hẹ ri, „he cannot have done it, because he was not there."

Páli, adv. „the whole day, all day;" e. g. ña tǫ́mǫ páli, „they danced all day."

Páli gbẹs, „all day and all night;" e. g. sạ tǫ́mǫ páli gbẹs, „we danced all day and all night."

Pạl, v. a. „forget"; e. g. ǫ pạl añ-lápra-ñ'ǫñ, „he forgot his cap."

Pạ́lnẹ, v. refl. a. „forget oneself, forget; e. g. ǫ pạ́lnẹ-tši, „he forgot it."

Pañ, v. a. „lack, want, need;" e. g. ǫ pañ hẹ r'áka ó r'áka, „he is not in want of any thing."

Pañ, kạ-, n. verb. „act of lacking (a thing); state of being in want, want, distress, lack;" e. g. ka-pañ-k'ǫñ, „his want."

Pánẹ, v. a. „carry in" or „on the arms" (as a child, or as wood); „embrace, press to one's bosom." Also used as a compliment on meeting with one a second time the same day, in the sense of „meet", when the subj. pronoun is dropped. E. g. ǫ pánẹ ẹ-tǫk, ǫ kérẹ-yi ro-set, „he took the wood in his arms, and carried it into the house." See also Colloq. Phras. p. 107 and 110.

Páñi-tr'eī, adj. comp. „harmless, innocent, being without fault;" e. g. w'úni páñi-tr'eī, „a harmless person."

Pạñk, a-, n. „folly, foolishness;" e. g. añ-pạñk-ñ'ǫñ, „his folly."

Pạñk, adj. „foolish"; e. g. w'úni pạñk, „a foolish person."

Pánkạl, a-, pl. ẹ-, n. „cithern" or „harp", also called „Krooharp." It has seven grass strings, is of a triangular form, and fixed in one half of a split calabash, and is played with the fingers. E. g. o fer am-páṅkal, „he plays the harp."

Páṅkal, a-, pl. e-, or tra-; or also o-, pl. tra-, n. „a large antelope exceeding in size the common native ox," with white spots, and long horns, commonly called „bush-cow". The female has no horns. It is said to put down its horns backwards when running through the bush; but when it is in a fury, it raises them upright for selfdefence.

Pant, a-, or i-, pl. ma-, n. „work, business; e. g. ma-pant ma-báki. „hard work." The sing. is hardly ever used.

Pántṅe, v. n. „raise oneself, rise up" (as one stooping or kneeling down); e. g. o pántṅe. „he rose up."

Pántrane, v. recipr. a. (rad. pantr), „mix" or „mingle together, put" or „lay together" (as people money for a common stock); „mix together promiscuously, confound;" e. g. 'a pántrane aṅ-kála-'a-ñaṅ, „they put their money together."

Par-par, adv. onom. „briskly, smartly," used with mára, „flame, burn;" e. g. an'ántr na mára par-par, „the fire burns smartly" or „the fire burns making par-par."

Patr, v. n. „cook; boil; be boiled, be stewed;" e. g. I poṅ patr, maṅ kóne di, „I have cooked, let us go to eat;" — am'ántr ma patr, „the water boils."

Patr, v. a. „cook, seethe; stew;" e. g. o patr o-šem, „he stewed the meat."

Patr, adj. „cooked; boiled; stewed;" e. g. o-šem o-patr. „boiled beef."

Pe, contraction of pa yi, „it is; e. g. tro pe-e?" how is it?" See Colloq. Phras. p. 105.

Pénša, = péša, v. n. answer in the negative, contradict, refuse, not concede, deny;" e. g. o pénša ho o trára-mi, „he disowned me." lit. „he denied that he knows me;" — tšẹ pénša, w'an! „do not deny, boy!"

Pénša, } v. a. „deny, refuse, reject, object to; give a negative
Péša, } answer to-, contradict;" e. g. o pénša-tši. „he denied it;" — tšẹ péša-tši, w'an! „do not deny it, boy!" — o péša o-trar, „he objected to the slave" (having a fault).

Péskiane, v. recipr. (rad. peski), „open in various directions, diverge from each other" (as roads); „lie in different positions" (as bundles); fig. „disagree, be at variance with each other; differ" (as words); e. g. e-pā-'e-mu e péskiane, „thy statements do not agree;" — as'oṅ tra péskiane ri, „the roads diverge from each other there."

Péskiane, adj. „diverging from each other, diverging off in various directions; being at variance with each other; different;" e. g. s'oṅ tra-péskiane, „roads diverging from each other;" — s'im tra-péskiane, „words being at variance with each other.

Petr, ka-, pl. tra-, n. „town"; e. g. ka-petr ka-bána ka yi ri, „there is a large town there."

Pi, pr, obj. „it"; e. g. I wai-pi, „I bought it" (i. e. rice).

Pía, pr. emph. „it, this;" e. g. apa-lā-pa-mi, pía yi tši, „as to my rice, this is it," = „this is my rice."

Piár', abbr. of piára, generally used before the int. ó. See the next word, and cf. Colloq. Phras. p. 106—107 for examples with this form.

Piára, v. n. „be all day, spend all day, be well all day, live, spend, be." It is often used as an aux. to express the adv. „all day." E. g. o piára yǫ ma-pant, „he did work all day;" — na piára tǫmǫ, „they danced all day;" — o piára ro Ma-lal, „he was all day at Malal."

Pika, v. n. „faint, swoon; get senseless" (as by a stroke on the head): o píka, „he swooned away."

Pil, ka-, n. „the west;" e. g. o yéfa ro-pil, „he came from the west." With the prep. ro- it becomes also a prep. or a postposition.

Pílor, a-, or i-, pl. ma-, n. „ball" (for a gun), „bullet"; e. g. a-pílor a-bána, „a large ball."

Pim, v. a. „pick, pluck, pluck off" (as flowers, fruit, or ears of rice), hence also „reap"; e. g. sa ko pim ma-lémre, „we go to pluck lemons."

Pima, v. inch. „break, get broken" (as rope); „tear, get torn" (as cloth); „get loose" (as a horse); e. g. aṅ-soi o píma, „the horse got loose;" — ak'óta ka píma, „the cloth got torn."

Pínkar, a-, pl. e-, n. „gun, musket;" e. g. a-pínkar a-fíno, „a fine gun."

Pólo, v. a. „crown"; also „crown-as-"; e. g. 'a pólo o-bai, „they crowned the king;" — 'a pólo-ko o-bai, „they crowned him (as) king"

P'ólpala, = p'ólpara, n. „gunpowder;" e. g. p'ólpala pa-lai, „much gunpowder."

P'oṅ, pr. poss. „his, her," lit. „of him, of her," being a contraction of: pa ko with the euph. ṅ; e. g. apa-la-p'oṅ, „his rice."

Poṅ, v. n. „have an end, take an end, be over; be finished, be done, be exhausted; be at an end; be expired, be up" (as a fixed time); e. g. apa-la pa poṅ, „the rice is exhausted;" — ma-pant-ma-mi ma poṅ, „my work is finished."

Poṅ, v. a. „finish, make an end to-; go all over" (as a country); „exhaust" (as provisions); „wear out" (as clothes); „destroy" (as a town); „rout" (as an army). As an aux. verb it serves to express the past tense in the sense of „have", or „have done;" and sometimes it expresses the adverb „entirely, completely, altogether." E. g. o yéma poṅ ama-pant, „he wants to finish the work;" — o poṅ e-lópra-y'oṅ, „he has worn out his clothes;" — 'a dim aka-petr, „they destroyed the town;" — o poṅ gbal, „he has written;" — o poṅ di am-bamp, „he ate the bird altogether," or: o poṅ ko di, „he ate it altogether."

Poṅ, v. impers. „be enough, suffice; be done;" e. g. pa poṅ, „it is" or „will be enough."

Pon', euph. form of poṅ, „finish", used before d, n and t; as o pon' na gbal, „he has written to day."

Póṅa, v. rel. „finish-for-, destroy-to-, destroy-for-;" e. g. 'a póṅa-ko aṅ-fam-ṅ'oṅ, „they destroyed him (all) his people."

Poṅ's, v. freq. a. (for póṅas), „finish, complete, accomplish; fulfil" (as a promise); „exhaust, spend" (as money); e. g. I tśi poṅ's ama-pant-ma-mi téṅoṅ, „I shall finish my work to day;" — o poṅ's ar'im ará o traṅ, „he fulfilled his promise," lit. „he accomplished the word which he pledged (said)."

Póro, am-, n. „the Poro association." See Pref. § 18. a.

Pǫrǫ, a-, pl. e-, n. „porro greegree." See Pref. § 18. b.

Pǫru, a-, pl. e-, n. „sperm, seed" (for generation); also „foetus, embryo" (as the result of sexual commerce). Both sexes, they say, have such a pǫru, and if one has no child, or if a woman does not bear children, they say: ǫ bā he a-pǫru, „she (he) has no seed," = she is barren;" — am-pǫru-n'oṅ ṅa kḁsa, „she had an abbortion." lit. „her embryo got spoiled."

Pǫti, a-, pl. e-, n. „cup, drinking vessel" (with a handle); e. g. kára a-pǫti, „bring a cup."

Pǫ́to, ǫ-, pl. a-, n. „a white man, a European;" e. g. ǫ-pǫ́to ǫ yi he ka ka petr aké, „there is no white man in this town."

Pǫ́to, adj. „european, belonging to a white man" or „to the white man's country;" e. g. a-bil a-pǫ́to, „a ship," lit. „a european canoe."

Púre, a-, pl. e-, n. „lover, sweet heart, concubine" (used of both sexes); e. g. ǫ bā a-púre, „he has a concubine," or also „she has a lover."

Putr, v. n. „rise" (as the sun, or moon above the horizon); e. g. aṅ'óf ṅa putr, „the moon rises."

Putr. v. a. „burst, open (as the leaves which enclose the ear of rice);" pierce, lance" (as a boil); „make known, divulge" (as the death of one); e. g putr am-bóya, „open the boil;" — 'a putr ara-fi, „they made known the death" (as by drumming). Also „bruise" (as a reed); „clean" (as fish by taking out the intestines and scraping off the scales).

Pútu, a-, pl. e-, n. „rectum", Ger. „Mastdarm"; also „tripe".

R.

R', pref. indef. and insep. „a, an;" e. g. r'ǫf, „a cerastes", for ra-ǫf.

Ra, pref. indef. „a, an;" e. g. ra-béṅa, „a rope."

Ra, pr. subj. „it"; e. g. ara-béṅa ra bǫ́li, „the rope is long."

Ra, pr. poss. „of"; e. g. ra-béṅa ra Sóri, „Sori's rope," lit. „a rope of Sori."

R'ȧ, = r'ȧka, which see.

Ra̤, prep. indef. „to, in, from, at." It is an indef. form of ra and ro. E. g. o yéfa ra̤-petr, „he came from a town;" ra̤ ka̤-petr, „in a town."

Ra-mi, pr. poss. „my", lit. „of me;" e. g. ara-béña-ra-mi, „my rope."

Ra-ñañ, pr. poss. „their", lit. „of them;" e. g. ara-béña-ra-ñañ. „their rope."

R'ā ra-bóti-som, „something delicious to devour" or „to eat;" e. g. I tši som r'ā ra-bóti-som, „I shall eat something delicious to devour."

R'ā ra-di, pl. y'etr e-di, „something to eat, food, victual;" e. g. o soñ-mi r'a ra-di, „he gave me something to eat."

Ra̤-tr'eī ó tr'eī, „from every harm." See: béne w'úni ra̤-tr'eī ó tr'eī under B.

Rábu, o-, n. „Lord". Adopted from the Ar. رَبّ, dominus. It is used of God only. E. g. o-Rábu-ka-su. „our Lord."

Raf, v. a. „establish, make, enact" (as a law); „fix" (as a spear in the ground); also „stab-with-;" e. g. o-bai o raf a-toñ. „the king made a law;" — o raf añ-sor ro-tof, „he fixed the spear in the ground;" — o raf-ko a-tis, „he stabbed him with a knife," = o ráfa-ko a-tis.

Ráfa, v. rel. „fix" or „put-for-; stab-with;" e. g. ráfa-mi añ-sor ro-tof, „fix the spear in the ground for me." See also the next word.

Ráfa w'úni a-bálma, „stab one with a dagger;" e. g. o ráfa-mi a-bálma, „he stabbed me with etc."

R'a̤fa, pl. s'a̤fa, n. „army of war-people, army;" e. g. r'a̤fa ra-bána, „a large army."

Ráfa̤r, v. rel. „fix" or „put-for-, put up-against-" (as the porro greegree against one). See Pref. § 18. b.

Rak-rak. v. n. „shake, be loose" (as a tooth, or a blade in a handle); fig. „be of a delicate health" or „constitution"; e. g. e-šek-y'oñ e rak-rak, „his teeth are loose."

R'áka, = r'a, pl. y'etr, n. „something, a thing, an article, a vessel; tool, instrument," pl. also „furniture"; e. g. I bá he r'áka tra som-mu, I have nothing to give thee."

Ráka, a-, pl. e-, n. „camp, place enclosed with a war-fence;" e. g. o yi ro-ráka, „he is in the camp."

R'áka-ó-r'áka, „every thing, any thing;" with a negative „not any thing, nothing at all;" e. g. o bā he r'áka-ó-r'áka, „he has nothing at all."

Ram, v. n. „pay, pay a fine;" e. g. o bā tra ram, „he has to pay a fine."

Ram, v. a. „pay, pay for, reward; requite;" e. g. I gbáli he sóto ak'óta, támbe I ram-ki, „I cannot get the cloth, except I pay for it."

Ram, a-, pl. e-, n. „pay, reward, recompence, wages, premium;" e. g. o sóto añ-ram-ñ'oñ, „he got his pay."

Ram tr'eï ka 'ra-bomp ra w'úni, „visit a thing upon one" (in scriptural language); „recompense" (in the way of punishing); lit. „pay (requite) a thing upon the head of a person," = „send evil upon one judicially."

Rámara, v. doubl. rel. (rad. ram). „heal-for-, cure-for-;" also: „cure-with-;" e. g. rámara-mi ow'ahét, „cure me the child," or „cure the child for me."

Rámne, v. refl. n. „pray"; e. g. o ko rámne, „he goes to pray," lit. „pay oneself off," then probably „perform one's duty" (as towards God, or towards a krifi), being derived from ram, „pay".

Rámne, v. refl. a. „pray to, worship; pray, beg, beseech;" lit. probably „pay one's duty towards" or „to-". It is used of the worship of God and of krifis. E. g. sa bā tra rámne K'áru, „we must pray to God;" o rámne o-krifi, „he worships a krifi." Cf. the preceding word.

Rámne, ka-, pl. tra-, n. „prayer, worship;" e. g. ka-rámne-ka-su, „our prayer."

Rámne a-krifi, ka-, n. „krifi worship," lit. „a worshipping krifis."

Rámi, v. n. long form of ram, „sound, tinkle;" fig. „be famous, be renowned;" e. g. am-bitiñ ña rámi o-fíno, „the drum sounds well." See the next word.

Rámi o-bóti-tral, „sound sweetly, sound pleasant to the ear" (as a song). See leñ, a-, „song".

Rań, pr. dem. rem. = arán, „that", used when it is the subject of a proposition without the noun; e. g. ra-béńa ra-fíno rań, „that is a good rope," lit. „a good rope that."

Rąń, adj. num. „two"; e. g. a-fąm ńa-rań, „two persons."

Rána, v. a. „carry on the back;" e. g. o rána ow'ahét, „he carried the child on the back."

Ráni, o-, pl. a-, n. „wife"; e. g. o-ráni-ka-mi, „my wife."

Rańk, a-, pl. e-, or tra-; or also o-, pl. tra-, n. „an elephant"; e. g. a-rańk a-bána, „a large elephant."

Rap, v. a. „surround, go round, go around; e. g. ńa rap ańkuńk, „they surrounded the yard."

Rąp, ką-, n. adultery, fornication" (used of both sexes); e. g. ka-rąp-k'oń, „his adultery;" — a-fąm 'a ka-rąp, „adulterous people," lit. „people of adultery."

Rárań, kạ-, n. „backpart, backside, hinder part" (of a thing); fig. „support, backing;" e. g. ka-rárań ka ań-set, „the back part of the house;" — o-baī o bá ka-rárań ka-bána, „the king has great support." With the prep. ro- it becomes a prep. or a postp., for which see rorárań.

Rárań, postp. „behind"; e. g. o yi-mi rárań, „he is behind me;" = rorárań.

Rárąń-ka-tši, ka-, see: ka-rárąn-ka-tši, and: ka ka-rárąń-ka-tši.

Ráre, ką-, pl. trą-, n. „door; shutter;" e. g. kánta ka-ráre, „shut the door."

Rąs, adv. „yet, still, first;" e. g. kár-mi rąs, „wait me first;" — o fet rąs, „he is still young."

Rása, a-, pl. e-, n. „a creeping plant (bearing a kind of tomata or love-apple), which winds itself round trees very thickly." The natives chew the inner white skin of the plant, after the outer green one is taken off, and swallow the juice of it. The fruit is eaten by animals, sometimes also by men. They also call this plant k'óroro. ¡ l. tr'óroro

Ráta, postp. „under, below, beneath," = roráta; e. g. o-wontr-ka-mu o yi ro-fuńk ráta, „thy brother is under the storehouse."

Ratróń, prep. and postp. „between, in the midst, amongst;" e. g.

o̦ las-ña ratro̦ń, „he passed between them;" — yira-su ratro̦ń, „sit between us;" — o̦ wur ratro̦ń ka añ-fa̦m, „he came out from amongst the people." There is a euph. form datro̦ń, which see.

Ratro̦ń, adv. „between, in the midst;" e. g. o̦ las ratro̦ń, „he passed between;" — fo̦f ar'im o̦-báka̦r ratro̦ń, „accentuate the word in the middle," lit. „pronounce the word strongly in the middle."

Rayé̦r, prep. or postp. „near to, close to, beside, near, at the side;" e. g. o̦ las-mi rayé̦r, „he passed near to me;" — o̦ trá̦ma-mi rayé̦r, = o trá̦ma rayé̦r-ka-mi, „he stands close to me;" — tše̦ yira rayé̦r ka am-mésa, „do rot sit near the table." There is a euph. form dayé̦r, which see.

Rayé̦r, adv. „aside; near;" e. g. o̦ trá̦ma rayé̦r, „he stood near;" — botr-yi rayé̦r, „put them aside."

Re —? adv. inter. „whereto?" e. g. re mań ko̦-e? „where art thou going to?"

Rē, ma-, n. „sleep"; e. g. ma-rē ma bā-mi, „I am sleepy," lit. „sleep has me." Also „vision"; e. g. o̦ na̦ńk ma-rē, „he saw a vision."

Re, = de, or = der. v. n. and aux. „come"; de is a euph. form of re. When used as an aux. it may sometimes be given by „go" and by „happen"; it is also used to express a remote Future in connection with the particles tši, or tra̦, or with ma, me and mo; sometimes also without them, if used for a Future in the Passive. Otherwise it indicates a purpose or intention to exercise the energy, expressed by the principal verb. It is construed with the short, and also with the long form of the Infinite. E. g. o̦ re he̦ nań, „he did not come," = o̦ de he̦ nań; — o̦ tra̦ re dif-ko̦, „he will kill him by and by;" — ya ña ma re yo̦-mu, „thus they will be doing to thee;" — ak'a̦ntr ka re gbútra̦s, or also: ak'a̦ntr ka tra̦ re gbútra̦s, „the stick will be shortened by and by;" — o̦ re tila, „he comes to trade;" — o̦ re gbal, „he (came) comes to write", or: o̦ re tra gbal, „he comes (came) for the purpose to write." When used for the Future it is best given by „by and by."

Rẹ, adv. „here"; e. g. ọ yíra re, „he lives here."

Rẹ, conj. „and", = dẹ, which is a euph. form. E. g. múnọṅ re mínaṅ sạ kọ́nẹ, „thou and I we will go;" — ọ-kas rẹ ọ-kára-k'ọṅ, „his father and his mother."

Rẹ, prep. = dẹ, which is a cuph. form of it, „with, by;" e. g. pạ yi he rẹ aṅ-fọ́sa ṅa kónọṅ, „it was not by the power of him," = „it was not by his power;" — ọ di re mínaṅ, „he ate with me."

Réï, a-, or i-, pl. ma-, n. „a day of 24 hours, a day;" e. g. aṅ-réï aṅé, „this day;" — ma-réï ma-sas, „three days."

Réka, a-, pl. ẹ-, n. „skin, hide; parchment, paper; letter, book;" e. g. aṅ-réka ṅa ka-lómẹ, „the skin of the sheep;" — ọ sóm'ra-mi a-réka, „he sent me a letter." The Mohammedans often use dressed skins to write upon; now they write also on paper.

Réke? adv. inter. „where?" e.g réke am-bil-'a-mi-e? „where is my canoe?"

Réke? pr inter. „which? what?" e. g. a-lóko réke ma der-e? = a-lọ réke mạ der-e? „what time didst thou come?" — ka-petr ka-réke? „which town?" — w'úni réke? „what person?"

Reṅ, or ren', ka-, pl. tra-, n. „a year"; e. g. ka-reṅ k'in, „one year;" — tra-ren' tra-sas, „three years." The g is sometimes cut off before d and t.

Ren',) v. a. „put on the top of-, load-with-, put; e. g. o reṅ-
Reṅ,) ko ka-trä, „he put the hand upon him;" — o reṅ-ko ka aṅ-soï, „he put him on the horse;" — o ren' ri ka 'ra-bomp-r'ọṅ, „he put it on his head." Ren' is a cuph. form, used before words beginning with d, r and t.

Reṅ, ka-, n. probably „night". It is always used with datrọ́ṅ, when the g is cut off for the sake of euphony. See next word.

Ren' datrọ́ṅ, ka-, n. „midnight". See Fables p. 62.

Rén'sa, (for rénạsa), v. freq. and caus. (rad. reṅ), „mount, ride upon, go" or „be on the top of, be upon," e. g. tsẽ rén'sa e-tok, „do not go on the top of the wood;" — o rén'sa a-soī, „he rides upon a horse;" — ka-trak aké ka rén'sa-mi, „this palaver is upon me."

Rén'sa, (for réñasa). v. freq. and inch. „get on the top, be on the top, rest, be;" e. g. o rén'sa ka añ-soī, „he got on the horse." Also „sit" (as a cap on the head); e. g. añ-lápra ña rén'sa o-fíno, „the cap sits well."

R'etr, pl. s'etr, n. „a sun", def. ar'étr, „the sun" (considered as the source of light; an'ef is the sun as the source of heat); e. g. ar'étr ra putr. „the sun rises." The pl. may be used if there is a reflection of the sun, as in the water, and there appear to be two suns.

Ri, pr. obj. = di. „it"; e. g. ara-béña gbútras-ri, „as to the rope shorten it." Di is a euph. form.

Ri, adv. loc. = di, „there"; e. g. tšĕ ko ri, „do not go there." Di is a euph. form of ri.

Ría, pr. emph. = día, „it, this;" e. g. ar'úma-ra-mi ría yi tši, „this is my shirt," lit. „my shirt this is it." Día is a euph. form.

Ri-a, adv. loc. emph. = di-a, „there"; e. g. ro añ-gbálañ na gbópe, rí-a o botr ara-bomp-r'oñ. „where the rock was rugged, there he put his head." Di- a is a euph. form of rí-a.

Rí-añ, adv. loc. abs. = di-añ, „there"; e. g. rí-añ o yi, „there he is;" — o yi ri rí-añ, = ri-añ ri o yi, „he is there" or „there he is." Di-añ is a euph. form. (Cf. -ñ under N.)

Ríañ, pr. abs. „it, this;" e. g ara-béña-ra-mi ríañ, „this is my rope," lit. „the rope of me it."

Riánna, n. „heaven" (as the residence of the blessed); Mand. aryena. From the Ar. جَنَّة, hortus, paradisus. E. g. ro-riánna, „in heaven."

Rígba, a-, pl. e-, n. „headwoman of the Bondo Institution. E. g. añ-rígba o kus am-bóndo, „the headwoman of the Bondo Institution discharged the Bondo girls" or „closed the Bondo ceremonies by a public procession."

R'im. = d'im, pl. s'im, n. „a word, voice; command;" also „promise"; e. g. ar'ím-ra-mi, „my word;" — l tra̱l r'im ra-bána,

„I heard a great (strong) voice;" — ar'ím ra K'úru, „the word of God." D'im is a euph. form of r'im.

R'in, adj. num. = d'in, „one"; e. g. r'im r'in, „one word;" — ra-béňa r'in, „one rope." D'in is a euph. form.

Ro, adv. loc. „yonder, at," or „to some distance;" e. g. kóne ro, „go yonder;" — ňa yi ri ro, „they are there yonder." Also „where, whereon, wherein;" e. g. ka-fant'r ro o fánta, „the bed whereon he lay down;" — o sŏm a-réka, ro o gbal-e ho etc., „he sent a letter, wherein he wrote that etc."

Ro, prep. loc. „at, in, to, from, upon, on;" e. g. o yi ro-set, „he is in the house;" — o yéfa ro-petr, „he came from town;" — o ko ro-Kamp, „he went to Sierra-Leone." The sense of this prep. is indicated by the verb with which it is used. There is a euph. form do-, which see.

Ro-be, „wherever"; e. g. ro ma ko be I (si tram-mu, „wherever thou goest, I shall follow thee."

Rodér, prep. and postp. „at the face;" e. g. rodér-ka-mi kadi, „before my face;" — o yi-mi rodér kadí, „he is before my face."

Rodí, adv. loc. „ahead, before; on, onwards, forwards;" e. g. sa ko he rodí, „we do not go ahead;" — ko rodí, „go forwards" or „go on" or „go before;" — tráma rodí, „stand ahead." Cf. also kadí.

Rodí, prep. and postp. „before, in front, beyond;" e. g. o yi-mi rodí, „he is before me," = o yi rodí-ka-mi; — kára-mi a ra-béňa ará fánta rodí ka aráň, „bring me the rope which lies beyond that one;" — o tráma rodí ka aň-set, „he stands before the house."

R'oť, pl. s'oť, n. „a horned viper, cerastes;" e. g. r'oť ra-báňa, „a large horned viper."

Rok, v. a. „cut, reap" (as rice); fig. „decide, settle, judge" (as a matter); e. g. 'a ko rok pa-la, „they go to reap rice," — o-bai o tra rok am-pa, „the king will settle the matter."

Rok, ka-, n. verb. „act of cutting" or „reaping, harvest; act of deciding" or „settling" or „judging;" e. g. ka-rok-k'oň pa-la, „his reaping rice;" — ka-rok ka-fíno, „a good harvest."

Rok an-tǫ́uka, ka-, n „the judgment" (as of the last day).

Róka, v. rel. „cut-for-; cut-with-; reap-for-, reap-with-; reap with-" (as with joy); fig. „decide-for-;" e. g. ọ rǫ́ka-kọ a-tis, „he cut him with a knife;" — ọ róka-mi pa-lā, „he reaps (cuts) rice for me;" — ọ-bai ọ trạ rǫ́ka-mi am-pā, „the king will settle the matter for me."

Rokáṅ, adv. loc. „without, out, out of doors;" e. g. wur rokáṅ, „come out;" — yira rokáṅ, „sit without;" — o trạma rokáṅ, „he stood without;" — 'a kére-kọ rokáṅ, „they led him out."

Rokáṅ, prep. and postp. „at the outside, without;" e. g. o yi rokáṅ ka aṅ-set, „he is at the outside of the house."

Kokín, adv. „together, to one place, at one place, at the same place;" e. g. ṅa tóṅklanẹ rokín, „they assembled together;" — botr-ṅa rokín, „put them together."

Rokǫ́m, adv. loc. „up, on high, upwards, above, from above;" e. g. ọ yi ri rokǫ́m, „he is there above;" — aṅ-gbal aṅá béka ma-raṅ rokǫ́m, „the second line from above." Cf. also roráta.

Rokǫ́m, = dokǫ́m, prep. and postp. „above, on the top, at the top;" e. g. o yi rokǫ́m ka aṅ-set, = o yi ka aṅ-set rokǫ́m, „he is on the top of the house." Dokǫ́m is a euph. form.

Rokór, adv. loc. „at the inside, within;" e. g. ṅa yi ri rokór, „it is there within."

Rokór, prep. and postp. „within, into, at" or „in the inside;" e. g. ṅa yi-mi rokór, „it is within me;" — botr-ṅi rokór ka am-pǫ́ti, = botr-ṅi ka am-pǫ́ti rokór, „put it into the cup."

Roléṅken, adv. loc. „yonder, to the neighbouring yard, to some distance, to the other side;" e. g. „sa kǫ́nẹ roléṅken, „we go to the neighbouring yard."

Roléṅken, prep. and postp. „on the other side, beyond;" e. g. ka-petr ka yi roléṅken ka ka-tšeṅ, = ka-petr ka yi ka ka-tšeṅ roléṅken, „the town lies on the other side of the hill."

Rom, a-, pl. ẹ-, n. „leprosy"; e. g. o bā a-rom, „he is a leper," lit. „he has leprosy;" = a-rom ṅa wop-kọ.

Romí, pr. comp. „to me, from thee, with me; towards me; against me; at" or „to my place, there" or „yonder at" or „to my place;" e. g. o der romí, „he came to me;" — o di romí, „he ate at my place."

Romóri, adv. loc. „to the other side" (as of a brook); e. g. o kóne romóri, „he went over to the other side" (of the water).

Romóri, prep. and postp. „to the other side, beyond, to the opposite side" or „shore"; e. g. o las romóri ka 'ra-boṅ, „he passed over to the other side of the river."

Romp, ka-, pl. tra-, n. „pestle" (for a mortar); e. g. ka-romp ka-lol, „a small pestle."

Romú, pr. comp. „to thee, with thee, from thee, at" or „to thy place, there" or „yonder to" or „at thy place; against thee; towards thee;" e. g. o yi romú, „he is there with thee;" — o tra der romú, „he will come to thee."

R'oṅ, or r'on', pl. s'oṅ, n. „way, road;" e. g. o trori-mi ar'óṅ, „he showed me the way." The euph. form r'on' is used before words beginning with d, as: trori-mi ar'óṅ' da ro Ma-lal, „show me the way to Malal;" — r'on' da-fíno, „a good road."

R'oṅ, pr. poss. „his, her," lit. „of him, of her;" e. g. ar'úma-r'oṅ, „his shirt."

Roṅ, a-, pl. e-, n. „image, figure, idol, mask" (usually made of wood and painted); e. g. o woṅ a-roṅ, „he put on a mask."

Roṅ, a-, or i-, pl. ma-; or also sometimes a-, in the sing. and e-, in the pl. n. „mountain"; the pl. ma-roṅ is used of a „chain of mountains," hence they call the Colony of Sierra-Leone: ro Ma-roṅ, lit. „at the mountains." E. g. a-roṅ a-bóli rokóm, „a lofty mountain."

Roṅáṅ, pr. comp. „to them, with them, from them; towards them; against them; at" or „to their place, there" or „yonder at" or „to their place;" e. g. o di roṅáṅ, „he ate at their place;" — 'a kálane roṅáṅ, „they returned home," lit. „they returned to their place."

Róṅkat, v. n. „be bitter; be harsh, be acerb" (as unripe limes); e. g. ma-ber ma róṅkat, „the palmwine is bitter."

Róṅko, ka-, pl. tra-, n. „branch of a palm-tree with" or „without the side-leaves, palm-branch;" e. g. o gbak ka-róṅko, „he cut a palm-branch."

Roṅóṅ, pr. comp. „to him, with him; towards him; against him; at" or „to his place, there" or „yonder at" or „to his place;" e. g. o der roṅóṅ, „he came to him;" — o pä roṅóṅ, „he said to him;" — 'a yéfa roṅóṅ, „they came away from him;" — o kálane roṅóṅ, „he returned to his place (home)."

Ronú, pr. comp. „to you, with you, from you; against you; towards you; at" or „to your place, there" or „yonder at" or „to your place;" e. g. o kóne ronú, „he went yonder to your place;" — o der ronú, „he came to you."

Ro-pil, see Pil, ka-, n.

Roráraṅ, adv. loc. „behind, at the place behind, behind" (the house); „abaft, aback;" e. g. o yi ri roráraṅ, „he is there behind;" — trama roráraṅ, „stand behind," or „stand abaft."

Roráraṅ, prep. and postp. „behind, at the back part;" e. g. o tráma mi roráraṅ. = o tráma roráraṅ-ka-mi, „he stands behind me," or also „he backs me;" — o yi roráraṅ ka aṅkuṅk, „he is behind the fence."

Roráta, adv. loc. „below, beneath;" e. g. ra yi anó roráta, „it is here below;" — ka rokóm ha roráta, „from the top down to the bottom."

Roráta, prep. and postp. „below, beneath, under, at the bottom;" e. g. re ma botr an-tis-e? I botr-ñi roráta ka am-mésa, „where didst thou put the knife?" „I put it under the table;" — owó yi roráta-k'oṅ, „who is under him" (i. e. under his power); — ka an-tof roráta, or: roráta ka an-tof, „under the earth"

Ros, v. n. „serve up food" (especially rice by taking it out from the pot, in which it was cooked, with a spoon into a dish, with or without e-nak, „rice"); e. g. o bap-ña 'a tra ros, „he met them serving up rice"

Ros, v. a. „dish up, serve up" (as food); e. g. 'a ros e-nak, „they served up rice."

Ro-tóroṅ, see Toroṅ, ka-, n.

Rū. v. a. „plait, weave;" e. g. o tra rū k'óta ka-fíno, „he is weaving fine cloth."

Rū, ra-. pl. tra-. n. „the world, the universe;" e. g. ka 'ra-rū ará ma der-e, sa tra rok ey'étr, eyé sa poṅ sak ano-rṅ, „in the world to come we shall reap the things, which we have sown in this world."

Rúba, v. a. „bless"; e. g. o rúba-ña, „he blessed them."

Rúba, a-, pl. e-, n. „a blessing"; e. g. añ-rúba-ñ'oñ, „his blessing;" — a-rúba ñañ, „that is a blessing." lit. „a blessing that."

Rúhu, o-, n. „Spirit" (of God). From the Ar. روح, anhelitus, spiritus. E. g. o-rúhu ka K'úru, „the Spirit of God."

R'úma, pl. s'úma, n. „a shirt, robe, the long garment worn by the Mandingos;" e. g. ar'úma aré ra fíno, „this robe is good." Also „afterbirth."

Rúni, o-, pl. a-, n. „a man, male;" e. g. a-rúni a-sas, „three men;" — añ-rúni, „the males."

Rúni, adj. „male"; e. g. a-fam a-rúni, „men", lit. „male persons;" — w'ahét rúni, „a boy," lit. „a male child."

Rúni o-bi, o-, pl. a-rúni a- bi, n. „a black male, black man, negro."

Rúni o-féra, o-, pl. a-rúni a-féra, n. „a white male, a white man, a European."

R'únia, pl. s'únia, n. „multitude, crowd;" e. g. r'únia ra a-fam ra-bána ra yi ri, „there was a great crowd of people there."

Rúṅkatr, v. a. „mix" (as solids with liquids); „knead" (as dough); e. g. rúṅkatr e-tof re m'antr, „mix the earth with water."

Rúsam, v. a. „bring up, raise up, nurse; nourish;" e. g. mína rúsam-ko, „I brought him up;" — e-nak e rúsam-su, „rice nourishes us."

S.

S', pref. indef. insep. „a, an;" e. g. s'ádka, „sacrifice;" as'ádka-tr'oñ, „his sacrifice." It is a form of tr', or tś' for: tra-. Cf. the form t' below.

Sa, pr. subj. „we;" e. g. sa ṅañ-ko dis, „we saw him yesterday."

Sábat, a-, pl. e-, n. „sabbath." From the English.

S'ádka, n. „sacrifice." Fr. the Ar. صَدَقَة, quicquid datur Deo sacrum. The pl. is indicated by joining with it the adj. laï or gbáti. „many," as: s'ádka tra-laī. „many sacrifices." In Vei: sadaka.

Sak, v. a. „scatter disperse; sow;" e. g. sa ko sak pa-lā ténoṅ, „we go to sow rice to day;" — o sak aṅ-fam, „he dispersed the people; — ará sa ma sak, ría sa bā ka-pim," what we are sowing, that we have to reap (pluck)."

Sak, ka-, pl. tra-, n. „rib;" also „side;" e. g. fánta ro trasak. „lie on the side;" — tra-sak-tr'oṅ, „his ribs "

Sáka. v. rel. „scatter-with-, scatter-for-; sow-for-, sow-with-; sow with-;" e. g. sáka e-tróko apa-lā, „scatter the rice for the fowls; — sáka-mi pa-lā, „sow rice for me."

Sáka, a-, pl. e-, n. „a country dish," also called „palaver-sauce," (being prepared of various herbs with fish and palm-oil); e. g. a-sáka a-bóti-di, „a delicious palaver sauce."

Sákane, v. spont. or rather recipr. (rad. sak), „disperse;" e. g. aṅ-fam ṅa sákane. „the people dispersed." Also „separate from each other. part," (as man and wife).

Sákar. v. rel. (rad. sak), „bespatter-with-, bespatter," also, „blot, stain;" e. g. o sákar ak'óta-k'oṅ d'ūba, „he stained his cloth with ink."

Sáke, v. n. „turn, turn oneself; become changed " or „altered," fig. „become converted," (with or without méra, „mind"); e. g. o gbáli he so sáke, „he cannot turn himself again;" — o-tem owé o sáke gba, „this old man is much changed."

Sáke, ka-, n. verb. „act of turning oneself; act of being" or „getting changed. change;" fig. „conversion;" e. g. ka-sákek'oṅ ro-tóroṅ, „his turning himself towards the east;" — kasáke-k'oṅ, „his conversion."

Sáke ma-der. „become flesh, become man;" e. g. o sáke mader, „he became man "

Sáki, v. a. „turn, change, make;" fig. „convert" (with méra); e. g. o sáki-ko o-móri, „he made him a Mohammedan;" — o sáki am-móra-ṅo'ṅ, „he converted him."

Sákine, v. refl. a- „turn oneself into-, change oneself into-," (as a person into a leopard): „make oneself-;" e. g. o sákine o-sántki, „he made himself a Santki (minister)."

Sal, v. a. „form, build" (as a house, or a pot of mud or clay); e. g. o sal a-sel, „he built a house."

Sal, a-, or i-, pl. ma-, n. „finger," also „toe" (of the foot); e. g. ma-sal-m'oṅ, „his fingers."

Sála, v. rel. (rad. sal), „form-for-, build-for-; build-with-, form-with-;" e. g. o sála-mi a-sel, „he built a house for me."

Sálma, a-, or i-, pl. ma-, n. „psalm;" e. g. ma-sálma ma-sas, „three psalms." Adopted.

Sálkar, adj. „salted, salt;" e. g. o-šem o-sálkar, „salt meat."

Sam, ka-, pl. tra-, n. „an open running sore, a sore, ulcer; wound;" e. g. ka-sam ka-bána, „a large sore."

Sam, adj. „sacred, holy;" e. g. d'er o-sam, „a sacred place."

Sámas, v, caus. (rad. sam), „make sacred, make holy, set apart from common use; sanctify;" e. g. 'a sámas od'er owé, „they made this place sacred."

Saṅ, ka-, pl. tra-, n „mouth, lip," (also used of the lips of a wound); fig. „advocate;" e. g. ka-saṅ-ka-mi, „my mouth," or also „my advocate;" — tra-saṅ tra ka-sam, „the lips of the wound."

Saṅ ka o-bai, ka-, n. „an ambassador, a herald." lit. „the mouth of a king."

S'áni, n. „acerbity" (as of unripe limes); „quality of setting the teeth on edge;" fig. „pity, regret;" e. g. s'áni tra yi ka e-šek-'e-mi, „my teeth are set on edge," lit. „acerbity is to my teeth;" — ma-lémre ma ba s'áni, „the limes are acerb." lit. „the limes have acerbity," or „such a quality as to set the teeth on edge;" — as'áni tra wop-mi „my teeth are set on edge," lit. „the state of having set the teeth on edge holds me;" — o ba s'áni tráka troṅ, „he has pity on account of him." See Proverb 1, p. 98.

Sánne, v. refl. for: sáṅne (rad. saṅ), „bow oneself down, bend oneself down, stoop; make a compliment", (of males only); „bend itself" (as the blade of a knife); „submit to one's authority, submit;" e. g. o sánne roṅóṅ, „he bowed down to him," or „he made a compliment to him." or „he submitted to him;" — an-tis ña sánne, „the knife bends itself;" — o sánne, „he stooped down."

Sántki, o-, pl. a-, n. „a minister (of a king);" e. g. o-sántki o-lạs, „a bad minister."

Sạntr, e-, n. „seed," (especially of rice). e. g. o bā e-sạntr trạ́ka kúta, „he has (rice) seed to plant (sow)."

Sántrạk, a-, or i-, pl. ma-; or also sometimes a-, pl. ẹ-, n. „nail," (of the fingers or toes); „talon, claw," (of beasts); e. g. o bā e-sántrạk ẹ-bọ́li, „he has long nails."

Sap, v. a. „strike, flog, beat," (as a person, or as waves a canoe); also „thresh" (as rice); „catch" (as a bird); „get," (as trouble); „scoop, lad out," (as water from a bowl, or food from a dish); e. g. 'a sap-kọ, „they flogged him;" — o sap a-rom, „he got leprosy;" — 'a sap ẹ-nak, „they took out the rice;" — o sap-mi kạ-tšiṅ, „he flogged me for nothing;" — o sap m'ọ́nẹ, „he got trouble," lit. „he catch trouble," (as the Liberat. Africans say).

Sap, v. n. or pass. „be flogged; be caught;" e. g. o sap robólo. „he was caught by the throat."

Sap, kạ-, n. verb. „act of flogging" or „of threshing, etc.;" e. g. ka-sap-k'ọṅ, „his flogging," (actively or passively); „also: a flogging; a threshing."

Sápa, v. rel. „flog-with-; thresh-with-; flog-for-; thresh-for-; lade out-for-;" e. g. 'a sápa-kọ k'ẹtr, „they flogged him with a whip;" — sápa-mi apa-lā, „thresh the rice for me."

Sápạr, a-, pl. ẹ-, n. „digger," (being a sort of hoe, but running parallel with the handle, and not forming an angle; it is used to dig holes with for the sinking of posts for houses); e. g. a-sápạr a-bána, „a large digger." Also „an iron bar" (used to dig holes with).

Sápạs, v. freq. a. (rad- sap), „catch in a trap, catch, ensnare, entrap;" e. g. ọw'áṅ ọwé o sápạs ẹ-bamp ṅa-rạṅ, „this boy caught two birds in a trap."

Sar, a-, or i-, pl. ma-, n. „a stone;" e. g. ma-sar ma-laī, „many stones."

Sára, v. a. „carry on the head, carry, put on the head, be loaded with on the head; put on" (as a cap); „take upon oneself" (as a palaver); „have upon oneself; suffer, have," (as trouble); e. g. I sára-kọ, or: I sára-kọ ro-bomp, „I carried him on the head;" — o sára a-lápra, „he put on a cap;" — mína sára atr'eï tra-tši, „I take that matter upon me;" — o sára m'ọnẹ, „he suffers trouble."

Sas, adj. num. „three;" e. g. a-fam a-sas, or: a-fam ṅa-sas, „three persons;" — ma-réï ma-sas," three days."

Sas, ra-, n. „state of being three, trinity."

Sẹ́bẹ, a-, pl. ẹ-, n. „an amulet, a charm" (as hung round the arm, or neck, etc., and enclosed in leather or cloth; e. g. o ba ẹ-sébẹ ẹ-laï, „he has many charms".

Šek, v. a. „tie, tie on." (as a person, or a charm); „gird-with-;" e. g. ṅa šek ama-trā-m'ọṅ, „they tied his hands;" — šek o-nā ka ak'ạntr, „tie the cow to the post;" — I šek-ko a-gbáto, „I girded him with a cutlass," or „I tied him on a cutlass;" — šek an-trol, „tie on the charm." Also „fasten," as: ko šek am-béla, „go fasten the sail."

Šek, ra-, pl. ẹ-, n. „a tooth;" e. g. ẹ-šek-y'ọṅ, „his teeth."

Šékẹ! } int. „I pity thee!" It is always followed by: ó, and is pro-
Šékẹ! } perly a noun signifying „pity." See Colloq. Phras. p. 108. 110., and cf. also mútši w'úni šékẹ.

Šéknẹ, v. refl. a. (rad. šek), „tie-on oneself, tie-round oneself, gird oneself with-;" e. g. o šéknẹ a-gbáto, „he tied a cutlass round himself;" — o šéknẹ a-trol, „he tied a charm on himself."

Šel, ma-, n. „laughter; scorn, scornfulness, mockery;" e. g. ma-šel-m'ọṅ, „his laughter." Also „object of mockery," as: 'a sạki-ko ma-šel, „they made him an object of mockery."

Šel-tr'eï, adj. „inclined to ridicule" or „mock at a thing, scornful;" e. g. w'úni šel-tr'eï, „a scornful person."

Sẹ́linẹ, v. refl. n. (rad. sẹ́li), „lean oneself on backwards, recline oneself, recline;" e. g. o sẹ́linẹ ka aṅ'ạntr, „he leaned himself against the tree."

Sẹ́linẹ, v. refl. a., „lean oneself upon-backwards, lean oneself back against-; rely on-, repose on-, trust on-;" e. g. o sẹ́linẹ aṅ-set, „he leaned himself back against the house;" — o sẹ́linẹ K'ạru, „he relies on God."

Šélo, v. n. „will, be willing, consent;" e. g. o pà ho: I šélo, „he said: I will."

Šélọ, ma-, n. „will, pleasure: readiness;" e. g. ma-šélọ-m'oṅ. „his will."

Sẹm, ọ-, n. „beef, meat," e. g. ọ-sẹm ọ-fíno, „good beef."

Sẹm, a-, pl. ẹ-, or trạ-; or also sing. ọ-, pl. trạ-, n. „a wild animal, venison, a beast of the chase, animal, quadruped;" e. g. o-sẹm ọ-nínis, „a fierce animal " See the two next words.

Sẹm ẹ-trọl, ẹ-, n. „cattle of the larger kind," lit. „beasts reared up." The small cattle are called: y'ẹtr ẹ-trọl, lit. „things reared up."

Sẹm ka ka-petr, ọ-, pl. trạ-sẹm tra ka-petr, n. „a tame beast," lit. „a beast of the town." The sing. may also take the form: a-sẹm 'a ka-petr, and the pl. ẹ-sẹm ya ka-petr. The pl. may be given by: „cattle."*)

Sẹm ka ro-kant, ọ-, pl. trạ-sẹm tra ro-kant, n. „a wild animal," lit. „a beast of in the wood." The sing. may also take the form a-sẹm 'a ro-kant, and the pl. ẹ-sẹm ya ro-kant. See the Note for the preceding word.

Sen'! ⎱ int. „welcome!" It is always followed by : ó, and is pro-
Séne! ⎰ bably a noun signifying „welcome." See Colloq. Phras. p. 107. 110.

Séne! int. answering to the English „God bless thee!" It is used after sneezing. See Colloq. Phras. p. 108.

Séña, a pl. ẹ-, n. „a greegree, charm," (used to detect thieves with). It generally consists of a goat's horn, to which some of its hair, strips of cloth, and some beads, etc. are tied. When it is made use of, fearful curses are pronounced against the offender, which the greegree is to execute upon the hidden criminal.

Séńc, n. prop. See Proverb. 3, p. 99.

Séne! int. see sen'! above.

Sẹńk, adv. „all, whole; fully, entirely." It has often the sense of an adj. = be; e. g. ọ tam ña sẹńk, „he conquered them

---

*) Note. There are still some other forms for the sing. and pl., as will be seen in the Grammar.

all," or „the whole of them;" — mo o poñ káno señk. etc, „when he had said all, etc."

Séno; a-, or i-. pl. ma-, n. „arrow." (made of a kind of cane with an iron beard); e. g. o ba ma-séno ma-lai, „he has many arrows."

Set, a-, pl. e-, n. „a house, abode, dwelling, building; nest," (as of birds); e. g. o sal a-set, „he built a house; — o yi ro-set, „he is in the house."

Setáni, n. „Satan, the devil." Fr. the Ar. شَيْطَانْ, satanas, diabolus.

Séte, ka-, pl. tra-, n. a rod, stick," (as to flog with, or to drive cows away with); e. g. ka-séte ka-bóli, „a long rod."

Šim, v. a. „break, break off, break in two," (as a stick); „break down, pull down" (as a house); o šim ak'antr, „he broke the stick in two."

Šimtar, adj. (rad. šim), „sudden, unexpected;" e. g. ra fi ra-šimtar, „a sudden death."

Sip, o-, pl. tra- n. „a leopard;" e, g. o-sip o-bána, „a large leopard."

Šíte, v. n. „break the wind."

So, adv. „again, also;" e. g. tsè so yó-tši. „do not do it again."

So, v. n „bend, bow" (as the knee); also „sting, pierce, stab; pierce-with-, stab-with-;" e. g. o so-mi a-tis, „he stabbed me with a knife." See next word.

So tra-wu, „kneel down." lit. „bend the knees;" e. g. o so tra-wu-tr'oñ, „he kneeled down."

Sófali, a-, pl. e-, or tra; or also sing. o-, pl. tra-, n. „an ass;" e. g. o rén'sa a-sófali, „he rides upon an ass."

Soi, a-, pl. e-, or tra-; or also sing. o-, pl. tra-, n. „a horse;" e. g. o waī a-soi, „he bought a horse."

Soi, adv. „softly, quietly, calmly, easily,; slowly; secretly;" e. g. o yo-tši soi, „he did it softly;" — o kot soi, „he walked slowly; — I gbáti yo-tši soi, „he can do it easily."

Sok, v. impers. „dawn;" e. g. yókane, pa sok! „get up, it dawns!"

Sókanȩ, v. refl. „hunt;" e. g. ọ kọ sókanȩ, „he goes (went) a hunting."

Sókanȩ, kạ-, n. „act of hunting, hunting;" e. g. ka-sókanȩ-k'ọṅ, „his hunting."

Súki, ọ-, pl. a-, n. „a seer, one having four eyes" (as they call it), „one having to do with familiar spirits, one possessed of second sight, augur, wizard," e. g. ọw'úni ọwé ọ yi ọ-sóki, „this person is a wizard."

Sókọ, v. n. „be awake, be sleepless, be up during the night, spend the night." As an aux. it expresses the adv. „all night." E. g. 'a sókọ tómọ, „they danced all night;" — ọ sókọ gbẹs. „he was awake all night," or „he was up all night; — ọ sókọ romí „he spent the night with me."

Sōm, v. a. „send;" also „cause;" e. g. Pā Sóri ọ sōm-kọ rọmí, „Mr. Sori sent him to me;" — tšía sōm-kọ ọ yō-tši, „this caused him to do it." Also „send-to-," as: ọ sōm-kọ a-réka, „he sent a letter to him."

Sōm, v. n. „send"; also „be the cause;" e. g. ọ́ sōm trạka tšéla-kọ, „he sent to call him;" — tšía sōm ọ dínnȩ, „this caused him to perish," lit. „this is the cause he perished."

Sōm, ka-, pl. trạ-; or a-, pl. ȩ-, n. „message;" e. g. ọ kérȩ-kọ a-sōm, „he carried a message to him."

Sọm, v. a. „devour, eat;" e. g. ọ sọm am-bamp tárạp, „he devoured the bird entirely." Also „nibble" (as a rat a wooden bowl.)

Sọm, euph. form of sọṅ, „give", used before m; see: sọṅ, below.

Sómpa, adj. „troubling"; also passively „punished, troubled;" e. g. tr'eí trạ-sómpa, „something troubling," or „something which causes trouble."

Sómpa, ka- pl. trạ-, n. „act of punishing, punishment" (inflicted); e. g. ka-sómpa-k'ọṅ, „his punishment."

Sómpanȩ, v. refl. „suffer," lit. „trouble" or „punish oneself; be afflicted;" e. g. ọw'úni ọwé ọ sómpanȩ ọ-laï, „this person suffers much."

Sómpanȩ, kạ-, pl. trạ-, n. „suffering, punishment" (endured);

"affliction;" e. g. kạ-sómpanẹ kạ-bána kạ wop-kọ, "he is greatly afflicted," lit. "great affliction holds him."

Sóm'ra. (for: sómạra), v. doubl. rel. (rad. sōm) "send-to-, send-for-;" also simply "send;" e. g. Pā Sóri ọ sóm'ra-mu-ńi, "Mr. Sori sent it to thee;" — ọ sóm'ra-kọ ro-k'ọr, he sent him to the farm."

Sōn, adv. "alone, only;" e. g. miń' sōn, "I alone;" — kọń' sōn, "he alone;" — kọń' sōn tábọ, "not he alone."

Sọń, v. a. "give, deliver;" e. g. ọ sọm-mi kạ-bō, "he gave me country-bread;" — ọ sọń ań-kála ka ọ-kas-k'ọń, "he gave the money to his father," — ọ sọń ọ-kas-k'ọń ań-kála.

Sọ́na, v. rel. (rad. sọ), "bend-for-, bow-to-," (as the knees to one. See next word.

Sọ́na w'úńi tra-wu," bow the knees to" or "for one, kneel down before one;" e. g. 'a sọ́na-kọ tra-wu, "they bowed the knees before him," = "they kneeled down before him."

Sóńala, a-, pl. ẹ-, or trạ-, or sing. ọ-, pl. trạ, n. "a lion:" e. g. a-sóńala a-bána, "a large lion."

Sọnd. v. a. abr. (rad. sọń), "deliver up, give up, give away; resign" (as an office); "part with; e. g. ọ-bai ọ sọnd ań-tọf, "the king gave the country away;" — 'a sọnd-kọ rọńań, "they delivered him up to them;" — I gbạ́li hẹ ńi sọnd, "I cannot part with it."

Sọr, adj. "daubed over with mud, mudded, made of mud; e. g. a-set a-sọr, "a mud-house."

Sor, a-, pl. ẹ-, n. "a Fula javelin, spear; a stick with an iron fork used for throwing;" also "a long staff tipped with brass" or "silver, borne by old men as a sort of badge of honour."

Sọ́rọ, ẹ-, n. "excrements of infants; e. g. ẹ-sọ́rọ ya ow'ahẹl, "the excrements of the infant."

Sọt, v. n. "sew;" e. g. ọ sọt o-bána, "he sews with large stitches;" — ọ sọt ọ-fino, "he sews well."

Sọt, a-, or i-, pl. ma-; or also a-, pl. ẹ-, n. "a trick, an artifice; cunning, stratagem;" e. g. ọ-trar owé ọ ba a-sọt a-lạs, "this slave has a bad trick." The pl. form ma-sọt, is also used in the sense of "craftiness, cunningness."

Sóte, v. n. „piss, urine, make water."

Sóto, v. a. „receive, get, acquire, obtain;" also „get into" (as into some state): e. g. sa poṅ sóto aṅ-ram-'a-su, „we have got our pay;" — o sóto i-nei, „he obtained mercy," or also „he is in a pitiable state so as to deserve pity."

Sóto, ka-, n. verb. „act of getting" or „obtaining."

Sóto a-méra, v. n. „get sense, come to the years of discretion;" e. g. o pon' to sóto a-méra, he has now come to the years of discretion."

Sótona, v. rel. „obtain-for-, get-for-;" e. g. som-mi aṅ-kála aṅá ma sótona-mi, „give me the money, which thou didst get for me."

Su, pr. obj. „us;" e. g. o sap-su, „he flogged us."

Sū, ka-, pl. tra-, n. „pipe" (as made of corkwood); „trumpet;" e. g. feṅ aka-sū, „blow the trumpet."

Súle, v. n. „have diarrhoea, have loose bowels; be loose" (as the bowels); e. g. ak'or-ka-mi ka súle, my bowels are loose."

Súle, adj. „loose" (as bowels); e. g. o ba k'or ka-súle, „he has loose bowels."

Súlima, o-, pl. a-, n. „one of the Sulima nation, a Sulima."

Sūm, a-, n. „a fast;" e. g. 'a wop aṅ-sūm, „they hold the fast," or „the Ramadan." Fr. the Ar. صُوْم, abstinentia a cibo, potu etc., ab aurora usque ad solis occasum, jejunium.

Súma, e-, n. „times." The sing. is not used; it always occurs in the phrase: e-súma yĕ, „now-a-days, now at this time;" e. g. réke Yísua o yi e-súma yĕ-e? „where is Jesus now?"

Sut, v. a. „rub" (as in washing or otherwise); „strike; stroke;" also „shoot with-, fire off-, discharge," (as a gun); „shoot;" e. g. I sut-ko, „I rubbed him;" — o sut ka-tra-k'oṅ, „he rubbed his hand;" — o sut am-píṅkar, „he discharged the gun."

Sútne, v. refl. „rub oneself" (as in washing); „strike" or „knock oneself;" e. g. sútne o-tot, „rub thyself well."

Sútar, v. rel. „shoot at-, fire at-, shoot," (with or without píṅkar);

e. g. o sútar-ko, or: o sútar-ko a-píṅkar, „he shot him," lit. „he shot at him," or „he shot at him with a gun;" — o sútar am-bamp, „he shot the bird."

Sútara, v. doubl. rel. „shoot at-with-, fire at-with-," e. g. 'a sútara-ko a-píṅkar, „they shot at him with a gun." Also „shoot at-for-," as „sútara-mi-ko, „shoot at him for me," = „shoot him for me."

Ṣyā, pr. emph. „we;" but also used for the sing. „I" when joined with other emph. pronouns, or with proper names, implying the copula „and;" e. g. ṣyā Pa Sóri sa kóne, „I and Mr. Sori we go;" — sya an-Témne sa t'ra he amatrei amé, or: ṣya 'n-Témne etc., „we Temnes do not know these things."

T.

T', pref. indef. insep. „a, an;" e. g. t'amasére, „an evidence;" it is an abbr. form of tra, which is evident from the fact that the adjective takes the pref. tra-, as t'amasére tra-gbáraṅ, „a clear evidence."

Ta, adv. „yet; more;" e. g. o ta der he, „he did not yet come." It sometimes serves to express the comparative degree, as: riañ pa-la pa ta lā, „there rice is more plentiful "

Ta, prep. „except, unless;" e. g. ma gḥáli he sóto r'áka, ta ma ko ri, „thou wilt not get any thing, unless thou doest go there."

Tabána, adv. „for ever, ever;" with a negative „never." E. g. an'ántr na ro-yahánnama na gbáli he dimṣe tabána, „the fire in hell will never go out."

Tabána, adj. „everlasting, eternal;" e. g. an'ántr na-tabána, „the everlasting fire."

Tabána táṅkaṅ, adv. emph. „for ever and ever, ever, at any time, to all eternity," = táṅkaṅ tabána, with a negative „never, at any time, not at any time." E. g. sa tra yi ro-riánna tabána táṅkaṅ, „we shall be in heaven for ever and ever;" — tabána táṅkaṅ I bun be an-toṅ'-a-mu, „I never at any time transgressed thy commandment."

Táhọ, adv. „not;" e. g. yẹ táhọ, „not so;" — kọn' táhọ yọ̄-tšị, „it is not he who did it," or „not he did it;" — min' táhọ, „it (is) not I;" — ey'ẹtr-'ẹ-ṃi yía táhọ, „these are not my things." This negative may be used more absolutely without a verb, which is not the case with hẹ, or fẹ, and tšĕ. It generally implies the substantive verb „be" like the Hebr. אֵין.

Tákas, v. n., „learn;" e. g. w'an, ṃạ tákas ọ-fíno! „boy, thou doest learn well!"

Tákas, v. a. „learn;" e. g. ṃạ tákas ka-gbal-i? „didst thou learn to write?"

Ták'sa. v. caus. „make-to learn, teach, instruct;" e. g. ṃạ yéṃa họ I ták'sa-mu-i? „doest thou wish me to teach thee?"

Ták'sa, v. rel. (for: tákạsa), „teach- for-;" e. g. ták'sa-mi-kọ. „instruct him for me;" — o ták'sa a-fam ka-tšemp ka-bána, „he taught people with great wisdom."

Ták'sa, ka-, n. verb. „act of teaching, teaching, instruction;" e. g. ka-ták'sa-k'ọn, „his instruction."

Tálanẹ, ọ-, n. „boundary, termination, end;" e. g. ọ-tálanẹ wa an-tọf, „the end of the earth;" — an-nésam-'a-su anọ-rū ṅa bā ọ-tálanẹ, „our life in this world takes an end," lit. „— — has an end."

Talọ́m, adv. „or;" e. g. ṃạ gbáli tran' do-gban talọ́m ro-ban. „thou canst go by land or by water."

Tam, v. n. „get the victory, conquer, be victorious;" e. g. am-bóna añé na tam ka ka-tšim lọ́kọ ó lọ́kọ, „this nation gets always the victory in war."

Tam, v. a. „conquer overcome, subdue, defeat;" e. g. an-Témnẹ ṅa tam am-Bólam. „the Temnes conquered the Boloms."

T'amasére, n. „evidence, witness, testimony; e. g. at'amasére-tr'oñ tráka ọw'úni ọwé, „his evidence about this person."

Támbe, prep. „except, unless;" e. g. I tši kálanẹ nínan, támbe k'ánkal ka bẹntr-ṃi, „I shall return tomorrow, unless a tornado prevent me."

Támbe, conj. „unless, except;" e. g. I gbáli hẹ sọ́tọ ak'ọ́ta, támbe I ram-ki, „I cannot get the cloth, except I pay for it."

Táme, v. n. „awake, be awake;" e. g. ọw'ahḗt o táme tọñ, „the child is awake now."

Támi, v. a., „awake, rouse from sleep;" e. g. tsē támi-kọ," do not awake him."

Támi, adj. „conquering, victorious." It may follow a proper name without a prefix, when it is emphatic and may be given by „the Conqueror," as: Farma Támi, „Farma the Conqueror."

Tamm, adv. spec. „quite, entirely, in profound silence, altogether, completely," used with trañk „be silent;" dim „destroy;" and yíra, „sit;" e. g. ọ-tem ọ yíra tamm, „the old man sat in profound silence;" — o trañk tamm, „he is quite still."

Tám'rọ, v. rel. inch. and pass. n. (for: támarọ or támara), (rad. tam), „get overcome, get routed, get defeated;" fig. „get tired, get beaten, not succeed, fail to obtain one's object, get baffled in one's attempts, be" or „get disappointed;" e. g. añ-Lọ́kọ ña tám'rọ, „the Lokos were defeated;" — I tūp tra sọ́tọ pa-la; kére I tám'rọ, „I endeavoured to get rice: but I failed to obtain my object."

Tám'rọ, v. rel. inch and pass. a. lit. „get conquered by-, get overcome by-," or „in-," (as an army in war); hence: „not obtain-, fail to obtain, not get, miss; lose;" e. g. 'a tám'rọ ọ-nā, „they missed the cow" (which they sought to catch); — ọ tám'rọ am-bōk, „he did not get the snake;" — I tám'rọ-kọ, „I missed him" (as in pursuing after one).

Tám'rọ, ka-, n. „defeat, overthrow; discomfiture; disappointment;" e. g. ka-tám'rọ ka ar'áfa-r'oñ, „the defeat of his army."

Tan, ọ-, adj. but used adverbially „(a) little;" e. g. I dira gbo ọ-tan, „I slept but little."

Tan, adj. „little, few;" e. g. m'antr ma-tan, „a little water;" — ma-réï ma-tan, „a few days."

Tan', for: tañk, which see. This form is used before d. See Fables p. 56. 58.

Tána, v. n. „be able, prevail." As an aux. it serves to express the Engl. aux. „can", and indicates ability to accomphish what is denoted by the principal verb, which follows in the short form of the Infinitve. E. g.ọ tą́na he, „he is not able;" — añ-fạm ańé ńa tą́na he yọ̄ ma-pant, „these persons are not able to do work."

Tą́na, v. n. „be able for-, prevail over, be a match for-, be equal to-, be able to keep up" or „to compete with-;" e. g. ọ-láṅba ọwé o tą́na he ọwóń, „this young man is no match for that one;" — I tą́na-kọ, I am able to compete with him;" — ọw'áń o tą́na-tši, „the boy is able for it."

Tą́nas, v. caus. „enable, make able;" e. g. I tą́nas-kọ tra yọ̄-tši, „I enabled him to do it."

Táni, conj. „lest, that not;" e. g. tšē ko ri, táni ńa šek-mu, „do not go there, lest they tie thee."

Táni, adv. „soon, shortly, by and by;" e. g. I tši der táni, or: táni I tši der, „I shall come soon;" — o tra sap-mu táni „he will flog thee shortly." It may be joined with nouns indicating time, to make that time more definite, as: táni tratrák, „to night," or „this night," lit. „soon to night."

Tańk, a-, pl. ẹ-. n. „root," (of a tree or shrub); e. g. a-tańk a bána, „a large root." Cf. Fables p. 56. 58.

Táṅka, } adv. „ever, for ever, always, at all times; some day,
Táṅkań, } one day, any time; much, very." With a negative „never." It is also sometimes used in the sense of an adj. denoting „much, many." E. g. mạ nạń'-kọ táṅkań-i? „didst thou ever see him?" — sạ tra yi ri táṅkań, „we shall be be there for ever;" — I tši tšéla-mu sọ táṅkań, „I will call thee again some day;" — ọ tra trū táṅkań, „he is very sick;" — tšē tši sọ táṅka yó, „never do it again," lit „do not do it ever again;" — ọ dif a-fạm táṅkań, „he killed much people." The form táṅkań is used more absolutely, or at the end of a proposition. (Cf. -ń under N.)

Táṅka be, „very much, exceedingly; e. g. ọ lásạr ak'óta táṅka be, „he spoiled the cloth very much."

Táṅkań ó táṅkań, „for ever and ever, to all eternity, eternally." With a negative „never, not at any time;" e. g. an'ántr na ro yahánnama na gbạ́li he dímse táṅkań ó táṅkań, „the fire in hell will not go out for ever and ever."

Táṅkaṅ tabána, — tabána táṅkaṅ, which see.

Tánta, ka-, pl. tra-, n. waterfall, cascade, cataract;" e. g. o yi ro-tánta, „he is at the waterfall."

Tápaṅ, adv. „formely, once, in former (old) times, long ago, before-time;" e. g. w'úni o yi ri ro-Ma-lal tápaṅ, „there was once a person at Malal;" — aṅ-fam aṅá yi ka ka-petr aké tápaṅ, „the people who were in this town in former times."

Tárap, adv. „entirely, altogether; completely, quite; well;" e. g. aṅ-kála-ń'oṅ ṅa dínne tárap, „his money is lost altogether;" — I trára-ko tárap, „I know him well."

Tas, v. impers. a „surpass, exceed." It may be used to express the Comparative and Superlative degrees, as: sa poṅ he bótar K'úru pa tas r'áka ó ráka, „we have not loved God above every thing," lit. „— — it surpasses every thing.

Tas, v. a. „surpass, pass, excel;" e. g. kóno tas aṅ-nábi be, „he is superior to all the prophets," lit. „he surpasses all the prophets;" — ma tas-mi tráka a-fósa, „thou art stronger than I," lit. „thou excellest me as regards strength." These examples will show that also this form is used to express the Comparative and Superlative. This is also the case with the next word, which see.

Tas, v. n. „go on, pass, pass on, pass along; pass away" (as smoke); also „exceed excel;" e. g. o tas ka aṅ-set-'a-mi, „he passed at my house;" — ak'íma ka tas, „the smoke passes away;" — I bā a-kála a-gbáti, kére kóno tas, „I have much money, but he has more," — „he has more money than I."

Tas, ka-, n. verb. „act of passing" or „of passing along" or „by;" e. g. ka-tas-k'oṅ aṅ-set-'a-mi, „his passing at my house."

Tása, v. caus. and pass. „exceed, pass, surpass;" e. g. I tása yi, „I am more than that," or „I exceed thus," lit. „I was made to exceed thus." Also this form may be used to express the Comparative and Superlative.

Tásale, a-, pl. e-, n. „a brass pan used for ablutions by the Mohammedans at their prayers, pray-kettle."

Tási, v. a. „surpass, exceed, be superior to, excel; e. g. añ-set-ñ'oñ ña tási añ-set-'a-mi, „his house is superior to my house." Also „be too much for-," (as food for a number of persons); e. g. ey'étr e-di eyé e tássi-ña, „this food is too much for them." Like tas above this form is also much used to express the Comparative and Superlative; for which purpose tási is also used intransitively. Tási is the long form of tas.

Teī, v. n. „rot, get rotten, decay, be rotten;" e. g. e-tok e teī, „the fire-wood gets rotten."

Téli, a-, or i-, pl. ma-, n. „a trap, snare" (for birds, or other animals, made of bamboo leaves, or of wooden rope); e. g. o gbątr ma-téli, „he set a trap."

Télma, adj. „chatting, prating, loquacious;" e. g. w'úni télma, „a loquacious person," = „a prater."

Télma, ką-, n. verb. „chatting, prating, loquaciousness;" e. g. ow'úni owé o bà ką-télma, „this person is fond of chatting;" — w'úni ką-télma, „a loquacious person," lit. „a person (of) loquaciousness."

Télma Módu, „a prater, a chatting person, babbler;" e. g. káne Télma Módu káma o trañk, „tell the prater to be silent." Cf. the word Módu under M, and Proverb 5, p. 99.

Tem, o-, pl. a-, n. „old man, Sir." It is a title of respect to old men; e. g. o-tem, kóri 'u! „I salute thee, Sir!" The indef. pref. ña- may be put also behind the noun, as is the case with a few nouns of this class, as: tem-ña, or: ña-tem, „old men;" but: a-tem-ña, „the old men."

Témne, o-, pl. a-, n. „one of the Temne nation, a Temne." About its derivation see Pref. §. 2.

Témne, adj. „belonging to the Temne country" or „people, of Temne origin, temne;" e. g. an-tof a-témne, „the Temne country."

Ten, v. a. „seek, look for-, try to obtain"; e. g. ko r'áka mą ten-e? „what doest thou look for?"

Ten, ką-, n. verb. „act of looking for;" e. g. ka-ten-k'oñ o-nā, „his looking for the cow."

Téna, v. rel. „seek-for-, get-for-, provide-for-; procure-for-; supply-with what is necessary;" e. g. w'an, ko téna-mi o-ṇä, „boy, go look me for the cow;" — o-tem o téna-mi y'etr e-di, „the old man supplies me with food;" — K'úru o téna-mi o-fíno, „God provides well for me."

Ténoṅ, adv. „to day, this day;" e. g. o yō-tši ténoṅ, „he did it to day."

Ténoṅ ra-foi, „this evening;" e. g. o trạ der ténoṅ ra-foi, „he will come this evening."

Ténoṅ ra-yaṅ, „to day at noon;" e. g. I tši kóne ténoṅ ra-yaṅ, „I shall leave to day at noon."

Ténoṅ tratrák, „to night, this night;" e. g. o kas-ka-mi o trạ der ténoṅ tratrák, „my father will come to night."

Tens, v. freq. or intens. a. (rad. ten), „search for-, look for- carefully, seek;" e. g. ko nạ tens ri-e? „what do ye search for there?"

Ténša, v. freq. or intens. and rel. „search for- in behalf of-; look for- diligently in behalf of-, seek carefully for-;" e. g. ténša-mi naṅ aṅ-lápra-'a-mi, „seek ye my cap for me." Also „seek an occasion for-" (as for war, or palaver); e. g. o ténša ka-tšim, „he seeks much for an occasion of war" or „of a fight."

Ténta, a-, pl. e-, n. „a hammock"; e. g. o fánta ro-ténta, „he lies in the hammock."

Téri, ma-, n. „wrong" (the contrary of: right), „injustice; impropriety, wrongness" (as of an action); „fault, blame;" e. g. o bā ma-téri, „he is in the wrong;" — 'a soṅ-ko ma-téri, „they gave him wrong;" — ma-téri ma atr'ci atrá o yō, „the impropriety of the thing which he did."

Tésa, v. n. „be pleased, be gratified; please, give pleasure, be acceptable, be agreeable;" e. g. K'úru o tésa traka as'ádka-tr'oṅ, „God was pleased with his sacrifice;" — as'ádka-tr'oṅ tra tésa ka K'úru, „his sacrifice was acceptable to God;" — aṅ-fef aṅé ṅa tésa he, „this wind is not agreeable."

Tésane, v. impers. refl. „please to-, give pleasure to-, delight," lit. „give pleasure to oneself;" e. g. pa tésane-mi trąka troṅ, „I am pleased" or „delighted with him," lit. „it gives pleasure to me on account of him;" — pą tésanę-kọ, „he is delighted," lit. „it delights him."

Tésąs, v. caus. „make to be pleased, gratify, delight, cheer; make acceptable, ingratiate oneself with-; e. g. są bā tra tésas ọ-baī, „we must make the king pleased;" — atr'eí atšé tra tésąs-mi, „this thing delights me."

Téte, adv. „presently, now, just now, immediately;" e. g. tro są ma yọ tete-e? „how shall we do now?" — kánę yọ téte atr'eí atšé-e? „who did now this thing?" — ọ-lánba ọ bēk téte, „the young man came just now;" — yọ-tši téte, „do it immediately."

Tétu, a-, pl. ę-, n. „a messenger, an apostle;" e. g. ọ sóm'ra a-tétu ka ọ-baī, „he sent a messenger to the kiug." Some use the pref. ọ- in the sing. and a-, in the pl., as: ọ-tétu-ka-mi, „my messenger," but this form is not much used.

Ti, ma-, n. „pus, matter" (as of a sore); e. g. ma-ti ma-laī ma wur ka ka-sam, „much pus came out from the sore."

Tíla, v. a. „sell"; e. g. ọ tíla ak'óta, „he sold the cloth."

Tíla, v. n. „trade"; e. g. ọ der tra tíla, „he came to trade."

Tińkąr, v. rel. „press down upon-, press upon-," (as upon a debtor); „force" (as one to do a thing); „bear upon-" (as on a sail); e. g. w'an, tińkąr am-beń, „boy, press upon the board;" — ọ tińkąr-mi tra ram-kọ ań-kála, „he pressed upon me to pay him the money;" — ọ tińkąr-ńa tra kọ ri, „he forced them to go there;" — tińkąr am-bę́la, w'an! „bear upon the sail, boy!"

Tis, a-, pl. ę-, n. „a knife, a country knife;" e. g. kára ba a-tis¡! „bring a knife here!"

Tit, v. a. „choose, select, make a choice of-, pick out;" e. g. ką́li, ę-lop ę-gbáti, mą gbą́li tit ę-lọm, „look, there are many fish, thou canst pick out some."

Tọ, adv. = tọń, „now, then, already;" e. g. ką́li tọ ak'óta aké, „look now at this cloth;" — ńa pon' tọ dis waī ey'étr, „they had bought the things already yesterday." See also tọń below.

Tọf, a-, pl. tṛa-, n. „country, land;" e. g. aṅ-tọf a-témne, „the Temne country."

Tọf, a-, n. „soil, ground;" e. g. a-tọf a-fino, „good soil." The def. form is also used for the terraqueous globe, as: aṅ-tọf, „the earth" or „the world;" e. g. aṅ-tọf be, „the whole earth."

Tọf, e-, n. „ground, earth" (as dug out to make mud with for to build houses); hence also „dirt, mud" (i. e. earth mixed with water); e. g. tšē sákạr-mi e-tọf, „do not bespatter me with dirt."

Tọ́fạl, adj. „peaceful, quiet, meek, soft, gentle" (of animate and inanimate objects); „tame" (as a horse); „mild" (as liquors); „cool" (as food); „safe, out of danger; etc.;" e. g. w'úni tọ́fạl, „a quiet person;" — aṅ-tọf a-témne ṅa yi a-tọ́fạl, „the Temne country is quiet;" — ma-réï ma-tọ́fạl, „peaceful days;" — a-soī a-tọ́fạl, „a tame horse;" — ọw'úni ọwé ọ bā a-méra tọ́fạl, „this person is of a soft temper."

Tọ́fạl, ọ-, adj. but used adverbially „gently, softly, easily; peacefully, in peace;" e. g. ọ yọ̄-tši ọ-tọ́fạl, „he did it softly;" — 'a baṅ-ko ọ-tọ́fạl, „they fetched him gently;" — kọ́ne ọ-tọ́fạl! „go in peace!"

Tọ́fạl, ma-, n. „peace; gentleness, meekness; tameness; mildness;" e. g. ọ bā ma-tọ́fạl ro-méra, „he has peace in his heart;" — ma-tọ́fạl ma aṅ-soī, „the lameness of the horse."

Tọ́f'lọ, } v. inch. (for: tọ́fạlọ), „get quiet, get easy, become pacified" or „quiet; get cool" (as the sun, or food, or
Tọ́f'la, } anger); „abate" (as pain); e. g. am-méra-'a-mi ṅa tọ́f'lọ he, be I nạm fe ọw'áṅ-ka-mi, „my mind does not get easy, if I do not see my child;" — aṅ'eí na tọ́f'lọ tọṅ, „the sun gets cool now."

Tọ́f'la, } v. impers. and rel. „get" or „become easy with-, get
Tọ́f'lọ, } better with-, get comfortable with-, get out of danger with-" (as with a sick person). It is difficult to give the literal sense of this verb in English, where the object becomes the subject; e. g. pạ tọ́f'lọ-kọ, „he gets better" (as a sick person), or more lit. „it gets better with him;" — pạ tọ́f'lọ-

mi ténoṅ ro-méra, „I feel easy to day in my mind," lit. „it got easy with me to day in the mind."

Tọī, v. a. „burn, set on fire" (as a house, or person); „scald" (as hot water one's hand); e. g. 'a tọī aṅ-sel, „they burned the house;" — ain'ántr ma-fại ma tọī ka-trā-ka-mi, „the hot water scalded my hand."

Tọīs, v. freq. or intens. a. „set on fire" (as many houses); „broil, roast on the fire" (not in a pot); „bake" (as bread); e. g. ar'ā́fa ra tọīs e-sel bẹ, „the war-people burned all the houses;" — tọīs ọ-šẹm, „roast the beef."

Tọīsa, v. freq. or intens. and rel. „set-on fire for-; broil-for-, roast-on the fire for-; bake-for-; e. g. tọīsa-mi ọ-šẹm, „roast the beef for me."

Tọk, kạ-, pl, ẹ-, n. „fire-wood;" e. g. mạ yéma waī ẹ-tọk-i? „doest thou want to buy firewood?"

Tọk, v. a. „extol, praise;" e. g. 'a tọk o-baī, „they extolled the king."

Tọ́kạs, kạ-, n. verb. „act of praising, praising, praise;" e. g. ka-tọ́kạs K'úru, „the act of of praising God."

Tọ́kọ, adv. „apart, by itself, separately;" e. g. ọ yíra tọ́kọ, „he lives by himself;" — botr atr'ántr atšé tọ́kọ, „put these sticks separately."

Tọ́kọ, \} adv. „now, then," = tọ, and tọṅ; e. g. kọ́nẹ tọ́kọṅ,
Tọ́kọṅ, \} „go now;" — aṅ-lọ́kọ ṅa poṅ tọ́kọ tas, „the time is now passed" or „is now up." The form tọ́kọṅ is used more absolutely, or at the end of a proposition.

Tọ́mọ, v. n. „dance"; e. g. aṅ-fạm ṅa trạ tọ́mọ ro-petr, „the people are dancing in town."

Tọṅ, adv. = tọ, „now, then, already;" e. g. der tọṅ, „come now;" — ka ka-kal-ka-ini I bạp tọṅ ṅa poṅ tīla aṅ-wut-'a-mi, „at my return I found then (that) they had sold my children." It is also sometimes used to express the adv. „too, too much," as: ra-béṅa ra bọ́li tọṅ, „the rope is too long," lit. „the rope is long now." Tọṅ is a more abs. form, and also always used at the end of a proposition, which is not the case with tọ. Cf. the form tọ above, and the letter ṅ under N.

Toń, a-, pl. e-, n. „a law, commandment;" e. g. e-toń ya K'úru, „the commandments of God;" — o-baī o raf a-toń a-fu, „the king made a new law."

Tóńka, v. n. „debate a matter, talk a palaver; expostulate, plead at the bar, litigate, judge;" e. g. Pa Sóri, múno tóńka, „Mr. Sori, do thou talk the matter."

Tóńka, v. recipr. „implead each other" (at law); „plead with each other, have a law-suit," or „go to law with each other, debate a case with each other;" e. g. ńa ko tóńka ro ka o-baī, „they go to have a law-suit with each other at the king's place."

Tóńka, a-, pl. e-, n. „a legal case, a law-suit, a matter" or „case to be settled, a case about which they plead at the bar;" e. g. Pā Sóri de mínań sa bā a-tóńka, „Mr. Sori and I have a law-suit;" — o-baī o tra rok an-tóńka, „the king will settle the case."

Tóńkas, v. caus. lit. „make to plead," hence „carry to law, implead, prosecute by law, give palaver to, sue, litigate with, expostulate with-; judge" (as a person, not matters), „try, enter into judgment with-;" e. g. o tóńkas-mi ka-tsiń, „he sued me for nothing;" — tšē mi tóńkas! „do not enter into judgment with me!"

Tóńkla, v. a. „collect, assemble, gather together;" e. g. 'a tóńkla ey'étr-'e-ńań be, „they collected all their things;" — o tóńkla ań-fam ńa ka ka-petr be, „he assembled the people of the whole town."

Tóńklane, v. recipr. or refl. „assemble, gather themselves, troop together, meet together;" also „accumulate itself" (as sand); e. g. ńa tóńklane téńoń, „they met together to day;" — ań-fam be ńa ro-petr ńa tóńklane rokín, „all the people of the town assembled together."

Tóńto, v. a. „coax, flatter, persuade, entice" (by sweet words); „beguile; allure, tempt;" also „soothe, appease" (as a child crying); e. g. ńa tóńto-ko káma koń' so o ko ri, „they coaxed him, that he also might go there;" — o tóńto gbo a-fam, „he only beguiles people;" — tóńto ow'ahét, „soothe the child."

Tónto, a-, pl. e-, n. „a trap" or „snare put by sweet and enticing words, allurement; any thing given to another for the purpose to procure his friendship again which was lost by having offended him, or in order to induce him to do a thing, or to comply with one's wish;" e. g. o bótra-mi a-tónto, „he put a snare for me."

Tor, v. n, „come down, go down, descend; set" (as the sun); „come away" (as the afterbirth); e. g. w'an, tor! „boy, come down!" — o tor ro-gbań, „he came down the country;" — ar'étr ra tor, „the sun set." With ro-bil, „embark", lit. „go down into the canoe." Cf. the Hebr. יָרַד, Jon. 1, 3.

Tóra, v. caus. „make to come down, bring down; let down, send down;" e. g. K'úru kóno tóra k'om, „it is God who sends down rain" or „who causes to rain;" — w'an, ko tóra ambéla, „boy, go let down the sail." Also fig. „humble, degrade, abase, bring down low;" as: kóno tóra-ko, „he humbled him."

Tórane, v. caus. and refl. or spont. „bring oneself down" or „come down of one's own accord;" fig. „humble oneself; come down in one's circumstances" or „affairs; be in a low state" (as one's body, or as regards outward circumstances). E. g. o tórane ro-set, w'úni tóra he ko, „he came down from the house himself, no one brought him down;" — o tórane háli, „he has come down much in his circumstances."

Tóroń, ka-, n. „the east, sun-rise;" e. g. o yéfa ro-tóroń, „he came from the East." With the prep. ro- it becomes also a prep. or a postp.

Tóroń, adj. „eastern"; e. g. a-tof a-tóroń, „an eastern country."

Tot, adj. „good, kind, good-natured, gracious;" e. g. w'úni tot, „a kind person."

Tot, o-, adj. but used adverbially, „kindly, well, good;" as applied to dying „happily"; e. g. o yō-mi o-tot, „he treated me kindly;" — sútne o-tot, „rub thyself well;" — o fi o-tot, „he died happily."

Tot, ma-, n. „kindness, goodness, good nature, graciousness;" e. g. o-tem owé o bā ma-tot ma-bána, this old man is very kind" or „very good-natured," lit. „this old man has great kindness."

Tr', pref. indef. and insep. (for: tra̧-), „a, an;" e. g. tr'a̧ntr. „sticks", for: tra̧-a̧ntr.

Tr', part. (for tra), „let", which see.

Tr' 'o̧ —! (for: trē ho̧ —!) or for: tšē ho̧ —! „mind that — not —!" do not —!" lit. „not that —!" See Fables p. 52.

Tra̧-, pref. indef. „a, an;" e. g. tra̧-bep, „spoons". It is sing. and pl.

Tra̧, prep. poss. indef. „of"; e. g. tra̧-bep-tra̧-mi, „spoons of mine," lit. „spoons of me," = „my spoons."

Tra̧, prep. indef. „for, as to, as regards; on account of; etc.," e. g. o̧ tási-mi tra̧ ka̧-yeṅk ma-der, lit. „he surpasses me in health," = „he is more healthy than I;" — pa̧ yi he tra̧ ra-trũ o̧ tšē bápar, „it is not on account of sickness that he was not present." It is the indef. form of tra, which see below.

Tra̧, pr. subj. indef. „it; they;" e. g. tra̧-bep-tra̧-mi tra̧ dinnȩ, „spoons of mine are lost."

Tra, part. to form the Present tense and the Participle with all persons in both numbers, excepting the 1st. pers. sing.; for which they use the form tši, or tri. E. g. o̧ tra der, „he is coming;" — o̧ tra sap-mu, „he will flog thee." This part. is used if the Future is to be expressed positively, i. e. if there is no doubt about the event, which is to take place; otherwise they use the forms: ma, mȩ and mo̧. Cf. the examples under the part. ma, 1.

Tra-, pref. def. „the", = atra-; e. g. tra-bep, or atra-bep, „the spoons."

Tra, prep. poss. def. „of"; e. g. tra-bep-tra-mi, „my spoons," lit. „the spoons of me;" — tra-bep tra Sóri, „the spoons of Sori."

Tra, prep. = tráka, „for, to, in order to; about, concerning, as regards, as to; with; on account of, by." It is also used as the sign of the Infinitive. E. g. a-fa̧m ña gbáli hȩ fúti tra ma-yo̧s-ma-ñañ ma-fíno, „men cannot be saved on account of their good works;" — sa ba tra kal sǫ ninaṅ, "we have to return again to morrow;" — Yísua ǫ fi tra aṅ-fam be, de tra trάnnu sǫ, "Jesus died for all people, and for you also." The form trα̨ka, which is used, definitely and indefinitely is more frequently employed. Tra is the def. form of trą which compare, as also trα̨ka. See more about this prep. in the Grammar.

Tra, pr. subj. def. "it; they;" e. g. tra-bep tra dínne, "the spoons are lost."

Tra, conj. = tša, which see.

Tra, part. "let", used to form the Hortative Mood. When used with the pr. ǫ, "he, she" or 'a "they", which is for ṅa, they generally drop the vowel of the part., and contract its consonants with the following pr., as tr' ǫ ko di, "let him go eat," or "let him go to eat," lit. "let he go eat," for: tra ǫ kǫ etc.; — tr' 'a dif-kǫ, "let them kill him," lit. "let they kill him," for: tra ṅa dif-kǫ; — tra są kǫ ro-Kamp, "let us go to Freetown."

Trā, ką-, pl. ma-, n. "a hand; handle;" e. g. ma-trā-m'ǫṅ, "his hands;" — ka-trā ka am-pǫ́li, "the handle of the cup."

Tr'a (for: trára), "know", which see. This form is used before the negative adverbs fe and he, "not", as: I tr'a he tši, "I do not know it."

Trą-mi, pr. poss. indef. "my", lit. "of me;" e. g. trą-trála-trą-mi, "hoes of mine" or "my hoes."

Tra-mi, pr. poss. def. "my", lit. "of me;" e. g. tra-trála-tra-mi, "my hoes," lit. "the hoes of me."

Trą-mu, pr. poss. indef. "thy", lit. "of thee;" e. g. trą-trála-trą-mu, "hoes of thine," = "thy hoes."

Tra-mu, pr. poss. def. "thy", lit. "of thee;" e. g. tra-trála-tra-mu, "thy hoes," lit. "the hoes of thee."

Trą-ṅaṅ, pr. poss. indef. "their", lit. "of them;" e. g. trą-bep-trą-ṅaṅ, "spoons of theirs," = "their spoons."

Tra-ṅaṅ, pr. poss. def. "their". lit. "of them;" e. g. tra-bep-tra-ṅaṅ, "their spoons," lit. "the spoons of them."

Tra̧-nu, pr. poss. indef. „your", lit. „of you;" e. g. tra̧ trála-tra̧-nu, „hoes of yours," = „your hoes."

Tra-nu, pr. poss def. „your", lit. „of you;" e. g. tra-trála-tra-nu, „your hoes," lit. „the hoes of you."

Tra-tši, pr. dem. log. „that, those;" e. g. tra-bep tra-tši, „those spoons" (spoken of before).

Trák' (for: tráka), prep. which see.

Trak, a-, pl. e- or tra-; or sing. o̧-, pl. tra̧-, n. „a harnessed antelope," commonly called „deer".

Tra̧k, ka-, pl. tra̧-, n. „a staff of authority, a walking staff, a staff;" also „palaver, matter;" e. g. ka̧-trak ka̧-bána, „a great matter."

Tr'ak, pl. of k'ak, which see.

Tráka, prep. = tra, and tra̧, which see; „for, for to, to, in order to; about, concerning, as to, as regards; on account of; with; etc." It is a def. and an indef. form, and may be used either for: tra or for: tra̧; but tráka is more frequently used than either tra or tra̧, and like tra it is also used as a sign of the Infinitive. E. g. o̧ fai o̧-nä o-fet o-bois tráka tron̄, „he killed the fattened calf for him;" — tráka kánę ma̧ yo̧ ma-pant-e? „for whom doest thou do work?" — amméra-n̄'o̧n̄ n̄a kira-ko̧ tráka atrá o̧ pon̄ yo̧, „his conscience troubles him about what he has done" or „on account of what he has done;" — yȩ pa yi tráka w'úmi ó w'úmi an̄-lo n̄a-tši, „thus it was with every man that time."

Note. Before the prefix a- the vowel of the prep. is often dropped, as: o̧ pä fo̧ o̧ tas-mi trak' a-fósa, „he says that he is stronger than I," lit. „he says that he surpasses me as regards strength."

Tráka 'ra-bomp ra —, „for the sake of —, on account of —," lit. „for the head of —;" e. g. ma̧ yéma dim aka-petr bę tráka 'ra-bomp ra ka-pan̄ ka a-fam tramát-i? „wilt thou destroy the whole town on account of the lake of five persons?"

Tráka tši, „therefore, wherefore, for this reason," lit. „for it" or „on account of it;" e. g. ma̧ ta pon̄ hę ram ak'óta; tráka tši I gbáli hę mu ki so̧n̄, or I gbáli hę som-mu-ki, „thou hast not yet paid for the cloth; therefore I cannot give it to thee."

Trạl, v. n. "hear; understand; obey;" e. g. mạ trạl mọ ọw'ér ọ sọm ak'áro-i? "doest thou hear how the rat nibbles the bowl?" — I trạl ọ-fíno, "I understand well;" — ọw'án ọwé ọ trạl he kō-kō, "this boy does not obey at all."

Trạl, v. a. "hear; understand; obey; listen to, hearken to;" e. g. ọw'án ọwé ọ trạl he ar'ím-ra-mi, "this child does not hear" or "listen to my word;" — ọ trạl he mi, "he does not obey me;" — añ-fẹt añé ña trạl ar'ím ra ọ-kas-ka-ñañ lọ́kọ ó lọ́kọ, "these children always hear (obey) the word of their father." This form is not used with a personal object, except in negative propositions; if there is a personal object in positive propositions the form trạ́la is used, which see.

Trạl, ọ-, pl. a-, n. "a hearer, one hearing;" e. g. kérẹ tšē nạ gbo yi a-trạl; kérẹ yi nạ sọ a-yọ̄ ña atrá nạ trạl, "but be ye not hearers only; but be ye also doers of what ye hear."

Tral, adv. spec. "quite, altogether;" it is used with tšiñ, "be naked," and with the noun kạ-tšiñ, as used adverbially in the sense of "for nothing, in vain, without cause;" e. g. ọ-béra ọwé ọ tšiñ tral, "this woman is quite naked;" — nạ rámnẹ gbo kạ-tšiñ tral, "ye pray but in vain altogether."

Trála, kạ-, pl. trạ-, n. "a country hoe, a hoe;" e. g. kạ-trála kạ-bọ́li, "a long hoe."

Trạ́la, v. a. "hear, hearken to, listen to, obey;" e. g. mạ trạ́la am-bamp-i? "doest thou hear the bird?" — ọw'án-ka-mi ọ trạ́la ar'ím-ra-mi, "my child listens to my word;" — ọ trạ́la he kọ, "he does not obey him." Also "feel" (as a smell, or scent); see next word. Cf. also trạl, v. a. above.

Trạ́la am-bọntr ña-, "get the scent of-, come upon the track of-" (as a dog upon the track of something lost, or of a person), lit. "feel the scent of-;" e. g. be an-trạn ọ trạ́la am-bọntr-ñ'ọñ, ro ọ kọ be, ọ tra trañ-kọ, "if the dog gets the scent of him, wherever he goes to, he will follow him."

Trála i-bọntr, "feel a smell" or "scent"; e. g. I trạ́la i-bọntr i-fíno, 1 feel a good smell.".

Tṛála w'úni i-bǫntr, „feel a smell on one;" e. g. ṅa tṛála he kǫ i-bǫntr ṅa an'ántr, „they did not feel a smell of the fire on him."

Tṛálnę, v. refl. a. „feel" (as pain etc.): e. g. I tṛálnę r'ä ra-las ka ka-trä-ka-mi, „I feel something bad on my hand;" lit. „hear" or „feel oneself."

Tṛálnę d'or, „feel hungry;" e. g. ǫ tṛálnę d'or, „he felt hungry;" lit. „feel hunger."

Tṛálpę, v. n. „jump down, light down, come down; step, go, jump;" e. g. am-bamp ǫ tṛálpę ro-tof, „the bird lighted down on the ground;" — ǫ-lánba ǫ tṛálpę ro-mantr, „the young man jumped (down) into the water." It is also applied to the lightning, or rather to the thunder, when striking into a house; because the Temnes believe that it is the thunder which comes down.

Tram, euph. form of traṅ, „follow", used before m, as: ǫ tram-mi, „he follows me." See traṅ.

Tram, v. a. „publish, give public notice of-, inform of-, make known, proclaim" (as a law); „tell" (as tales); e. g. kǫ tram-tši ro-petr bę, „go publish it in the whole town;" — ǫ tram-tši ka aṅ-fam bę, „he gave notice of it to all the people;" — ǫ tram-kǫ, „he made him known;" — man der naṅ tram m'ump, „come let us tell tales."

Tṛáma, v. n. „stand; be." As an aux. it serves to express the English „be about, be on the point," to exercise the energy, denoted by the principal verb, which follows in the long form of the Infinitive. E. g. ǫ-tem ǫ tṛáma ri ro-set, „the old man stands there in the house;" — ǫ tṛáma tšiṅ, „he is naked;" — ǫ-bęra ǫ trama tṛáka fi, „the woman is on the point of death," lit. „ - stands to die" or „is about to die;" — ǫ tṛáma ǫ-fíno, „he is well off." — Also „stop" (as one walking); „stay, live" (as at a place); e. g. r'im ra tšéla-kǫ: Tṛáma! „a voice called to him: Stop!" — ǫ tṛáma ras ro-Báke Lóko, „he still stays at Port Loko."

Tṛáma, a-, or i-, pl. ma-, n. „attitude, posture; state, condition; situation, place, lot; independence; estate, dwelling; etc.;"

e. g. ma-trǎma-m'oṅ ma tésa he, "his attitude does not please" or "is not agreeable;" — o bā ma-trǎma ma-fíno, "he is well off," lit. "he has a good condition;" — ma-trǎma-m'oṅ ma yi ro-tšen' dokóm, "his estate is on the top of the hill." The sing. is seldom used; as: aṅai-trǎma-ṅ'oṅ ṅa tésa he, = ma-trǎma-m'oṅ ma tésa he.

Trǎma kadí, = trǎma rodí, "stand before" or "beyond, go before, walk before, be ahead, be first, precede" (as to space or time), "lead the way, place oneself at the head;" also "be contrary" or "unfavourable" (as wind): e. g. k'in ka tralóme, owó trǎma kadí, etc., "one of the sheep which led the way, etc.;" — aṅ-feſ ṅa trǎma kǎdí, "the wind is contrary."

Trǎma rayér, "stand near, stand close by, stand aside;" e. g. o-wontr-k'oṅ o trǎma rayér, "his brother stood close by."

Trǎma rodí, = trǎma kadí, which see; e. g. o trǎma rodí ka ka-rǎre, "he stood before the door."

Trǎma rokáṅ, stand without;" e. g. o-tem o trǎma rokáṅ, "the old man stands without."

Trǎma w'úni kadí, = trǎma w'úni rodí, "stand before one" or "beyond one, go" or "walk before one, be at the head of one, be in front of one, precede one" (in distance or time); also "be in one's way, oppose one;" as applied to wind "be contrary to one, be against one." E. g. kóno trǎma-ṅa kadí, "he goes before them;" — Bō Fóki o trǎma Alikáli Mórba kadí, "Bey Foki preceded Alikali Morba;" — o-láṅba owé o trǎma-mi kadí, I gbáli he sóto r'áka, "this young man is in my way, I cannot get any thing;" — aṅ-feſ ṅa trǎma-su kadí ténoṅ, "the wind is against us to day."

Trǎma w'úni rayér, "stand close to one, stand near (to) one;" e. g. o-tem o trǎma-mi rayér, "the old man stands close to me."

Trǎma w'úni rodí, = trǎma w'úni kadí, which see.

Trǎma w'úni roráraṅ, "stand behind one," hence "defend, take one's part, plead one's cause, back;" e. g. o-baī o trǎma-ko roráraṅ, "the king takes his part."

Trǎmar, v. caus. "make to stand, set up, raise" (as a house of timber); „place, put, put up; make;" e. g. trámạr ak'ạntr, „set up the post;" trámạr ka-túli ro-bil, „put up the mast in the canoe;" — ko̱ trámạr am-pǫ́ti ka- am-mẹ́sa, „go put the cup on the table;" — o̱ trámạr o̱w'ahẹ́t tši̇̀n, „he made the child naked."

Trámạr, v. rel. (rad. tram), „proclaim-to-, make-known to-, publish-to-; acquaint-with-, inform- about-; e. g. an-tétu o̱ trámạr añ-fạm ara-keī, „the messenger made known the theft to the people."

Trámạs, v. freq. or intens. a. „proclaim, make known, publish-all about; „e. g. o̱-baī o̱ trámạs an-to̱ń ka añ-fạm-ń'o̱ń be, „the king proclaimed the law to all his subjects," lit. „to all his people."

Tramát, adj. num. „five;" e. g. a-fạm tramát, „five persons."

Tramát de̱ rạń „seven," lit. „five and two;" e. g. a-fạm tramát de̱ rạń, „seven persons."

Tramát re̱ sas, „eight," lit. „five and (with) three;" e. g. tra-bep tramát re̱ sas, „eight spoons."

Tramát ro kin, „six," lit. „five to one;" e. g. e̱-gbáta tramát ro kin, „six mats."

Tramát ro ń'ánle̱,) „nine," lit. „five to four;" e. g. e̱-tis tramát
Tramát ro ń'ánle̱,) ro ń'ánle̱, „nine knives."

Tramtrámne̱, v. refl. a. „medidate upon-, think about-, reflect upon-, muse upon-, consider of-;" e. g. o̱ tramtrámne̱ atr'eí tra-tši, tro añ-uáne̱-ña-tši ña yi-e, „he thought about that thing, what the meaning of it might be."

Trạn, a-, pl. e̱-, n. „a dog;" e. g. a-trạn a-bána, „a large dog."

Tran', euph. form of trañ, v. n. „follow," which see. It is used before d and n; e. g. I tši tran'-nu, „I shall follow you," See another example under talǫ́m.

Trañ v. n. „follow; pass, go;" e. g. o̱ trañ roráráń, „he followed from behind;" — o̱ trañ fe̱ ro-r'oń, „he did not pass in the road."

Trañ, v. a. „follow, go after-, follow after-," also „pass, go upon-; follow up-, trace;" e. g. I trañ-ko̱ ro-r'oń, „I followed him in the road;" — o̱ trañ-ña ro-Báke̱-Lǫ́ko̱, „he followed them to Port Loko;" — ọ trañ ar'óñ aré, „he passed this road;" — I tši trañ atr'eí tra-tši, „I shall follow up that matter." It has the euph. or abbr. forms tram and tran', which see in loco.

Trañ, v. a. „lock," (as a door); „fasten-with a nail, nail" (as a board);" drive in," (as a nail); „make costive," (as medicine the bowels); „tell, pledge," (as a word); „pledge-to-," (as a word to one); see the two next words. E. g. trañ aka-rárẹ, „lock the door;" — ọ poñ trañ am-bil, „he has nailed the canoe."

Trañ r'im, „make a promise," lit „pledge a word;" e. g. ọ trạl fọ ọ-baı ọ poñ trañ r'im, fọ w'úni ó w'úni ọwó mọ dif ọ-lánba, ọ trạ nántra ọw'án-k'ọñ ọ-béra, „he heard that the king had made a promise, that whosoever kills the man, shall have his daughter to wife."

Trañ w'úni r'im, „make a promise to one;" e. g. ọ trañ-mi r'im trạka añ-kála, „he made me a promise about the money."

Tráñanẹ, v. caus. and refl. lit. „make oneself to follow after," hence „follow up-. go after-," (as after the scent of a thing); „trace, track;" also „hold to-, keep to-," (as to one's word, or to a road), hence „fulfil; follow after-, follow, do according-; imitate, follow the habits of-;" e. g. ọ tráñanẹ ar'ím-r'ọñ, „he held to his promise;" — ọ tráñanẹ 'ma-ni ma ọ-kas-k'ọñ, „he followed the footsteps of his father;" — tšē tráñanẹ ọ-kas-ka-mu, „do not imitate thy father." See also next word.

Tráñanẹ am-bọntr ña-, „follow the scent of-, follow the track of-;" e. g. an-trạn ọ tráñanẹ am-bọntr ña ọw'ọ́r, „the dog followed the track of the fillentamba."

Tränd, v. abr. a. (rad. trañ), „chain, fetter, put-in chains;" e. g. ọ-baī ọ tränd-kọ, „the king chained him."

Tränd, v. abr. a. (rad. trañ) „follow, follow after-; resemble, be like to" (as one to another in character, or otherwise); e. g. ọ tränd-kọ, „he followed after him."

Trándọ, adj. „succeeding, following, second;" e. g. ka añ-réï a-trándọ, „on the following day."

Trańk, a-, pl. e-, n. „a species of anteater" or „antbear," living principally on the termites. It is of the size of a goat, with a long small mouth, long claws, and lives in holes under the earth. It has no teeth.

Trańk, o-, n. „a cold, coldness" (as of water); „freshness, greenness," (as of a tree or leaf); also „an ague;" e. g. o-trańk wa am'ántr, „the coldness of the water;" — o-trańk o wopmi, „I got an ague fit;" — o-trańk o wop-ko na tratrák, „he got a cold last night." Also „rawness" (as of meat).

Trańk, v. n. „be silent;" e. g. trańk nań! „be ye silent!"

Tr'ánle, } adj. num. „four;" e. g. tra-trála tr'ánle, „four hoes;" Tr'ánle, } — tr'antr tránle, „four sticks;" — tra-gbā tránle, „four scores" = 80.

Trańń, adv. spec. „steadily, attentively, indeed." It indicates continuance, and is used with káli, „look at-, look; be alive;" e. g. o káli-mi trańń, „he looked steadily at me;" — sa nań'-ko o-kali trańń, „we saw him alive indeed."

Trańńán, pr. comp. „for them; about them; against them; etc.;" It is always preceded by: tra, or tráka. E. g. o faī o-nā tráka trańńán, „he killed a cow for them."

Tránnu, pr. comp. „for you; about you; against you; etc." It is always preceded by: tra or tráka; e. g. tra tránnu táho o dif o-nā, „it is not for you" or „on account of you (that) he killed the cow."

Tr'antr. pl. of k'antr, which see.

Trap, v. n. „begin, commence;" e. g. 'a ta trap he tra rok, „they did not yet begin to reap;" — o ta trap he, „he did not yet begin." — It is often used as an aux. to indicate the commencement of an action, or of the exercise of the energy, denoted by the principal verb, which follows in the long form of the Infinitive; or the aux. may also be construed with the verbal noun; as: o trap ka-gbal ań-réka, = o trap tra gbal ań-réka, „he began to write the letter," lit. „he b. writing the letter;" — o trap ka-pań r'áka, „he began to be in want," lit „he began to lack a thing."

Trap, v. a. „begin, commence;" also „invent;" e. g. o trap ka-yọ ma-pant, lit. „he began the doing (of) work," = „he began with the work;" — kọ́nọ trap ka-sal e-bọl, „he invented the making of earthen pots." When trap v. n., as an aux., is construed with the verb. noun, it might also be considered as a transitive form, and as belonging here.

Trạp. kạ-, pl. trạ-. n. „beginning. commencement;" also „fashion, manner; sort, kind, species;" e. g. „ka ka-trạp ka 'ra-rū aré, „at the beginning of this world;" — ọ kúta pạ-lā mọ kạ-trạp kạ-fu, „he plants rice according to a new fashion;" — ọ bā e-bamp ka trạ-trạp trạ-gbánte, „he has birds of various species."

Trap, v. a. „chop, wound;" also „fell," (as a tree); „chop" or wound-with-;" e. g. ọ trap-mi, „he chopped me;" — 'a trap-kọ a-gbátọ, „they wounded him with a cutlass; — ọ trạp n'ạntr, „he fell a tree."

Trápa, v. rel. „chop" or „wound- for-; chop" or „wound-with-; fell-for-; fell-with-;" e. g. ọ trápa-mi a-gbátọ, „he cut me with a cutlass;" — trápa-mi an'ạntr ané, „fell this tree for me;" — trápa-mi-kọ, „chop him for me." Also used with one Acc. in the sense of „chop" or „cut with-," as: 'a trápa kạ-bap ka tra-sạk, „they cut the ribs with a hatchet," lit. „they cut with a hatchet at the ribs."

Trạ́pi v. a. „create, begin; be the author of-, make-from the first; also „invent, contrive, beget," (of the male); e. g. K'úru kọ́nọ trạ́pi at'rúru dẹ an-tọf, „it is God who created the heavens and the earth;" — Pā Sóri kọ́nọ trạ́pi-mi, „Mr. Sori he begat me." It is the long form of trạp.

Trạpi kạ-fi, „be the author of death," lit. „begin dying;" e. g. kọ́nọ trạ́pi kạ-fi, „he became the author of death."

Trạ́pi, kạ-, n. „act of creating (a thing, or person), creation;" e. g. ka-trạ́pi ara-rū aré, „the creation of this world," lit. „the creating this world."

Trạ́pia, v. rel. „create-for-; create-with-;" e. g. ara-rū aré K'úru ọ trạ́pia-ri ar'ím-r'ọń, „as for this world God created it by his word."

Trar, o-, pl. a-, n. „a slave;" e. g. o waī a-trar ńa-rań, „he bought two slaves;" — o-trar o-rúni, „a male slave."

Tıar, ra- n. „slavery, bondage;" e. g. o woń ra-trar, „he got into slavery."

Trar o-béra, o-, pl. a-trar a-béra, „a female slave."

Tr'ar, pl. of k'ar, which see.

Trára, v. n. „know, understand; be acquainted;" e. g. o trára o-fíno, „he understands well;" — o trára ro-petr, „he is acquainted in town." It is often used as an aux. to indicate skill in the exercise of the energy, denoted by the principal verb, which follows in the short form of the Infinitive, as: o-béra o trára yak, „the woman understands washing," or „knows to wash clothes;" — o-láńba owé o trára ták'sa, „this young man can teach well," lit. „— — understands teaching," or „to teach." With negative propositions the contr. form tr'a is used, as: o tr'a he táksa, „he does not understand to teach." Cf. also tr'a above.

Trára, v. a. „know, understand, be acquainted with; be aware of-; e. g. „I trára-ko o-fíno, „I am well acquainted with him;" — o trára-tsi, „he knows it;" — ma trára am'ólo ma ak'óta-i? „doest thou know the price of the cloth?" — o tr'a he tr'ei ó tr'ei, „he knows nothing at all;" — I trára ka-rámne o-fíno, „I understand the prayer well." — Cf. the preceding word about the contr. form tr'a.

Trára, ka-, n. verb. „faculty of knowing, knowledge;" ka-trára-k'oń, „his knowledge."

Trára-tr'ei, v. comp. n. „be learned, be accomplished, be clever;" e. g. ow'úni owé o trára-tr'ei, „this person is learned."

Trára w'úni r'áka, „care for one, regard one, treat one according to rank" or „circumstances," lit. „know something for one;" e. g. o-láńba owé o tr'a he w'úni r'áka, „this young man does not care for a person."

Trásam, v. onom. n. „sneeze;" e. g. o tra trásam, „he is sneezing."

Trásam-trásam, v. onom. freq. or intens. n. „sneeze much, sneeze repeatedly;" e. g. o-tem o tra trásam-trásam, „the old man was sneezing repeatedly."

Trássu, pr. comp. „for us, about us; on account of us; against us; etc." It is always followed by tra, or trąka. E. g. Yísua ǫ fi tra trássu bę. „Jesus died for all of us," or „for us all."

Tratrák, n. „night;" adverbially „at night, in the night;" e. g. ǫ tšéla-mi tratrák, „he called me at night;" — I díra hę na tratrák, „I did not sleep last night." Its prefix is ka-, but it is seldom used. See more about this form in the Grammar.

Tr'átrąk, pl. of k'átrąk, which see.

Tratšéń, adj. „true; righteous, just;" e. g. an-tratšéń, „the righteous." It is properly the noun tra-tšeń, „truth," but used as an adj., the pref. of the noun being taken as a radical part of the word, (when used adjectively), which is sometimes the case.

Trē, = tšē, adv. „not, do not." See tšē; and cf. the Note after kótši.

Tr'eī, pl. ma-treī, n. „a thing, matter, palaver, case; trouble, harm;" e. g. atr'eī atšé, „this matter;" — tr'eī tra yi hę „there is no palaver;" — trạ bā hę tr'eī, „it does not matter," = „it is of no consequence;" — ma-treī ma nǫ-rū, „the things of this world." — See also: wǫn' do-treī. It is sometimes also used in the sense of „character," especially in the pl. This word has an insep. pref. in the sing., and a separable one in the pl., the insep. pref. of the sing. being taken as radical in the plural.

Trei, v. a. „leave, abandon, forsake; leave off, desist from;" e. g. ar'áfa ra treī ań-ráka ténǫń tra kǫ tšim, „the war-people left the camp to day to go to war;" — ǫw'úni ǫwé ǫ poń treī ǫ-ráni-k'ǫń, „this man has left his wife; — ǫ treī ka-sap ǫw'ahét, „he desisted from flogging the child." Also „leave behind," (as property); „cede; etc.;" as: tšē treī am-pińkar-'a-mu, „do not leave thy gun behind."

Tr'eī ó tr'eī, „any thing, every thing; any matter; only trouble, nothing but trouble;" with a negative „not any thing, not any matter;" e. g. ǫ-lańba ǫwé ǫ trára tr'eī ó tr'eī, „this young man knows every thing;" — tra bā hę tr'eī ó tr'eī, „it does not matter at all." — See also: bęnę w'úni ra-tr'ei ó tr'ei.

Tr'ei trạ-lạs, „sin;" also „danger;" lit. „a bad thing," or „something bad"; e. g. trei trạ-lạs trạ yi he ri, „there is no danger there;" — o yọ tr'ei trạ-lạs, „he committed sin."

Tr'ęmę, pl. of k'ęmę, which see.

Tr'ęmę tramát rę sas, „eight hundred;" e. g. trạ-reṅ tr'ęmę tramát rę sas, „eight hundred years."

Tręmę tramát ro k'in, „six hundred."

Tr'ęrę, pl. of k'ęrę, which see.

Tri, pr. obj. for: tši, which see. Cf. the Note after kótši.

Trī', pr. emph. abbr. „it, this; these." for: tría; e. g. tra-bep atrá mạ yéma tšía-tšē-i? De, trī' táhọ; „are these the spoons which thou doest want?" „No, not these."

Tro? adv. inter. „how? of what kind? how much? how many?" e. g. tro sạ ma yō-e? „how are we to do?" — tro na yi-e? „how many are ye?"

Tro? pr. inter. „what?" e. g. tro sōm o pa yaṅ-e? „what is the cause (that) he says so?" or „what is the cause (that) he speaks thus?" — tro mạ nánę? „what doest thou think?"

Tro, kạ-, pl. trạ-, n. verb. „act of beating rice (in a mortar);" e.g. aṅ-lókọ kạ-tro, „the time of beating rice (for supper)," (which is done from 4—6 o'clock P. M., hence also „the time from 4—6 o'clock." The pl. form of ka-tro is used of a plurality of places, where rice is beaten.

Tro pe-e? for: tro pạ yi-e? „how is it?" or „what news?" or also „how art thou?" = tro pę mu-e? Cf. Colloq. Phras. p. 105. See next word.

Tro pę mu-e? for: tro pạ yi-mu-e? „how art thou?" or „how is it with thee?" Cf. Colloq. Phras. p. 105.

Trọfátr, adj. num. „ten;" e. g. a-fam trọfátr, „ten persons."

Trọfátr ṅ'in, „eleven;" e. g. ma-sar trọfátr ṅ'in, „eleven stones."

Trókọ, a-, pl. e-, n. „a fowl;" e. g. a-trókọ a-bána, „a large fowl."

Trọl, v. a. „rear," (as cattle); „tend, mind, attend to, take care of," (as of cattle, or also of men); e. g. ọ trọl e-trọ́kọ, "he rears up fowls;" — ọ-baī ọ trọl tra-nā-tr'ọṅ ọ-fíno, "the king minds his cows well;" — K'úru ọ trọl-mi, "God takes care of me."

Trọl. adj. "reared, reared up." (as cattle); "tended, minded, taken care of;" e. g. y'etr e-trọl, "things reared up," = "small cattle."

Trọl. ọ-, pl. a-, n. "one tending cattle, herd's man, shepherd;" e. g. ọ-trọl ka ọ-baī, "the herd's man of the king."

Trol. adj. "clever, skilful;" e. g. w'úni trol, "a clever person," = "an artisan."

Trọl. a-, pl. e-, n. "medicine;" also "charm, amulet, country-medicine;" — e. g. ọ di e-trọl, "he took medicine;" — ọ śékne a-trọl, "he tied a charm round himself."

Trọm, v. n. ruminate, chew the cud;" e. g. ọw'ír ọ irạ trọm, "the goat is ruminating."

Tr'ọṅ, pr. poss.. "his, her." lit. "of him, of her;" e. g. tra-bep-tr'ọṅ, "his spoons."

Trọṅ, kạ-, pl. trạ, n. "middle, midst, centre; trunk of the body, waist;" e. g. ka-trọṅ ka ka-petr, "the middle of the town;" — ka-trọṅ-k'ọṅ, "his waist." With the prep. ra-, it becomes a prep. or a postp. — See ratrọ́ṅ, prep.

Trọṅ, pr. "him, her," this form is used after tra or trạ́ka, as: ọ faī ọ-na trạ́ka trọṅ, "he slaughtered a cow for him."

Trọṅ ka —, ka-, used as a prep., see ka-trọṅ ka —. under K.

Trond, v. abr. a. "cook for-," (as for a krifi, or for the dead, being considered as a sacrifice); e. g. 'a kọ trond ọ-krifi, "they go to cook for the krifi."

Trọ́ṅkạr, v. rel. (rad. troṅk), "abscond with-, run away to-, flee to-, take refuge with-;" e. g. o-trar o trọ́ṅkạr Pā Sóri, "the slave absconded with Mr. Sori."

Trọ́ṅkạr, v. rel. n. "abscond, run away;" e. g. ọ-trar ọ trọ́ṅkạr ka ọ-baī, "the slave run away to the king." With this form the suff. is rather redundant.

Trọ́ri, v. a. "show, inform; show-to- inform- of-;" e. g. I kọ trọ́ri-mu ar'óṅ, "I go to show thee the road;" — an-tétu o̱ tró̱ri-mi atrá o̱-baï o̱ káne̱-ko̱, „the messenger informed me of what the king told him;" — w'úni lo̱m o̱ tró̱rí-mi, fo̱ o̱-baï o̱ poṅ fi, „some person informed me, that the king has died."

Tró̱troko̱, adj. „first," e. g. aṅ-réï a-tró̱troko̱, „the first day;" — aṅ-fa̱m a-tró̱troko̱, „the first people."

Trū, v. n. „be sick, be ill;" e. g. Pā Sóri o̱ trū, „Mr. Sori is sick."

Trū, ra- pl. tra̱, n. „sickness, illness;" e. g. ra-trū ra-báki ra wop-ko̱, „he is very ill," lit. „a heavy sickness holds him."

Trū k'or, „have the menses;" e. g. o̱-bé̱ra o̱ trū k'or, „the woman has the menses."

Truī, v. impers. „be hard, be difficult;" e. g. pa̱ truī he̱ tra yó̱ atr'cí atšé, „it will not be hard to do this thing."

Trutr ka̱-, pl. tra̱-. n. „envy, jealousy;" e. g o̱ bā ka̱-trutr tra̱ka o̱-ráni-k'o̱ṅ, „he is jealous on account of his wife." lit. „he has jealousy on account of his wife."

Tš', pref. indef. and insep. for: tr'; see the Note after kótši. It is an insep. form of: tra̱-; e. g. tš'ek. „beards," = tr'ek, for: tra̱-ek.

Tša, conj = tra, „for, because;" e. g. K'úru o gbá̱li su na̱ṅk, tša o̱ yi d'er ó d'er, „God can see us; for he is everywhere." — I nésa, tša min' tšiṅ, „I was afraid, for I am naked." See the Note after kótši.

Tšē, adv. = trē, „not, do not." Often used with the Imperative; as: tšē tši yo̱, „do not do it;" — tšē fatr ri, or: tšē ri fatr, „do not approach there;" — tšē fatr-ṅa, „do not go near to them;" — tr' 'a tšē ko̱ bé̱ne̱ ro-petr, „let them not bury him in the town."

Tšē-wop ar'ím ra-, ka-, „the not holding (obeying) the word of-;" e. g K'úru o̱ tra só̱mpa-nu tra̱ka ka-tšē-wop ar'ímr'o̱ṅ, „God will punish you for not obeying his word."

Tšel, adj. „not related, strange, foreign, other;" e. g. a-fa̱m a-tšel de aṅ-fa̱m-ṅ'o̱ṅ gbeṅ na bó̱ta̱r he̱ ko̱, „strange people and his own people do not like him;" — k'antr ką-tšel, „a foreign language."

Tšéla, v. a. „call, invite;" e. g. kǫ tšéla am-bǫī-'a-mu, „go call thy servant." Also „hail," as: añ-fam añáñ ña tra tšéla-su, „those people are hailing us;" also „name," e. g. 'a tšéla-kǫ Sóri, „they called him Sori."

Tšemp, v. n. „get wise, get intelligent, get sense, get prudent; get sober; be wise, be intelligent, etc.;" e. g. o-láñba ǫwé ǫ ta tšemp he, „this young man has not yet got wise;" — múnǫ ma tšemp he, „thou hast no sense." It is the short form of tšémpi. Cf. the Note after wos, v. n.

Tšemp, ką-, n. „wisdom, intelligence, prudence, sense; discretion; soberness;" e. g. Yísua ǫ lák'sa a-fam ką-tšemp ką-bána, „Jesus taught people with great wisdom;" — ǫw'úni ǫwé ǫ bā ką-tšemp, „this person has intelligence."

Tšémpi, v. n. „be wise, be prudent, be intelligent, be discreet, have sense; be sober;" e. g. o-tem ǫwé ǫ tšémpi, „this old man is wise;" — o-láñba ǫwé ǫ tšémpi sǫ, „this young man is sober again."

Tšémpi, adj. „wise, prudent, intelligent; sober;" e. g. w'úni tšémpi, „a wise person." It may follow a proper name without a prefix, in which case it is emphatic, and may be given by „the Wise," as: Bē Fǫ́ki Tšémpi, „Bey Foki the Wise." Cf. Proverb 3, p. 99.

Tšen, v. a. „cut up" (as an animal slaughtered), „cut, carve" (as a fowl), lit. „separate the joints of-," (as butchers do with cattle slaughtered);" e. g. 'a poñ tšen o-nā, „they have cut up the cow."

Tšeñ, tra-, n. „truth, veracity; justice." Also used adverbially in the sense of „indeed, truly, in truth." E. g. atra-tšeñ tra am-pā-ñ'ǫñ, „the truth of his statement;" — ǫw'úni ǫwé ǫ ba ką-tšemp tra-tšeñ! „this person has sense indeed!"

Tšen', ka-, pl. tra-, n. for: tšeñ; this form is used before d. See next word.

Tšeñ, ką-, pl. tra-, n. „a hill;" e. g. ǫ yi ro-tšen' dokǫ́m, „he is on the top of the hill;" — ką-tšeñ ką-lǫl, „a little hill."

Tšę́ntšęnę, adv. „indeed, truly, surely;" e. g. „o̱ tra̱ der tę́ntšęnę, „he will surely come."

Tšep, v. a. „plant;" e. g. I tši tšep ri y'intr," „I shall plant trees there."

Tšˇer, pl. of w'er, which see.

Tšer, v. a. „let go, let, dismiss, let loose; forgive; allow, permit;" e. g. tšer-ko̱, „let him go;" — o̱-baī o̱ tšer an̊-fam, „the king dismissed the people;" — I tšer-mu a-méra fíno, „I forgive thee with all my heart," lit. „— — with a good heart;" — tšer an-tis, w'an! „let go the knife, boy!"

Tšéra, v. rel. „let go- for-; remit- to-" (as a debt to one); „forgive- to-;" e. g. tšéra-mi an-tis, w'an! „let go the knife for me, boy!" — o̱-tem o̱ tšéra-mi atr'eí tra̱-la̱s, atrá l yō-ko̱, „the old man forgave me the evil thing, which I did to him;" — I tšéra-ko̱ ara-beī-r'o̱n̊, „I remitted him his debt."

Tši, part. = tri, to form the Participle, and the Future tense in the 1st pers. sing. — E. g. I tši der romú nina̱n̊, „I shall come to thee to morrow." Cf. the Note after kótši; as also what has been stated under the part. tra; because what has been said there, applies also to this form.

Tši, pr. sub. and obj. = tri, „it; these; they, them;" e. g. atr'a̱ntr kára-tši ano̱, „as for the sticks bring them here."

Tšía, v. n. „remain, stay; be left;" e. g. o̱ tšía ro-Ma-lal, „he remained at Malal;" — o̱-tem o̱ tšía ri sōn, „the old man was left there alone;" — ma-réï ma-sas ma tšía gbo, „only three days remained;" — n̊a tra̱ tšía nan̊ ka-rára̱n̊-ka-tši mo̱ ho̱ ma n̊a yi tá̱pan̊, „they would remain afterwards as they were before."

Tšía, v. a. „leave, let remain, spare;" e. g. pa-la apá an̊-fa̱m n̊a pon̊ tšía, „the rice which the people have left;" — an̊-fa̱m n̊a tšía a-kála a-gbáti ro-set, „the people have left much money in the house" (for themselves).

Tšía, v. rel. „leave, leave-to-, bequeath-to-;" e. g. ma-tó̱fa̱l mía I tšía-nu, „peace I leave to you;" — o̱-kas-ka-mi o̱ tšía-mi gbo a-kála a-tan, „my father left me but little money;"

— o-tem o tšía-mi k'e kạ-bána, „the old man left me a large property."

Tšía, pr. emph. „it, this; they, them, these;" tra-bep-tra-mi tšía yi tši, „these are my spoons," lit. = the Germ. „Meine Löffel diese sind es."

Tšía bā, „therefore, for this reason, this is the reason," lit. „it has," or „this has;" e. g. ra-bomp-ra-mi ra bań-mi; tšia bā mạ nańk fẹ mi ténọń, „my head pained me; this is the reason (that) thou didst not see me to day."

Tšía bā tši, „therefore, this is the reason," lit. „it (this) has it;" e. g. ọw'ahẹ́t-k'ọń ọ lạ̣sạr apa-lạ; tšía bā-tši ọ bạ́ń'sa, „his child spoiled the rice; this is the reason (that) he got angry."

Tšíań, conj. „therefore, for this reason, this is the reason," lit. „it, „or" this." It is properly the abs. form of the pr. tši, „it." E. g. ọw'áń ọ pọń yọ tr'eï trạ-lạs; tšíań ọ mańknẹ, „the boy has done something bad; therefore he hides himself."

Tšik. o-, pl. a-, n. „a male stranger, pilgrim, guest;" e. g. ọ-tšik ọ der romí ténọń, „a stranger came to me to day."

Tšik. ra-, pl. trạ-, n. „state of being a stranger, strangership, sojourn, pilgrimage;" e. g. ra tšik-r'ọń ro-Kamp, „his sojourn at Freetown."

Tšim, v. n. „war, fight, strive, struggle;" e. g. ọ kọ tšim, „he went to war;" — ọ tra tšim ri, „he is fighting there." It is, however, more frequently used in a recipr. sense, „fight together, war against each other, wage war against each other, strive together;" e. g. tšía sōm ńa tšim, „this is the reason they carry on war with each other;" — ńa tšim· ri ma-reï ma-rạń, „they fought there for two days."

Tšim, v. a. „fight with-; war against-, wage war against-, invade;" e. g. I kọ tšim-kọ, „I go to fight with him;" — ań-fạm ńa tšim-kọ, „the people fought against him;" — Alikáli Fátima Bréma ọ tšim an-tọf a-lọ́ko. „Alikáli Fatima Brema waged war against the Loko country."

Tšim. kạ-, pl. trạ-, n. „war, fight, battle, combat;" e. g. 'a tšim ri kạ-tšim kạ-báki, „they fought a great battle there;" —

ọ fi ka ka-tšim, „he died in the battle." — 'a tám'rọ ka-tšim, „they lost the battle."

Tšíma, adj. „belonging to fighting" or „to war;" e. g. y'etr e-tšíma, „arms," or „war-implements," lit. „things belonging to war."

Tšímnẹ, v. refl. lit. „fight with oneself," hence: „struggle, agonize," (as a dying person); fig. „exert oneself much, try hard;" e. g. ọ tšímnẹ tra sọ́tọ pạ lā, „he exerted himself much to get rice." Also used in a recipr. sense „compete" or „contend with each other," as: 'a tšímnẹ trạ́ka ọ-bẹ́ra, „they contend with each other about the woman."

Tšímonẹ, v. rel. and refl., or v. spont. lit. „fight for oneself," or „fight of one's own accord," hence „make haste, hasten, be quick;" e. g. tsímonẹ, káma mạ kọ́nẹ, „make haste that thou mayest go;" — ọ tšímonẹ trạ́ka kálanẹ, „he hastened to return."

Tšiṅ, v. n. „be naked," (as the body); „be bare," (as the head); „be empty," (as a bottle); e. g. ra-bomp-r'oṅ ra tšiṅ, „his head is bare;" am-bítra ńa tšiṅ, „the bottle is empty."

Tšiṅ, adj. „naked; bare; empty;" e. g. ra-bomp ra-tšiṅ, „a bare head; a-bítra a-tšiṅ, „an empty bottle."

Tšiṅ, kạ-, n. „emptiness." It is often used adverbially in the sense of „for nothing, without cause, in vain; gratis." E. g. ka-tšiṅ ka am-bítra, „the emptiness of the bottle;" — ọ yò-tši gbo kạ-tšiṅ, „he did it just for nothing;" — I gbáli he sọm-mu-ńi kạ-tšiṅ, „I cannot give it to thee gratis."

Tšir, ma-, n. „blood;" e. g. ma-tšir ma wur-kọ, „he bleeds," lit. „blood comes out from him."

Tšis, v. n. „be drunken, be intoxicated;" e. g. ow'úni owé ọ tšis, „this person is drunken."

Tšis, adj. „drunken, intoxicated;" e. g. w'úni tšis, „an intoxicated person."

Túbi, v. n. „repent;" Mand. tubi. Fr. the Ar. نَابَ, conversus fuit a peccatis; poenitentiam ob delictum ostendit. E. g. sạ bä tra túbi tráka ra-bomp ra ma-treī-ma-su ma-lạs, „we have to repent on account of our sins."

Túbi, kạ-, n. verb. „repentance;" e.g. ka-túbi-ka-ńań, „their repentance."

Tuk, a-, pl. ẹ-, n „rice straw, stalk of rice after the ears are plucked off," which is generally left standing in the ground, sometimes also cut off, and taken home; and from the roots of which the rice called. ẹ-pásạr (second crop) comes out, which is of an inferior quality.

Túli, kạ-, pl. trạ-, n. „a mast," (as of a canoe or ship); also „the turret" or „spire on the top of the conical roof of a country house," which is properly the post supporting the conical roof in the middle, reaching down to the ground, and projecting at the outside of the roof on the top, forming, as it were, a little spire. E. g. ka-túli kạ-bána, „the main mast," lit. „the great mast;" — trạ́mạr ka-túli ro-bil, „put up the mast in the canoe."

Tunt, v. a. „measure, weigh;" e. g. tunt ak'óta, „measure the cloth."

Tūp, v. n. „endeavour, try, try hard, exert oneself," (as to get something); e. g. I tūp tra sóto pạ-la; kẹ́rẹ I tám'rọ, „I endeavoured to get rice; but I was disappointed."

Túpạs, v. n. prob. a freq. form from an obs. tup, „practise divination, divine, make country fashion," (as they call it), „tell fortune," (by means of sand, or small stones of different colours) ; e. g. ọ trạ túpạs tráka Pà Sóri, „he is making country fashion for Mr. Sori."

Túši, v. a. „pull out," (as roots, or the feathers of a fowl); „unroot," (as plants); „pluck," (as a fowl); „extract," (as a tooth); e. g. „túši ẹ-yóka, „pull out the cassadas;" — ọ-bẹ́ra ọ túši am-bamp, „the woman plucked the fowl." Cf. the Ar. نَتَشَ, and the Hebr. שָׁתַם, extraxit.

U.

U-, pref. indef. „a, an;" used by some as an indef. form of ọ-; but it is not generally used, ọ- being used definitely and indefinitely; it seems to have crept in from the Bolom. E. g. u-šem, „meat;" but o-šem, „the meat"

'U, abbr. form of: mu, „thee," used with kóri, „salute," as: kóri 'u, Pā! „I salute thee, Sir!"

W.

W', pref. indef. and insep. „a, an;" as: w'ir, „a goat," for: wo-ir.

Wa, pr. poss. „of;" e. g. o-trank wa am'ántr, „the coldness of the water."

W'ahét, pl. a-fet, n. „a little child;" e. g. a-fet a-rúni, „boys;" — w'ahét rúni, „a boy;" — an-fet na tra wol, „the children are playing together." Sometimes they use for the sing. the form o-fet; w'ahét is probably a contraction of: w'an fet, „a young child."

Waī, v. a. „buy, purchase;" e. g. „I waī k'óta, „I bought cloth."

Waía, v. rel. „purchase- for-, purchase" or „buy-with-;" e. g. waía-mi k'óta, „buy me cloth;" — I waía-ni k'óta, „I bought it with cloth," (as a mat).

W'an, pl. a-wut, n. „a child," (larger than w'ahét). It is also used, without any adjunct, in the sense of „son; boy; young man, youth; friend"; = the Gr. παῖς and ἑταῖρος. E. g. ow'án-ka-mi o-rúni, „my son;" — w'an, yéntra-mi an-tis, „boy, hand me the knife." It is sometimes even applied to an old person in the sense of „friend;" and the pl. is also used of the „young ones" of beasts.

Wan, ka-, pl. tra-, n. „a chair, a seat;" also „throne;" e. g. o bémpa ka-wan, „he made a chair."

W'an dúni, pl. a-wut a-rúni, „a male child, boy;" also „a man."

W'an béra, pl. a-wut a-béra, „a female child, a girl."

Wándi, ka-, tra-, n. „instruction, speech, preaching: lesson;" e. g. o fof ka-wándi ka-las ténon, „he delivered a bad speech to day;" — o gbaīr an-fam ka-wándi, „he preached to the people," lit. „he imparted instruction to the people."

Wánki, v. revert. a. „take away the protecting charm from-, deprive- of the protecting charm," (as a farm or fruit-tree);

fig. „deprive of protection, outlaw, proscribe;" e. g. ọ wáṅki aṅ'ạṅtr, „he took away the protecting charm from the tree;" — ọ-baī ọ wáṅki-mí, „the king outlawed me."

Wáraṅ, v. n. „be bright, be clear," (as the sky or atmosphere); e. g ak'úru ka wáraṅ, „the sky is clear."

Wẹk, v. a. „draw," (as milk from a cow); „wring out, squeeze out," (as wet cloth, or a sore); e. g. wẹk ak'óta," wring out the cloth;" — mạ bā trạ wẹk aka-sam, „thou must squeeze out the sore."

W'er, pl. tš'er, n. „a rat;" e. g. ọw'ér ọwé, „this rat."

Win, adv. „once, one time; one, one and the same, alike, the same;" e. g. I nạṅ'-kọ gbo win, „I saw him but once;" — an-tọṅ-ṅ'ọṅ yẹ ma-šélọ-m'ọṅ ma yi gbo win, „his law and his will are just the same." With a negative „never," as: I tr'a hẹ mu win, „I never knew thee."

Win win, „now and then;" Ger. „hie und da," lit. „once once;" e. g. ọ yọ-tši gbo win win, „he did it only now and then."

W'ir, pl tš'ir, n. „a goat;" e. g. ts'ir trạ-bána, „large goats."

Woī! int. „alas!" It is expressive of pain, grief, lamentation or pity. E. g. woī mínaṅ! „alas for me!" See Colloq. Phras. p. 108.

Woī! Woī! int. emph. „alas! alas!" See Colloq. Phras. p. 108.

Wol, v. n. „play, play together;" e. g. aṅ-fẹl ṅa trạ wol, „the children are playing together." As to its sense it is rather recipr., but not as to its form.

Wóma, adj. „in the husk" (applied to grain); e. g. pạ-lā pạ-wóma, „rough rice," or „rice in the husk."

Wọn, v. a. „shake out, shake" (as cloth, or the law-broom); „shake off" (as something from one's cloth); „flap, clap" (as the wings); „ply" (as a whip); e. g. wọn ak'óta, „shake the cloth;" — ọ wọn am-bōk, „he shook off the snake."

Wọn, v. n. „be long, stay long; last long, last;" e. g. ṅa wọn di, „they stayed long there;" — aṅ-sel aṅé ṅa trạ wọn, „this house will last long;" — ọ wọn he, „he will not be long." It is the short form of wóni.

Woṉ', euph. form of woṉ, „go in," used before the prep. do-, as: o woṉ' do-sel, „he went into the house; — woṉ' di, „go in there." See next word.

Woṉ, v. n. „go in, come in, enter;" of the sun „set, go down," = the Hebr. בוא. E. g. o woṉ ka aṉ-set. „he went into the house," = o woṉ' do-sel; — o woṉ gbo, „he went just in;" — ar'étr ra woṉ, „the sun set."

Woṉ, v. a. „get into, enter into, get into" (as into some state, or something into one's body); „enter" (as a house); „join" (as a company); „embrace" (as a religion); „put on, wear" (as clothes); also „get" (as a sore pus); e. g. o woṉ ra-trar, „he became a slave" or „he got into slavery;" — o woṉ' da-nēs, for: o woṉ ra-nēs, „he got afraid." lit. „he entered into fear;" — ṅa woṉ aṉ-set, „they entered the house;" — o woṉ a-wóṅanę, „he joined a company;" — o woṉ' da-móri, „he embraced Islamism;" — ka-sam ka woṉ ma-ti, „the sore suppurates" or „gets pus;" — o woṉ ar'úma-r'oṉ lóko ó lóko, „he puts on (wears) his shirt always;" — e-tof e woṉ-mi ro-for, „some earth got into my eyes." lit. „earth got into me at the eyes." With the last ex. the obj. pronoun of the verb serves to express the poss. pronoun.

Note. It may be observed here, that this verb is very frequently used in connection with an abstract noun, to form comp. inch. verbs; when woṉ may often be given by „become, get, get into." Also wur in the sense of „bring forth, produce, get", is often used in a similar way, as will be seen from the Temne Grammar and Dictionary. Cf. also wóṅa below.

Woṉ, = owóṅ, pr. dem. rem. „that, that one;" this form is used if the pr. without the noun is the subject of a proposition, as: w'úni las woṉ, „that is a bad person," lit. „a bad person that."

Woṉ ka a-fam, „become fashion among people," lit. „enter into people."

Woṉ' do-tr'ei, „get into trouble;" e. g. o-láṅba o woṉ' do-tr'ei, „the young man got into trouble."

Woṅ w'úni yáńfa, for: woṅ w'úni a-yáńfa, „form a conspiracy against one, conspire against one;" e. g. 'a woṅ-ko yáńfa, „they conspired against him."

Wóṅa, v. caus. „make to go in, cause to enter, bring in, lead in;" e. g. o wóṅa-mi ro-sel, „he brought me into the house;" — o wóṅa-ko ra-trar, „he enslaved him," lit. „he led him into slavery;" — o wóṅa-ko ma-lap, „he made him ashamed" or „he brought shame (disgrace) upon him."

Note. By this caus. form the comp. inch. form with woṅ may be made transitive or causative.

Wóṅane, a-, n. „a company, a society," (especially one whose members have engaged to assist each other in farm-work); e. g. o woṅ aṅ-wóṅane, „he joined the farming company."

Wónane, v. spont. (rad. won), „get fever, get warm" or „hot, have fever;" e. g. ow'ahél o wónane, „the child got fever."

Woṅ's, v. caus. (rad. woṅ) „make to go in" or „to enter, put-on-, clothe-with-;" e. g. woṅ's-ko ar'úma, „put him on the shirt," = „clothe him with the shirt;" — I woṅ's-ko e-lópra, „I put him on the clothes;" — o woṅ's-mi y'etr, „he clothed me," lit. „he made me to enter things." (woṅs showing here that wearing apparel is intended by y'etr; for this caus. form of woṅ is to be kept distinct from the other caus. form wóṅa above; because woṅ's is always used of putting on clothes, or wearing apparel, or war implements.)

Wont, v. n. „graze, feed;" e. g. tra-nä ńa tra wont ro-lal, „the cows are grazing on the grass-field."

Wont, v. a. „graze, feed on; look for-," (as for medicine); e. g. I ko wont e-trol ro-kant, „I go to look for medicine in the bush;" — tra-nä ńa poṅ wont od'er be, „the cows have grazed the whole place."

Wont, ka-, n. verb. „act of grazing, act of feeding, a grazing;" e. g. ka-wont ka tra-nä, „the grazing of the cows."

Wontr, o-, pl. a-, n. „a brother" or „sister"; also „brother" (without any adjunct), „one born of the same parents;" Germ. „Geschwister".

Wǫntr o-béra, o-, pl. a-, n. „a sister"; e. g. o-wontr-ka-mi o-béra, „my sister."

Wǫntr o-rúni, o-, pl. a-, n. „a brother"; e. g. o-wontr-ka-mi o-rúni, „my brother."

Wop, v. a. „take hold of-, hold, seize, apprehend; hit" (as the ball of a gun); „keep, obey" (as a law); e. g. 'a wop-ko, „they seized him;" — aṅ-rom ña wop-ko, „leprosy has seized him;" — o wop an-toṅ ña K'úru, „he keeps the law of God." Also „catch" (as fish), as: ma wop e-lop-i? „didst thou catch fish?"

Wop, ka-, n. verb. „act of taking hold of-," or „of seizing, capture; a holding, a keeping;" e. g. ka-wop-k'oṅ an-toṅ ña K'úru, „his keeping the law of God."

Wop a-sům, „hold a fast, fast;" e. g. 'a wop a-sům, „they hold a fast."

Wópa, v. rel. „take hold of-by-, hold-with-, hold-for-, seize-for-;" e. g. wópa-mi-ko, „seize him for me;" — o wópa-ko ka-trā, „he held him with the hand."

Wópa wúni t'amasére, „bear evidence against one," lit. „hold one with an evidence;" e. g. o wópa-ko t'amasére, „he bore evidence against him."

Wópne, v. refl. a. „hold oneself to-, take hold of-, hold oneself on-, trust in-, cleave to-; take refuge with-;" e. g. I bun fúmpo; kére I wópne ak'ǫntr, „I almost fell; but I held myself on the stick;" — o wópne-mi tra némteṉe-mu, káma ma tšē ko sap, „he took refuge with me to beg thee, that thou mightest not flog him."

W'or, pl. tr'or, n. „a species of deer generally called fillentamba" (being a beautiful animal with long slender legs, and a white and brown spotted skin); e. g. I naṅk w'or, „I saw a fillentamba."

Wǫrap, v. n. „dream"; e. g. I wǫrap na tratrák, „I dreamed last night."

Wos, v. n. „get dry; be dry; get hard, be hard" (as bread); „get parched, be parched" (as soil); e. g. ad'úba ra wos, „the ink gets dry."

Note. This is the short form of wósi, and expresses the inch. form also, as is the case with all the short forms of this class of verbs; while the long form is used more positively, and never in negative propositions.

Wos, ọ-, pl. a-. n. "a husband"; e. g. ọ-wos-k'ọṅ, "her husband."

Wósa, v. a. "answer to-, answer for-, answer; answer to- in the affirmative," Ger. "bejahen". Also "acknowledge, confess; be willing for-;" e. g. ọ wósa he kọ, "he did not answer him;" — tšē wósa-kọ, "do not answer him;" — 'a wósa-tši, "they confessed it;" or also "they were willing for it;" — ọ wósa atr'eí-tr'ọṅ trạ-lạs, "he acknowledged his sin." Also "be accountable for-."

Wósa, v. n. "answer, answer in the affirmative; confess; be willing, consent;" with tráka "account for-;" e. g. ọ wósa he, "he did not answer;" — múnọ bā tra wósa tráka atr'eí tra-tši, "thou hast to account for that matter."

Wósa, kạ-, n. verb. "act of answering" or "of answering for-, etc.;" e. g. múnọ bā ka-wósa atr'eí tra-tši, "thou hast to account for that matter," lit. "thou hast the accounting for that matter."

Wósi, v. impers. "be dry;" e. g. pạ-wósi, "it is dry." This form was only met with in a Proverb. See Proverb 2, p. 98.

Wósi, v. n. "be dry, be hard;" e. g. ka-bō aké ka wósi, "this bread is dry." See: wos above, of which this is the long form.

Wóso, kạ-, pl. trạ-, n. "a yellowish" or "whitish clay, with which the Bondo girls rub their body, while under the charge of the Bondo head-woman, and of which they make chalk."

Wóto, kạ-, or ra-, pl. trạ-, n. "a baboon, the African orang-outang, chimpansee." (simia satyrus, or simia troglodytes). The „grey baboon" is called: kạ-dúmbu, or: kạ-rúmbu (cynocephalus hamadryas).

Wotr, v. a. "break to pieces, break, smash" or "dash to pieces;" e. g. tšē wọtr am-bọl, "do not break the earthen pot to pieces."

Wu, kạ-, pl. trạ-, n. "knee"; see: so, v. a. "bow, bend."

Wul, a-, pl. ẹ-. n. "a thousand"; e. g. ẹ-wul ẹ-sas, "three thousand."

Wul, a-, pl. e-, n. „a loop, noose, trap" (to catch venison and birds in); e. g. ọ sap a-bamp ka añ-wul, „he caught a bird in the trap."

W'úni, pl. a-fam, n „a person; man, one, some one;" e. g. w'úni k'in, „one person;" — w'úni lọm ọ trọ́ri-mi-tši, „some person informed me of it."

Wúni, ra-, n. „manhood, human nature;" e. g. ra-wúni-r'ọñ, „his human nature."

W'úni bána, pl. a-fam a-bána, n. „a giant," lit. „a big person."

W'úni bom, pl. a-fam a-bom, or: bom-ña, n. „a woman." lit. „a female person." Cf. bom, ọ-, under B.

W'úni lọm, „some person, some one, a certain person." Cf. w'úni above.

W'úni ó w'úni, „every one, any one;" with a negative „not any person, no man, none, no one;" e. g. w'úni ó w'úni ọ gbáṅi he yō atr'eí atšé, „no man can do this thing;" — w'úni ó w'úni owó tšē kọ láne, „every one who does not believe in him."

Wur, v. n. „go out, come out, go forth, come forth;" also „jut out" (as a stone from a wall); „project" (as a point of land into the sea); „rise" (as the sun, = the Hebr. יצא); etc. With the prep. ro- this verb may have the sense „go out to-" or „from-" or „in-" or „into-," or „come out to-" or „from-" or „in-" or „into-"; thus: ọ wur ro-petr, may signify „come" or „go out from the town." or also „come out (from some place) into the town." E. g. ọ wur ro-sel, „he came out from the house," = ọ wur ka añ-sel; — ña wur he ténoñ, „they did not come out to day;" — ar'étr ra wur, „the sun rises."

Wur, v. a. „put forth, send forth, produce, emit, get;" also „come out from-;" e. g. ma-léñi ma wur i-bọntr i-fíno, „the flowers smell sweetly," lit. „the flowers put forth a good smell;" — añ-sal-ñ'oñ ña wur ma-tšir, „his finger bleeds," lit. „his finger emits blood;" — añ-fatr ña wur ma-gbak, „the iron gets rusty;" — añ'ántr ña wur e-bópar, „the tree gets leaves;" — añ'ántr ña wur ma-léñi, „the tree gets blossoms;" — añ-nēs ǫ wur tr'átrǎk trǎ-laī, „the spider got many legs" (i. e. when it came into existence, cf. Fable II. p. 56); — ma-tšir ma wur-kǫ, „he bleeds," lit. „blood comes out from him." See also the Note after wǫñ, v. a.

Wur i-bǫntr, „emit a smell, smell." See ex. under the preceding word.

Wúra, v. caus. „make to come out, pull out, draw out, take out; put forth, stretch forth" or „out; find out, invent;" e. g. ǫ wúra a-tis, „he took out a knife;" — kǫ́nǫ wúra añ-gbátǫ ka am-bom-ña-tši, „he drew out the cutlass from its sheath;" — ǫ wúra gbo ara-bomp-r'ǫñ, „it only stretched forth its head."

Wut, a-, pl. of w'an, which see.

Y.

Y', pref. indef. and insep. „a, an," as y'ętr, „things", for: ye-ętr.

Yā. ǫ-, pl. a-, n. „mistress, lady, madam;" also „mother" (when addressing her, otherwise ǫ-kára is generally used); e. g. kǎli ǫ-yā-ka-mi, „see my mistress;" — kóri 'u, Yā! „I salute thee, Madam!" This form corresponds with pa, „master, etc."

Ya, prep. poss. „of"; e. g. ey'ętr ya Sóri, „Sori's things," lit. „the things of Sori."

Ya, adv. = ye and yǫ, „thus, so, in this way, in the same manner, the same kind." This form is used before words with the vowel a, as: ya ña yō-e, „thus they did;" — ya ña pā, „thus they said;" — ya a-fǎm ña ma lā yǫ, „so people are always doing."

Ya-tši, pr. poss. neut. „its; their," lit. „of it;" e. g. e-bǫ́par-ya-tši, „its leaves" (as of a tree).

Ya-tši, pr. dem. loc. „that; those;" e. g. ey'ętr ya-tši, „those things" (spoken of).

Yahánnama, n. „hell, place of torment;" Mand. yahaniba; Ful. tšahannima. From the Ar. جَهَنَّم, gehenna, inferni ignis, infernus. E. g. ro-yahánnama, „in hell."

Yaī, adj. „worthless, of no value, trifling, vain, vile, mean;" e. g. w'ǔni yaī, „a mean person;" — r'a ra-yaī, „a worthless thing."

Yaī, ra-, n. „worthlessness, vanity, vileness, meanness;" e. g. ra-yaī-r'oṅ, „his meanness."

Yak, v. n. „wash clothes;" e. g. 'a ko yak ro-bat, „they go to wash clothes at the brook;" — o-béra owé o trára yak, „this woman can wash well," lit. „knows to wash."

Yak, v. a. „wash" (as clothes); „cleanse" (as a sore); e. g. yak aka-sam-ka-mu, „cleanse thy sore;" — I ko yak ey'étr-'e-mi e-lópra, „I go to wash my clothes."

Yáka, ka-, pl. pa-, n. „rice of a superior quality," also called: pa-la pa-krifi, „krifi rice." Cf. the word krifi, adj.

Yal, a-, pl. e-, or tra, n. „a boat"; e. g. a-yal a-fino, „a fine boat."

Yaṅ, ra-, pl. tra-, n. „middle part of the day, noon, midday;" also „the clear part of the day from sun-rise to sun-set;" e. g. o der na ra-yaṅ, „he came to day at noon." The pl. is hardly ever used.

Yaṅ, adv. == ya, „thus, in this way;" e. g. I yéma he ki yaṅ, „I do not want it in this way," (as a wooden bowl). Yaṅ is the abs. form of ya. (Cf. -ṅ under N.)

Yáṅfa, a-, pl. e-, n. „a trick; deceitfulness, deceitful character, deceit, treachery;" e. g. ow'úni owé o ba yáṅfa, „this person is deceitful," lit. „this p. has deceitfulness;" — o yo-mi yáṅfa, „he played me a trick," lit. „he did me a trick" or „deceitfulness".

Yáṅfa, adj. „deceitful, treacherous; e. g. w'úni yáṅfa, „a deceitful person."

Y'áṅkra, n. „long trowsers, as worn by the Mandingos and Susus;" e. g. y'áṅkra y'in, „one pair of trowsers;" — ey'áṅkra-y'oṅ, „his trowsers."

Y'áṅle,
Y'áṅle, } adj. num. „four"; e. g. e-tis y'áṅle, „four knives."

Yánte, ma-, n. „a kind of millet," also called: k'éne, pl. p'éne.

Yáo, adv. „yes; well;" e. g. ma yéfa ro-Báke Lóko-i? Yáo. „doest thou come from Port-Loko?" „Yes."

Yári, a-, or i-, pl. ma-, n. „a cat"; e. g. a-yári a-fet, „a kitten."

Yáro, a-, pl. e-; or a-, or i-, pl. ma-, n. „a diamond snake," also called „devil" or „magic snake" (much dreaded by the Natives). See Pref. § 13. b.

Yáwe! int. „oh dear! alas! ah! oh!" indicating disappointment or regret. E. g. yáwe, pā-ka-mi! „alas, my father!" This expression is used by women when crying after the death of their husband.

Ye, pref. indef. used with the num. adj. raṅ, „two", and with other adjectives in the def. state; e. g. e-gbáta ye-raṅ, „two mats."

Ye, adv. = ya, yọ, „thus, so, in this way, in the same manner, the same kind;" e. g. ye táhọ-i? „is it not so?" — ye pạ yi, „thus it is;" — ye I me lā yọ̄, „thus I am always doing." It is generally used before words with the vowels e, i and ạ.

Yē, pr. dem. prox. (for: eyé), „this; these;" used with the comp. dem. pronoun yía-yē, „it (is) this; they (are) these;" and in the phrase: e-súma yē, „at this time." Cf. súma, e-. — It is also often used after: fọ, or: họ, „say"; about which see: fọ yē.

Yéfa, v. n. „come away, go away" (from); „depart; descend, originate;" e. g. ọ yéfa ro-pelr, „he came away from the town;" — ọ yéfa roṅóṅ, „he went away from him," or „he turned away from him."

Yéhudi, ọ-, pl. a-, n. „a Jew"; e. g. a-yéhudi a-laī, „many Jews."

Yéli, ọ-, pl. a-, n. „a public singer" (who extols or degrades one by singing); also „minstrel, courtjester, merry Andrew" (as kept by chiefs for their amusement); „a public beggar."

Yem, ra-, pl. trạ-, n. „a lie, a falsehood;" e. g. ọ bā ra-yem, „he is a liar," lit. „he has falsehood."

Yéma, v. n. „tell a lie" or „falsehood, lie;" e. g. ọ yéma gbo, „he told but a lie."

Yéma, v. n. „want, wish." As an aux. it has often the sense of „be about, be upon the point." E. g. I yéma mun, „I want to drink;" — ka-sam ka yéma yeṅk, „the sore wants to heal" or „is about to get heal;" — pạ yéma sọk, „it is about to dawn" or „it wants to dawn;" — ma-lémre ma yéma lọl-aṅ, „the limes are about to get ripe." When used as an aux., it is construed with the short form of the Infinitive.

Yéma, v. impers. „want, be about." See the preceding form.

Yéma, v. a. „want, need, be in need of;" e. g. I yéma-ni háli, „I want it much."

Yém'sa, v. freq. and rel. (rad. yéma), „tell a lie about-" or „against-" or „of-"; e. g. o yém'sa-mi gbo, „he only told a lie about me."

Yéñeñ, Yéñen, } adv. „now"; e. g. pā yéñen tókoñ! „speak then now!"

Yeñk, v. n. „get well, get heal" (as a sore); with negative propositions also „be well, be heal;" e. g. ka-sam ka poñ yeñk, „the sore has got well." It is the short form of yéñki, „be well, be heal." See the Note after wos, v. n. above.

Yeñk ma-der, „get well in body, get restored to health."

Yeñk ma-der, ka-, n. „state of being well, health;" e. g. ka-yeñk-k'oñ ma-der, or: ka-yeñk ma-der-k'oñ, „his health."

Yéñkas, v. caus. „heal, cure, make well," (often used with ma-der, „body"); e. g. o som-mi e-trol tra yéñkas-mi, „he gave me medicine to cure me." See next word.

Yéñkas w'úni ma-der, „cure a person's body, make one well, restore one's health;" as: o yéñkas-mi ma-der, „he restored me to health," lit. „he cured me (as to the) body." The obj. pr. serves here, as it were, for a poss. pronoun.

Yentr, v. a. „deliver, hand over, give, give up, deliver up;" e. g. o yentr añ-réka, „he delivered the letter;" — 'a yentr-ko, „they delivered him up." Also „deliver up-with-" or „by-", as: 'a yentr-ko a-sol, „they betrayed him," lit. „they delivered him up by a stratagem."

Yéntra, v. rel. „deliver-to-, hand-to-, hand-for-;" e. g. w'an, yéntra-mi a-tis, „boy, hand me a knife."

Yer, v. a. „share, give; divide, share out to-, distribute, apportion;" also „share-with-;" e. g. yer-mi mun, „give me to drink;" — o yer o-sem, „he shared the meat;" — o yer-mi ka-bo, „he gave me of the bread," or „he shared the bread with me."

Yérane̩, v. a. recipr. „share among each other;" e. g. ńa yérane̩ ak'óta, „they shared the cloth among each other."

Yérane̩, v. rel. and refl. „share in-, have a part" or „share in-, partake of-oneself;" e. g. o̩ yérane̩ o̩-s̩e̩m, „he has a share in the meat."

Yés̩e, v. n. „get loose" (as rope); „get" or „be in disorder, get" or „be scattered" (as a bundle of sticks); „go to ruins, decay, dilapidate, fall to pieces," (as a house); e. g. ań-set ńa yés̩e, „the house goes to ruins;" — ka-fa̩nt'r ka yés̩e, „the bed is not made."

Y'e̩tr, pl. of r'ā, or r'áka, which see.

Y'e̩tr e̩-di, pl. of r'ā ra-di, which see.

Y'e̩tr e̩-lópra, n. „wearing apparel, clothes;" e. g. o̩ bā y'e̩tr e̩-lópra e̩-fíno, „he has fine clothes."

Yi, adv. „thus, so;" it may be sometimes given by „this"; e. g. káńko̩ K'úru pa̩ ts̩ē mu yi yi! „God grant that it may not be thus with thee!"

Yi, v. impers. „be"; e. g. ye̩ pa̩ yi, „thus it is."

Yi, v. n. „be, exist;" e. g. Pā Sóri o̩ yi he̩ ri, „Mr. Sori is not there;" — o̩ kas-ka-mi o̩ yi ro-pe̩tr, „my father is in the town."

Yi, v. a. „be to-, be-for-, be with-; consist of-; happen to-, befall;" e. g. tr'eī tra̩ yi-mi ro-méra, „I have something at heart," lit. „something is with me in the mind;" — tra̩ yi-mi tráka ko̩ ro-kamp, „I intend to go to Freetown;" — o̩ káne̩ ńa atrá ma yi-ńa, „he told them what would befall them."

Yi, ma-, n. „state, condition;" e. g. ma-yi-m'o̩ń ro-krífi, „his condition in Hades."

Yi, pr. obj. „it; them;" e. g. e̩y'e̩tr-'e̩-mi kére̩-yi ro-set, „as to my things carry them into the house."

Yía, pr. emph. „it, this; they, them, these;" e. g. e̩-gbáta-'e̩-mi yía-yē, „these are my mats," lit. „my mats they these;" — e̩y'e̩tr e̩yé yía l yéma, „these things them I want."

Yíań, pr. abs. „it, this; they, them, these;" e. g. e̩y'e̩tr-'e̩-mi yíań, „these are my things," lit. „my things they" or

„these". These abs. forms imply the copula „be". (Cf. -ṅ under N.)

Yif, v. a. „ask; ask-for-, beg-for-;" e. g. o̱ yif-mi tra̱ka aṅ-réka ló̱ko̱ ó ló̱ko̱, „he always asks me for the letter;" — o̱ yif-ña r'äka, „he begged them for something;" — ña yif-ko̱ ho̱ ye̱: Tra sa̱ ko̱-i? „they asked him: Shall we go?"

Yíki, a-, n. „glory, majesty; d'gnity, state, honour;" e. g. aṅ-yíki-ñ'oṅ, „his glory;" — o̱-bai o̱wé o̱ bā a-yíki a-bána, „this king has a great state."

Yíkis, v. caus. „glorify, dignify, honour;" e. g. aṅ-fam ña yíkis-ko̱, „the people glorified him."

Yím'ra, v. dim. and inch. (rad yim), „wither, fade" (as leaves), lit. „get reddish;" e. g. e̱-bó̱pa̱r ya aṅ'o̱ntr e̱ tra̱ yim'ra, „the leaves of the tree are withering."

Y'in, adj. num. „one"; e. g. y'aṅkra y'in, „one pair of trowsers."

Y'intr, pl. of ñ'o̱ntr, which see.

Yíra, v. n. „sit down, sit; live, dwell; also „settle" (as dreggs); e. g. o̱ yíra ano̱, „he sits here," or „he lives here;" — ko̱ yíra ri, „go sit down there." It is probably a rel. and caus. form of: yi.

Yísa, v. a. „hoist" (as a sail); „cock" (as a gun); e. g. w'an, yísa ri am-bé̱la, „boy, hoist the sail there."

Yo̱, v. n. „act, do;" e. g. yo̱ o̱ yō̱, „thus he did."

Yo̱, v. a. „do; make," (as a table); „raise," (as an army); „do-with-, do-to-, treat;" e. g. o̱ yo̱ ma-pant, „he does work;" — I yo̱-ko̱ mo̱ a-bo̱i, „I treated him as a servant;" — tše so̱ yo̱-tši, w'an! „do not do it again, boy!" As an aux. it indicates causation of the energy, denoted by the principal verb, and is construed with the def. verb. as: kó̱no̱ yo̱-ko̱ o̱ keía, „he caused him to steal." lit. „he made him be steal;" — múno̱ yo̱-ko̱ o̱ fi, „thou wast the occasion of his death."

Yo̱. ka-, n. verb. „act of doing" or „making, a treating, a doing;" also „habit, fashion;" e. g. ka-yo̱-k'oṅ atr'eí alšé, „his doing this thing;" — ka-yo̱-k'oṅ kía-kē, „this is his fashion."

Yọ, o̩-, pl. a-, n. „a doer"; e. g. añ-yọ ña ar'ûn ra K'úru, „the doers of the word of God."

Yo, adv. „thus, so, in this way, in the same way" or „manner, the same kind;" e. g. yo o̩ pä, „thus he said;" — yo o̩ yọ, „thus he did." This form is used before words with the vowels o and u.

Yọ o̩-la̩s, „act wrong, do wrong;" e. g. o̩ yọ o̩-la̩s, „he acted wrong."

Yọ w'úni ka̩-tšiñ, „treat one in a mean" or „vile manner;" e. g. o̩ láñba o̩ yọ-mi ka̩-tšiñ, „the man treated me in a vile manner."

Yọ w'úni o̩-báki, „deal hardly with one, treat one severely;" e. g. 'a yō-ko̩ o̩-báki, „they treated him severely."

Yọ w'úni o̩-bañ, „hurt one, harm one, injure one," lit. „treat one painfully;" e. g. añ-fa̩m ña yọ-ña o̩-bañ, „the people hurt them."

Yọ w'úni o̩-la̩s, „do wrong to one, treat one badly;" e. g. o̩-w'úni o̩wé o̩ yọ ña o̩-la̩s, „this person treated them badly."

Yọ w'úni o̩-to̩t, „do good to one, treat one kindly" or „well"; e. g. añ-fa̩m añé ña yọ-mi o̩-to̩t, „these people treated me well."

Yọ w'úni tr'ei tra̩-fíno, „treat one well," lit. „do one a good thing;" e. g. o̩-tem o̩ yọ-mi tr'ei tra̩-fíno, „the old man treated me well."

Y'of, pl. of ñ'of, which see.

Yófa̩t, adj. „soft" (as a pillow); e. g. ka-fant'r ka̩-yófa̩t, „a soft bed."

Yóka, v. a. „take, take up, take away; take on oneself, assume" (as an office); e. g. o̩ yóka ak'a̩ntr, „he took up the stick;" — o̩ yóka an-tróko̩, „he took away the fowl;" — o̩ yóka ra-yóla, „he made himself a gentleman," lit. „he took (assumed) the rank of a gentleman;" — o̩ yóka ma-der ma w'úni, or simply: o̩ yóka ma-der, „he took on himself a human body," = „he became man."

Yóka, a-, pl. e̩-, n. „a cassada root;" e. g. e̩-yóka e̩-fíno, „good cassadas."

Yóka k'or, „conceive, become pregnant," lit. „take a belly;" e. g. o-béra o yóka k'or, „the woman conceived."

Yókane, v. refl. n. „take oneself up," hence „rise, get up; rise up as —;" e. g. w'an, yókane, pa sok! „boy, get up, it dawns!" — añ-fam be ña yókane, „all the people got up;" — o yókane o-kélfa, „he rose up as a war-officer;" — o yókane ka ra-fi, „he rose from death." Also fig. „recover, get well again" (rise up, as it were, from a sickness), as: o-tem o poñ yókane so, „the old man got well again."

Yókane, v. rel. and refl. „take to oneself, take on" or „upon oneself, assume;" e. g. o yókane ra-kélfa, „he took on himself the office of a captain of the army," = „he made himself a captain of the army;" — o yókane ma-der ma w'úñi, „he took on himself a human body," = „he became man" or „he became incarnate," for which they may also say simply: o yókane ma-der.

Yóla, o-, pl. a-, n. „a gentleman, a rich man;" e. g. o yi o-yóla o-bána, „he is a great gentleman."

Yóla, ra-, n. „state" or „rank of a gentleman, gentlemanship;" e. g. o bā ra-yóla, „he is a gentleman."

Y'oñ, pr. poss. „his, her," lit. „of him, of her;" e. g. ey'étr-y'oñ, „his things."

Yoñ, adv. = yañ which see. This form is not much used; they rather use yañ for it.

Yoñ, ka-, pl. tra-, n. „a bamboo stick hollowed out to about the middle of its length;" it is used to catch fish with. On one of its ends it is widely opened, and then gets more and more narrow; at the other end it is tied together. If the fish goes in at the open end, and reaches the middle of it; it cannot come out again. The stick is left in the water for this purpose sometimes a whole day.

Yóna, v. rel. (rad. yo), „do-for-, make-for-; do-with-, make-with-; do work with-;" e. g. o-láñba o yóna-mi ma-pant, „the young man does work for me;" — o yóna-mi a-mésa, „he made a table for me;" — o yóna ka-bap, „he does work with the axe;" — yóna ka-bap aké ma-pant, „do work with this axe."

Yóna, adj. „belonging to doing work with, doing with, using for;" e. g. y'etr e-yóna ma-pant ro-tọf, „tools to do work with in the ground," = „agricultural implements."

Yóne, v. refl. (rad. yō̱), „happen, come to pass, take place;" also „be fulfilled" (as a prophecy); lit. „do itself;" e. g. atr'eí atšé tra yóne ténọṅ, „this thing happened to day;" — atrá K'úru o pả tápaṅ-e, tra yóne ténọṅ aṅ-lo aṅé, „what God spoke long ago, has come to pass at this day," or „what God foretold, has been fulfilled at this time."

Yọs, a-, or i-, pl. ma-, n. „a deed, work, achievement, action; custom, habit, manners;" e. g. ma-yọs-mọṅ, „his deeds;" — ma-yọs ma am-bóna aṅé, „the customs of this nation;" — ma-yọs-m'ọṅ ma-kabáne, „his wonderful deeds;" — aṅ-yọs aṅé aṅá o yō̱ ṅa tésa he, „this deed which he did does not please."

---

www.ingramcontent.com/pod-product-compliance
Lightning Source LLC
Chambersburg PA
CBHW022018240426
43667CB00042B/937